PSYCHOLOGICAL COMMENTARIES

VOLUME ONE

Other books by Maurice Nicoll, all published by Shambhala:
Living Time
The Mark
The New Man

PSYCHOLOGICAL COMMENTARIES
on the Teaching of
GURDJIEFF
& OUSPENSKY

Volume One

by *Maurice Nicoll*

SHAMBHALA
Boston & London 1984

SHAMBHALA PUBLICATIONS, INC.
314 Dartmouth Street
Boston, Massachusetts   02116

9   8   7   6   5   4   3
Distributed in the United States by Random House
and in Canada by Random House of Canada Ltd.
Printed in the United States of America

Library of Congress Cataloging in Publication Data
Nicoll, Maurice, 1884-1953
  Psychological commentaries on the teaching of Gurdjieff and
Ouspensky.
  Reprint. Originally published: Psychological commentaries on
the teaching of G.I. Gurdjieff and P.D. Ouspensky. London: Robinson
& Watkins [1952?]—
  1. Gurdjieff, Georges Ivanovitch, 1872-1949.
  2. Uspenskiĭ, P.D. (Petr Demianovich), 1878-1947.   I. Title.
B4249.G84N55   1984   197'.2   83-25194
ISBN 0-87773-269-8 (pbk.)
ISBN 0-394-72395-3 (Random House: pbk.)

CONTENTS

Birdlip, 1941

Birdlip, 1942

Birdlip, 1943

FOREWORD

These Commentaries were written on the Teaching which Dr. Maurice Nicoll received personally from Ouspensky, whom he met in 1921, and Gurdjieff, whom he met in 1922. He studied under Ouspensky and then in 1922 went to Gurdjieff's Institute at Fontainebleau for a year, after which he returned to London and studied under Ouspensky until 1931 when Ouspensky gave him permission to teach the System. Dr. Nicoll's teaching has continued from 1931 until the present day. The Commentaries which form this book were begun during the war years and continued afterwards.

Dear Bush,

I was very interested to have your report of the meeting on March 20th. I think it would be best if I wrote to you on the basis of the questions that you have reported to me and the personal notes that you made yourself.

In the first place what must be understood is that man on this earth is in a very strange situation. When I first heard about this idea of man it affected me very much. Ordinarily, of course, we imagine that man can grow and develop in what I might call the natural normal way, simply by education, example, and so on. Yet, if we look at history, we find that man has not really developed, and particularly if we look at the present day we cannot boast that man has reached any real further stage of development. Look for a moment at the horrors that humanity imposes on itself nowadays. Yet people are prone to imagine that time means progress and that everything is getting better and better as time passes. And as a rule people take the obvious contradictions as *exceptional*. That is to say, people are always inclined to think that what are really the usual and ever-present circumstances of life, in a bad sense, are exceptional. You will agree with me perhaps that people usually regard war as exceptional. Yet you must admit that if you pick up any book of history you will find that it deals with war in the main, with war, intrigue, people seeking power, and so on. Actually, unless we have the strength of mind to see what ordinary life on this planet is like, we will remain in imagination, or illusion, if you prefer the word. As you know, in this system of work, amongst many sayings which have a great density of meaning—namely, that take a long time to understand—there is one saying that "the level of being of a man attracts his life". This saying applies to humanity in general—that is, the general level of humanity with regard to its being attracts the form of life that it experiences. It is useless to think that wars and horrors and revolutions, etc., are exceptional. What is at fault is the level of being of people. But nobody is willing to understand this and whenever war takes place, as I said, people take it as exceptional, and even speak about a future free from war, as soon as the existing war is over. We can see the same process at work now. History repeats itself because man remains at the same level of being—namely, he attracts again and again the same circumstances, feels the same things, says the same things, hopes the same things, believes the same things. And yet nothing actually changes. All the articles that were written in the last war are just the same as the articles written in this war, and will be for ever and ever. But what concerns us more is that the same idea applies to ourselves, to each individual person. As long as there is no change in the level of being, the personal history of a man remains the same. Everything repeats itself in his own life: he says the same things, he does the same things, he regrets the same things, he commits the same things. And all this belongs to this immensely deep idea that the level of being attracts his life.

Let us come to some of the main ideas which deal with the question of how a man can change his being. The whole of this work is about a change of being—that is, a change of the level of being at which a man naturally is—in ordinary life. What must be first realized here is that every one of us is at a certain level of being. In this connection we must visualize a vertical direction or a ladder extending as it were from below upwards and having many rungs on it. People—all of us—are on one or another of the rungs of this ladder that stands vertically below and above us. This ladder is quite different from time—namely, from past, present and future which we can imagine as a horizontal line. In order to make my meaning clearer, I would like to ask you how you imagine time—that is, the passage of time from the past into the present and into the future. Usually, the kind of mechanical hope that people hold on to is connected with the idea of time—namely, that in the future things will be better, or they themselves will be better, and so on. But this ladder of which we are speaking and which refers to different levels of being has nothing to do with time in this sense. A higher level of being lies immediately above all of us at this very moment. It does not lie in the future of time but in ourselves at this very moment, *now*. All work on oneself, all personal work which deals with stopping negative emotions, with self-remembering, with not being identified with one's woes and troubles, with not making accounts, etc., etc., is concerned with a certain action that can take place in oneself at this moment—now—if one tries to be more conscious and remembers what it is we are trying to do in this work. That is to say, the work is about a certain transformation of the instant, of the moment, of the present, through the action of this work. For example, a man finding himself in the depths of despair, if he observes the situation and tries to remember himself, or tries to give himself any other kind of conscious shock at that particular moment, such as remembering his aim—that is, in other words, if he tries to "transform himself", to transform his mechanical reaction to the circumstances that surround him at that moment—may find to his astonishment that quite suddenly everything is changed, his mood of depression vanishes, and he finds himself in a new atmosphere from which he wonders how he could have been in his former state. This represents a momentary change in the level of being because everything has, not an exact level of being, but a general average level of being in which there are higher and lower degrees. But here we are talking about the application of the work to change in regard to the level of being. We are talking about what I might call the third stage of a man and now I will explain what I mean by this.

As was said, a man is born as essence and this constitutes his real part, the part from which he can really grow and develop. But this part in him can only grow in a very small way. It has not the strength to grow by itself any further after, say, the age of three or four or five. Let us call this the *first* stage of a man. That is, the first stage of a man is pure essence which by itself is capable of a certain amount of growth but reaches a point very soon in which it can grow no further. I notice in some of the questions asked in your letter to me that this point about man has not been understood so I am going to repeat it again. As I said, this system teaches that the essence in a man can only grow a very short way by itself. You have to try to see what I mean. People naturally think that growth and development is something continuous or that it should be, but here is this extraordinarily interesting idea taught by this system that this is not the case. Man's essence can only grow by itself unaided to a very small extent, and as such a man is nothing but a little child. Now in order for it to grow further something must happen. Something must form itself round essence and this is called personality. Essence must become surrounded by something that is really foreign to itself, acquired from life, which enters through the senses. A little child must cease to be itself and become something different from itself. As you were told, the centre of gravity of itself begins to pass from essence into personality. It learns all sorts of things, it imitates all sorts of things, and so on. This formation of personality around essence which is necessary for the development of essence can be called the *second* stage of man. But let us clearly understand what is meant here. The future development of essence depends on the formation of personality around it. If a very poor personality, a very weak personality, is formed round it, there is very little to help further growth of essence which we will speak of when we come to the *third* stage. In the second stage, the formation of personality is taking place, and, as was said, the richer the personality the better. But I notice that some of you do not understand what is meant here. The reason why you do not understand what is meant here is because you do not see this extraordinary situation that man is in—namely, that man cannot grow continuously from essence because essence is too weak to grow by itself. The further growth of essence depends first of all on the formation of personality and the richer the personality the better eventually for the growth of essence, but, ordinarily speaking, the formation of personality is quite sufficient for the purposes of life. A man finds himself in a good position, able to deal with life through the formation of a rich personality in him. And if he is satisfied, he is, for all life purposes, adequate. But this work, this teaching, is about a further stage of man, and this stage I will call the *third* stage.

You must understand that this work is not really about life; it is about something else that a man can begin to attempt quite apart from whether he is a successful politician, a famous scientist, or a well-respected butcher or baker or candlestick-maker. This work starts from man as good householder—namely, from a man who has developed personality and can deal with life in his own particular way, reasonably enough. That is to say, it starts from the level of good householder, which belongs to the second stage of a man's development. This third stage is all concerned with a possible further development of essence and that is why so many apparently paradoxical or at least strange things are said in the Gospels—such as are contained in the Sermon on the Mount—about man. They are all to do with allowing essence to grow at the expense of personality and this is the only way in which essence, which is too weak by itself to grow, can continue to develop. In this sense, personality, which is formed around essence, and must be formed round essence, becomes eventually, if this third stage is entered upon, the very source from which essence can grow further. Let us suppose that personality is in a particular person very richly developed. He is, then, a rich man, in the sense of the Gospels. He knows about everything, he is an important person, and so on. What is poor in him? What is poor in him is his essence. He is not yet a real man. What he does, he does to acquire merit, or from fear of loss of honour or reputation, and so on, but he does nothing from himself, nothing from the love of doing it, quite apart from praise, authority, position, popularity, or any other gain in the eyes of the world. Suppose that this man feels, in some way, like the Prodigal Son—namely, that he is eating nothing but husks. I mean simply that he may feel in himself very empty in spite of all his "richness". He has got the finest house or jewels, he has got a well-known name, he has in some way got the better of everybody else, and yet he feels empty. Such a man is approaching the third possible stage of development. He has now reached a position in which his essence—namely, his real part—can grow, and thus replace his feeling of emptiness by a feeling of meaning. But in order to bring about in man this further development he must begin, as it were, to sacrifice his personality and to go in a sense in the opposite direction to that in which he has gone up to now. In other words, a kind of reversal must take place in him which is well-expressed in the Parable of the Prodigal Son, and unless we understand that this third stage is possible and leads to a man's real development we will never understand what the Gospels are speaking about or what this system is speaking about.

* * *

The other day, at a meeting here, the following lines were read: "Let us take the Sermon on the Mount and try to understand what it means. As was said before, in the last talk, "religion"—as it is called— that is, as the psychological ideas taught by Christ about the individual evolution of man and his transformation into a new man are usually called—is concerned with the development of essence *after personality has been formed*. A man in whom a rich personality has been formed by experience, education and interests, is a "rich man" in personality. But essence remains poor. For it to develop, personality must become

4

work.

1. Stopping negative emotions

2. Self-remembering

3. not being identified
   w/one's work & thoughts

4. not making accounts

TO _____

DATE _____ TIME _____

WHILE YOU WERE OUT

M _____

Of _____

Phone _____

_____

TELEPHONED ☐   PLEASE RETURN CALL ☐

CALLED TO SEE YOU ☐   WILL CALL AGAIN ☐

RETURNED YOUR CALL ☐   RUSH ☐

MESSAGE _____

PENNSTATE

1855

Signed _____

passive." This was not understood, but it is very important that every-one in the work should understand what this paragraph means. It means that religion in the real sense—and we only know Christianity ourselves—refers to the third stage of a man, *the making of personality passive so that essence can grow.* I must repeat again that the inner meaning of the Gospels has nothing to do with life. Their teaching starts at the point where personality has been formed already in a man and refers to this *third* stage of possible development. A man must first of all become developed as regards personality by the action of life. This work is sometimes called a second education. It is for those who are looking for a second education. The first education is an education that life gives us; and this is absolutely necessary. The better a person is educated by means of life, the more he learns, the more intelligent he is, the more experienced he is, the more he knows about people, and about affairs, the more he knows about manners, the better he can express himself, the more he is able to use the different sides of life, the better for him. This is the first education. This forms personality. We have said before that man consists of different centres and each of these has different parts; these centres and parts should be well furnished and the better furnished they are with inscriptions on rolls, the better for him. But a point comes in a man's development where, as was said before, he feels empty, and it is at this stage that the teaching of the Gospels and all this work comes in. I do not know whether any of you have ever thought about this very deeply. But it is quite possible that some of you who have done your duty in life often wonder what it is exactly you are doing, what the meaning of it all is. Speaking in this personal way for a moment I would like to ask you this question: Do you think that life and the meanings that it affords us are enough and have you felt that in some way life does not quite give you what you expected? I am not saying that life is meaningless; it has obviously many meanings. But have any of you come to the point of feeling a certain meaninglessness even in those interests that you follow and try to hold on to? Why I am saying this is because if life afforded us our full meaning then there would be no point, in fact, no meaning, either in what the Gospels talk about or in what this system talks about. If you are quite content with the meanings that life affords, quite self-satisfied, then there is no point in trying to understand what this system teaches, and, let me add, there is no point in your trying to understand what Christ's teaching really means. Now, if man were nothing but a well-formed personality and this were his *end*, then we might very well believe in all those doctrines of humanitarianism and other scientific ideas that say that man is nothing but a creature turned towards external life and having to adapt himself as intelligently as possible towards it. But if you have followed what has been said in this letter about the idea of man in this system you will see that the development of personality is merely a stage, and an absolutely necessary stage, towards a further stage. It is directly comparable with the formation

5

of a mass of food round a seed, as in the case of a nut. The nut has an essential part in it—namely, the seed itself that can grow—but it cannot grow until it is surrounded by a mass of nourishing material, just as an egg has a seed in it surrounded by a mass of yolk, and so on. Take the latter example: how can a chicken grow unless it has all the substances surrounding it for it to feed on? And remember that it grows inside the egg-shell and finally emerges a complete chicken and this complete chicken has been made out of the substances that the living germ has attacked and eaten. Now the fate of acorns is one thing, but the fate of oak-trees is a different thing, and, as was said, man surrounded by personality resembles an acorn and suffers, as it were, the same fate as the acorn, unless he begins to grow, and growth in a man corresponds to what we are calling the third stage in a man after personality has been formed round essence. If we take man at this second stage where essence is surrounded by personality he is just like an acorn, maybe a larger or a smaller acorn, but nothing but an acorn. He is perhaps very important; he has learnt many things; he feels he knows; he is, in short, full of personality, and that is his level, and at that level he suffers, not really a proper human fate, but the fate of an undeveloped organism, the fate of a person who is not yet fully-grown, just as an acorn is not a fully-grown tree. And unless we understand very clearly about this third stage—namely, the development of an acorn into a tree by its living essence or seed feeding on the substances formed round it—we shall never understand, as I said before, what this work is about, nor shall we understand what the Gospels are about. You have already heard that man is a *self-developing organism* and is created as such. But now you can see that his development is not continuous. It must be interrupted by the formation of personality. I would be very glad if you all can understand this question of essence and personality up to this point. Later on, we will talk about what it means to develop essence at the expense of personality in more detail, but already you know a few points about this development. But let me ask you once more before I end this letter: have any of you ever thought what the Sermon on the Mount means? Do you seriously mix it up with the second stage of man's development or have you already got some sense of scale? Do you not understand that the Sermon on the Mount, about being humble and so on, has nothing to do with ordinary life but applies to this third stage of a man when he comes to the point of feeling empty, since personality does not satisfy him and he wishes to find new meaning for his own existence? I will try later on to write to you in more detail.

I hope now that you understood what I called at the beginning of this letter the extraordinary situation of man on this earth in regard to his development. He is born with essence and that is real and is the living germ in him, but it can only develop by itself to a very small extent. Personality must then form itself around essence and essence has no chance to grow further unless this personality forms itself round essence. But if a man remains in that state which we have called the

6

second stage—namely, in which personality is now active in him— h is not yet a man and is comparable with an acorn or a seed that has formed around itself nourishment for its eventual development. The third stage of a man is when he comes to make his personality passive so that the essence in him can grow. And there are, as it were, three forms of teaching that a man meets with in consequence. As essence, as a little baby, he hears simple ideas from his mother, and as we shall see later these simple ideas are important. Then he passes into life and learns the opinions of the period of the world he happens to be born into. This is his second stage; in this stage he takes up memory systems, correspondence courses, passes examinations, and so on. Personality is being formed. But there exists in this world a very strange class of teachings, one of which is clearly exemplified in the Gospels. What is their place? What are they about? They belong to the *third* stage of a man's development, to the new growth of essence that can now take place at the expense of personality. Unless we grasp this, we cannot understand either this system or the Gospels. They belong to this third stage which is defined by Christ when he says to the rich man: "Go, sell that thou hast, and give to the poor." And we must remember that the "poor" in us is this poor development of essence and the "rich man" is personality. Now you perhaps understand better what the phrase in this work means which says that man is unfinished or incomplete. He is unfinished exactly as an acorn is unfinished. At the second stage when personality has formed itself round him he is incomplete just like an acorn and in an exactly similar sense. If you have understood something of what all this means you will be in a much better position for me to talk about what false personality means and will be able to understand what it means to try to go against false personality.

And now I wish to add one word more, even at the risk of your feeling that I am repeating myself too much. Do you really begin to understand some of the implications of this idea about essence and personality? Can you begin to see what it means? What does it mean? No matter what form of education you have in life, what political colour you belong to, it can only form personality in a man. You may arrange for the best possible teaching of science, economics, history, literature, etc., but it will only form in a man personality; it cannot lead him to his real eventual development. And so perhaps now you understand more clearly why there exist, in life, two kinds of influences acting on a man, as all you older people in the work remember. One kind of influences are called A influences: these are created by life and they are forms of education that belong to the period that we are brought up in, all the viewpoints that belong to the particular age in which a man is born. These are A influences and form personality in him. But there are also, as we can see for ourselves even to-day, other influences which are ageless. For us the Gospels and their teaching are the chief example. These, as you know, are in this system called B influences and these hold good for any age because they are always about the same thing

7

—namely, this third stage of development of a man, in which essence begins to grow at the expense of personality. Unless we really understand this apparent paradox we will never get a very clear idea of the place of this system. It begins at the end of the second stage, when personality has been formed and a man has tasted life and seen what things are like and feels dissatisfied and begins to seek for something additional, for something that will make him understand better, something that will help him and give him a direction and eventually complete him.

Yours,
MAURICE NICOLL

★   ★   ★

The Knapp,
Birdlip.
Gloucestershire.
27th April, 1941

Dear Bush,

As we were speaking at the meeting here at Birdlip on Saturday, April 25th, on a subject that is important, I would like to write to you a little about it. It concerns the way in which people take this work and how and in what spirit they work on themselves.

I will begin with myself. I was brought up, in regard to religious ideas, with the sense that only the conviction of sin was important. Everything was sin, briefly speaking. In consequence, religion was a very gloomy business and personally I loathed it. Morality was only sexual morality. Virtue was only continence, and so on, and, in general, sin and the feeling of being a sinner was the main idea of religion. I never understood anything else in regard to religion as a boy and so was either afraid or worried or hated the whole thing. I began to stammer badly. I listened to the scriptures, mostly drawn from the Old Testament, which always seemed indescribably horrible. God was a violent, jealous, evil, accusing person, and so on. And when I heard the New Testament I could not understand what the parables meant, and no one seemed to know or care what they meant. But once, in the Greek New Testament class on Sundays, taken by the Head Master, I dared to ask, in spite of my stammering, what some parable meant. The answer was so confused that I actually experienced my first moment of consciousness—that is, I suddenly realized that *no one knew anything.* This is a definite experience and was my first experience of self-remembering—the second being the sudden realization that no one knew what I was thinking—and from that moment I began to think for myself, or rather knew that I could. As you know, all moments of real self-remembering stand out for ever in one's inner life, and one's real life is not outer events, but inner states. I remember so clearly this class-room, the high windows constructed so that we could not see out of them, the desks, the platform on which the Head Master sat, his scholarly, thin face, his nervous habits of twitching his mouth and jerking his hands—and suddenly this inner revelation of *knowing that he knew nothing*—nothing—that is, about anything that really mattered. This was my first inner liberation from the power of external life. From that time, I knew for certain—and that means always by inner individual authentic perception which is the only source of real knowledge—that all my loathing of religion as it was taught me was right. And although one always goes to sleep again after a moment of real self-remembering, and often for years, yet such moments of consciousness stand always in higher parts of centres and remain and await, as it were, the further moments of realizing, more consciously, what life actually is—that is to say, they are never lost, and, although forgotten in one way, stand in the background of oneself always, and come forward at critical moments to guard you.

Now I wish to speak to you about how you work on yourselves and in what spirit you take the work. You cannot easily work from the ordinary religious ideas and moods. You recall the saying about new wine in old bottles. This work, this system of teaching, these ideas we are studying, are the most beautiful things you can possibly imagine —and they are new to us. No, they are far more lovely and beautiful than anything you can imagine. They accuse you only of being asleep. They hold no conviction of sin in them. They ask you quite gently to observe yourself. It is you yourself who must accuse yourself. Let us take one of the ideas of this teaching—an idea about *essence*. This teaching tells us that the essence of each of us comes down from the stars. You will remember the Ray of Creation. Essence comes down from the note *La* (Starry Galaxy) and passing through the note *Sol* (the Sun) and then the note *Fa* (the planetary zone) enters the earth. We are not merely born of our parents; our parents create the apparatus for the reception of this essence that comes from the stars. And all work, whether personal work, work with others in the work, or work for the work itself—and these are the three necessary lines of work for anyone who wishes to remain in this work—is to lead us back to where we have originally come from. Now each one of us is down here, on this dark planet, so low down in the Ray of Creation, because he or she has some special thing in themselves, some special factor, or *chief feature* to see, to observe, to become conscious of and to begin to dislike, and so to work against. It may be meanness, or cruelty, or lying, or self-pride, or fear, or ignorance, and so on. And if a man or woman dies without seeing why they are here and what is the real reason of their lives, can it be called anything but a tragedy? Each one of you is here, on the earth, because from the work point of view you have something very special and very important to see in yourselves and struggle against with all your skill and ingenuity, with all your strength of mind and will and soul and heart and body. But of course if you pride yourselves on your virtues—well, what can happen save that self-righteousness and so false personality will be increased every day you live: and the result will be that you will crystallize out in such narrow viewpoints and attitudes and become *dead people*. You have heard me speak of the meaning of the *dead* in the Gospels—for example, as in Christ's remark: "Let the dead bury their dead." The dead are those dead to all possibility of working on themselves and so changing themselves. Now the work can only be done in the spirit of its own beauty and light, in the spirit of its true message and significance. Life on earth is nothing but a field for working on oneself, so that one can return from whence one came. To take life as an *end* in itself is not to understand the work, and it may cause a wrong attitude which may be the source of many negative emotions and of useless efforts made in negative states. For to work in a negative way is useless. It is only through some kind of delight, some feeling of joy or pleasure or some genuine affection or desire, that a person can work and bring about any change of being in himself. Fear, for example, will not act in this way. A man may have some knowledge of truth, but unless he *values* it, unless he feels some delight in it, it cannot affect him. It cannot act on him, for a man unites with truth only through his love, as it were, and in this way his being is changed. But if he is negative, then his love-life—that is, his emotional side—is in a wrong state and it will be the same if he is in a state of fear and feels compelled to do something against his will. To do a thing willingly, from a delight in doing it, will effect a change in you. And when a person begins to take up his own "cross"—that is, the burden of some difficult thing in himself that he has at last come to observe—and does it in such a spirit, then he will get results. But if he does it heavily, out of the conviction of sin, nothing will ever come out of it, and especially if he shews others what he is trying to do, and likes to look miserable or grave or sad. And in this connection you will remember what Christ said about fasting—namely, that if you fast, you should anoint your head and wash your face "that thou be not seen of men to fast." To work on oneself from the conviction of sin puts the work into negative parts of centres, and to work in a negative way can lead to a worse state of oneself than not to work at all. Some tend to take the work in this heavy way. But no one can fathom the delight people take in making themselves miserable and in enjoying their negative states. You all know and have often heard me say that negative parts of centres create nothing. When I first heard Mr. O. say that negative parts of centres cannot *create* anything and that people who try to work in a heavy, dreary, negative way could only make their inner state worse than it was—then I think I experienced almost another moment of consciousness. I understood that what I had felt about religion had been right. It was suddenly formulated and explained. This work, if you will listen to it and hear it in your hearts, is the most beautiful thing you could possibly hear. It speaks not of sin, but of being asleep, just as the Gospels do not really speak of sin, but only of *missing the mark*—the Greek word means that. Can we hear the work? There is an old book that I have, composed by a man in the work of his time. It depicts a man lying fast asleep flat on the earth, and a ladder stretching to heaven, and angels on it blowing trumpets almost in the man's ear. Yet he hears nothing. He is asleep in life—perhaps he is a millionaire or some very important person, or simply a harassed clerk, or a worried mother, and so on.

This work is beautiful when you see why it exists and what it means. It is about liberation. It is as beautiful as if, locked for years in prison, you see a stranger entering who offers you a key. But you may refuse it because you have acquired prison-habits and have forgotten your origin, which is from the stars. How, then, will you ever be able to *remember yourself* with only prison-thoughts and interests, and hand back your life whole and not twisted and soiled by negative emotion and every form of identifying? It will then be only natural for you to refuse the key that will unlock all the doors of the prison, one by one, because you prefer to remain in prison—that is, as you are in yourself. Nay, even more, you may be indignant and seek to kill the stranger and fight for your prison-life and even sacrifice your life in order to remain in prison.

Yours,
MAURICE NICOLL

Birdlip, May 4, 1941

THE FOURTH WAY

It is very necessary at this moment to understand something of what the Fourth Way means. There are four ways of work on oneself. We belong to the Fourth Way which is the most difficult way of all because it must be practised in the midst of life. The Way of Fakir—that is, the First Way—the Way of Monk, that is, the Second Way—the Way of Yogi, that is, the Third Way, is not our way. We have to speak on the small scale of ourselves, but the point is that we are, even on this small scale, trying to follow the Fourth Way which comes down into external life always when there is a period of special disorder and chaos.

Now I would like to say to you all that some of you do not understand the idea of the Fourth Way—for example, you appear to me to expect that the conditions that have existed at one time must or will always exist. This is quite wrong. The Fourth Way must always be related to the varying circumstances of life and can never become fixed and habitual. Suddenly it may be necessary to alter the whole external scheme of things. I want especially at this moment to have around me people who understand this and who can relate themselves to different conditions and still maintain in themselves all the principles and ideas of the work. We have no idea how things will go in the future. But we understand that the work must continue in the future. And that means that people must be able to adjust themselves to completely different external conditions and yet maintain the sense and feeling of the work.

In the Fourth Way the first main achievement is to become No. 4 man—that is, balanced man or all-sided man. Now if some of you have formed an idea of what the external form of the work is from past associations and you find yourselves confronted with an entirely new external state of affairs and become negative you are really useless to me in so far as the Fourth Way is concerned. You must learn that every change in the work externally is always useful to you, whatever form it takes, and all of you must be prepared to follow the work in its changing outer manifestations, and at all moments maintain a clear inner attitude towards it. At the present moment it is quite impossible to reproduce the situation that existed in Essex. The present Headquarters of our branch of the work are now situated in the full glare of publicity—that is to say, the two houses that we have taken are literally on the highway, especially the house in Birdlip itself, which is right in the village. For that reason it is quite impossible to live our life as we did in Essex at the Farm and everyone must realize this and adjust himself to circumstances, and also everyone must realize that we are in, so to speak, a "foreign" county, and particularly a conservative county, and must contribute to making a reasonable and normal impression on people. Under such circumstances we cannot have the same external life as before, but I see no reason why people who visit us should not understand that this quite small difficulty can be overcome and that apart from it everything is exactly the same as before.

I said a long time ago to you and repeated it several times that the work does not necessarily include coming to the Farm and that the Farm was distinct in a sense from the teaching of the work. The work exists through everyone's attitude towards it and no matter what the external situation may be it should make no difference to work in this sense. I am sorry that I have to say this but it is necessary to do so. For all that I know, we may find ourselves again in quite different circumstances, which again will require a proper understanding, and then again, and then again. People must understand that they are in the Fourth Way and that they must always be able to be "all things to all people" and to develop every side of themselves, in relation to society and to all forms of external life, to a reasonable point; otherwise they do not understand the idea of the Fourth Way which maintains itself right in the midst of life amongst everything that goes on, adjusting itself and yet always maintaining itself internally. The Fourth Way is and must be always the most "flexible" of all, but it requires a most flexible inner understanding and unless a person can be flexible, and yet maintain the feeling of the work, he is a rather difficult subject in connection with this line of work. Every change in circumstances provides a very useful chance for everyone to learn something. When I have sufficient people round me whom I can trust, in the sense of their being able to deal normally with every kind of person they meet and with every situation in life, I will feel that I am able to extend the work in the way that I wish to extend it eventually. And here I will remind you of one meaning of *"mechanicalness"* in the work. If you cannot relate to one side or another in life you must make this one of your aims. There is not a single thing in life about which a man in the Fourth Way should not be knowledgeable, or capable of maintaining himself in connection with it. This Fourth Way is not romantic and it is no use having romantic feelings about the Farm in Essex. This Fourth Way is quite ruthless and as soon as something is finished—that is, gives no longer any real value, it is abandoned. By this I do not mean that we cannot go back to the Farm, but that this is a great chance for everyone to adjust himself to the external form and physical situation of the work at the moment. This applies equally to those who cannot come here and to those who can.

I would be very glad if you would all try to understand what I mean because it is important to draw attention to this point owing to the fact that so often everyone begins to "settle down" after a time into some form of the Fourth Way work which he thinks is going to go on and on just like that. Unfortunately, such mental and emotional habits can be formed.

I once said to G.: "Why don't you build more solidly?" (we were building a theatre). He said: "This is only temporary. In a very short time everything will be different. Everyone will be elsewhere. Nothing can be built permanently at this moment." So it is necessary for everybody to understand in a way what this means. Many times G. had no work "externally"—that is, no place, no habitation. Everything seemed to have been dissolved away and from the external or sensory point of view to have vanished, yet, as you know, the work went on and was finally transmitted to this country, and yet this had nothing to do with the external form of the work, with the actual house or situation and so on, and in view of what G. told me privately I fancy that we can have no permanent home for the work and that we shall have to adjust ourselves to every kind of situation in the future. But all of you who have heard the teaching over a sufficient time should be able now to be quite tranquil about change in the external form or the external demands of the work and to relate yourselves instantly to them from the work point of view. The trouble is that things become mechanical and it is necessary for a shock to be given so that things are no longer quite mechanical. But the work continues in the same way and speaks with the same voice and gives the same force to those who acknowledge and practise it.

I must add that the centre of gravity of this talk to you lies in the meaning of what is called the Fourth Way. We are not Fakirs holding out our arms year after year; we are not monks living in monasteries; we are not Yogis going to remote schools or sitting and meditating in caves in the Himalayas. We belong to what is called the Fourth Way which is right down in life. So we have to work in the midst of life, surrounded by all the misfortunes of life, and eventually life becomes our teacher—that is to say, we have to practise non-identifying in the midst of the happenings of life; we have to practise self-remembering in the midst of affairs; and we have to notice and separate ourselves from our negative emotions in the midst of all hurts and smarts in daily life. And for that reason it is said that a man who follows the Fourth Way must become No. 4 man—that is, a man who has developed his centres. It means a man who can be all things to all men, and it means a man who has developed all sides of himself so that he can meet with every situation reasonably, with every class, with every kind of person, with every point of view, with every theory, with every practical thing or theoretical thing or philosophical thing up to a certain point. From one point of view he is a man of the world. It is wrong to say this, but it probably gives the first idea of what No. 4 man is. No. 4 man does not really mean a man of the world. It means something deeper than this, but certainly it includes this—that is to say, it means that a person is able to meet with all the events and situations of life in a reasonable way and is not a fool about life and people. There are many things to learn from ordinary life that everybody ought to learn and in view of the idea of No. 4 man all these things become interesting. This person mechanically hates this side of life or that person mechanically hates that side of life. Actually a man must get his full development from life in conjunction with the work in order to reach the stage of No. 4 man —for no man can become No. 4 man unless the work illuminates him and at the same time no man can become No. 4 man unless he relates himself to all sides of life. Ask yourselves, all of you, in what sides of life you are very undeveloped, and here I simply mean ordinary external life. Would you be able to take charge of an army suddenly? Would you be able to run a hotel? Would you be able to talk effectively to the Prime Minister? Could you produce a play or sail a ship or give an important dance and keep quite quiet and know what to do? Could you give a good criticism of a book? Could you maintain yourself in conversation amongst ordinary educated people? Although all this is not important and no one must take it literally, everyone must have ideas of what No. 4 man means, because No. 4 man does not mean what I have said exactly. It means the attainment of a quite wonderful allsidedness so that, although you have never talked to the Prime Minister, when the moment comes you can do it from your inner development and your inner strength.

The Fourth Way lies in life and people must be strong enough to maintain it in their wills and their understanding because it has no temples or churches or ritual, only rules. So therefore please understand that if external conditions of the Fourth Way change for you and even change again and again, you must always try to keep your balance and accept the new conditions as work and believe that however much I like a man or woman personally I cannot do anything if change of external circumstances makes him or her negative in the work.

And I will add this quite simple sentence. Please do not think, some of you, that the work means the Farm. The work is not an external thing lying at the Farm. Often people connect themselves with the work through outer sensory images so that they forget even what the work is about. The work is not a place, the work is not a thing that you can touch or handle, the work is not in France or England or America, or in any *place* in the world. The work is in your hearts and in your own understanding, and wherever a man has to go, the work can always go with him, if he maintains the right attitude towards it. The work is only kept alive by a man's own efforts. Only if he is willing to receive it can the work touch a man; and it then slowly begins to transform him. Therefore the work is not in space nor even in time. It is in something that we do not understand, which is neither space nor time, place nor moment, for which a word was invented long ago, a word that is always completely misunderstood, called *eternity*.

Birdlip, May 29, 1941

INTRODUCTORY NOTE TO
COMMENTARIES ON WORK IDEAS

In the teaching of the ideas of this system of work, it is necessary to give the work-ideas in pure form—that is, the work-ideas as originally taught must be handed on just as they were taught. This is the task of anyone who is given permission to teach the work to others. Otherwise people begin to alter the ideas a little according to their own level of understanding, with the result that in process of time they become quite different, according to each person's prejudices, buffers, bias, and so on. In the talks about the work itself, the ideas are given in their original form. But the object of the work-ideas is to make people think for themselves by means of them, for none of the ideas of the work can really take hold of a person unless he or she begins to think about them and tries to see what they mean individually, and begins to value them and think about life and its meaning and themselves from the standpoint of these ideas. And it must be added here that no one can be different from what he is now unless he begins to think in a new way. The work is to make us think and awaken our individual minds or what is called in this system the *driver* in us, which in the vast majority of people is fast asleep and remains fast asleep throughout life in spite of all troubles and disasters, one reason being that man prefers to live in the *basement* of himself, in the lower part of him—in the instinctive and moving centres—that is, in sensation, appetites, and muscular activity. But since the first object of the work is to make people think for themselves about its ideas and from its ideas, what are called *commentaries* have a place in the work.

Commentaries are reflections about the work, individual thoughts arising out of it through personal observation and application of the work-ideas practically, additional illustrations, and so on. These *commentaries* form, therefore, an additional side of the work, but they are, so to speak, personal contributions to the general system of ideas of the work and therefore must never be taken as being the actual teaching of the work itself or confused with it, and they can be accepted or not, according to individual choice. The teaching of the work-ideas is one thing: the commentaries are another thing. The teaching of the work-ideas is permanent. The commentaries are of another order and more in the nature of suggestions, possible amplifications, explanations, and so on. But as a body, the commentaries are merely additional and may be changed according to circumstances. The important thing is to be able to remember what is the work itself and what belongs merely to *commentaries*, as they are called. In this respect, it must be understood that there are several things in the work, as it has been given so far, that are obscure and need some additional thoughts, in order to try to make their meaning more distinct. But such additional thoughts are nothing but *commentaries*. They are additional material, and nothing more, and, as I said, can be accepted or not according to individual choice. If they assist in understanding the work better, they are useful, and if not, they need not be taken as the work itself. The commentaries on the work fall under two headings. The first is: commentaries which contain ideas not definitely found in the work itself. The second is: commentaries which are merely additional reflections and illustrations directly referring to one or another aspect of the work—such as commentaries on self-observation, self-remembering, and so on.

COMMENTARY I—*Birdlip, May* 29, 1941

ON ADDITIONAL MEANS OF SELF-OBSERVATION

I

Can you observe the difference between your own lives and life in general? What do you mean by the term *my life*—as when you say: "My life has been a happy life" or "My life has been an unhappy life"? Do you mean that outside things have been pleasant or otherwise, or inside things—that your moods and feelings and so on have been pleasant or otherwise? You will agree with me that sometimes a person who is in a good external situation in life with enough money and with pleasant surroundings, and without any serious trouble, etc., is unhappy and miserable, and on the other hand that a person in very different and even adverse circumstances is often quite the reverse. Let us look at this situation more closely. What is one's life—this thing we talk of so glibly without seeing what it is? When people gratuitously wish to tell the history of their lives, what do they speak of? They speak of *events*, of other people, of external things. But one's life consists of two distinct things, which for the purposes of self-observation must be realized. One's life consists not only of events, but of *states*. States are inner and events are outer. States are states of oneself, that is, inner states, such as bad moods, habits of worrying, habits of fear and super-stition, forebodings, depression, on the one hand, or, on the other hand, better states, states of feeling happy, states of enjoyment, and mercy. They are in oneself—that is, all states are states of oneself. Events are external and come in to us from outside. Now one's inner state may correspond to an external event, or may be caused by it or may have no relation to it. But it is necessary to try to see that states and events are two different things, first of all, before thinking of how they may be connected together. Take, for instance, a pleasant event. Does your inner state correspond with it? Can you say for certain that when the outer event occurs your inner state corresponds to it? Say you know some desirable event is going to happen and you look forward to it. Can you say that when it does come about, your inner state can meet with it in a delightful way? Or will you admit that, though the event happens perhaps even as you hoped, something frequently is lacking? What is lacking? What is lacking is the corresponding inner state to combine, as it were, with the outer event that was so eagerly anticipated. And, as you probably all know, it is usually the entirely unexpected event that affords us our best moments.

Now let us take this idea—namely, the correspondence of inner states and outer events. Unless we have in ourselves the right state we cannot combine rightly with the happy event—that is to say, something in us must exist to engage with and so enjoy the outer event. Yet people are very much inclined, in thinking of their lives, as I said, to believe that their lives are only *outer events* and that if a certain number of *outer events* of one kind or another have or have not happened to them, their lives have been unfortunate. But a person's capacity for life depends on his inner development—that is, on the quality of his inner states. For internally, in regard to our states, lies the *apparatus for living*, and if this apparatus is, for example, swamped by self-pity and worries and other negative emotions, no matter how delightful the outer events, nothing can happen rightly, simply because the *apparatus for living*—that is, the person in himself—is quite unable to combine in a fortunate way with such events that come from external life that might give him some pleasure and delight. A person may look forward to a trip abroad and when it comes about, it is an *event*. But he may be so mean, so careful about small unimportant things, etc., that the whole trip is nothing but a disaster. And in such a case it will be the man's *inner state* that is at fault. So if we ask ourselves what *our life* consists of, we cannot say merely of *events*, but that it consists far more of *states*. Suppose that a man, whose chief love is to be pessimistic and melancholy and gloomy, complains to you that life is a bad business and not worth living, will you suppose that this is caused by a lack of suitable *events* or by the man's inner *states*, and will you be so silly as to think by arranging a nice party for him he will change? The disease is in the man himself—and how many people do you not observe every day who make their own life and the lives of others miserable owing to their wicked inner states— and who, in fact, deserve imprisonment because they have not begun to see what their own inner lives really are and imagine life, as it is called, as being something altogether outside them?

Now in self-observation, try to distinguish between outer events and inner states and notice where you are standing both in relation to your inner state and to the nature of the outer event. Outer events are of any kind. Outer life is not a smooth sheet of paper that we are crawling over like ants. It is full of hills and valleys, of good weather and bad weather. This is the nature of life—but, as a rule, all events we take as exceptional, or at least unpleasant ones, as illness, war, etc. Life is a series of different events coming along, on larger and smaller scales, to meet you, and each event has its special nature. And inner states are again of every kind. All personal work is about inner states and you have all heard of what wrong states one must work on and try not to identify with. If you work on these wrong states and try to separate yourselves from them, then the unpleasant events of life will not catch you, as it were, so easily, and draw force from you. Events are *influences* changing at every moment in their various combinations, and some are better than others, but all have to be taken consciously, even good ones—at this low level, where we are in the universe—namely, on the earth—and some of them are very dangerous and must not be identified with at all costs. From what has been said, it will become clearer that one's life is more to be thought of as one's *inner states* and a true history of one's life would be a history of one's inner states and negative emotions especially. To live *anyhow* in *oneself*—in this internal vast world accessible only to each person through individual self-observation and always invisible to others—is the worst crime we can commit. So this work begins with self-observation and noticing wrong states in oneself and working against them. In this way the inner life becomes purified and since our inner life attracts our outer life, by changing our inner states, starving some and nourishing others, we also alter not only our relation to *events* coming from outside but even the nature of the events that come to us day by day. Only in this way can we change the nature of events that happen to us. We cannot change them directly, but only through changing *states*—that is, through beginning to put this disorderly house we live in into some order. It is not the events of to-day that happened to you that matter—such as that you lost something or something went wrong or someone forgot you or spoke to you harshly, etc., etc.—but how you reacted to it all—

that is, what states of yourself you were in—for it is here that your real life lies and if our inner states were right nothing in the nature of external states could overcome us. Try therefore to distinguish, as an exercise in living more consciously, between inner states and outer events, and try to meet any outer event, after noticing its nature, with the right inner attitude—that is, with the right state. And if you cannot, think afterwards about it—first try to define the nature of the event and notice if this kind of event often comes to you and try to see it more clearly in terms such as "This is called being late" or "This is called losing things" or "This is called receiving bad news" or "This is called unpleasant surprises" or "This is called hard work" or "This is called being ill". Begin in this very simple way and you will soon see how different personal events, and so how in this respect one's outer life, are changing all the time, and what you could not do at one moment, you can at another. For events as it were are like the opening and shutting of doors. Then you will be able to see, in regard to the small events of daily life, what events are partly due to your own cause, and what are accidental, and so on. And then think about your state and with what state you usually meet some rather typical event and whether the state is, as it were, the right tool to use, the right ticket to offer, the right method to employ for that event. Towards very many events one has to learn to be *passive*—i.e., not react at all, not do anything. But to be passive demands a great inner activity of consciousness, to prevent any mechanical reaction taking place when the event, coming in as a mechanical impression, touches the purely associative machinery of mind and feeling which we mistakenly take as ourselves.

COMMENTARY II—*Birdlip, June* 6, 1941

ON ADDITIONAL MEANS OF SELF-OBSERVATION

Section I—The following is a commentary, which refers to the idea of different 'I's in us. As you know, in this system of teaching, man is not regarded as a unity. The lack of unity in a man is the source of all his difficulties and troubles. Man's body is a unity and works as an organized whole unless it is sick. But man's inner life is not a unity and has not organization and does not work harmoniously as a whole. Man, in regard to his inner state, is a multiplicity, and from one angle in this teaching, this inner multiplicity is spoken of in terms of 'I's or egos in a man. Man has no one permanent 'I' but a host of different 'I's in him that at each moment take charge of him and speak out of him as if in his voice: and from this point of view man is compared with a house in disorder in which there is no master but a crowd of servants who speak in the name of the absent master. As you have probably all heard, it is the greatest mistake that can be made either to suppose that oneself or others have one permanent unchanging 'I' —or ego—in them. A man is never the same for long. He is continually changing. But he imagines that if a person is called James he is always James. This is quite untrue. This man whom we call James has in him other 'I's, other egos, which take charge of him at different moments, and although perhaps James does not like telling lies, another 'I' in him—let us call it Peter—likes to lie and so on. To take another person as one and the same person at all times, to suppose he is one single 'I', is to do violence to him and in the same way is to do violence to oneself. A multitude of different people live in each of you. These are all the different 'I's belonging to personality, which it is necessary to observe, and try to get to know, otherwise no *self-knowledge* is possible —that is, if one really seeks *self-knowledge* and not invention and imagination about oneself. Not one of you here has a real permanent, unchanging 'I'. Not one of you here has real unity of being. All of you are nothing but a crowd of different people, some better and some worse, and each of these people—each of these 'I's in you—at particular moments takes charge of you and makes you do what it wants and say what it wishes and feel and think as it feels and thinks. But you already know all this and I want to speak in more detail about this *doctrine of many 'I's* in a man and suggest to you something about its deeper meaning and significance. If some of you cannot understand what follows, it is either because you have not yet had sufficient practice in self-observation, in which case you must be patient and wait a little, or it is because, if you have been longer in the work, you have not even begun seriously to observe yourselves yet—that is, you have not begun to work on yourselves and perhaps even have never seriously thought what it means. In the latter case, I can only say that you must really try to make an effort to understand what it means, through actual self-observation, and as soon as possible, for time is counted in the work, and opportunities begin of themselves to get fewer and if one does not take them while it is possible it may, in the very nature of things, become too late to do anything with oneself in the way of inner change, which is only possible through self-observation and the self-knowledge that comes from it.

The first point to which I will draw your attention in connection with the doctrine of many 'I's in a man is that as long as a man takes himself *as one* he cannot change. But have you thought for yourselves —that is, from your own private thinking—why this is so? You all know that this work is to make a man think for himself and that to hear the ideas of this system without thinking about them for oneself and so making them become part of oneself is so much waste of time. The work is not something external, but internal, and people who imagine that the work, as an external organization, will carry them along are sadly mistaken about its meaning. The very fact that the work begins with *self-observation* surely is sufficient to shew that it demands a personal effort on the part of each individual and only each of you can observe himself or herself and no one else can do this for you. Now it is only through the effort of self-observation that a man can eventually see for himself that he is not one and so break the illusion that he is one permanent unvarying individual. For as long as a man has this illusion that he is always one and the same person, he cannot change —and, as you know, the object of this work is to bring about a gradual change in one's inner life. In fact, the whole of this work is based on the idea that self-change or transformation of oneself is a definite possibility in everyone and is the real goal of existence. But the starting-point of this self-change remains hidden as long as a man is under the illusion that he is *one*. A man must realize for himself that he is not *one* but *many* and he can only do this by means of uncritical observation of himself. But for a long time the illusion that he is always one and the same person will struggle with his attempt to observe himself uncritically and make it difficult for him to realize the significance of his observations. He will find excuses and justify himself and so cling to the idea that he is really one and has a permanent individuality and that he always knows what he is doing and thinking and saying and is always conscious of himself and in control of himself at all times. It will be very difficult for him to admit to himself that this is not the case. And on the other hand, it will be quite useless if he pretends to believe that he is not *one* and does not see the truth of it for himself. It is a part of the *knowledge* of this system of teaching that man is not one but many. But merely as knowledge it lies only in a man's memory. Unless a man sees the truth of this knowledge by applying it to himself, by working on his being, it cannot become understanding. A man may say: "I know I am not one but many—the work says so." But that is nothing. The knowledge remains external to the man himself. But if he applies this knowledge practically and through long self-observation begins to see the truth of it, then he will say: "I understand I am not one but many"—and this is quite a different thing. The knowledge will have borne fruit in him, so to speak, and will no longer be merely knowledge, but understanding, because the man has applied the knowledge to himself and by means of it worked on his own being. And you will remember the great emphasis laid in this system on the difference between knowledge and understanding and how often it is said that in these times to-day knowledge has gone far beyond understanding, because man has developed only on the side of *knowledge* and not correspondingly on the side of *being*.

When a man begins to observe himself from the angle that he is not one but many, he begins to work on his being. He cannot do this if he remains under the conviction that he is one, for then he will not be able to separate himself from himself, for he will take everything in him, every thought, mood, feeling, impulse, desire, emotion, and so on, as himself—that is, as 'I'. But if he begins to observe himself, he will then, at that moment, become two—an observing side and an observed side.

And unless he divides himself in this way and struggles to make this division more and more distinct, he will never be able to shift from where he is, because, always taking everything that takes place in him as himself, he will say 'I' to it all and so everything will then be 'I' in him, and by identifying himself with everything that happens in himself, and taking it all as 'I', he will make it impossible to change everything, for everything will hide itself behind this illusion of 'I' and continue to live in him. In fact, the whole crowd of people in a man—the crowd of separate 'I's in him—both the useful and useless—will have, as it were, equal rights and be equally protected by him because he will be quite unable to distinguish them from one another since he takes them all as himself. This is merely one way of putting the situation within a man who remains convinced that he is *one*. Now a man cannot begin to change until he is able as the result of self-observation to say: "*This is not I*". As soon as he can begin to say this internally to something he observes in himself, he begins to separate it from himself. That is, he begins to take the feeling of 'I' out of it and the result is, eventually, and often only after a struggle, that what he has observed begins to move away from him and so pass, as it were, into the distance in his inner world. But this is impossible if he thinks that what he has observed is *himself*, for then it will still be 'I' in him and 'I' cannot change 'I', for then no separation will be possible and he will remain united with what he has observed, by taking it as 'I'—that is, as himself—instead of taking it as an 'I' in him.

When a man is thinking he believes that it is himself thinking. But our thoughts come at random, unless we are thinking deeply and with attention, which is very rare. The thoughts that pass across our minds come from different 'I's in us. Let us suppose a man notices that he is having negative thoughts about the work or about a person or something that has happened. Let us suppose that he takes these thoughts as his own—as himself—that is, as 'I'—and let us also suppose that he feels some discomfort about them. He says to himself: "I must really not think in this way." This may have some result or it may not. But the point is that he is making a mistake—namely, the mistake of taking all that happens within him as himself, as 'I'. If he observes himself rightly, he notices these thoughts not as himself but as coming from a negative 'I' in him, which perhaps he knows something about already. Let us suppose he knows this 'I' in him fairly well. He recognizes at once that this 'I' is talking in him and communicating its thoughts to him through the mental centre and stirring up at the same time a particular kind of negative emotion. He does not for a moment take this negative 'I' as himself but sees it as something in him apart from himself. As a result what it says does not get power over him, because he is separate from it. But if he goes to sleep in himself—that is, if he ceases to be conscious of what is going on in him and which 'I's are close to him—he falls under its power and, becoming identified with it, imagines that it is he himself who is thinking in that way. By doing this, he strengthens the power of this negative 'I' over him—because, as you know, whatever we identify with at once has power over us, and the more often we identify with something, the more we are slaves to it. In regard to the work itself, our temptations lie exactly in negative 'I's—that is, in 'I's that hate the work because their lives in us are threatened by it. These negative 'I's start certain kinds of thoughts through acting on the mental centre and using the material stored there in the form of rolls. If we go with these thoughts—that is, with these negative 'I's that are at the moment working in us—we are unable to shake off their effect. Their first effect is to make us feel a loss of force. Whenever we feel a sudden loss of force, it is practically always due to the action of a negative 'I' which has started a train of thought from our memories and, by carefully selecting its material, represented something in a wrong light—and it must be remembered that all negative 'I's can only lie, just as all negative emotions can only distort everything, as, for instance, the emotion of suspicion. Unless we can observe the action of the negative 'I' in the mental centre, it will gain power over us. It will gain power instantly if we take it as 'I'—as ourselves. But if we see it as an 'I' at work in us, it cannot do so. But in order to realize that it is an 'I' in us, we must already have become certain, by practical work on ourselves, that many different 'I's exist in us, and that we are not one, but many.

* * *

Section II—Let us return to the illusion everyone has that he is one. This illusion exists in each of you. It can only be discovered gradually by personal observation. Each of you ascribes to himself the possession of individuality and not only individuality but full consciousness and will. But as you know this system of ideas that we are studying teaches that man is not one, but many—that is, he is not one individual, but many different people—and also that he is not properly *conscious* but nearly always asleep in dreams, in imagination, in considering, in negative emotions, and so on, and as a result does not remember himself and so, as it were, wastes and destroys his inner life, and lives in a sort of darkness and finally that he does not possess *will* but has many different wills which conflict with one another and act in different directions. If man were a unity instead of being a multiplicity, he would have true individuality. He would be one and so would have one will. The illusion, therefore, that a man has about himself that he is one refers to a possibility. Man *can* attain unity of being. He can reach his true individuality. But it is precisely this illusion that stands first of all in the way of man's attainment of this possibility. For as long as a man imagines he has something, he will not seek for it. Why should a man strive for something that he has never doubted for a moment that he possesses already? This is one of the effects of the imagination, which fills up, as it were, what is lacking or makes it appear that we are like this, or like that, when actually we are the reverse. In this work it is

we will have jam to-morrow. But it is always to-morrow. If a man says: "I will begin to work on myself to-morrow", then he will never work on himself, for it is always to-morrow that he will work and never to-day. This is sometimes called in the work the disease of *mañana* —to-morrow. As long as a man says always *mañana*—that is, *to-morrow* —he will never change.

In order to work on oneself it is necessary to circumscribe the field of work—that is, not to dream idly of working in the future on some grand occasion but to work to-day—to circumscribe practical work to to-day, to this very day with its events, and not think in terms of to-morrow. Have you begun to observe yourself in regard to the day —the ordinary every-recurring day that is the cosmically determined miniature of the year and of one's whole life? You all know that saying: "Sufficient unto the day is the evil thereof". But have you thought what this saying means and have you considered the context in which Christ made this remark? What, for instance, does it mean when it is said *sufficient*. Sufficient for what? It is sufficient to work on the evil of to-day. If a man begins to work even a little on the day and its vexations and troubles, he then begins to work practically on himself. But he must get to know his day and get to know himself in relation to his day. There is a certain average day that each person passes through, apart from very unusual events. The events of the ordinary day have, as you will admit, a certain recurring similarity for each person. Now suppose that a man never realizes this and never observes himself in connection with the typical events of his average day, how can he even think he is working on himself and how can he even suppose he can change himself? Change of being begins with changing your reactions to actual incidents of the day. This is the beginning of taking your life in a real and practical sense in a new way. If you behave in the same way every day to the same recurring events of the day, how can you believe that you can change? To get to know yourself, begin with observing your behaviour towards the events of a single day in your life. Notice how you react—that is, notice your *mechanical reactions* to all the little events that happen and to other people and notice what you say, feel, think and so on. Then try to see how you can change these reactions. Of course if you are certain that you always behave consciously and rationally and that you are never in the wrong, and so on, nothing will ever change in you, for you will never be able to realize that you are a machine, a mechanical person, always saying and feeling and thinking and doing typical things according to changing circumstances over and over again. But perhaps, owing to a grain of modesty or a sense of humiliation or, better still, owing to increasing consciousness of yourself, you may realize that you are not *one*—not a fully conscious individual, willing his life consciously at every moment, but at one moment a mean person, at the next an irritable person, at the next a benevolent person and the next a scandalous or slanderous person, at the next a saint, at the next a liar. Try to make the work-exercise of behaving *consciously* for a small part of one day in your life. Because everything we do affects us for ever. A single moment in which one is conscious enough not to behave mechanically, if it is done *willingly*, can change many future results. If you learn, say, a little French to-day, you will know more to-morrow, but if you do nothing to-day, you will know nothing more to-morrow. It is the same with work on oneself. But one must work willingly on oneself and not because one is told to. To work sullenly or for merit, is one thing; to work on oneself because one dislikes something in oneself and longs to alter it, is another thing.

Our whole manner of taking a day in our lives is wrong because by habit it gets fixed and so mechanical. Then indeed we are mechanical and so have no real feeling of what we are doing and our days pass in a strange unfelt way—i.e., we follow the mechanical habits of the day and so have no real life and take in no new impressions. "It" acts— that is, the machine. But if a man starts his day *consciously*, the whole day may be rather different for him. But he must get to know what it means to work on himself, taking his life *as a day*—to see, observe, and realize what a *day* is for him, and not think that a day for him is unimportant because it is so usual and that work means something in the future—or that work is something "he has no chance yet to apply to himself, because he is so busy with his day's work", as someone once said to me in a serious manner. How do you get up, in what mood are you at breakfast, what always upsets you, etc., etc.? Please do not think that to change yourself is merely to smoke less or eat less. Remember this work is psychological. Our daily life, our profession, our trade, our occupation, etc., are nothing but a dream with which we identify. But this understanding comes slowly—when we understand better what *sleep* and mechanicalness mean and why mankind is called *asleep* and life is called mechanical. To work on yourself, begin to work on daily life and then you will understand what is meant by the strange phrase: "Give us this day our daily bread" in the Lord's Prayer. For the word "daily" here means in the Greek supersubstantial bread or "bread from above". The ideas of this work are to give us *bread for life* in the double sense of ideas and force to meet with the troubles of daily mechanical life and so supersubstantial "bread"; and to feed a new life beginning in oneself, for in the work everyone seeks to become a new person. Now no one can alter his life or change anything in regard to his mechanical reactions to his daily life unless he has the help of new ideas and is helped by the force coming from these new ideas and the new thoughts that are born in his mind if he begins to understand them. Remember that the slightest thing counts in regard to mechanical reaction to ordinary daily life—the slightest negative reaction matters, and the slightest wrong thinking about oneself or another, or internal consider- ing, or negative imagination, and so on. To prepare lower centres to receive the ideas and force always coming from higher centres (but not heard, as it were, owing to our heavy inner state of sleep) is long work

27

—but every attempt, done willingly, to correct or separate from a negative reaction, every attempt to remember oneself in the presence of a difficulty, every act of sincere observation of oneself, as when one is lying or shewing off or making oneself over-important from false personality, or twisting the truth to injure another, helps to make right connections in lower centres and so to prepare them for conjunction with higher centres and the help that comes from them.

NOTE ADDED

Now let us speak for a moment on personal work at the present moment in which the added fact of war exists. A man in this work has to insulate himself from the effects of life, otherwise he is eaten, as it were, by life. All work on oneself is connected with insulating oneself so that something can grow and develop which cannot do so under the influence of life because life does not develop anything beyond personality in us, and this, though necessary, is not yet the development of the real part of us, but is something artificial. If a man does not insulate himself, but identifies with everything and wastes his force in negative emotions and considering, imagining and mechanical talking, and so on, nothing can develop in him beyond what he is, mechanically. Actually, in esotericism, a man must become hermetically sealed, as an ancient phrase puts it, and this refers to something internal, of which we will speak at some other time, connected with the power of silence. The phrase belongs to the language of ancient times when there existed a teaching on man's inner evolution connected with the name of Hermes. Apart from this, you can understand that if you leak all the time, and have no insulation from life, there will never be enough force in you to lead to the growth of anything in you. You will not be able even to develop ordinary accomplishments. So it is necessary to learn how to hold off things and struggle *against life* each day. That is why it is said sometimes that this work is *against life*—at least, this is one meaning. But if you have fundamentally a wrong attitude to life, and believe that everything should go right in life, you will take even the most ordinary troubles as exceptional and be continually disappointed and upset and lose force and simply be a weak person—that is, weak in life. A great deal of sentimental nonsense is spoken and written about life. But you do not meet this in the work. The work says life is mechanical and humanity is asleep and men cannot *do* and everything happens. Yet people cannot believe this, even when terrible things take place, and imagine it is due to this or that person and that it is exceptional, and so on. All this is due to a wrong attitude. You remember what the definition of *good householder* is in this system—a man who does his duty and is a responsible person, etc., but who *does not believe* in life. Now you will see that here lies a very difficult thing to understand, so difficult that I am not going to say anything more about it, except that, in these times, it is very important not to let *what happens in life* weaken your thoughts and feelings and experience of the work itself, in the way that it does to so many ordinary folk, who, seeing the horror of war, feel convinced that there can be no meaning in things and no God. Remember the work says that life is mechanical and man is asleep. It does not, in other words, start from any false ideas of the nature of life or the nature of man. If you take the outer scene—that is, life—as your criterion and standard, do you not see how this war can drag you down and make you lose force? Now can you see how, if you have a work-attitude to life, this war can increase the reality of the work? Try to find out what is meant in what I have briefly said and try to act upon it—that is, try to *think* from the ideas of the work and so get the right attitude to this life on earth, where, as you know, we are under so many laws—where, indeed, we are in almost the worst part of the whole creation. You have often heard it said that in this work it is necessary to *transform impressions* and that this is the essence of the first conscious shock, as it is called. I know that many of you do not understand the nature, in a practical way, of the first conscious shock, and simply say that it means self-remembering. But a word does not explain what it means. The transformation of daily life, that is, of its impact upon us, depends on understanding all that has been taught you about practical work—about self-observation and work on negative states, work on identifying, and so on. It is this that *insulates* you. When you realize that you need not take a thing or a person in the way you are taking them, you transform something and at the same time you insulate yourself. *Self-remembering*, *non-identifying* and *not-considering* all help to insulate us from the influences of life. Acting consciously at a difficult moment has the same effect. Similarly, if you experience a moment of real consciousness, a moment of self-remembering, you will feel that it is just as if you were insulated from life and that nothing could touch you. And such would be the case if we were always in a state of self-remembering. Our task is to try to *imitate* higher states of consciousness, so as to attract them.

COMMENTARY IV — *Birdlip, June* 17, 1941

ON A, B and C INFLUENCES

Part I.—It is necessary for everyone to think often about what he understands for himself of the meaning of this system of teaching. What does this teaching imply? What is it about? Why, for example, is it necessary to struggle with identifying, with negative states, with imagination, with internal considering, with self-justifying and other forms of mechanical lying, with mechanical talking, and so on. Why should one try to observe and break buffers or notice mechanical attitudes, or detect pictures of oneself? Why must false personality be struggled with in all its unpleasant manifestations? Why should it be necessary to remember oneself?

In the first place, you must understand that this system forms an organic whole. To take a small part without connection with the rest is not enough. It is not enough because the meaning of the whole teaching reflects itself into every part of it, and in order to feel the meaning of any one part of it—such as what it says about self-justifying, for instance—it is necessary to have some idea of the whole. Merely to say to oneself: "I must observe self-justifying in myself and try to stop it", while it may not be useless if it is done sincerely and may shew something to oneself that one had not realized, can easily become a mechanical action—that is, one that is done without conscious meaning.

Consider, for a moment, what it means that this system is an organic whole. The meaning of this work as a whole and the related meanings derived from the general meaning, right down to the smallest meanings, all stand in connected relation to and within one another. Its organization is like that of all living things, as for example that of the body. In the body the smallest parts unite to form larger parts, and these combine to form the body as a whole. Everything is connected with and related to everything else.

Knowledge of this system demands knowledge of the details *and* the parts *and* the whole; and if this system were not organic in the sense explained above, this would be impossible. People often say of one or another detail or part of this system: "Oh, that is like something I read in a book", or they say: "Oh, that is like what so and so teaches, or what this or that philosophy or religion says", etc., etc. It is quite true that if you read certain kinds of literature you will find a sentence here or a sentence there which reminds you of something in this work. But all these are fragments. They are merely separate bits, not in any organized relation with any whole, and, isolated by themselves, are useless. Let us suppose someone comes across a sentence in some old book in which it is said that "man is asleep". He may imagine for a moment that he has found the system in the book, but if he looks more closely he will see that it is an isolated statement. It is without connection, and so without any organic relation with any other ideas. And if he compares this detail with all that this work says about sleep and about awaking, about different states of consciousness, about mechanical and conscious humanity and about all that it is necessary to do in order to awaken out of sleep, he will realize that the man who wrote the book had merely heard something, but had no real knowledge. What, then, is *real* knowledge?

Real knowledge implies a knowledge of the part in *relation* to the whole—that is, real knowledge is relative in this sense. This is the real meaning of the principle of relativity in knowledge, from the standpoint of this system. A rough illustration of what is meant is as follows: A man may know all about the little village he lives in, but nothing about the town or county or country he lives in, or of other countries, or the world in general. He has no relative knowledge and so can neither see anything in its right proportion, nor can he have greater knowledge. This is very important to understand. By having real knowledge—that is, relative knowledge—a man's knowledge can grow in a right way, otherwise only one-sidedness results, with all the evils that follow, that are more obvious to-day than at any time in the world.

Now let us apply what has been said to any single part of the work. Let us take the example of *self-justifying*. As you know, it is said, in connection with practical work on oneself, that it is necessary to observe self-justifying. But if a man does not see why he should observe self-justifying in himself and work against it, he is trying to do what has no meaning for him, save that he is told to do it. If that is the case, he will be working in the most external way possible. What he is doing will be superficial, not really connected with him through any inner meaning. To work in this way is little else than to give a sort of lip-service to the work. And, still worse, he may be doing it for the sake of meritoriousness just to say that he is working, especially if he speaks of it. And he will not see that it is exactly self-justification that is at the root of feeling pleasure in meritoriousness, which only strengthens false personality, having nothing real or genuine in it. You will now understand why it was said at the beginning of this commentary that it is necessary for everyone to think for himself about the meaning of this teaching. Unless he does so, he will do everything in a vague external way, without seeing or understanding what it is all about, and without having any *force* to work. Meaning gives force and the more meaning this work has for you the more it will affect you emotionally and the more force will you obtain from it. For it is from the awakening of the emotional centre that the greatest force is derived.

Now let us begin with the meaning of this work on the highest scale. Let us begin, as it were, from the top. What does this work mean? You have all heard it said that there are two quite different kinds of influences existing in life, entitled respectively *A* and *B* influences in this system. *A* influences are created by life. They arise within the life of mechanical humanity from the interests of business, money-making, science, sport, politics, from the interests of conquest, intrigue, crime, power, from the interests of wealth, position, display and possessions, and from all the necessary interests of food, clothing, housing, law, order, and so on. You have only to open the newspaper to see what *A* influences are and to understand how they are created by life and arise within the life of humanity. All these interests develop personality, and in time, from personality, especially false personality, other interests arise, which become part of human life and which again are *A* influences. But there exist also in life influences of a quite different kind, called in this system *B* influences. These do not arise from life. Their source of origin is different. They have nothing to do with business, money-making, politics, sport, and so on. They come from outside the circle of mechanical life. In all ages and at all times we can find evidence of their existence in a certain class of literature, in certain religious ideas, in many ancient writings, in teachings that have been preserved to us, often in all sorts of disguised forms, in allegories, in fairy-stories, and so on. It is a very startling experience for anyone who has become familiar with the ideas of this work and has begun to understand something of its real significance to open a book written, say, a thousand or two thousand years ago or even more, and find some sentence which is, so to speak, "the pure work". What is the explanation? Why is there so great a background to the ideas of this system? What does it mean? It means, to begin with, that this system of work which we are studying is nothing new. It is nothing new in the sense that it is not something that some man or other invented recently and concocted out of his own mind, like some passing modern psychological theory. The system we are studying is the presentation in a form adapted to the times of something that was long ago understood, and long ago taught, about man and his inner possibilities. It has been understood and it has been taught not only since the beginning of known history, which is only a brief portion of all human history, but long before it, reaching us only in legendary form, in myths and allegories. The same teaching has *always* been given, but it has been given in different outer forms, in different dress, according to circumstances, according to the times and according to the nature of the people or race to which it is being given. It has changed only in regard to the general *state* of people—that is, their level of being and the depth of their sleep in the things of the external senses and so of their opportunities in respect of inner evolution.

Now all the traces in history concerning the idea that man is capable of reaching something of incalculable value, a treasure that cannot be estimated, through inner work on himself, constitute what are called in this system *B* influences. Since they do not relate to life, their existence in life is inexplicable unless we understand that they are essential for humanity—unless humanity wishes to perish totally in hate and destruction, which is a possibility closer to us than ever before. In the next commentary I will speak of the source of origin of *B* influences in the light of the ideas taught by this system. But if anyone wishes to ask for a clear example of *B* influences now existing in life, let him take as an example the New Testament, or rather, the four Gospels, which alone contain the teaching of Christ, and let him only take the recorded words of Christ. It will be obvious to him that the ideas contained in these words are not similar to the ideas belonging to *A* influences—to the newspapers—and are obviously about something different from the ordinary aims and interests of life, although, in a subtle way, they bear on the latter. Let him only reflect that he is taught to struggle with hatred and look into himself and see what he is like.

So far we have seen that this system of work is an organic whole, and every part and detail of it, such as the detail of self-justifying, is connected with ideas which have *always* existed and have been taught in every age. These ideas and teachings always are the same thing. They are always about the transformation of life. They are not about life and life-interests, but about the transforming of *yourself* in relation to all that happens to you every day in life, in the light of an entirely new set of ideas and entirely new aims and entirely new efforts. And when you begin to try to do all this, remember that you are beginning to do something that has always been taught to those capable of understanding and that the meaning of what you are doing is so great, so deep, so eternal, that, even if you can catch a mere glimpse of it, your emotions will awaken and you will see in a flash what is meant by evaluation of the work, and what is meant by greater mind, and what is meant by the sleep of humanity.

COMMENTARY IV—*Birdlip, June 24, 1941*

ON A, B and C INFLUENCES

Part II.—Last time the existence of two distinct kinds of influences in life, called *A* and *B* respectively, was spoken of. In this commentary, of which this is the second part, we are speaking of the need for connecting any part or detail of this system with the whole meaning. In order to get force to work, what you do in working on yourself must have *meaning* and the more meaning the system conducts for you—that is, the more it means to you and the more the evaluation of it grows— the more force you will get from it. If you do not value it, if you like to doubt it, if you never really think about it, and do not try to see its significance more and more as time passes, by working along both the line of knowledge and the line of being, and so on, then whatever you do in connection with the work will have no meaning for you and so no force. You know that when anything has intense meaning for you it generates force in you, and if it has little or no meaning, then there is no force.

At present we are speaking of the general meaning of this work— that is, on the highest scale. In this connection it is now necessary to speak of the source of *B* influences. As was said in Part I, *B* influences do not arise within life as do *A* influences. Their origin is from a source outside mechanical life. Actually, their source is in *C* influences. What does this mean?

As you know, in the teaching of this work, mankind is not taken as being all on one and the same level. Man is divided into different categories. Quite different kinds of men exist. There is, first of all, the circle of mechanical humanity, as it is called, in which No. 1, No. 2 and No. 3 men exist. They are respectively men in whom mainly one centre is used—the instinct-moving centre in the case of No. 1 man, the emotional centre in the case of No. 2 man and the intellectual centre in the case of No. 3 man. These instinct-moving men, emotional men and intellectual men, because they are mainly "one-centred", see everything differently, each from one side, from one centre. They form together the circle of mechanical humanity which is characterized by the fact that people belonging to this circle are based on violence and do not understand either themselves or one another. It is called sometimes the circle of "confusion of tongues" or Babel, in which misunderstandings, quarrels, strife, persecutions, and war of every kind must always exist without leading to anything different. Next comes an intermediary circle formed of No. 4 man. This circle does not arise in life but as the result of work. No. 4 man is developed in all the ordinary centres so he is not one-sided and so is called "balanced man". No. 4 men begin to be able to understand one another and begin to overcome violence in themselves. Then comes the conscious circle of humanity formed by No. 5, No. 6 and No. 7 men who understand one another, who are not based on violence, and who are not only developed in the ordinary centres but who have the power of being conscious from a lesser to a greater extent in *higher emotional* and *higher mental centres*. These centres transmit influences to which mechanical humanity—that is, sleeping humanity—are insensitive, or rather, which they cannot "hear". It is from the circle of conscious humanity that B influences originate. But they originate, not as B influences, but as C influences. It is only when they are sown into mechanical life that they become B influences. This happens, because, as C influences, they cannot exist in mechanical life, but become changed and altered in such a way that they only approximate to their original form. Just as the ideas and emotional perceptions belonging to higher centres cannot be caught or understood by the "formatory centre", so conscious teaching cannot exist in the sphere of mechanical life by itself. But it can be kept alive and transmitted by means of schools *having a direct connection* with people who have reached that degree of inner evolution and consciousness belonging to the circle of conscious humanity. In these schools, C influences can exist and be transmitted orally—that is, by oral teaching—from one person who understands, to another, who begins to understand, and so to another who does not yet understand. This *chain* must exist. And in such a case, these influences can be transmitted orally as C influences, handed on from one person to another.

Let us take the example of the Gospels. As was said in the first part of this commentary on *A, B* and *C* influences (which was read last time) the Gospels constitute an example of *B* influences. People sometimes ask a question of the following nature: "Why", they say, "are the Gospels an example of *B* influences? Surely Christ was a conscious man? Why, then, are the Gospels not an example of *C* influences?" We must remember that the Gospels appeared a long time after Christ died— from fifty to one hundred years after. It is not at all certain who were their authors. It is incorrect to suppose they are merely records written on the spot by eye-witnesses. Luke, for example, never heard Christ. He was a pupil of Paul, who of course never heard Christ, and who quarrelled with the school at Jerusalem and apparently got his teaching in some school near Damascus. But it is unnecessary to go into historical questions. You have only to read the Gospels to see that it is said that Christ taught his disciples in private and only said a certain amount to the public, and nearly always in the form of parables. In the Gospel of Matthew, after the Parable of the Sower has been related, it is said that the disciples asked Christ why he spoke to the people in parables: "And he answered and said unto them, Unto you it is given to know the mysteries of the kingdom of heaven, but to them it is not given. For whosoever hath, to him shall be given, and he shall have abundance: but whosoever hath not, from him shall be taken away even that which he hath. Therefore speak I to them in parables; because seeing they see not, and hearing they hear not, neither do they understand." — (*Matthew* XIII *xi-xiii*)

The kingdom of God is the circle of conscious humanity. It means the circle of those who have evolved beyond violence, of those whose knowledge is practical—that is, *what they know, they will*, and so *do*—of those who understand one another because they speak a common language—(and let us remember that we, in this work, are learning a common language). Everyone knows and feels that there must be some place, some society, some beings who live without mutual violence, criticism, dislike or hatred. I will quote, in this connection, a passage in the Mahometan esoteric literature. A pupil came to Mahomet for instruction. Mahomet said: "What is the substance of thy faith and the reality of thy understanding of it?" The pupil said: "I have seen Hell and Heaven three times in a vision. In Hell everyone was attacking his neighbour. In Heaven they were visiting one another." Mahomet said: "Thou hast seen aright".

I have said enough in this commentary now to shew you what is the supreme meaning of the work. Everyone who wishes to can read and think for himself about the parables in the Gospels concerning the Kingdom of Heaven—that is, the circle of conscious humanity. These parables are very extraordinary when you think of them in the light of the work. For the work is necessary to understand the fragments of teaching given in the Gospels. It is then possible to understand why it is said, in this system, that what we seek above all things is *Light*—and Light means *consciousness*. We seek to live more consciously and to become more conscious. We live in darkness owing to lack of light—the light of consciousness—and we seek in this work light on ourselves. Everything this system says about work on oneself—about self-remembering, about struggling with negative emotions, about internal considering, about self-justifying, and so on, has as its supreme aim to make a man more conscious—to let *light* dawn *in him*. And it is a very strange thing, this *light*. It is first to become more conscious of oneself and then more conscious of others. This is a strange experience. I mean

35

by this that the direction in which the work leads you through increasing consciousness, increasing light, is not at all the direction you might imagine as a person asleep, a person who knows only ordinary consciousness—that is, the first two states of consciousness in which humanity lives. To become more conscious of yourself is a strange experience. To become conscious of others is just as strange and even more strange. The life you yourself lead with passions and jealousies, meannesses, dislikes and hatreds, becomes utterly ridiculous. You wonder, in fact, what on earth you have been doing all your life. Have you been insane? you ask yourself. Yes, exactly. In the deep sleep we live in, in the light of the Kingdom of Heaven, we are all utterly insane and do not know what we are doing. The work begins to teach you what to do. To awaken—that is the object of this work. And for a man who awakens even to one single thing that the work teaches it means that he is no longer the same man. In this way the work changes us. But the work cannot change anyone unless its meaning is felt. You can feel the meaning of the work through another at first, but the time comes when you must feel it through yourself. And then every detail of the work becomes alive to you because you see it as a book of instruction, as a plan, as a map, and as a compass, that must be followed if you wish to awaken to another life and another way of living on this earth. Take quite simply this one single instruction: *do not identify*. Follow this instruction. Follow it to the end and see what happens and what changes take place in you and what light begins to reach you. But if this work has no real meaning to you and if the meaning of life is always far greater and more real to you than the meaning of the work, then no change in yourself can ever happen and you will only know life-emotions and remain in the circle of mechanical life, in the circle of confusion and strife and quarrels and disappointments and complaints and war.

COMMENTARY—*Birdlip, June 29, 1941*

MAN IS NOT A UNITY BUT MULTIPLE

(1) If a man takes himself as *one*, no struggle can develop within him. If no struggle develops within him, he cannot change.

Why is this so?

(2) If a man supposes there is only one thing that acts, thinks and feels in him—that is, one 'I'—then he cannot understand that there should be one thing that commands and another that obeys.

This means that if man regards himself as a unity, nothing can change in him. The work says: "Unless a man divides himself into two, he cannot shift from where he is in himself"—that is, he cannot be different in himself.

36

(3) If a man is so hypnotized and therefore so asleep as to think he is *one*, he cannot receive the ideas of the work. What is the object of the practical side of the work—that is, the ideas and instructions relating to *work on oneself*? This object is to make a man work on himself by dividing himself into a work-side and a mechanical side—that is, to observe himself from the angle of the work ideas. In that case, the observing side looks at the side to be observed. So a man becomes two —an observing side and an observed side.

(4) If a man thinks he is one and a unity, and that it is always the same self that acts and thinks and does, how can he observe himself? He cannot, because he imagines he himself is one and so nothing is to be observed about himself. In such a case, a man often believes that *observation* means observation of something outside himself—of 'buses, streets, people, scenery, etc. But self-observation is not done *via* the external senses which shew only what is *not oneself*—i.e., the outer world.

(5) Unless the work is established in a man by means of Observing 'I', nothing can change in him. Observing 'I' is more *interior* than life as sense. But if Observing 'I' is not supported by some depth of continual and renewed understanding of the *work*, it weakens and, in stress of outer life-circumstances, fades away—then a man finds himself simply back in life and if life is favourable at the moment to his self-interests, he does not suffer.

(6) The establishing of Observing 'I' is to make something more interior in a man, so that it can observe what is more exterior *in him* (exterior not in the sense of outer exterior life, but *in him*, in his personality, in Johnson, if his name is Johnson). Unless this Observing 'I' is established—that is, unless a man is willing to observe *himself* (and *himself* is not anything in outer sense-given life, his house, his furniture, his money, his dinners, his garden, his business, his social position, his medals, his pedigree, his clothes, etc.)—unless he can begin this inner act, nothing can change *in him*. He remains the *same person*.

(7) After a long time in the work the inner system, which starts from *willing* Self-Observation—that is, from a willing Observing 'I'—begins to act and control the mechanical man. It does this by means of collecting round it all 'I's in Personality which wish to and can work. This stage is *Deputy-Steward*. If this persists in spite of temptations, something very strange begins to happen. Temptations in this first stage of the work are wholly struggling against doubts, evil interpretations, slander, scruples, finding fault, making requirements, and so on, for no other temptations exist for us at this stage. This is where a man must first be tempted in this way to be any good for any further awakening. Observing 'I' collects round it 'I's that can work and understand the work. They form a small group of 'I's called Deputy-Steward, which have to struggle and fight, not only with False Personality but with undeveloped Essence. If Deputy-Steward, in spite of endless failures, becomes strong enough, "Steward" draws near. "Steward" belongs to something *above* man. It comes at first in flashes and often when it draws

37

near, people have great difficulties either externally or in struggles with negative states in the form of illness, etc. "Steward" comes from a different level. To receive, as it were, "Steward", a man must undergo a new setting of himself, a new ordering of his mind, or even brain cells. But this always takes place in the way best for the individual and can be endured. The work is to get in touch with higher centres. But they work in their own way so changes have to take place in a man. A man cannot produce these changes himself for he knows nothing of the new connections necessary. It is through his personal work and the struggle of Deputy-Steward in him that they are brought about—that is, what is trying to enter from above a man brings this about when the conditions are right. Once brought about, the man is a different man. His feeling of 'I' is different. His ideas and thoughts, his reasoning and his actions are different. He has undergone the self-evolution latent in him. He is "born again" as the phrase in the Gospels puts it.

But all this is impossible unless a man establishes *Observing 'I'* to begin with and has the help of the work, *via* the understanding of it for himself, which means the clustering of other 'I's in him round Observing 'I', so that a small band of 'I's is formed in the chaos of his inner life called "Deputy-Steward".

But, of course, if a man remains in the conceit that he is *one* and can only be *one*, and that there is always *one* thing that acts, feels, thinks, speaks, etc., in him, all that has been said above remains impossible of realization.

Birdlip, July 7, 1941

A NOTE ON SELF-REMEMBERING

It is useful to make a memorandum in one's mind about what practical work means.

The most important thing is self-remembering. You must try to remember yourselves at least once a day, and you must do it willingly, from yourselves. All other work on oneself ultimately depends on self-remembering. Only half a minute is necessary, and even if it consists in nothing else than stopping your thoughts and trying to relax everything, it is better than nothing. Don't *think* about self-remembering, but *do* it. At first it is best to do it at some definite time that you decide upon. The first sign that you are doing it rightly is that you have a distinct feeling of force entering you, as if something had opened in you. Immediately you feel this, stop. You must stop instantly, and forget about the whole thing.

Another form of self-remembering is called making "inner stop" in oneself. This is done in connection with self-observation. For example

38

you observe that you are beginning to talk in a certain mechanical way, or that you are getting annoyed with somebody, etc. You then make "inner stop", as it is called, but this must be made completely, as if something were cut off. It does not matter if later on the things you are trying to stop come back.

Let me say before going on that all self-observation should be accompanied by some degree of self-remembering. Remembering why you are observing yourself and feeling the presence of the work in your mind while observing yourself is a degree of self-remembering. Actually it brings carbon 12 up to the place in the human machine at that point where the First Conscious Shock can be given.

Next comes practical work on the centres. Let me remind you that all work means effort.

Work on Intellectual Centre

Everyone should have intellectual work of some kind. Any form of thinking that requires attention puts you into the conscious side of Intellectual Centre, such as thinking over something you have heard and trying to recall it, reading a book that needs attention, even writing letters or doing your accounts, etc., etc. There is a saying in this work that everybody must move his brains every day.

Work on Emotional Centre

The observation and the inner separation from all sorts of subtle depressions apart from the more obvious negative emotions, stopping imagination, working on negative states, and using your Intellectual Centre to remember exactly what was said, apart from what you imagined: all this is work on the Emotional Centre.

Work on the Moving Centre

Everyone in daily life should have some form of work that requires the use of Moving Centre. Some effort of the body is necessary and must be done willingly. If you do a thing willingly you do it from yourself—that is, you do it consciously; and everything that is done consciously is saved for you—it belongs to you. What you do unwillingly simply because you are told to do it is worse than useless. You have to tell yourself to do things. Again if you do things mechanically you get no benefit for yourself.

Work on Instinctive Centre

This is not necessary at our stage because the Instinctive Centre is far more clever than we are and knows far more than we do, but if something is wrong with the body we must try to help the Instinctive Centre as far as we can. Instinctive Centre regulates the inner work of the physical body and warns us that something is wrong, either by pain or discomfort. One of the worst things is to interfere with the work of Instinctive Centre when there is no cause to do so.

Of course many things have been left out in this short note. But you must all try to make some memorandum of this kind and apply it during the day-time. Remember that when you cannot work on one centre then you can work on another centre. Apart from your general aim you should have more or less three subsidiary aims connected with the Intellectual, Emotional and Moving Centres respectively.

Birdlip, July 16, 1941

CONCEPT OF CONSCIENCE IN THE WORK

Consciousness and *Conscience* are similar in their respective spheres, one being in the *Intellectual Centre*, the other in the *Emotional Centre*.
Consciousness is *Knowing all together*;
Conscience is *Feeling all together*.

CONSCIENCE

As you know, in the experiment of *religion* as a means of conveying teaching from Conscious to sleeping humanity, one of the sources of failure is that each person sets up his own dogma as absolute truth, and so people persecute, despise, and kill each other in the name of God. They may do so very earnestly and say they act from Conscience. But this is False or Mechanical Conscience and is formed in *Personality*. This False or Acquired Conscience is not based on *inner* understanding. It is related to False Personality and so to feeling merit and therefore feeling that one is right and better than others, and that others who have different religious beliefs are inferior or wicked and contemptible and worthy to be killed.

The difference between Real Conscience and Mechanical or False Conscience is that Real Conscience is the same in all men and speaks, as it were, the same language. Mechanical or False Conscience is different in different people, according to their nationality, upbringing, customs, forms of belief, etc.

If all men could *awaken*, Real Conscience would speak in them all and they would agree with one another, because it would speak in the same way to everyone.

Real Conscience exists in everyone but is buried and so out of reach. Personality has grown over it and as a result our feelings, our sense of ourselves, has shifted to Personality. Therefore to "feel all together" is impossible and indeed would be unendurable as we are. To "feel all together" would mean that we were one. But Personality is divided into little bits, as it were. The fundamental thing to grasp about Personality

40

is that it is multiple. For this reason you now feel in one way and now in another way, but separately and not together—and without even remembering—just as you think now in one way, then in another, or behave now in one way and then in another. And to all this shifting kaleidoscope within you, you say 'I'. That is, you imagine you are one person. As long as a man takes himself *as one person he will never move from where he is*. To awaken to Conscience you must begin to see the contradictions in yourself. But if you try to see contradictions in yourself taking yourself all the time as *one person* you will get nowhere. Indeed, you will stand in your own way and instead of stepping aside will create an impossible situation. It would be just as if you believed everything you saw in front of you was a part of your body.

What especially prevent a man from seeing contradictions in himself are *buffers*. In place of having Real Conscience a man has *Artificial Conscience* and *buffers*. Behind everyone there stand years and years of a wrong and stupid life, of indulgence in every kind of weakness, of sleep, of ignorance, of pretence, of lack of effort, of drifting, of shutting one's eyes, of striving to avoid unpleasant facts, of constant lying to oneself, of abuse and blaming of others, of fault-finding, of self-justifying, of emptiness, of wrong talking, and so on. As a result the human machine is dirty and works wrongly. Not only this, but artificial appliances have been created in it due to its wrong way of working. And however a person may wish to wake up and become another person and lead another life these artificial appliances interfere very much with his good intentions. They are called *Buffers*. Like the contrivances on railway carriages, their action is to lessen the shock of collision. But in the case of buffers in man their action is to prevent two contradictory sides of himself from coming into consciousness together.

Buffers are created gradually and involuntarily by the life around us, in which we are brought up. Their action is to prevent a man from feeling *Conscience*—that is, from feeling "all together". For example, very strong buffers exist between our likes and dislikes, between our pleasant feelings towards someone and our unpleasant feelings. To break a buffer it is necessary to observe oneself over a long period and remember how one felt and how one is feeling. That is, it is necessary to see on both sides of a buffer together, to see the contradictory sides of oneself that are separated by the buffer. Once a buffer is broken it cannot form again.

Buffers make a man's life more easy. They prevent him from feeling Real Conscience. But they also prevent him from developing. Inner development depends on shocks. Only shocks can lead a man out of the state he is in. When a man *realizes* something about himself, he suffers a shock, but the presence of buffers in him will prevent him from realizing anything. For buffers are made to lessen shocks. The more a man observes himself the more likely will it be for him to begin to see buffers in himself. The reason is that the more you observe yourselves the more you will catch glimpses of yourselves *as a whole*. If you observe different moments of your lives, after a time you catch a glimpse of yourself *over a period*, all together—that is, your consciousness of yourself increases. But first you must try to observe everything in yourself *at a given moment*—the emotional state, thoughts, sensations, intentions, posture, movements, tone of voice, facial expression and so on. All these must be photographed together. This is full observation and from this begin three things: (1) a new memory of oneself, (2) a complete change in the conception one previously had of oneself, (3) the development of *inner taste* in regard to the *quality* of what one is observing internally. For instance, by inner taste you can recognize that you are lying or in a negative state without difficulty, although you are justifying yourself and protesting you are not. Here the whole thing turns upon whether you possess inner sincerity or not. If not, then best to give up the work. *Inner taste* can be said to be the faint beginning of Real Conscience, because it is something that *recognizes the quality* of one's inner state. Self-observation and inner taste are not the same but may coincide. The more you understand the work, the more it is arranged rightly in your mind and its meaning seen, the more does it pass into Real Conscience. It is sometimes said that if we had Real Conscience the work would be unnecessary for we would know it already.

COMMENTARY—*Birdlip, July* 19, 1941

SOME THOUGHTS ON THE WAR
FROM THE STANDPOINT OF THE WORK

Part I.—War is an event which drags millions of people into its vortex whether they wish it or no. People, however, imagine that they are free. All man's life is based on the idea that he is free to choose. If a man could see clearly that he is mechanical—that is, that he is not free—he could not endure the realization. It is necessary to understand that mankind on the earth is under 48 laws, and each person is actually under 96 orders of laws. This is at first sight difficult to see unless you remember the Ray of Creation and realize from it that the part is under more laws than the whole. The fact, however, that man on earth is under many laws can be understood in general. These laws or influences, some waxing and some waning, as it were, or intercrossing and forming different combinations, produce the events that form the drama of human existence on the surface of the earth. Before an event occurs, it is quite easy to think that one is free from it. But when the event comes the case is different. It is almost as if it tried to drag as many as possible into its range and feed on them. People forget what they thought. The event attracts them into its sphere of influence. By means of buffers and self-justifying, they enter the event and pass under its power. A man may decide he will never fight again in any war. He is sure he will not. But when the drums begin to beat, when the horrors and madness of war start and he sees them or reads about them, he forgets all his resolutions. And it is the same not only with events on the scale of war, but events on the scale of his ordinary daily life. For events are on many different scales. There are, for instance, collective events—that is, events implicating nations or a single nation, such as wars or revolutions. And at the other end of the scale there are the little cycles of events that form an ordinary man's private life which turn like small wheels, repeating themselves endlessly—that is, in the same way, more or less, unless the man begins to struggle with himself and change himself. And although no one is really satisfied with his life, he does not see that his own level of being attracts his particular kind of life—that is, this repeating cycle of small events. Collective events —namely, events which involve millions of people—are like big wheels. But a person's life is like a small wheel turning somewhere in a vast machinery of bigger and smaller wheels—and all these wheels, big and little, form "life", which drives everyone.

This work speaks often of the necessity of isolating ourselves from collective events. We are connected with them by attitudes, as by invisible threads. To isolate oneself from collective events, it is necessary to change attitudes in oneself. It is through beginning to have a right attitude to the work that mechanically formed attitudes can be seen and altered or even alter themselves. One can only observe a thing in oneself by means of something else. A thing cannot observe itself. To observe, one must stand away from what one observes. The whole system of work and all its ideas, which belong to the age-old teaching about man and his possible development and inner freedom, give the full possibility of *self-observation*—that is, one observes oneself from the teaching and the ideas and knowledge of the work. A man in life cannot do this, for he has been formed by life and so can only observe himself from the ideas belonging to life.

War, in this system, is said to be caused by extra-terrestrial influences, not by people. It is said simply that planetary influences create war on earth. But it adds that these influences create war on *sleeping humanity*. Because man is so deeply asleep, these influences act on him in a particular way. If he were awake, they would act on him in another way. The greatest mistake and the greatest injustice we do, in regard to one another, is to imagine that everyone is conscious. This work also says that in life everything happens. It seems that man does and can do, but this is not the case, but an appearance. Actually, everything happens, just as the last war happened and this present war has happened. But the work also says that everything happens on earth because man is asleep. Everything happens in a world of sleeping people. Everything that takes place takes place in the only way it can. Millions kill each other, suffer incredible misery and so on, because they cannot help it, and it all leads nowhere, and can lead nowhere. The

43

direction that can lead somewhere is awakening from sleep. In every small part of time, some people are ready to awaken. If they do not try to do so, they block the way for others. It is like a ladder on each rung of which people are standing. If those above do not move up, those below cannot move. Awakening is the individual task of everyone. But only a few can awaken at a time or find the possibilities offered them. If these begin to awaken the effect spreads and others begin to understand what work means and what awakening means.

The hypnotism of life is at all times very powerful. The object of nature is to keep man asleep and keep him based on violence, so that he serves the purposes of nature. The work is a force coming into life from conscious sources from outside life. To-day the hypnotism of war is very strong. It is necessary to resist it. In order to resist it, the influences reaching us through this work must be kept alive. In order to keep the influences of this work alive, it is necessary constantly to think about it, to concentrate on different sides of it, to renew it daily, and put it into practice. The work must be kept alive and everything that keeps it alive is useful and everything that has the contrary effect is bad. Every one of you must think what it means to keep the work alive at this time and what effort it requires on the part of those who are teaching this system. Only those who think seriously of the work and see all its difficulties and have realized for themselves how very easy it is to forget everything and fall back into ordinary life can understand what is meant. One thing can be added—you all know that everyone must play his part in life in this way—that is, the fourth way—that we are studying. But it is one thing to identify with what one must do in life and another thing to take life as a means of working on oneself. Life and the work must not be mixed up. If a man mixes the work with life and cannot see the difference, he cannot feel the action of the work on him. It will fade and become as nothing in his mind. As you know, this point has been emphasized in many of the readings given since this present war began. The reason is obvious, but although this is so, we easily forget it and so must struggle all over again to remember the work and re-set it in our minds, see its inner meaning once more and understand again what this work is and what life is, and why this work has always, in one form or another, been taught to suffering humanity in every age. Above all, you must not adapt to war any more than you must adapt to this system. To adapt to war is to go to sleep in regard to war.

SOME THOUGHTS ON THE WAR
FROM THE STANDPOINT OF THE WORK

Part II.—Everything based on violence can only create violence. There is not a single school of real teaching that teaches violence. Even the schools of *Hatha-Yoga*, such as the doubtful schools of Ju-Jitsu, do not actually teach violence but the method of overcoming violence, but this is often misunderstood and there is very much in *Hatha-Yoga* schools that is wrong and useless. Man—natural man—is based on violence and that is why he conducts certain planetary influences in the particular way that produces war. The planetary influences are one thing—neither good nor evil. It is man's inner state that translates them into good or evil. Man must overcome violence in himself. This is a very great issue, and a man must first of all study identifying in himself to its roots before he can understand what the overcoming of violence in himself means. War exists because man is based on violence. If he receives influences he does not know how to use and does not understand owing to his defective and undeveloped apparatus of reception, he cannot deal with them, and so they pass into irritation, anger or violence. Man is thus like a bad transmitter. He is evil because he transmits badly. If a man begins to deal with the small cycle of recurring events in his personal life more *consciously* and does not identify with some of them, he begins to be able to transform his life on a small scale. He transmits a little better and begins to be a little more free of the machinery of life—of the turning wheels surrounding him. If everyone did this, planetary influences acting on man would not so easily bring mankind to war. People could then resist war.

When war comes people find reasons for it and consent to it and feel almost as if they were willingly taking part in it. Whereas war, as a vast collective event, a vortex, has grasped them into its powerful influence and made them take part in it. But if necessity imposes itself on a man in this respect, even then he need not serve nature. He need not serve nature if he practises *Karma Yoga*—that is, if he does not identify with what he has to do and must do. But if he feel it is a fine thing to do what he is doing, he will identify and even go so far as to wish for rewards for his meritorious actions. To practise non-identifying can lead somewhere: to serve nature leads nowhere. There are no outer rewards for non-identifying. Everything a man does in regard to working on himself has no relation to the rewards of outer life. Only *you* know what *you* do in this respect. If called upon to do something as a good householder, a man must do what is expected of him as far as possible. But you must remember that the definition of a good householder is that he is a man who feels his responsibilities and acts accordingly, but *does not believe in life*. This, at first sight, is an extraordinary definition. Let us consider what it signifies from one side. A good householder, in the work sense, is a man who acts conscientiously, as when, for example, he holds office—not from himself, but from fear of his reputation or for gain or in case he might lose power, etc. He does not believe in life. but sees life in a certain way and acts well, but not from himself. He does the right things perhaps but in a wrong way. This is why the path, or, as it is called, "The Way of Good House-holder", is so long, and requires so many repetitions. You all know there is an important class of people who do their duty, not because they believe in life, but because they are influenced by merit, reward, ambition, power, money, and so on; and perhaps even by better ideals. They ascribe everything to themselves. Their attitude to life enables them often to act as if they were not identified. But they are identified in their own way. Yet they are very useful in life and give the impressions often of sincere action. And to themselves, they seem sincere and honest. But in any situation that demands real sacrifice of their position, etc., they hesitate and find various reasons why they should not act in this or that way. They are in life. But they do not believe in life. The Way of Good Householder is long because what is good in such people must be shifted from its basis and must become real and essential. A man may be a very good man *mechanically*, from personality, yet his goodness is not real. If a man does his duty in life as a good house-holder, he seems to come near to acting without identifying. Yet actually he is very far from acting without identifying. In the Gospels Christ attacked the good householder especially, when he attacked the Pharisees, and you must read for yourselves all that was said there about them and their meritoriousness. And perhaps Christ attacked them so powerfully just because they were the very people who could have understood and who would have been most useful. As you all know, this work attacks false personality, because it is unreal—that is, because it cannot form the starting-point of inner evolution. It would be possible to say very much more on this subject, but enough has been said to raise questions in your minds about the war and about under-standing it from the ideas of the work.

THE DIFFERENCE BETWEEN OBSERVATION
AND SELF-OBSERVATION

To *observe* and to *observe oneself* are two different things. Both need *attention*. But in observation, the attention is directed outward through the senses. In self-observation the attention is directed inwards, and there is no sense-organ for this. This is one reason why self-observation is more difficult than observation.

In modern science only the observable is taken as real. Whatever cannot be a matter of observation by the senses or by the senses aided by telescopes, microscopes and other delicate optical, electrical and chemical instruments, is discarded. It has been sometimes stated that one of the general aims of this work is to unite the science of the West with the wisdom of the East. Now if we define the starting-point of western science on its practical side as the *observable*, how can we define the starting-point of the work? We can define the starting-point of the work as the *self-observable*. It begins, on the practical side, with *self-observation*.

These two starting-points lead in entirely different directions.

A man may spend his whole life in observing the phenomenal world —the stars, atoms, cells and so on. He may gain a great amount of this kind of knowledge—namely, knowledge of the external world—that is, of all that aspect of the universe that can be detected by the senses, aided or not. This is one kind of knowledge and by means of it *changes* can be made. The changes are in the external world. Outer, sense-experienced conditions may be improved. All sorts of facilities and conveniences and easier methods may be invented. All this knowledge, if it were used in the right way, could only be for the benefit of mankind by changing his external environment to his advantage. But this kind of knowledge of the external can only change the external. It cannot change a man *in himself*.

The kind of knowledge that can change a man internally cannot be gained merely by means of *observation*. It does not lie in this direction— that is, in the direction of the outwardly turned senses. There is another kind of knowledge possible to man and this knowledge begins by *self-observation*. This kind of knowledge is not gained through the senses, for, as was said, we do not possess any organ of sense that can be turned inwards and by means of which we can observe ourselves as easily as we observe a table or a house.

While the first kind of knowledge can change the external conditions of life for a man, the second kind of knowledge can change the man himself. *Observation* is a means of world-change, so to speak; *self-observation* is a means of *self-change*.

But although this is so, in order to learn anything, we have to start from knowledge itself and knowledge of whatever kind begins from the senses. The knowledge of this system of teaching begins with hearing it—that is, it begins through the senses. A man must be told to observe himself and in which direction he must observe himself and the reasons why he should observe himself, etc. And whatever he hears or reads in this connection first of all must enter through his senses. From this point of view the kind of knowledge of which the work speaks begins from the plane of the *observable*, just as does the teaching of any science. A man must begin by giving *external attention* to the work. He must observe what is said, what he can read of it and so on. In other words, the work touches the plane of the senses. For this reason it can very easily become mixed up with the kind of knowledge that can only come through the study of what the senses shew, and as it were lie alongside it or become stifled by it. And unless a man has the power of distinguishing the nature or quality of the knowledge taught by this work and the knowledge taught by science—that is, unless he has *magnetic centre* in him, which can differentiate the qualities of knowledge—this mixing up of two planes or orders of knowledge will produce a confusion in him. And this confusion will remain even though a person continues in the work, unless some effort is made to let the work pass on to where it belongs in himself. That is, he will judge of the work only by what he sees, by other people outside him and so on. The work will remain, so to speak, on the level of the senses. *What then is the nature of the effort a person must make in this connection?* He must effect a separation in his mind between two orders of *reality that meet in him.* Man stands between two worlds—an external visible world, that enters the senses and is shared by everyone: and an internal world that none of his senses meets, which is shared by no one—that is, the approach to it is uniquely individual, for although all the people in the world can observe you, only you can observe yourself. This internal world is the second *reality*, and is invisible.

If you doubt that this second reality exists ask yourself the question: are my thoughts, feelings, sensations, my fears, hopes, disappointments, my joys, my desires, my sorrows, real to me? If, of course, you say that they are not real, and that only the table and the house that you can see with your outer eyes are real, then *self-observation* will have no meaning to you. Let me ask you: in which world of reality do you live and have your being? In the world outside you, revealed by your senses, or in the world that no one sees, and only you can observe—this inner world? I think you will agree that it is in this inner world that you really live all the time, and feel and suffer.

Now both worlds are verifiable experimentally—the outer observable world and the inner self-observable world. You can prove things in the outer world and you can prove things in the inner world, in the one case by observation and in the second case by self-observation. In regard to the second case, all that this work teaches about what you must notice and perceive internally can be verified by self-observation. And the more you open up this inner world called "oneself" the more will you understand that you live in two worlds, in two realities, in two *environments*, outer and inner, and that just as you must learn about the outer world (that is observable) how to walk in it, how not to fall off precipices or wander into morasses, how not to associate with evil people, not to eat poison, and so on, by means of this work and its application, you begin to learn how to walk in this inner world, which is opened up by means of *self-observation.*

Let us take an example of these two different realities to which quite different forms of truth belong. Let us suppose a person is at a dinner-party. All that he sees, hears, tastes, smells and touches, belongs to the first reality; all that he thinks and feels, likes, dislikes, etc., belongs to the second reality. He attends two dinner-parties recorded differently, one outer, one inner. All our experiences are the same in this way.

There is the outer experience and our inner reaction to it. Which is *most real?* Which record, in short, forms our personal lives?—the outer or the inner reality? Is it true to say that it is the inner world? It is the inner world in which we rise and fall, and in which we continually sway to and fro and are tossed about, in which we are infested by swarms of negative thoughts and moods, in which we lose everything and spoil everything and in which we stagger about and fall, without understanding even that there is an inner world in which we are living all the time. This inner world we can only get to know by self-observation. Then, and only then, can we begin to grasp that all our lives we have been making an extraordinary mistake. All that we have taken as "oneself" really opens into a world. In this world we have first to learn how to see, and for this purpose light is necessary. It is by means of self-observation that this light is acquired.

ADDED NOTE

Let us represent the matter in the following diagram. Diagrams are useful because one can easily remember them and so they can act as means of recalling ideas.

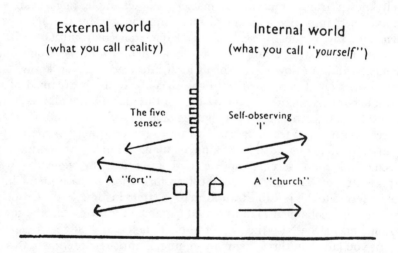

As regards the internal world, what blocks our contact with it is all that this work teaches that we must struggle with—false personality and so on. All these wrong things in ourselves form, as it were, a thick cloud that prevents us from right contact with the influences reaching us from the internal world. When the work forms a definite point or "organism" in use, it begins to make a relation to the "internal world". This I call a "church" for the moment. It is comparable to what we have to form towards outer life—namely, what I call here a "fort". This is added owing to the conversation that ensued after the above paper was read at the meeting on Saturday last at Birdlip. The most important thing to grasp is that we live in two different realities or worlds, one shewn by the senses, the other only revealed through work on oneself—through the purification of the emotions from false personality and the right ordering of the mind through the ideas of the work, so that *relative* thinking is made possible and a proper system of thought is built up.

Birdlip, July 30, 1941

THE IDEA OF TRANSFORMATION IN THE WORK

Part I.—As some of you know, it has been suggested by Mr. Ouspensky that this work might be called by the name *Psycho-transformism.* The idea of the work is psychological transformation—the transformation of *oneself.*

Transformation means the changing of a thing into a different thing. Chemistry studies the possible transformation of matter. There are well known transformations of matter. For example, sugar can be transformed into alcohol, and alcohol into vinegar by the action of ferments: this is the transformation of one molecular substance into another molecular substance. In the new chemistry of the atoms and elements, radium slowly transforms itself into lead. As you know, the transformation of base metal into gold has always been dreamed of as possible by the alchemists of the past. But this idea did not always have a literal meaning, because the language of alchemy was sometimes used by secret schools of teaching as referring to the possibility of the transformation of man into a new kind of man. Man as he is—that is, mechanical man serving nature and grounded in violence—was represented as base metal and the transformation of base metal into gold referred to this possible transformation latent in him. In the Gospels, the idea of mechanical man as a seed capable of growing has the same significance, as has also the idea of re-birth, of a man being born again.

As you know, in this system of teaching, man is regarded as a three-storey factory, taking in three foods—ordinary food on the lower floor of the factory, air on the second floor, and impressions on the third floor.

The food we eat undergoes successive transformations. The process of life is transformation. Every living thing lives by transforming one thing into another. A plant transforms air, water and salts from the earth into new substances—into what we call potatoes, beans, peas, nuts, fruit, and so on—by the action of sunlight and ferments. The sensitive living film spread over the earth, which conducts force from the universe—that is, organic life—is a vast transforming organ.

When we eat food it is transformed successively, stage by stage, into all the substances necessary for our existence. This is done by that

50

mind called instinctive centre, which controls the inner work of the organism and of course knows far more than we do about it. We can understand that when food is taken, digestion begins. Digestion is transformation. The food is changed into something different in the stomach. This is only the first stage of the transformation of food and is designated in the work as the passage of *Do 768* to *Re 384*. It will be sufficient to use this first stage as an example without going further. It is a stage everyone can understand without difficulty. Everyone can see that the food taken into the lowest compartment of the three-storey factory—namely, the meals we eat—undergoes transformation. Now suppose the food passed into the stomach and nothing happened : what then? The body, which is like a huge town, will make no contact with it. How can an undigested piece of meat or a potato enter the blood stream and supply the necessary fine substance, say, to the brain?

This situation is more or less the case, however, in regard to the third food, the food of impressions. They enter and remain undigested —that is, there is no transformation here. Impressions come in as *Do 48* and stop. Save for a very small amount of transformation, nothing takes place. There is no adequate transformation of impressions. It is not necessary for the purpose of nature that man should transform impressions. But a man can transform his impressions himself, if he has sufficient knowledge and understands why it is necessary.

Most people think that external life will give them what they crave and seek. Life comes in as impressions, as *Do 48*. The first realization of the meaning of this work is to understand that life, coming in as impressions, must be transformed. There is no such thing as "external life". What all the time you are receiving is *impressions*. You see a person you dislike—that is, you get *impressions* of this nature. You see a person you like—that is, you get *impressions* once more. Life is impressions, not a solid material thing such as you suppose and believe is *reality*. Your reality is your impressions. I know this idea is very difficult to grasp. It forms a very difficult crossing-place. You are, perhaps, sure that life exists as such, and not as your impressions. The person you see sitting in a chair wearing a blue suit, smiling and talking, you think is real. No, it is your impressions of him that are real for you. If you had no sight, you would not see him. If you had no ears, you would not hear him. Life comes in as impressions and it is here that it is possible to *work on oneself*—but only if you realize that what you are working on is not external life but the impressions you are receiving. Unless you can grasp this, you will never understand the meaning of what in the work is called the First Conscious Shock. This shock relates to these *impressions* which are all we know of the outer world, that we are taking in, that we take as actual things, actual people. No one can transform external life. But everyone can transform his impressions, namely, the third and highest food taken in by the three-storey factory. For this reason this system of teaching says that it is necessary to create a transforming agency at the point of intake of impressions. This is the meaning of the work regarded in the light of *psychological transformation* and this is the point at which work begins. It is called the *First Conscious Shock* because it is something not done mechanically. It does not happen mechanically—that is, it needs a conscious effort. A man who begins to understand what this means, at the same time begins to be no longer a mechanical man, serving nature, a man asleep and merely used by nature for its own purposes, which are not in the interests of man. If you now think of the meaning of all you are taught to do in the way of effort, beginning with self-observation, you will see beyond any doubt that everything on the practical side of this work relates to transforming impressions and the results of impressions. Work on negative emotions, work on heavy moods, work on identifying, work on considering, work on inner lying, work on imagination, work on difficult 'I's, work on self-justifying, work on states of sleep, and so on, is all connected with *transforming impressions* and the results of them. So you will agree that in a sense work on oneself is comparable to digestion in the sense that digestion is transformation. Some transforming agency must be formed at the place of the intake of impressions. This is the First Conscious Shock and it is given the general description *remembering oneself*. If you can, through the understanding of the work, take life as work, then you are in a state of self-remembering. This state of consciousness leads to the *transformation of impressions*—and so of life as regards yourself. That is, life no longer acts on you in the old way. You begin to think, and to understand, in a new way. And this is the beginning of your own transformation. For as long as we think in the same way we take in life in the same way and nothing changes in us. To transform the impressions of life is to transform oneself, and only an entirely new way of thinking can effect this. All this work is to give you an entirely new way of thinking. Let me give you one example. You are told in the work that *if you are negative it is always your own fault*. The whole situation as recorded by the senses must be transformed. But to understand this, it is necessary to begin to think in an entirely new way.

You all can understand that life is continually causing us to react to it. All these reactions form our life—our own personal life. To change one's life is not to change outer circumstances: it is to change one's reactions. But unless we can see that outer life comes in as impressions which cause us to react in stereotyped ways, we cannot see where the point of possible change comes in, where it is possible to work. If the reactions that form your own personal life are mainly negative, then that is your life. Your life is chiefly a mass of negative reactions to the impressions that have come in every day. The transformation of impressions so that they do not always provoke negative reactions is then one's task, if one wishes to work on oneself. But for this, self-observation at the point where impressions enter us is necessary. Then one can let the impressions fall in a negative mechanical way, or not. If not, then that is to begin to live more consciously. If one fails to transform impressions at the moment of their entry, one can always work on the results of these impressions and prevent them from having their full mechanical effect. All this requires a definite feeling, a definite evaluation of the work, for it means that the work must be brought forward, as it were, to that point where impressions enter and are being distributed mechanically to their customary place in personality to evoke the old reactions. We will speak later much more about transformation, but it can be added that no higher level is possible of attainment unless there is *transformation*, and the very idea of transformation is based on the fact that different levels exist, and refers to the passage from one level to another level of being. No one can reach a higher level of development without transformation.

Birdlip, August 14, 1941

THE IDEA OF TRANSFORMATION IN THE WORK

Part II.—The personality that we all acquire receives the impressions of life. But it does not transform them because it is dead. If impressions fell on essence they would be transformed because they would fall on centres. Personality, which is the term applied to all that we acquire, (and we must acquire personality), translates impressions from every side of life in a limited and practically stereotyped way according to its quality and associations. The personality in this respect is sometimes compared in the work with a secretary who sits in the front room, dealing with everything according to her own ideas. She has a number of dictionaries and encyclopedias and reference books, etc. round about her and rings up the three centres—that is, the mental, the emotional and the physical centres—according to her limited ideas. The result is that the wrong centres are nearly always being rung up. This means that incoming impressions are sent to the wrong places and produce the wrong results.

A man's life depends on this secretary, who mechanically looks up things in her reference books without any understanding of what they really mean and transmits them accordingly without caring what happens, but feeling only that she is doing her duty.

This is our inner situation. What is important to understand in this allegory is that this personality which we all acquire and must acquire begins to take charge of our lives. And it is no use imagining that this only happens to certain people. It happens to everyone. Whoever we are, we find ourselves, through self-observation, possessed of a certain small number of typical ways of reacting to the manifold impressions of incoming life. These mechanical reactions govern us.

Everyone is governed by his own set of *reactions to impressions*—that is, to life—whether he is revolutionary or conservative, or good or bad

53

in the ordinary sense. And these reactions are his life. Mankind is mechanical in this sense. A man has formed in him a number of reactions which he takes as himself and his life experiences are the result of them. If you can relax enough physically, and drop away mentally from all ideas of yourself (which is mental relaxing) you will be able to see what I mean. You will see that, as it were, there are a number of things below you—namely, *external* to you—that you keep on taking as yourself. In such a passive state you can see them dimly. At first sight they seem to be above you. Immediately you tense your muscles or begin to talk you become them. They become you or you become them, and off you go again. But you must not try to do this exercise too much at first.

Actually they are like little grasping machines that insist on taking charge of you and demand that you should enter them again. They are set in motion by this "secretary"—that is, by the habitual way this secretary responds to impressions. And the reactions which follow we take as life. We take our typical reactions to impressions as life. We take our reactions to a person as him or her. All life—that is, outer life, which is what we usually think "life" is—namely, what we see and hear— is for each person his or her reactions to the impressions coming in from it. And as I said in the last talk, it is a great mistake to think that what is called "life" is a solid fixed thing, the same for everyone. No one has the same impressions of life. Life is our impressions of it and these can be transformed. But as was said, this is a very difficult idea to reach, because the hypnotism of the senses is so powerful. We cannot help thinking that it is only the senses that give us reality. So our inner life —our real life of thought and feeling—remains dim to our mental conceptions. Yet at the same time we know quite well it is where we really live—that is, in our thoughts and feelings. To establish a point in the work, to make it *more real* than life, we must observe ourselves and make our inner life of thoughts and feelings a fact more powerful than any "fact" given by our senses. This is the beginning of transforming. One cannot transform anything in oneself if one is glued to the senses. As I said, in the last talk, the work teaches that if you are negative it is your own fault. The sensory point of view is that this or that person in the outer world, that you see and hear by means of your eyes and ears, is at fault. This person, you will say, because he or she does this or talks like that, is to blame. But actually, if you are made negative, what you have to work on, what you have to observe, is this negative emotion intruding itself into your inner life—that is, into the inner invisible "place" where you really exist. Your real being is in the inner invisible world of yourself. Do you wish to argue this point? Well, are the thoughts and feelings and emotions and hopes and despairs you have less real to you than the tables and chairs in your dining-room? Do you live, as it were, in this dining-room? You may be very much identified with your particular tables and chairs, but even so, is it not your *feeling* about these tables and chairs that is real to you? Suppose you are ill and feel perhaps death is near you, do you bother any more about them? Of course not. And why? Because you have no longer any *feelings* about them. It is your feelings and your ways of identifying that make you regard this or that thing as important. It is not the *things* that you see with your physical eyes. Let us suppose that a person notices that he is identified, say, with his furniture: do you think that he must get rid of his furniture in order to change? Of course not. That would be silly. What he can change is his being identified so much. If he works on this, if he begins to transform this reaction in himself, he can still enjoy his furniture but he will not commit suicide if it is destroyed in a fire. Do you see the difference? You cannot transform life, but you can begin to transform the way you take life. The first conscious shock means *work on yourself* in general. The point of this work is to try to give oneself this shock. Everything that is taught in this system, on the practical side, belongs to the first conscious shock —non-identifying, non-considering, and so on. This may lead to a real moment of self-remembering—as a reward. Then one has insight into what one must do, and realization of the truth of the work.

But work must be done in the spirit of the work—that is, in the sense and feeling and valuation of the work. This must enter into every effort of work, for no one can work for himself alone, otherwise the results go only into false personality and so into merit. A man must work from *love* of the work. This brings Hydrogen 12 up to the place of incoming impressions. Incoming impressions are Hydrogen 48. They cannot pass to Hydrogen 24 without Hydrogen 12 as active force. If this hydrogen is present at the place of reception of impressions— that is, at the place we are conscious—Hydrogen 48, which comes in as passive force, passes to Hydrogen 24, the triad being completed by the Carbon 12. Hydrogen 12 is not present naturally at this point in the human machine. It has to be brought up to this point. If a person takes life as usual, in the ordinary way—that is, always receives impressions in the same mechanical way and speaks from them in the same mechanical way and acts from them in the same mechanical way—then nothing can change in the person. Such people cannot evolve. They do not see where the point of working on themselves lies. They think work is something outside them. A person must bring a very powerful hydrogen to the point where impressions are coming in. This is Hydrogen 12.

THE IDEA OF TRANSFORMATION IN THE WORK

Part III.—In order to continue these talks about Transformation let me take a question of this kind : "What prevents impressions from transforming themselves in us? Why does this not always happen?" Let us again study this subject.

Impressions should pass on in their octave until they reach Mi 12. You will remember that they come in as 48, but do not continue to evolve. (See Fig. 1). Remember also that the First Conscious Shock is to make impressions pass on in their evolution, namely, to Hydrogen 24 and then to Hydrogen 12. That is, by means of the First Conscious Shock, Do 48 becomes Re 24 and then Mi 12 (Fig. 2).

Fig. 1 Fig. 2

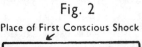

Place of First Conscious Shock

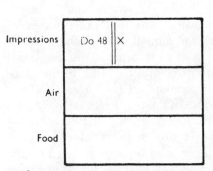
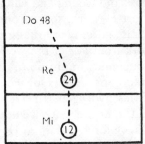

Situation when the First Conscious Shock is absent. Situation when the First Conscious Shock is given.

Now two things must be borne in mind and clearly understood:

(1) The First Conscious Shock does not happen to man asleep. It is a *conscious effort* requiring special knowledge and self-observation and given in connection with the incoming impressions of life and a person's mechanical reactions to them. Roughly, it consists in seeing the object and seeing one's reactions to it simultaneously and without being identified. This process is sometimes put diagrammatically as follows:

$$\longrightarrow$$
$$\longleftarrow$$

(2) The First Conscious Shock to the human machine increases the energies of the machine in the form of Hydrogen 24 and Hydrogen 12. The result is actually to give every cell in the body different food —that is, higher hydrogens. In regard to this second point let me remind you here that neither the psychical nor the physical functions of man can be understood unless it is grasped that they can both work in different states of consciousness. If the First Conscious Shock is applied,

the Third State of Consciousness is touched, with the result that the human machine works in a different way, owing to new energies, both as regards its psychical and its physical functions. The Third State of Consciousness is the state of Self-Remembering, which man should possess but which he has gradually lost because of the wrong conditions of his life. To-day it can be said only to occur in the form of very rare flashes. It is the creation of this Third State of Consciousness that forms the First Conscious Shock—that is, the first object of the work is to recover this lost state, namely, to make a man *remember himself* until eventually he does not merely have rare flashes of increased consciousness (over which he has no control) but can create in himself increasing degrees of self-remembering by deliberate efforts. These efforts, which belong to the First Conscious Shock, gradually cause the machine to work more rightly. Many wrong functions, both in the psychic and physical spheres, acquired by the wrong working of the machine in the two lowest states of consciousness—that is, in darkness—then begin to disappear of themselves.

Let us now return to the question as to what prevents Do 48 from passing on to Re 24 and then to Mi 12. Why does not this always happen? It does happen in childhood ; and to a certain extent Mi 12 is created in the body in early youth. We may remember its action. But as Personality grows more and more thickly round Essence, it happens less and less. That is, impressions are more and more intercepted by Personality, which is represented in the diagram by the double line marked X. Impressions coming in through the senses fall, as it were, on a thick net which catches everything (save a very small part, which passes onwards and produces a very small amount of Mi 12).

This net is the Personality, with its strong Buffers, its fixed Attitudes, its mechanical Associations, its Rolls automatically set in motion, and its ideas that it knows and can do, with all its contradictory 'I's, with all the different forms of negative emotion, which it has acquired by imitation, with all its habits of identifying, considering, self-justifying, imagining and lying, centred in the False Personality. All these prevent impressions from passing on in their normal transformations. In other words, something opaque, as it were, has formed itself at the place where impressions enter, and closed up the way for their passage onwards.

Now from the standpoint of Triads, impressions entering as Hydrogen 48 cannot pass to Hydrogen 24 unless Hydrogen 12 is present. Hydrogen 12 must be brought up to the place where impressions are entering. Personality is constructed mainly out of Hydrogen 48—the Formatory Hydrogen—so you have impressions 48 falling on Personality 48, and since the necessary elements of a triad are therefore lacking, no transformation is possible. In the case of food—ordinary food—that is, Hydrogen 768—on being taken in, it meets with the gastric juices, and their active ferments, belonging to the order of Hydrogens 192, and the result is the transformation of 768 into 384. But in the case of impressions once Personality is formed, no corresponding active "ferment" meets them (in this case Hydrogen 12). The work itself must be brought up to the place to act as a "ferment", for the work is to make a man think in a new way and to awaken him.

What does this mean? How can a man bring the work up to the place of incoming impressions? In brief, *by remembering the work emotionally.* The more a man through right self-observation feels his own helplessness, the more he realizes his ignorance, the more he sees his mechanicalness and that he is a machine, the more he preceives his own utter nothingness, the more emotional will the work become to him. The work can exist in us as Hydrogen 48. Then it is merely in Personality, as something formatory, in the memory. It can exist in us also in terms of Hydrogen 24. Then it is emotional. It can also become so valuable, so important to us, that it begins to have the intensity of meaning and significance that belong to Hydrogen 12. In that case, False Personality will begin to collapse and a man will become "as a little child". This is one meaning of the saying : " Except ye become as little children". If a man's love no longer runs always into himself, into his habitual ideas of himself, his strange vanity and esteem of himself—that is, into False Personality—then the direction of his will alters—that is, the resultant of his desires alters. When the valuation of the truth of esoteric teaching becomes stronger than self-valuation, it begins to act on a man. He begins to take everything differently. The whole way in which he reacts to outer life changes. (Why cannot you all understand that life is impressions?) He no longer reacts to impressions from his mechanical personality by always saying the same things, feeling the same things, and so on. He begins to act from the work—that is, in quite a new way.

The work comes up to the place where life is entering him as impressions and stands beside him. He begins to see life through the work and instead of wasting his time in hundreds of forms of useless internal considering or negative reactions, or of identifying, he seeks for the power of the work to help him to change these mechanical reactions which he is now aware of by observation and to transform his habitual ways of taking things. He begins to live more consciously at this point where life is entering as impressions.

THE IDEA OF TRANSFORMATION IN THE WORK

Part IV.   Section I.—Let us take the idea of *Work on Oneself.* As you all know, by now, we take the thing which we call *Oneself*—that is, myself, yourself—as one thing. We think *we* are *ourselves.*

Work on Oneself is thus made quite impossible. How can *you* work on *you,* if *you* and *you* in each case are one and the same thing? But *you* and *yourself* are not the same thing. If *you* and *yourself* were the same thing, work on yourself would be impossible. Think for a moment— if you and yourself are identical—that is, one and the same thing— how can *you* observe yourself? Would it not be impossible? A thing cannot observe itself. How could it do so? So if you take *you* as *yourself* and *yourself* as *you,* and think that *you* and *yourself* are the same thing, then how do you propose to begin to observe yourself? *You* will try to observe *you*—and how can that be possible? A thing cannot observe itself. A thing identical with itself cannot see itself, because it is the same as itself, and a thing which is the same as itself cannot possibly have a standpoint *apart from itself,* from which to observe itself.

I say all this in order to emphasize how difficult it is for people to begin to work on themselves. The reason is that they take themselves as themselves. If a man takes himself as himself he cannot observe himself. Everything is himself. He says 'I' to everything. And if a man says 'I' to everything in himself, then everything in him is 'I', and how can he observe himself? How can 'I' observe 'I', if they are one and the same thing? At one moment he is irritable and rude, at the next kind and polite. But he says 'I' to it all. And so he cannot see it all. It is all *one* to him. He cannot see it apart from himself and he and himself are one and the same thing to his mind—that is, to his way of thinking. This massive stumbling-block lies across everyone's path and long, very long overcoming of it is the task of *Work on Oneself.* And how long it takes before a man can begin to see what it all means, and what the work is always saying. I have watched people in the work often for many years, who have not yet caught a single flash of the meaning of self-observation—that is, people who still take everything that takes place in them as 'I' and say 'I' to every mood, every thought, every impulse, every feeling, every sensation, every criticism, every feeling of anger, every negative state, every objection, every dislike, every hate, every dejection, every depression, every whim, every excitement, every doubt, every fear. To every train of inner talking they say 'I', to every negative monologue they say 'I', to every suspicion they say 'I', to every hurt feeling they say 'I', to every form of imagination they say 'I', to every movement they make they say 'I'. To everything that takes place within them they say 'I'. In such a case the work can only be something listened to externally, something they hear said to them, the words of which they remember, or not, as the case may be. But they have no idea of what work on themselves means because they have no idea as yet that there is such a thing as " themselves". They look out of their two eyes, and they listen with their two ears, and see and hear what is outside them. Where, in this case, is this thing called *themselves*? Is not everything *outside* them, save something they call 'I'? Is not life a lot of things outside, and something they take for granted as 'I'—that is, themselves? And if this work is not about things outside, that they can hear and see and touch, what is it about really? For there is surely nothing else save outside things and something that is 'I'. At the same time they may feel the work emotionally. They may feel that it is about something strange and genuine and real. But they cannot see exactly what it is about. They continue to talk as they have always talked and say 'I' to it all. They continue to feel and to think as they have always felt and thought, and they say 'I' to it all. To all their manifestations, to all their mechanicalness, to all their inner life, they say 'I'. And since everything is 'I', what is there to work on ? This is quite true. For if everything connected with a person in outer manifestations and in inner life is 'I', and if there is only 'I', if everything connected with him is 'I', then there is nothing to work on. For who can work on 'I' if everything is 'I'? What can observe 'I' if everything is 'I'? The answer, of course, is that nothing can. A thing cannot observe itself. There must be something different in it for the thing to observe itself. And in our own cases, in the case of everyone, if there is nothing in us different from ourselves, how can we observe ourselves, and work on ourselves? For to work on oneself, it is necessary to begin to observe oneself. But if 'I' and 'myself' are one and the same, how can this ever be possible? I will have nothing to work on, for the reason that I regard everything I do, everything I say, everything I feel, everything I think, as 'I', so that if you speak to me of *myself* I will take it that you are speaking of me—of what I call 'I'—and whatever you say about me, I will take it as myself—that is, as 'I'—for to my way of thinking 'I' and 'myself' are identical. To my way of thinking, they are one and the same thing.

Birdlip, September 21, 1941

THE IDEA OF TRANSFORMATION IN THE WORK

Part IV. Section II.—Last time a paper was read about the necessity of not taking everything as 'I' in oneself. You have heard it said before that "unless a man divides himself into two he cannot shift from where he is." This saying, often used in the work, refers to the beginning of the process of what is called *inner separation*. A man must first divide himself into two. But the further stages of *inner separation* are more complex than this.

Let me give you an example. It was recently said to me by someone that he had begun to see what self-observation and separation meant for the first time. He said: "I have always been taking negative emotions as a nasty bit of myself. I realize my mistake." Self-observation will shew us our negative states. But something further is as a rule necessary than mere observation of them and that is *inner separation*. And no one can separate himself from anything he observes in himself if he regards what he observes as being himself, for then, inevitably, the feeling of 'I' will pass into what he observes in himself and this feeling of 'I' will increase the strength and power of what he observes. He has to learn to say *in the right way*: "This is not me—not 'I' ". Now if he takes his negative emotions as a nasty bit of himself, he will not be able to separate himself from them. Do you see why? He will not be able to separate himself from them because he is taking them *as himself* and so giving them the validity of 'I'. And as was said in the last talk, if we give to everything in ourselves the feeling of 'I', if we say 'I' to everything we think or feel or say or imagine, nothing can alter. For 'I' cannot alter 'I'. And if we practise self-observation on this basis, everything we observe will be 'I'. Whereas the case really is that everything in us, practically speaking, is "It"—that is, a machine going by itself. Instead of saying "I think", we should realize it would be far nearer the truth if we said "It thinks". And instead of saying "I feel" it would be nearer the mark to say "It feels".

What we call ourselves, what we say 'I' to, is actually an immense world, larger and more varied than the outer world we behold through our external senses. We do not say 'I' to what we see in the outer world. But we say 'I' to everything that takes place in our inner world. This mistake takes many years even to modify a little. But sometimes we are given the clear light of understanding for a moment and we realize what it means and what the work is continually telling us. If a man ascribes evil to himself he is in the wrong position in regard to it, just as if he ascribes good to himself and the merit of it. Every kind of thought can enter your mind; every kind of feeling can enter your heart. But if you ascribe them to yourself and say 'I' to all of them, you fasten them to you and cannot separate internally from them. One can avoid negative thoughts and feelings if one does not take them as oneself—as 'I'. But if one takes them as 'I', one combines with them—that is, one *identifies* oneself with them—and then one cannot avoid them. There are inner states—states within us all—that we must avoid just as one avoids walking into mud in the external visible world. One must not listen to them, must not go with them, must not touch them or let them touch you. This is inner separation. But you cannot practise inner separation if you ascribe everything that takes place in your inner invisible life—where you really all live—to yourselves. I have often been struck by people asking me about themselves in regard to thoughts that plague and worry them. For example, people who pride themselves on being what is called "clean-minded" often find themselves

61

tortured by indecent thoughts and images; this is exactly what happens if a person insists on thinking that everything in him or her is 'I'. In this connection, I remember that after we left the Institute in France we went to Scotland, to my grandfather's house. He had collected an immense library, among which were a great many theological and moral volumes. They were, of course, entirely formatory. But having nothing else to read I spent some of the long winter evenings there in trying to understand what they were about. There were the usual endless acrimonious arguments about the nature of the Trinity, the nature of heresy, and so on, but I noticed that one subject of debate that often came up was whether we are responsible for our thoughts. Some of the most severe moralists insisted that we were, but a few of these now long-dead theologians took the point of view that we were not. Some said that the devil sent us our thoughts. But no one of those writers whom I read took a psychological view of this question.

At any moment the strangest thoughts and images can enter us. If we say 'I' to them, if we think that we thought them, they have power over us. And if we then try to eliminate them, we find it impossible. Why? I will repeat one of my own illustrations of this situation. Suppose you are standing on a plank and trying to lift it and struggling as hard as you can to do so. Will you succeed? No, because you yourself are trying to lift yourself and this is impossible.

It requires a considerable re-orientation of one's whole conception of oneself to be able to realize what all this means. So many buffers and forms of pride and stupid ways of thinking prevent us from seeing what the situation within us is really like. We imagine we are in control of ourselves. We imagine we are *conscious* and always know what we are thinking and saying and doing. We imagine we are a *unity*, and that we have a real permanent 'I' and so have *will*, and we imagine many other things besides. All this stands in our way and before we can practise *inner separation*, a quite new feeling about oneself and about what one really is, is necessary.

Birdlip, September 21, 1941

COMMENTARY ON MEANING

Part I.—We can all get so tired of one another that we have no meaning for one another. A man and a woman can get so tired of each other that they have no meaning for one another. One can get so tired of a subject that it has no longer any meaning for one. A person can do his daily work dutifully for years until it has no longer any meaning for him. A man may search for new adventures until they have no meaning for him and he does not know what he is doing, and so on.

Let us ask ourselves about the meaning of meaning and the source of meaning. Let us consider, first of all, whether meaning is important or not. If we decide after reflection that meaning is important, then let us ask ourselves *what we want*. A very good formulation of what we want is this: "I want to find meaning in everything", or "I seek more meaning" or "I dread a state of meaninglessness and pray to have more meaning in my life", and so on. Some years ago I was speaking to Mr. O. about aim. The conversation was about the possibility of recurrence—that is, living one's life again. It is a possibility, and if nothing changes in our *essence*—that is, in our deepest and most real part—then the recurrence of one's life, if this happens, will be identical with the life one has passed through. One will live the same life, and perhaps live it over and over again, but have no memory of it. This means that at death one returns to that part of Time where one was born, and is born into the same surroundings, etc., and lives again the same life—in fact, lives again and again the same life because nothing has changed in oneself.

Mr. O. asked me what my aim was in connection with this possibility of re-living my life and I said: "Thinking of my life as far as I can remember it, I see that I took very little in. It was like a dream. It had very little meaning, and in fact whole years are blotted out in my mind. I would like to have the power of feeling meaning in all the experiences I had, if I re-lived my life." He said: "Yes, this is right. As a rule we are not there. As Mr. G. said of someone: 'He is never at home'.". He continued in something like the following words: "And this really applies to us all. We are never at home, or very rarely. We are nearly always out. So our experiences have little or no meaning for us." I said: "But I am sure that you, for example, remember your life far better than I remember mine, and that your life has had more meaning." He replied: "Yes, but not quite in the way you mean. I have noticed how much you have forgotten. In my case, as a child I did not play with toys. I was less under imagination. I saw what life was like at a very early stage." I said: "Well, in my case, I must confess that I never thought of life as a thing to think of. I took it all for granted." He said: "Yes, that is why it had little meaning for you. You were simply carried along by it, as by a torrent, thinking you were going somewhere—to some clear goal. It is only when you realize life is taking you nowhere that it begins to have meaning."

At that time I thought this conversation a very strange one. I have given it as I remember it, in regard to the ideas expressed. I carried away two clear impressions: one was that to formulate your aim in regard to the *possibility* of having to re-live your life at death, in terms of wishing to have more meaning, was right, and the second idea was that unless you saw the nature of life you could not get more meaning in living it.

I realized that he had answered the question I had not asked—namely, " How can life have more meaning?"

Let us take this conversation as the basis of an attempt to speak about *meaning*.

Although people do not realize it necessarily, they live by meaning, and when things become meaningless, they feel hopeless and useless. Life gives certain meanings, otherwise everyone would be unable to live or would feel that suicide were better. The meanings life gives are not permanent. Perhaps you have all noticed this. Imagination enhances meaning, but reality tends to exhaust it. There is no correspondence, of course, between imagination and reality. The one can never pass into the other, because they are utterly different things. It takes people a long time to see this—namely, that imagination can never be fulfilled in reality. Imagination is on one plane, reality on another. However, most people get a great deal of meaning solely from imagination. Imagination feeds meaning. It is one source of meaning. But the meaning that is formed by the action of the imagination does not correspond with reality. On the other hand, reality itself has its own meaning, quite apart from imagination. For example, a good dinner is "reality" and not imagination. It has meaning of its own. If you try to separate meaning derived from imagination and meaning derived from life— that is, from reality, speaking in the ordinary sense of the word—you will begin to see the great difference between these two sources of meaning.

Let us consider this phrase: "You have destroyed all my illusions." This phrase is used in the sense of suffering, of being wronged, of being seriously damaged by someone, of being, as it were, ruined. Illusions lie in the imagination. If all the meanings you derive from your imagination are destroyed, is that a loss? The answer is: Yes and No. It is quite possible to destroy a person's meanings too violently and do harm. Yet meaning derived from imagination eventually only complicates life and often, later on, actually prevents any real situations and relationships from developing. When I first made my private début into life—that is, when I first advanced more or less independently (as I supposed) into the world—I had absolutely no idea that my imagination about life and people was in any way different from the possibilities offered by reality and obtainable from it. That is, of course, nothing extraordinary. I do not regard myself as exceptional in having such an attitude. At that age I was chiefly in imagination. That is to say, my meanings were chiefly derived from that source. As a result my experiences were "like a dream". By this term I mean that reality did not correspond with imagination and since I was chiefly in imagination, everything was "like a dream". In fact, I was dreamy. I was not there. I was not at home. I was always out. Because if your meanings are formed in the imagination you are living all the time in imagination, so that life is a far away unpleasant thing. Reality is unreal. In fact, you cannot come in contact with the meanings that reality offers you. You have heard me often say that everyone has his dream-woman, or her dream-man. Such dreams are intensified nowadays in many ways

64

—by the cinema, by novelettes, and so on. But such dream-creatures, formed in the imagination, only feed on your own energies, for your own energies are required to keep them alive. All such forms of imagination derive their strength from yourself. But it is quite true to say that all this takes place in most people, often throughout their lives, and exhausts them in many different ways, making them unfit for any real relationships or right contact with real people. As you know, *imagination* is one of the things that the Work speaks of as having to be struggled with and fought with continually. And there are some drastic Work-parables about the imagination that some of you may remember. I will give them in another place.

Now let us return to this idea expressed by Mr. O. : "A person is usually out. He is rarely at home." If a person is in the imagination and its meanings, he is then always out. He is not at home. Such a person does not see *you*. He sees his dream of you, his imagination of you, his illusion of you. This is not a very satisfactory basis for any real relationship. A tremendous shock has to be undergone for a person to pass from the meanings derived from imagination to the meanings that reality offers. Reality in this respect is at first sight a poor small thing compared with all the wealth of meanings that the imagination supplies a person with, day and night.

You know that in the Work it is taught that you have to try to see yourselves apart from your imagination of yourselves. This is a long task and very difficult and painful. You may think you are charming but not notice you are usually rather rude and always lazy. And just in the same way, you have to try to see others without imagination. And this is also very difficult. It is imagination that blinds everyone in every direction. It blinds all mankind. You have heard one of the sayings of the Work about imagination in regard to mankind in general. It compares mankind with people in a hall of turning mirrors. These mirrors are so arranged that everyone thinks he is going forward toward some goal. But actually the mirrors are turning and people are going round and round in an ever-repeating circle. It is imagination that makes people believe in progress. Look only at this century! And this imagination has its roots in individual people's imagination of themselves and the entirely false meanings they derive from their imagination. Imaginary people meet imaginary people. Imaginary people dress up to meet other imaginary people dressed up. Imaginary people converse politely with imaginary people. Imaginary people marry imaginary people. Imaginary people kill imaginary people—and so on. And since people are based on false personality, which is entirely composed of imagination, it is not so surprising that this is the case. All their meanings, in fact, most of the meanings people live by, are derived from false personality and therefore from imagination. Real meanings exist apart from the meanings derived from imagination. But it is difficult to find them without the help of something that is not based on imagination. The action of this Work is gradually to destroy imaginary

65

meaning and substitute real meaning. *Work on oneself* signifies, among other things, destroying imagination, for the Work is to make the real side of a person to become active and grow, and the false side of the person to weaken and become passive. This is called *awakening from sleep*.

We have spoken about meaning derived from imagination and meaning derived from reality. We have now to speak of meaning derived from the Work.

*   *   *

Part II.—The whole of the Work, all the ideas connected with the Work, all that it says about man being asleep, about the possibility of man's awakening, about life, about mechanicalness, about man's inner state, about efforts on oneself, about consciousness, about being, about new ways of thinking, new ways of understanding, new ways of taking things —all this can become the greatest source of meaning a man can possess. The meanings that the Work—that is, the meanings that esotericism and its unchanging concepts about man and his possible inner re-birth —can give a man, belong to an order of ideas that can transform all the meanings that life gives us. If a man begins to take *life as work*, then his whole relationship to existence begins to change, because the *meaning of life* changes for him. He sees life in another light, not as an *end*, but as a *means*, and this enables him not to identify with life and its happenings, as he formerly did. He does not necessarily expect that life is going to take him anywhere, but knows that if he takes life in the light of the Work, it becomes his teacher. That is, the Work gradually shews him how to take what happens in life so that he learns from life and all that happens in life and in this way life becomes his teacher. Whatever happens, he has the Work to hold on to, and he knows that the explanation it gives him of the real meaning of his own life cannot be destroyed by anything in life itself. But if he takes life as an *end*, the case will be different: then he will never understand the Work and never have any new meanings. From the Work viewpoint, then, life is a means, and all the Work teaches about self-evolution is the real end. This, however, is not easily understood, nor are we to suppose that it is easy to take *life as work*. When an unpleasant situation arises in life, one does not easily take it from a Work viewpoint, especially if it touches the meanings of ourselves through which we feel our self-satisfaction and which we derive from imagination and false personality, and abide in as easily as if they were really ourselves. No one, of course, *understands* the work. We know a little about it. But few have applied it to their being. That is, the Work is not *third force* for us. Life is. Only in a vague way and at times and by means of another's help, is the work *third force* for anyone—that is, a *neutralising force* stronger than the neutralising force of life and the forms of imagination derived from life.

It is very difficult to change and no change is possible as long as life and imagination are the source of meaning for you. To think in a new

66

way is the starting-point of inner development. And this, as you all know, is exactly what the Gospels say. The Gospels are also "esoteric teaching"—that is, teaching about man's possible inner evolution. The Gospels say: "Unless a man thinks in a new way, he cannot gain the Kingdom of Heaven." This is unfortunately translated: "Unless a man repent." To think in a new way is to find new meanings, and to be given new ideas is to have new thoughts. But people do not quite see what is meant. They hear this work and still think as before. So they believe that many of the ideas of this work are odd or fantastic. But it is they who are so. None of the ideas of this system is odd or fantastic. How long it takes us, and how many hard and horrible experiences we need before we catch glimpses of the fact that the Work, and the Gospels, and all Esotericism, are not saying anything odd or fantastic, but are actually saying something real and absolutely necessary to us.

Once we begin to be aware of this, in individual experience, new meaning enters us, and at once our relationship to life alters a little. Old meanings lose a little of their force. Psychologically we live in a world of different meanings and new meanings enter us only when old meanings die. Do you see that one cannot serve all one's old meanings and expect to have *new meanings*? But all this is very difficult to understand. You all have your meanings—the meanings that you follow. Perhaps you even believe that your meanings are the only ones, and are absolutely right: or perhaps you believe that there are fixed meanings for everything—in fact, *standardised meanings*? Of course, this is not the case. The meaning of every single thing can change. Think of some general changes in meaning since this war began. A thing can lose all meaning for you; then it is meaningless and then you will have no relationship to it. You are related to a person through his or her meaning for you. If this meaning changes, your relationship changes.

Meaning relates us to a thing or a person and, if all meaning fades, there is no relationship. But it will depend on the source of your meaning. Life divides people: the Work unites people.

If a man takes *life as Work*, everything can come to have new meaning. As a result of new meaning, new parts of centres are touched and new connections made internally, and new interpretations are possible. That is, the man becomes a little more free, not so mechanical. But since the source of these new meanings reaches him through the ideas of the Work, this change depends on how much he feels the ideas, how much he evaluates the Work. Therefore, you must think of the meaning of the Work and what evaluation of the Work means, in order to understand better this third inexhaustible source of meaning, whose origin lies beyond mechanical life, in the conscious circle of humanity.

SOME NOTES ON WRONG WORK OF CENTRES

Part I.—One of the most interesting ideas found in this system of teaching
is that man has several different minds and that the intellect is only one
of the minds he possesses. Let us take the diagram of the different
centres in man according to the teaching.

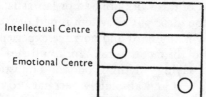

Intellectual Centre

Emotional Centre

Instinctive-moving Centre

Each of these centres is "mind". Each of them represents a *different
kind of mind*.

Centres can be roughly compared with very delicate and extremely
complex machines, each machine being designed for a different purpose
and use. Moreover, each machine is made of separate smaller machines
or of machines within machines, and these can work by themselves.
That is, the whole centre or whole machine can work, or only a small part
of it. Everyone possesses these highly complex and delicate machines,
but knowing nothing or next to nothing about them, people are liable
to use them wrongly. In fact, they think they have only *one* mind and
that this *one* mind can deal with everything. And the idea of *one mind* is
linked up with the illusion that man is *one*—that is, with the form of
imagination that everyone carries about with him—namely, that he is
internally one, a unity, having one will and one permanent 'I', and
possessing full consciousness and self-knowledge and the power to do.
It is a very strange and interesting thing that no one can reflect upon
deeply enough—for it leads to the source of man's inner "sickness"—that
it takes so long before people can bear to realize that internally they are
not one but many, that they are not a unity and harmony but a multiplicity and disharmony, that they have not one permanent and real 'I'
but hundreds of different and quite contradictory 'I's that take charge
of them at different moments, that they have no real will but a host of
changing conflicting wills, belonging to each of these 'I's, that only
rarely do they have moments of consciousness but usually are in a
peculiar state of waking-sleep, and that as a result of all this they have
no real power of doing and so live in a world where everything happens
and no one can prevent it from happening. Even the idea that a man has
not *one* mind but different centres or minds can be resented or regarded
as being as fantastic as the saying that people are not conscious. No one
in fact will face himself and his real situation.

So a man clings to what he imagines himself to be, and by clinging
in this way to what does not exist, to what is unreal, makes it impossible

for himself to exist and to become real—that is, what he might become and actually is created to become. You perhaps have heard a saying in this Work that everyone can be a millionaire but in order to be a millionaire he must first realize that he is not a millionaire. In this respect everyone is like the rich young man in the parable, the man rich in feeling his own merit, who ascribed goodness to himself as his own possession and was deeply identified with his virtues. You remember that he was told to go and sell it all and give to the poor—that is; to the real or essential ungrown inner part of him, starved by the "rich personality". Now a man is not likely to take in anything that is said about the wrong work of centres unless he has reached the point of recognizing for himself that different centres really do exist in him. You must all understand that this is not a fantastic idea or a merely theoretical idea. It is a fact and it is a fact of the greatest importance to anyone who wishes to use his life well and not make it something blurred, unformed and largely meaningless. For this reason the first thing you are told to do in regard to practical work on yourselves is to observe which centre or centres are working at any particular moment. That is, you are told to practise self-observation, which is the only road leading to self-change, first of all in relation to noticing the different centres in you. But even this is very difficult and people do not, even after a long period, really see for themselves that these centres exist in them. Or they try to observe them for a moment and think that is all that is needed. There are three different people in everyone, to begin with—the Intellectual Man, the Emotional Man, and the Instinctive-Moving Man, corresponding to these three centres or minds. That is, a man thinks one thing, feels another, and "senses" a third—that is, his sensations, which belong to his Instinctive Centre, are different from his feelings, which belong to the Emotional Centre, and his thoughts, which belong to the Intellectual Centre. Let us suppose you are trying to keep an aim, and have taken the trouble to make this aim clear to yourself. Now suppose you get upset by something: what will happen, taking the matter only from the standpoint of different centres? If you are upset it means that the Emotional Centre has become negative. You feel angry, cross, disappointed, or perhaps you feel nothing is worth while. Now suppose you follow the mind of the Emotional Centre as it is *at the moment* will you be likely to keep your aim, whatever it is? No, of course not. But if you will get into your Intellectual Centre—if you can—and think about your aim and what made you make it and so on, then you may still keep your aim. Why? Because you are using the right centre for the occasion. You are not using the wrong centre, for to use, to follow, the Emotional Centre when it is *negative* is *always* to use the wrong centre. But all this has been spoken of sufficiently before. To-day we have to speak of the wrong work of centres not so much in the sense of the wrong centres being used for any particular task, as for example, in trying to *think* how to run quickly downstairs, but in the sense of using the wrong part of a centre. As you know, each centre is divided into three parts and each of these parts into three further parts. I am not now speaking of the division of some of the centres into positive and negative sides. Each centre reflects itself and the others in its three divisions and three sub-divisions. For example, the Intellectual Centre has three divisions, which represent the Instinct-Moving Centre, the Emotional Centre, and the Intellectual Centre itself, but all on a *smaller scale*. And these again are subdivided in the same way on a still smaller scale.

The Instinct-Moving part of any centre is the most mechanical part and it is in these mechanical divisions of centres that people spend their lives as a rule. But before we speak in detail about divisions of centres in general, one principle must be grasped relating to their divisions. Why do people spend their time in mechanical divisions of centres? The answer is simply that they require *no attention*. When attention is prac- tically zero, one is in the lowest most automatic parts of centres. The result is that a person says and does things without any idea of what he is doing. Another result is that a person cannot adapt to any change or use his knowledge but behaves absolutely mechanically on all occasions and repeats what he knows like a machine. You all notice how hard it is for many people to adapt themselves to any new ideas or conditions, and how they repeat all they have been taught as if they were school-children.

To get into higher divisions of centres the effort of *attention* is necessary. This is the *principle*. Now let us take the mechanical part of Intellectual Centre as a starting-point. Its function is the work of *registration* of memories and impressions and associations and this is all it should do normally—that is, if *rightly used*. It should never reply to questions addressed to the whole centre. Above all it should never decide any- thing important. Now here we have the first example of wrong work of centres in regard to their parts and divisions. The mechanical division of Intellectual Centre, which is called the Formatory Part or Formatory Centre, is continually replying to questions and is continually making decisions. It replies anyhow, in slang terms, typical phrases and jargon of all sorts. It replies automatically and says just what it is most accustomed to say, like a machine. Or on a slightly higher scale, it replies always in a stereotyped way, like a schoolmaster or government official, using well-known sentences, party maxims, slogans, proverbs, wise saws, and so on. And the strange thing is that many people always reply in this way and never notice it, either because they cannot think about anything and rely on mechanical and even automatic expressions of the Intellectual Centre, or because they do not see the importance of thinking for themselves and freeing their thoughts from the mechanical words and expressions that belong to the lowest divisions of the centre.

We now come to *attention*. Attention puts us into better or more conscious parts of centres. Attention is of three kinds:

(1) zero-attention, which characterizes mechanical divisions of centres;

(2) attention that does not require effort, but is attracted and needs only the keeping out of irrelevant things;

(3) attention that must be directed by effort and will.

As was said, the first kind of attention, zero-attention, accompanies the work of mechanical divisions of centres; the second kind puts us into the emotional divisions of centres, and the third kind into the intellectual divisions. Let us take briefly the Intellectual Centre again as an example, as we shall have to return to this subject next time. The emotional part of the whole Intellectual Centre consists chiefly of the desire to know, the desire to understand, to seek knowledge, to discover, to increase one's understanding, to grasp and find out, to have the satisfaction of knowing, the desire for truth, the pleasure of learning, of reaching out; and, inversely, the pain of not knowing, the dissatisfaction of being ignorant, uninformed, and so on. The work of the emotional part requires full attention, but in this part of the centre attention does not require any effort. It is attracted and kept by the interest of the subject itself. The intellectual part of the whole Intellectual Centre includes a capacity for creation, construction, invention, finding methods, seeing connections, and bringing together apparently isolated things into an order or unity or formulation so that we see the truth of something hitherto obscure. This part cannot work without *directed attention*. The attention in this part is not attracted but must be controlled and kept by effort and will; we usually avoid doing the work belonging to this part of the centre, which is thus often *unused*.

Now from this we can notice in what parts of centres we are. Next time we will speak further on this subject.

Birdlip, October 23, 1941

WRONG WORK OF CENTRES

Part II.—Last time we spoke of wrong work of centres from the point of view of using wrong divisions of centres and from the principle of *Attention*.

As was said, people inhabit or live in small divisions of centres— that is, in mechanical divisions. You must understand that all the different 'I's in us live in smaller or larger divisions of centres. That is to say, we have more mechanical or less mechanical 'I's. In the small divisions, in the mechanical or even automatic parts of centres dwell most of the 'I's that control our ordinary life. In this sense, people inhabit or live in small mechanical divisions of centres. That is, our ordinary life is largely controlled by very little mechanical 'I's, that inhabit these small subdivisions of centres. These should be servants and not our masters, for we have 'I's of different power or quality or capacity. For example, the 'I's that live in small subdivisions of centres are incapable of understanding this Work. They are very limited. They cannot change. They are like peasants who suspect anything new. The little 'I's that you use in ordinary life—the 'I's that quarrel and feel dis-

71

contented, that are occupied with little plans, little suspicions, little things, little interests, and so on—are in mechanical parts of centres. They are quite useful for little things. But they cannot understand the Work. They belong to little parts of centres. And sometimes you find people who are so much in these small daily 'I's that they are incapable of understanding anything save what belongs to their immediate small interests and to the outlook of these little 'I's that occupy themselves only with the small things of daily life, which are very important *on that scale*—namely, on the scale of small things. That is to say, these little small 'I's have their right place and if they deal with what belongs to them, they do their work as they should ; and everyone must possess trained 'I's of this sort. As you know, a person must be developed to some extent in all parts of centres in order to become No. 4 man or balanced man. But, as was said, these small 'I's cannot grasp this Work, they cannot adapt themselves to the ideas of this Work, and if the Work-ideas fall only on these little small daily-life 'I's the Work cannot be received and rightly placed in a person's being. In short, this Work, if taken in only by these small self-interested daily 'I's, will only be understood at their own small level of understanding—at the "level of being" of these little 'I's. This Work must fall on bigger 'I's and never be allowed to sink to small 'I's. This is a very real and important side of work on oneself—that is, it is very important not to let small 'I's living in small parts of centres think and decide about the ideas of this Work. Since this is so important and from a practical point of view constitutes so direct an example of the wrong work of centres, which is the subject we are now studying, we must try to understand better what is meant. For, as was said, the study of wrong work of centres is not merely a matter referring to the wrong use of a centre, such as using the thinking centre for running quickly downstairs—in which case one will fall—but also a question of using the right *part* of a centre in relation to what has to be done at any particular time. For there are quite different *kinds* of things that we are called upon to deal with at different times and we possess not only different centres or minds—the intellectual for complex comparisons and thoughts, the moving for complex movements far quicker than thought, the emotional for seeing the quality of things and relations and meanings hidden from the intellectual, and so on—but each centre is divided and subdivided into parts, each having its right place in the scheme of things and its proper function.

To return to the intellectual centre. The *mechanical* part includes in itself all the work of *registration of memories, associations and impressions*, and this is all the work it should do normally—that is, when the other centres and parts of centres are doing *their* proper work. It should only do the work of registration or recording, like a secretary taking down what is said and arranging it, etc. And, as was said, it should never reply to questions addressed to the *whole centre* and should never decide anything important: but unfortunately it is always deciding and always replying in its narrow limited way, with ready-made phrases, and it continues to say the same things and work in the same mechanical ways under all conditions. This is the fixed part of a man and when a man dwells intellectually in the mechanical divisions of intellectual centre, he will not change, and nothing can be new in him, but he will see life always in a certain way and say the same things, like a gramophone. But if he has another part of him developed in a larger division, the case will be quite different. He will then have a very mechanical dead side and a different side, that is more conscious and living—namely, that lies in either the emotional or intellectual divisions. Actually, a balanced man in the Work-sense is developed to some extent in all parts—mechanical, emotional and intellectual—of all centres. That is, he is represented in them by some 'I's and they are not like empty rooms. This distributes his energy, and brings the psychic life into harmony, but it is only through ideas similar to those of this Work—namely, ideas coming from "C" influences, from the *conscious circle of humanity*, from those who have reached full internal stature—that the harmonious development of centres is possible. Life-interests alone are bound to lead to one-sided development; and no man can develop only through self-interest for then he will only develop certain parts of emotional centre.

Now if the Work falls on the mechanical side of the intellectual centre it will fall among 'I's that deal with the ordinary daily affairs of life. These 'I's are fed by "A" influences and are for use in life, and they cannot understand what the Work is about or why the Work is necessary. They are turned to outer visible life which is the sum total of reality for them. For them only what they can see and touch is real. There is therefore no *soil* for the *Work-ideas* to grow from, for the Work is not about the things of sense that can be seen or handled, but begins with *self*-observation—that is, with what cannot be seen or handled. So you will understand how dangerous it is for those who have been given the opportunity of receiving the Work in larger parts of centres, in bigger 'I's, to allow its ideas to fall down in themselves into little mechanical 'I's where they will be divided or even torn to bits, as it were. This is really the basic idea in sacrilege or profanation—that is, it belongs to wrong work of centres. The Work must always be thought about with *attention*, for this puts a man into intellectual parts of centres.

As regards the hearing of the ideas of the Work with little narrow 'I's, you all know the parable about the Sower and the Seed. The person who lives only in very small parts of centres, in little personal things, on hearing this Work will only understand it in a very little small way. This situation is mentioned in the parable. The seed means the ideas of esotericism, the ideas of this Work. If the ideas of this Work fall, as living seeds, on very small 'I's, on very little parts of centres inhabited by very small, very little 'I's, it is as if the seed—that is, the ideas of this Work—fall "by the wayside". Let us remind ourselves of this parable:

"The sower went forth to sow his seed: and as he sowed, some fell by the wayside; and it was trodden under foot, and the birds of the heaven devoured it. And other fell on the rock; and as soon

73

as it grew, it withered away, because it had no moisture. And other fell among thorns; and the thorns grew with it and choked it. And other fell into the good ground, and grew, and brought forth fruit a hundredfold." (*Luke*: VIII *v-viii*)

In interpreting this parable to his disciples, Christ says: "The seed is the word of God. And those by the wayside are they who have heard; then cometh the devil, and taketh away the word from their heart, that they may not believe and be saved." Do you understand why it is called the wayside? It means that the ideas of the Work fall amid the traffic of one's mind, among the ordinary thoughts of one's life, and are taken in the *mechanical* side of the mind which Christ calls the *devil*—for mechanicalness is the devil.

Now you all know that, in the Work-sense, a person can only understand at his level of being. This means that if you meet a man on a higher level of being than your own you will not understand him. And if you live in very little, very small, very limited, mechanical 'I's, then that represents your level of being. You will then only understand what is very small, very little, very personal, and, as was said, if you centre yourself in these little 'I's, these small 'I's that relate to the small business of your daily life and to your little jealousies, little hatreds and desires and meannesses, you will be unable to adapt yourself to anything new, so the ideas of the Work will "fall by the wayside" and either be quite meaningless to you or even ridiculous, silly, unnecessary and fantastic. This means that you will understand the Work at this level of your being. But everyone has a *scale* of being. That is, a man has, *provided he has magnetic centre*, a better level and better 'I's in him, if he tries to find them, through which to understand the Work. And one sign of this is the possession of "magnetic centre" which can distinguish between "A" influences and "B" influences.

Birdlip, November 9, 1941

WRONG WORK OF CENTRES

Part III.—The mechanical divisions of centres have their proper work to do and they can work rightly without attention, or with very little attention. When you walk, the action requires very little attention, and only from time to time, and all the complex movements involved in the act of walking are done rightly by the mechanical divisions of *moving centre*. You can prove that this is done by the mechanical division of moving centre because while walking your hands can be engaged in movements that require conscious direction—i.e. attention—as in sharpening a pencil or unravelling string, and so on. But just because the mechanical parts of centres can work with zero-attention or very little, occasional, attention, they often act independently—e.g. a man goes to dress for dinner

74

while thinking over a problem and eventually finds himself, to his surprise, getting into bed. Everyone must have noticed similar examples.

Now the whole human machine is made in such a way that one part can in an emergency do the work of another part for a certain time. This is expressed, in this system, by saying that *centres overlap* to some extent in regard to function. And although it is because centres overlap to a limited extent that the human machine can meet with certain emergencies and is therefore more capable of adjustment, it is actually because of the overlapping that occasions for the wrong working of centres are given. To take an example: we know that breathing can be carried on without our attention. Here the moving centre, which contracts and relaxes the muscles used in breathing, is controlled by the instinctive centre, which estimates the condition of the blood at every moment and increases and decreases the rate of respiration accordingly. But we cannot observe this directly. We cannot observe the instinctive centre and its intricate task of attending to the inner work of the organs. But we can observe the results of its work—namely, that after running we breathe more deeply or if we are feverish we breathe more rapidly and realize that this is because the instinctive centre needs more oxygen, and so on. But breathing is not only carried on by the instinct-moving centre. There is an overlapping of control for we can breathe deliberately—that is, voluntarily. A man cannot hold his breath voluntarily beyond a certain time because the instinctive centre will take over his breathing for him as soon as he begins to lose consciousness. But a man can interfere with his breathing and make himself breathe more slowly or more deeply, and so on. This is a dangerous thing to do but there are moments when it is very important and when, in fact, it can save a man's life. If, however, a person tries to control his breathing without understanding what he is doing, and without knowledge, he may interfere with the normal working of the instinct-moving centre, which then becomes lazy, and, as it were, hands over the business of breathing in part. I remember hearing G. say more than once that people who expect to gain increased powers by means of breath-control were fools unless they had gone through long preliminary training under a teacher and had been selected by him. They were fools because they interfered with a function which, once wrongly interfered with long enough, might never work normally afterwards.

The question of the wrong work of centres is a matter of life-long study through self-observation. In order to understand anything you must realize its nature, otherwise you will approach it wrongly or have the wrong attitude to it. You cannot understand about centres and their right and wrong work just in a moment. If you think you can, you will ask the wrong questions and indeed never take in anything about the subject. Think a moment. All your *life* is a function of, and is controlled by, centres—your thoughts, your feelings, your ideas, your hopes, fears, loves, hates, your actions, your sensations, your pleasures, your comforts, and so on. How, then, can you expect to understand all about right and wrong work of centres in a short time? To do so is like expecting

75

to understand all about life after hearing a lecture or two on it. What has been said so far is only to give you some indication of what is meant and to make you begin to study the subject, and unless you study it by self-observation, then even if you hear a thousand and one lectures on the matter, you will not *understand* a single thing.

Now it is necessary to give the division of other centres so that people have some general chart to use, to find their way by, and to which they can refer some of their own observations of themselves and find where they belong—for this heips one to see oneself more clearly.

I will now have to divide certain centres into positive and negative divisions, first of all, and then fill in, here and there, at present only some of the subdivisions, giving *approximate* definitions of their functions. Let us begin with the Intellectual Centre.

Figure I— Intellectual Centre

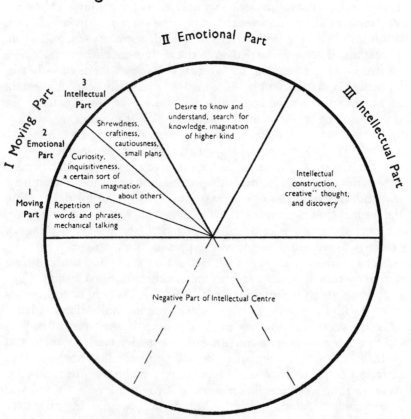

Note.—Only the Moving Part of the Intellectual Centre is in any detail charted in this diagram. Note here the difference between Emotional Part of Moving Part of Intellectual Centre and the Emotional Part of Intellectual Centre as a whole. Notice what is meant.

Figure II — Emotional Centre

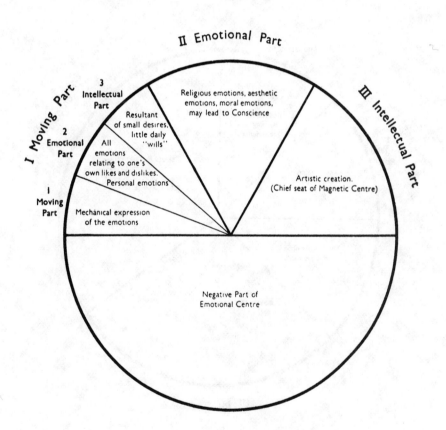

II Emotional Part

I Moving Part

3 Intellectual Part

2 Emotional Part

1 Moving Part

Resultant of small desires, little daily "wills"

All emotions relating to one's own likes and dislikes. Personal emotions

Mechanical expression of the emotions

Religious emotions, aesthetic emotions, moral emotions, may lead to Conscience

Artistic creation. (Chief seat of Magnetic Centre)

III Intellectual Part

Negative Part of Emotional Centre

Figure III — Moving Centre

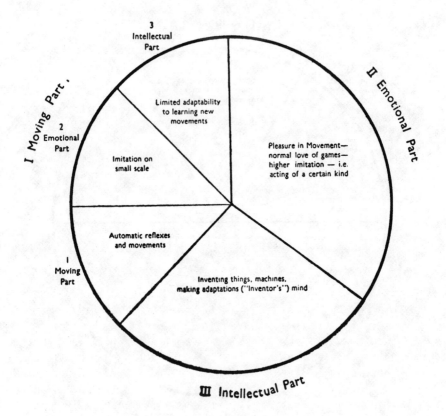

Figure IV — Instinctive Centre

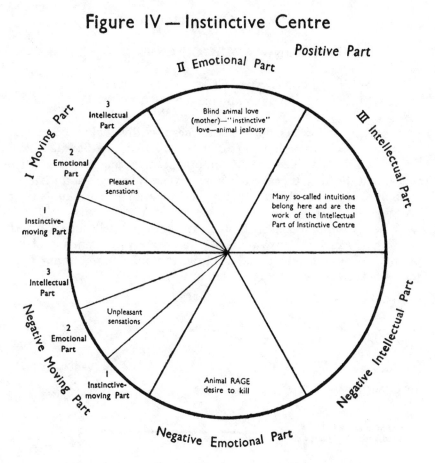

As we said, in these diagrams of the centres and their divisions only a few parts are charted to serve as a guide to the observation of centres and their work. It was part of our work several years ago to observe parts of centres and collect and compare our observations.

All that has been given so far requires careful study. First it is necessary to *register* what is said about the centres and parts as given and then to think about what it all means and get an individual idea of the subject—for this puts it in higher parts of centres—and then to find examples and try to place them. *Please do not ask questions about the parts of centres not mapped out.* It is always a sign of negative thinking and automatic questioning which is worse than formatory questioning, to ask about Asia when a lecture is being given on America or to ask about the exception when a rule is being explained.

Birdlip, November 18, 1941

WRONG WORK OF CENTRES

The Intellectual Centre as Divided into Positive and Negative Parts

Part IV.—Let us now begin to study the negative divisions of centres and what they mean. In order to do so, let us speak to-day of the Intellectual Centre which is divided *naturally* into a positive side and a negative side and at the same time speak a little of what thinking is and what the Work means in regard to arranging the Intellectual Centre in its right order.

What is the function of the negative part of Intellectual Centre? Roughly, its function is to think *No*, to negate. The function of the positive part of the Intellectual Centre is to think *Yes*, to affirm. Thus the whole centre can be represented in this way.

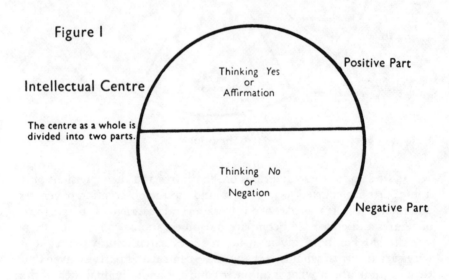

Figure I

Intellectual Centre

The centre as a whole is divided into two parts.

Thinking Yes or Affirmation — Positive Part

Thinking No or Negation — Negative Part

Without a negative part in the Intellectual Centre, it would be impossible to *think*. What is thinking? The first definition this system gives is that thinking is *comparing*. Thinking is comparing one thing with another, one proposition with another, etc. But if a man only has *affirmation* or *Yes* as an instrument to think with, comparison will not be possible. Comparison requires a quality, or a choice between two things, to one of which one says *Yes* and to the other *No*. All the questions we ask beginning with *why* (as distinct from those beginning with *how*) mean that we seek a reason for something: and all reasoning involves comparison and choice—that is, selecting this and rejecting that. And it would be impossible to select or reject unless there were in the Intellectual Centre a twin-power—namely, the power of affirmation and the power of negation. Now the two parts of the centre should be able to work together, somewhat in the same way as the two blades of a pair of scissors work, one acting against the other. That is, a man should be able to see what affirms, as well as what negates, whatever he is thinking about, and hold them together, and between the two opposite sides find a *path* for his thoughts, for all genuine thinking *leads* in some direction in the mind (and should lead to a new place in the mind and not always along the old paths to the old places where one has been before and which are really reached without any thinking but simply by habitual association). I am speaking of genuine thinking which requires an *effort* and is something people rarely do. As you have no doubt heard, everyone in this Work is advised to "move his brains" once every day and this means to make a real effort to think. What we ordinarily call thinking is merely an automatic flow of associations, a flight of vague ideas and memories and phrases interrupted by an occasional slight effort to *recollect* something such as what we have to buy or where we have to go to-day. When the Intellectual Centre is working as a whole, all its different parts and divisions and subdivisions fall into their right order and functions but this rarely happens. The whole centre is rarely lit up. As a rule only small parts and subdivisions work—that is, it works at low pressure with only a little light and in small parts, and so cannot deal with any thoughts and ideas which need the activity of the centre as a whole. And again, people as a rule do not know what to think about. Now this system with all its ideas and principles, its tremendous background, and its practical details,—in fact, the whole teaching—is a connected organic system constructed to make a man think and teach him how to think and give him something through which to develop his own thinking. For some of the ideas are easy to grasp and on a small scale, others are more difficult and on a bigger scale, and the connection between them may not be seen for a long time, but the *whole* Intellectual Centre, with all its parts, small and great, is eventually needed to hold the system together in its right order so that it can work aright and transmit force as an organized and living whole. This is not a question of memory only, for memory is, first of all, a function of the mechanical or formatory division of the Intellectual Centre, which *registers*, and this part is not enough to comprehend the ideas of the teaching fully. It is also a question of evaluation and seeing and tasting its truth. At the same time, unless this system is *registered* properly in a man it cannot develop and grow rightly in him to receive and transmit the vibrations of higher centres. You must understand that there is no force in the Work itself taken as words and diagrams but in what the Work transmits through its being voluntarily understood. For when the Work is understood, then it has formed something in a man that he did not possess before and this instrument, so to speak, thus formed in him, can respond to influences of which he was not formerly conscious. And it is these influences that modify, change and eventually transform the man. You will see, therefore, how important it is to keep the Work alive in oneself and to hear its ideas over and over again and think of them again, and again try to act from them. For if the Work dies out in a person through the overwhelming pressure of life and its daily demands, it may be difficult to awaken it again. People easily fall asleep ; and it takes very much time, study, effort and sacrifice before the Work forms itself strongly enough in a man to remain alive of itself, so people must keep in touch with those who can keep it alive and whose task it is to do so.

I have made this digression in order to shew how the Intellectual Centre working as a whole is necessary for the full comprehension of this system and how the system is constructed for this purpose and can organize the whole Intellectual Centre aright into an instrument that can begin to respond to the influences coming from Higher Centres. But as this subject belongs to "Relative Thinking" (which alone brings the Intellectual Centre into right action) we will now here return to the divisions of the centre into *positive* and *negative sides* and consider them in regard to the wrong working of centres (and parts of centres).

Let us take *negative thinking*. Negative thinking occurs when a man thinks only or mainly from the negative side of the Intellectual Centre. He uses the negative part to think with. As was said, the two sides, positive and negative, should work together and check each other. Now if a man starts to think, let us say of this Work, from the negative side of the Intellectual Centre and lets this side continue its activity *unchecked*, he is bound to reach a denial of the Work, because the negative side can only join things together in the form of increasing *negation*. The end-result will therefore be *No*. This *negative thinking*, about matters such as the Work is concerned with, is very common to-day, but in order to flourish it must discard or reject or disparage anything which does not agree with it.

Negative thinking takes many forms in different people. Some people have well-developed systems of entirely unchecked negative thinking about different things—about themselves, about others, about life, about the world, the Universe, and so on. These systems have formed themselves independently of the positive side of the Intellectual Centre and are therefore one-sided, unchecked, unchallenged by any *opposite* thinking and often a source of illness.

One of the easiest things is to *disagree*. To habitually disagree is to use the negative part of the centre. Habitual disagreeing, finding fault, picking holes, splitting hairs, etc., is to use the negative side unchecked: and a negative thinker is, in brief, a man to avoid, for whatever you say to him he will try to destroy it. He cannot help doing so for he is, so to speak, intellectually *in reverse* and can only go backwards. All this is *wrong use of a centre*. On the other hand, a person who thinks, let us say again of this system, only on the side of affirmation, will never grasp it. It will never become real to him, for he will not have passed through any temptations in regard to it and struggled and worked it out for himself by slow degrees.

There is a story in the Work that once upon a time man was perfect. Man was in touch with "higher centres". In fact, it is said he conversed with gods. But he was very weak, because, never having denied and always having affirmed, he did not know how to meet with *denial*. So he fell easily from his high position, for he had no strength of thinking and understanding from himself. Now he has to find his way back to where he once was, with the power of denial to help him.

ADDITIONAL NOTE

There are some very interesting things that can be said in regard to the two divisions, positive and negative, of the Intellectual Centre, if we take them in conjunction with other centres, such as the Emotional Centre. For example, a man may have *negative thinking* and *positive feeling or will* towards a thing. Or, on the contrary, he may have *positive thinking* and *negative feeling or will*. In order to illustrate this, the example given in the Gospels is useful to think about:

"A man had two sons; and he came to the first, and said, Son, go work to-day in the vineyard. And he answered and said, I will not: but afterwards he repented himself and went. And he came to the second and said likewise. And he answered and said, I go, sir: and went not. Whether of the twain did the will of his father?"

(*Matthew* XXI *xxviii-xxxi*)

A person who has a too-mechanical *affirmation* from the Intellectual Centre will say "Yes" but that belongs to his thought—not to his *will*. The basis of the will is in the Emotional Centre. So he says "Yes" with his thinking, but eventually "No" with his Emotional Centre. Or a man has negative thinking and positive feeling. He says "No" with his mind but his feeling says later on "Yes". The parable or psychological definition can be understood differently. But it means that a man is not *one*—and has two distinct sides which do not necessarily agree.

Another thing that can be said is that if a man has no *Magnetic Centre* (which *affirms* the existence of two kinds of influences in the vortex of life—namely A and B) he may start only from the negative side of thinking once he meets work of this kind and so spend all his time in *disproving*. A feeling starts a certain kind of thinking. Our intellectual apparatus as it is, divided into positive and negative, can give *any result* according to whether one side or the other is set into action. It can prove or disprove *anything*. It is *valuation*—the Emotional Centre—that is decisive. Regarded as a pure machine, the two sides of the Intellectual Centre are mutually destructive. This is why it is said that a *third factor* is necessary for the proper working of the centre.

WRONG WORK OF CENTRES

Part V.—In this paper, which is the last of the series on the Wrong Work of Centres, we will begin with the Emotional Centre in regard to its negative side, but I am going to digress a good deal on the subject of negative emotions themselves.

It was said in the last paper that the Intellectual Centre has, naturally, a negative part. But this is not the case with the Emotional Centre. The negative part of the Emotional Centre is the seat of *negative emotion*. But *naturally* there is no such part in the centre : it is acquired. And it can be said at once that whenever this acquired negative part of the Emotional Centre is active, it means wrong work of the centre. And it is no exaggeration to say that the Emotional Centre very rarely works in the right way, owing to the action of this acquired negative part with which it has become, as it were, infected from its contact with life. For negative emotions govern life, perhaps especially to-day, and people cling to their unhappy negative emotions more than to anything else. Now the infection of negative emotions (like the infection of negative thinking) introduces itself gradually into a growing child, for a child is born awake (on its own scale) into a world of sleeping people, and, by imitating them, learns only to fall asleep in its turn: and among many other things it imitates negative emotions—that is, the facial expressions, the intonations, the words and phrases that spring out of the negative states of other people. The child imitates all these and so gradually begins to feel what they represent. In this way, the negative feelings of its elders gradually communicate themselves to the child and after a time the child begins to shew negative emotions and to sulk and brood and nag and feel sorry for itself and so on. After all, what else can the child do? And again, what else can those who are already infected with negative emotions do, since they are entirely unaware that they are negative and have never heard of the idea, and, as a rule, if they ever do hear it, are certain that they are never negative. So you see how difficult it is to alter this repeating, ever-recurring chain of cause and effect, this continual inevitable infection and reinfection, which is worse than any other infection, physical or moral. Who is going to break it? Or what can break it? The only thing that can break it is for a man to hear, see, understand and realize what negative emotions are and start *with himself*. For if even one person shifts his position in this respect in the close mesh-work of life, in the immoveable jam of human beings, he will give room to others. But this will only be the case when he works on his negative emotions genuinely from the deepest, inner, individual perception of the truth of the horror and uselessness of negative emotions, for that is the point where real work starts, from this inner vision. You must all understand that you can work from different places, or, as it were, depths, in you. You can work for superficial reasons or for deeper reasons. When a man works on himself for rewards or praise or position or duty, or from a certain kind of conceit or pride or self-merit, or some picture of himself, or from honour or from trying to please, or imitation, or fear, as from fear of loss of reputation, fear of criticism, fear of losing friendship, and so on, and so on—all these *motives* or *sources of his will* in him (some better and some worse) are not yet the *man himself* working *from himself*. He is working externally to *himself*. These motives are a series of substitutes for the *real 'I'* in a man—substitution 'I's, some of which form Deputy Steward and, as I said, some are better and some are worse, some are useful and some are hindrances—that is, some are more internal and so more towards essence or the *real* part of a man and some are more external and so towards false personality or the imaginary person we take ourselves as and on whom we all spend so much force, thought, time and money in keeping going, amidst such clouds of negative emotions and frictions.

It is only *real* work and not imaginary work on personal negative emotions that will allow others to shift their position for otherwise the negative emotions are still there, in another form, for they resemble Proteus who was always changing his shape and turning into something else. But it is a necessary part of this Work, that everyone must eventually pass, to see in himself by sincere observation, how he clings to his negative emotions with one hand and tries to free himself with the other. The Work inevitably leads everyone to the same places and the same experiences. A man must reach the point of discerning his own helplessness—of realizing his own mechanicalness. And this, if it is not a negative experience, will bring him into a state of *self-remembering*. Through seeing his helplessness he attracts help. For realizing one's own helplessness puts a man into the Third State of Consciousness where help can reach us. And since I am on this subject I will add for those of you who still do not yet quite understand what it means to work more "externally" and what it means to work more "internally" that the case is like this. The object of the Work is to arouse "buried conscience"—I am not speaking of acquired conscience which is different in every race and is a matter of custom, training, class and nation. *Buried conscience is the same in all people* but it is buried—that is, out of reach. Unless there were this "buried conscience" in us, the Work would be useless—nothing more than a new craze, a new fashion, a new jargon. Now if we could touch this buried and real conscience, we would know instantly that all negative states were wrong—and, in fact, poison to us. It is exactly by "inner taste", as it is called in the Work, that we begin to realize this for ourselves. "Inner taste" makes a man realize when he is negative. Then a struggle starts. He wishes to say something—and cannot. When this happens, when the Work brings him to this point, the Work is then "working in him". It is no longer something he accepts, but something he must fight for in himself. Then he begins to see that he must work on his negative emotions more internally, and then conscience will help him. But if he works on his negative emotions because he is told he should, or because he is ashamed before others at having them, and so on, then he is working more "externally" upon them, and not genuinely from himself. But for the faint indications of real conscience that this Work begins to evoke in people, and its inner help, the struggle with negative emotions would be impossible. That is, *unless we had conscience somewhere in us, negative emotions would be unconquerable.* Life would be too strong. But fortunately for us existing on this earth, placed so far down in the Ray of Creation, so that it is only one degree removed from the worst possible place in the whole Universe—fortunately for us, we have *within us* the means of awakening, though it is buried, and on the other hand we have *outside us* the forms of teaching about awakening, handed on age by age through the efforts of the circle of conscious humanity outside life, that can arouse us to awaken ourselves.

*   *   *

Let us now return to a brief consideration of the Emotional Centre in its negative part. It can be represented, although not entirely correctly, in the same way as in the case of Intellectual Centre.

Emotional Centre

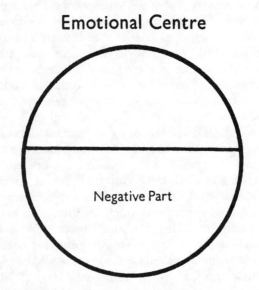

This represents the centre after it has acquired a negative part from contact with life. I do not propose at this stage to say any more on the different parts of the negative aspect of the Emotional Centre, save that the starting-point for your personal thinking on the subject is the idea that everything in the negative part works the wrong way round, as if in reverse. Let us take *suspicion*. Suspicion is an emotional state which soon involves the negative part of the Intellectual Centre and leads it to form conclusions of a negative kind. I said last time that one thing we have to understand about the Intellectual Centre is that each side of it—the positive side or the negative side—if it works independently of the other can come to *any conclusion*. This must be very clearly grasped. Now if suspicion arises in the negative part of the Emotional Centre, for suspicion is first of all an *emotion*, then it will bring into operation the negative side, and only the negative side, of the Intellectual Centre, in which case *everything will go to prove that your suspicion is right*. Now suppose your suspicion is changed suddenly into a more agreeable emotion by hearing something you did not know. What happens? Then the positive or affirmative side of the Intellectual Centre will start working and your conclusions will be quite different. You know the expression "the wish is father to the thought". But this is not a sufficient formulation. Any of our emotional states tend to govern our thinking. This is an example of one centre hypnotizing another and so of wrong working of centres. So we must try to free our thoughts from our emotions when they are negative. But all this is a matter for observation and to speak about it fully would require a long time.

I will add one or two things about negative emotions. They are very powerful. They can infect everyone. That is one reason why they are so prevalent and why people like to be negative, because then they can hurt everyone so easily. You will remember that there is a very hard saying in the Work—namely, that it is always your fault if you are negative. This is difficult to realize. It always seems the other person's fault. I will also remind you that the peculiar characteristic of negative emotions is that they go on and on by themselves, always creating fresh negative emotions, long after the cause is removed. Also they take so much energy and waste it uselessly that people often become ill as a result. And finally, if a person has well-marked negative thinking and negative emotions, it is a very dangerous state to be in. If a man works at the perception of his Emotional Centre he will find his whole life takes on a new meaning and he will experience moments of awakening that he will never forget and gain a glimpse of what it might mean if the Emotional Centre worked in its right way. But by himself he cannot do this. It is only through a new force and through new ideas and a new way of looking at himself that this can begin to be possible. All the efforts that the Work speaks of are necessary, particularly self-remembering, and the whole background of the Work must be felt as well.

KARMA-YOGA

A TALK GIVEN BY DR. NICOLL

Karma-Yoga is the science of action with non-identifying. This phrase must be remembered by everyone. It must not be changed into "the science of action without identifying". The essence of the idea of Karma-Yoga is to meet with unpleasant things equally with pleasant things. That is, in practising Karma-Yoga, one does not seek always to avoid unpleasant things, as people ordinarily do. Life is to be met with non-identifying. When this is possible, life becomes one's teacher; in no other sense can life become a teacher, for life taken as itself is meaningless, but taken as an *exercise* it becomes a teacher. It is not life that is a teacher, but one's relation through non-identifying makes it become a teacher. Nothing can change *being* so much as this practice—namely, to take the unpleasant things in life as an exercise. And anything that acts on being at once increases our force. To take life with non-identifying does not mean empty acting; it means to act from a real basis, from aim and from understanding the ideas and meaning of the Work.

It is impossible to understand life in terms of itself. Taken by itself it is a gigantic muddle. Something must be fitted over life, a system of ideas, such as the Work, to make it have any meaning. Karma-Yoga gave life a meaning. But by itself it was not enough. All the ideas of the Work are necessary to *transform* life into meaning for oneself.

HOW CAN A PERSON FIND HIS OWN MEANING?

Everyone is born into the world with one lesson to learn from the Work standpoint, one task to perform in regard to himself, and unless he begins to see it, his life is really meaningless. We have to remember something we have all forgotten. Life is very short; we lose ourselves too early in life. Do not drift. Take hold of yourself and ask: "What am I doing? Where am I going? " Think what you must do before it is too late; think what it is important for you to work on. Everyone has to distinguish in himself what has to be worked on, his reason for living this life. Man is born into this planet with an inner task and life is so arranged that he cannot find himself and his meaning through life alone, but only through seeing what this inner task is. The Work says that everyone is born into, and is in, exactly the best circumstances in regard to this task, and that if a man meets this Work his conditions are just what is best for the purpose of work. But of course everyone thinks that if only he were in different circumstances everything would be easy. This is not the case. Birth is from fate, not accident, and all fate has to do with oneself and one's possible evolution. One has to work against the circumstances one finds oneself in. To be born poor entails difficulties and to be born rich entails difficulties. As life is, it always goes differently from what we expect, and everything goes, as it were, criss-cross. If life itself were the object, this would not be the case. But when we think of our lives from the standpoint that we and all other people have a chief thing to understand and transform, the whole meaning of existence changes. Life is very brief—a moment or so of confusion and muddle —but even so it is possible by the action of the Work to catch a glimpse of what it is one has to work upon and what one's existence here really means. This Work, if rightly felt and applied, gradually brings into view what a person has to do, what lesson he must learn, what chief thing in him he has to understand and transform. This is called Chief Feature. But a man cannot come into the inner perception of his Chief Feature until he is ready for it. All his separate observations and aims in regard to his own work on himself, if done sincerely, will gradually combine and shew him what it is that he has to work against and will give him the reason why he is down here on earth. This is finding one's meaning, or rather, the meaning of one's existence. But it is useless striving to find one's Chief Feature directly. You must quite honestly begin always to work on one or another thing that you have observed and try to change it sincerely. People feel the Work sincerely often, but never think of starting sincerely from something they notice in themselves and working on it. They want everything together, and without paying.

But if you feel emotional about getting to know your Chief Feature, and really want to know about it, you may catch glimpses. Sometimes you can see Chief Feature in other people. Ask yourselves: "What is it in this person that would make him different if it were changed?" Sometimes it is possible to see this in someone else. And if you can only see how you have been wrong in your own life, how you have always reacted in the same way in certain circumstances, if you can suddenly catch a glimpse of this, then you can have an aim which will inevitably lead you to Chief Feature. You will find that it is something that you have always known about and suspected, but you have never quite recognized it as that very thing. Perhaps you will see it in a flash for a moment, and you will think: "So it's that after all; it has been that all the time." You have always known it but not guessed that that was the thing to be changed. And you will see then that if you can change exactly that thing you will be able to change other things. After the first glimpse you may not see it again for some time. Then you will see it again. It is the axle on which your personality turns, and it is the wrong axle, so, unless you build up something behind your personality, you cannot find yourself. But if you can get a trace of real 'I' to bear upon Chief Feature, you will see what makes your life wrong. And if you feel that the discovery of this is the real meaning of life for you, then life can never become meaningless.

RIGHT AND WRONG

It is difficult for people, especially people who are crystallized in their sense of right and wrong, to understand that there is no absolute right and wrong, but that right and wrong are relative. People are offended when told this, especially people who are vain enough to think they are right. Right and wrong depend on a third factor. As they are themselves, they are merely opposites, which cancel each other. The third factor is *aim*. If your aim is to go to Edinburgh, then it is right to go north and wrong to go south. But if your aim is to go to Brighton it is right to go south and wrong to go north. But people like to be told that it is always right to do this or that—e.g. to go north—and always wrong to go south. Many inflexible ideas of this kind dominate people's minds and render their development sterile. The general formulation of right and wrong in the Work is that everything that awakens you is right. But this formulation requires a great deal of understanding in order to understand it.

SELF-REMEMBERING

People keep on *thinking* of self-remembering, but they do not do it. It is necessary to stop the chain of automatic associations every day. This can be done by *inner stop*—that is, stopping everything, all thoughts, etc. This is the beginning of self-remembering. But people, as I say, keep on *thinking* of remembering themselves, and never *do*. To remember oneself one must stop everything and lift oneself into total silence and total loss of all ordinary sense of oneself. This takes a little time. But most people cannot spare even one minute to do it because they are slaves to their machines, so they are bound and glued to the ceaseless and useless flow of mechanical thoughts, negative emotions, personal accounts, etc. It is a great pity, especially to-day, when the external hypnotism of life is so strong that people even think such thoughts as that the war will make everything better, that people do not give themselves the first conscious shock. Help can reach a man only as the result of this shock. It cannot reach him in the flood of his personal thoughts and troubles and emotions. Help, which comes from the direction of higher centres, cannot reach the Second State of Consciousness ; it can only reach as far as the Third State of Consciousness. To-day, when so many people are hypnotized by war, there is more force available in the world than at other times for those who seek it, if they can only touch it. But it cannot be touched by associated thinking which only keeps a man on the same level as if he were saying again and again : "I must jump", not realizing that if he wishes to reach a higher level he must really jump. It is no use saying : "I must remember myself." You must actually remember yourselves.

90

COMMENTARY ON EFFORT

Part I.—When a person in this Work has ceased to make any efforts, he is often said to be drifting. To drift means to have no direction. In other cases he is said to have fallen asleep. To fall asleep in the Work means simply to forget all about it. For example, a person may become so immersed in life that he forgets everything relating to the Work. He is then not merely drifting, but fast asleep. In this conversation I am going to speak about effort. The Work depends on effort. It is based on effort but effort of a certain kind. First of all, effort is, in general, distinguished into two kinds, mechanical and conscious. In a general sense, mechanical effort is what we have to do, what life makes us do. All animals, all nature, all organic life, of which we form a small part, have to make mechanical effort. Let us take an example. If it is raining you must put up your umbrella. This is exactly what is meant by mechanical effort, and by such efforts we adapt to life.

Conscious effort means effort that is not necessary in life and is not occasioned by life. That is, life is not the cause of it; the source of its origin does not lie in life. This means that some source other than the interests of life is necessary in order to make conscious effort, through which conscious effort becomes possible. Have you ever asked yourself if you really believe that there are any influences not belonging to life and coming from another source? Let me remind you of what this teaching says. There are two kinds of influences in life itself called A and B influences. A influences are created within life—by its clash and friction, by its jealousies and hatreds, by its ambitions, its wars, its crimes, its commerce, its interests, its laws, and so on. But B influences exist in life and they speak another language because they originate from a source outside life—from what are called C influences—that is, from people who have undergone individual evolution. C influences do not come from the circle of mechanical humanity, but from the conscious circle of humanity. But it is impossible for C influences to reach life directly. They would not be understood. Theirs is another language, one which we must learn slowly. Life alters them into B influences. But the point is that this system is based entirely on the existence of these other influences, distinct from life, called B and C influences—actually on C influences. That is why we have to learn a new language. You must understand that if man had not an inner secret destiny, if man were not a seed, and often a very unhappy one, there would be nothing for him save life and its interests. But the inner destiny of man does not lie in life. This seed that is man is capable of its own evolution and only certain kinds of light and heat can develop it—not the light and heat of the sun which governs external life and is the source of it. I say all this here because unless the two destinies of man are formulated in your own minds it is difficult to understand what the Work is about. The Work is what is called the *Fourth Way*, as distinct from the three other Ways. It is in life and so a person must know how to be in life and how to use life and get what he wants from life and at the same time be in the Work. This is only possible for certain kinds of people—namely, "Good Householders"—who are those who do their duty in life but do not believe in life. And you must realize that in this Work it is not demanded of you that you give up life or anything of that kind. On the contrary, this Work makes you realize that you must use life as far as you can for experience. But you must not trust life and get lost in it and think that the goal lies in life-experiences.

Conscious efforts are efforts to awaken from the sleep induced by life in humanity. As you know, it is not in the interests of nature that man should awaken, for then he ceases to serve nature. Such efforts would be impossible if man were merely a product of nature, whose sole function was to adapt to life. Why I say this at this point is that if you do not see for yourselves and are certain that there are in life two quite different sorts of influences, two kinds of things, two kinds of literature, two kinds of historical figures, then it will be impossible to make conscious efforts beyond a very limited degree. This is because in making the effort of personal work, the emotional centre must open out and must take its right part: and if it is only turned to life and personal ambitions, etc., it cannot come into its right action.

In making effort it is necessary to consider from what part of oneself the effort springs. A person may make effort against negative emotion in public, for example, for fear of making a fool of himself before others or of losing his job, etc. This is mechanical effort. As soon as he is at home, he will express his negative emotions. Conscious effort is quite different and springs from a different part.

When a man feels the existence of A and B influences and realizes that C influences must exist outside life, to account for the presence of B influences within life, he begins to feel the existence of something higher than himself. This begins to awaken the emotional centre and to make conscious effort possible. Otherwise the man will only feel self-emotions and remain in the narrow sphere of himself.

The most important conscious effort is to remember oneself. This always is difficult because we all forgot ourselves long ago, but it is quite impossible if a man has no sense of higher influences and cannot see the difference between A and B influences in life. Self-remembering must have an emotional factor, not of self, not of personality, but of something deeper, or, if you prefer it, higher than one's ordinary self. The factor of *will* enters in self-remembering—not self-will, but conscious will.

There are two sides to the Work where *effort* can be made, and these are the only two sides on which a man can evolve. The first is on the side of knowledge, and, in the case of this Work, the effort lies in thinking about the ideas and forming one's own individual intimate and inner connection with their meaning, and nothing is more important to start with. A man must think, speculate and ponder, take into his mind, dwell on in his own way, imagine and form his phantasies, his own sense of the Work, as a genuine *starting-point* in himself. For once he forms some starting-point, if it is wrong it can be modified. The Work then begins to shed a light in the mind. The second is on the side of one's being. Efforts on the side of knowledge are different from efforts on the side of being. It is quite easy to find this out for oneself. Man can develop in two directions and two only—on the side of knowledge and the side of being. Only these must go hand in hand. The resultant is *understanding.* As was said earlier, this Work must be based on understanding. One cannot adapt to it, as one does to life, outside oneself. Understanding is the most powerful force we can create in ourselves. Nothing better can be sought for in the long run than understanding: and in the Work a man is defined as his understanding. *A man is his understanding.* To-day I wish to speak only *of effort on the side of being.* Efforts directed upon one's being are different, as was said, from efforts directed to thinking about the knowledge of this system. The two sides of a man—the side of his knowledge and the side of his being—must be united to form understanding. This Work gives us more knowledge than we have being for. But it is very difficult to unite this knowledge with being. The whole task, however, is to do so, and the first necessity is to value the knowledge—that is, to like it, to wish it, to feel a desire for it. Knowledge can only unite with being through some emotion, through some desire, through willingness. One must will what one knows. Otherwise knowledge cannot unite with being. You cannot work on your being apart from the knowledge of this system and you cannot have any practical knowledge of this system unless you apply it to your being and you cannot apply it to your being—that is, it cannot enter your will and so act on you—if you do not wish it, desire it. A man's ordinary state is that he does not will what he knows. We act from our state of being, not from our knowledge. It is our will that acts and our will arises from our level of being. So a man knows better but acts worse, and as long as he is in that state, he has no unity in himself and so no understanding, because there are two separate sides in him. For knowledge to act on being there must be desire, or delight, or pleasure, in the ideas of the Work, for nothing can pass from the side of knowledge to the side of being without desire or pleasure or longing—that is, without willingness. Then a man will wish to live with what he knows, to live his knowledge, and his will and his knowledge will begin to coalesce. It is here that the whole valuation of the Work and its inner background comes in. Everything in the Work starts from *valuation* and this means *wanting something,* for you do not value a thing if you do not want it. This brings in the will, and it is through the will—through willingness—that you begin to apply the knowledge to your being. If you do apply it, then your knowledge will begin to turn into understanding through a union between the will of your being and the knowledge in your mind. As you know, *understanding* is defined clearly in this system. *Understanding* is the arithmetical mean between your knowledge and your being. So you see that to have know-

93

ledge of these ideas is not enough. It is quite easy to see when a person only has knowledge but not understanding of this Work. If you understand something you can speak of it in different ways; if it is merely knowledge you will speak of it from memory.

Now as regards *efforts on being*. Everyone must make conscious effort on his being every day, and especially at this period of time when everyone is going to sleep. If you wish to take life as your teacher, then, as was said in a previous paper, you must practise *non-identifying* with what life brings you, pleasant or unpleasant, for a certain time every day. Life demands mechanical effort, but if you practise non-identifying, it becomes conscious effort. Only do it for a certain time—say an hour—and keep conscious and observe yourself carefully. For instance, make your aim not to object to anything for an hour. This helps you to see what non-identifying means. Afterwards you can relax as regards work and do what you want if you like. But either work or don't work, and know what you are doing. Do not be in between centres. Do not drift for lack of any mental direction—and do not at this time fall asleep. To relax is not necessarily to fall asleep.

Now as regards working on special things in yourself and making effort in regard to them—that is, on the side of your being, on the kind of person you are and the way you react. First take your negative self—that is, your daily negative emotions. Try to see first of all that you are negative and acknowledge it. This helps by itself. Now, as you know, it takes another person to make you negative. So ask yourself some questions such as these :

(1) Do I think I am badly treated by someone?
(2) Am I jealous of someone?
(3) Is it mechanical disliking?

This helps you to formulate your situation to yourself. Now try to formulate the answers to yourself. Then try to think what *external considering* means. External considering means putting yourself in another person's position and realizing his or her difficulties. It is one way of *transforming* life. So now *become* the person you think has treated you badly or the person you are jealous of, etc. Try to do this sincerely. It requires a conscious effort. Visualize yourself as the person and reverse the position—that is, you become the person you dislike or hate or criticize, and you are now looking at another person, called yourself. As a rule this will cure you very quickly, if you can do it. But if you are in an evil state of negative emotion—as we all are at times—nothing will help you save realizing what you yourself are like—that is, what evil you have in you and what you are really like. This is painful. But we cannot change without pain. The Work is a mirror and everyone in it can help you to see your own self in that mirror. But you will not understand this unless you see yourself in others or others in yourself. *External considering* is the main way to deal with negative emotions. But it is necessary to understand what it means. It depends on visualization. External considering takes some time. It is difficult to do sincerely—

94

that is, rightly. It requires always a very great effort to do it. But it acts on being directly. Some find it impossible because they cannot imagine they might be someone else, especially a person they despise. This makes the Work difficult for them after a time.

Now let us speak of efforts on depression. Depression is not the same as being negative. There is one interesting thing about depression to be noticed—namely, that it affects all centres, even the instinctive centre. Depression is not due only to loss of hope and belief in the future, although this is a common cause. It can arise simply from making no efforts of any kind so that the centres are water-logged, so to speak, and on the other hand the state itself, however caused, is one in which the energy in centres turns sour. It can arise simply from a picture of oneself, as when one imagines one is always, let us say, successful, and finds one is not. But whatever its cause, the state of depression must be recognized and every kind of effort made to overcome it. I say *effort*, because effort only will change the state, even the effort of doing just ordinary small necessary things. But it is the conscious effort of remembering yourself that will instantly lift you out of depression. The reason is that it brings you into Work 'I's—that is, into the 'I's that feel the influences of the Work—and out of life 'I's in which the depression is centred. And here I must add that you must fight to have the Work in you. You must fight in your mind for the Work, to keep it alive, otherwise it begins to get cold.

Now take the question of conscious effort on *mechanicalness*. This is a very big question. Begin with *talking*, outer and inner. Talking is the most mechanical thing in a person. Remember it does not only mean talking *at the time*, but talking afterwards. I must warn you that it is always easy to see when a person has been talking badly. And talking is not merely saying things, but writing them or shewing them in some way by intonation, by gesture, by hinting, and so on. Hinting is a very bad example of wrong talking. Finally, it means talking *inside oneself*. Try to think over what you have said during the day and then think of the rules. People often infect one another by bad talking—that is, they are dangerous to one another. And remember here that what I say to anyone in private is not to be talked about. That is a definite rule. Now take another mechanical habit apart from talking. First you must observe whether it is a bad habit—i.e. if it puts you asleep. There are good habits which are mechanical—but why try to alter them? Distinguish between good and bad mechanical habits. Notice a clear example—i.e. laziness, greediness, etc. Try to overcome it *for a short time*—that is, while you have the force to do so. Never work on yourself beyond the point that it is useful, for then effort ceases to be conscious and becomes in turn mechanical. Everything becomes mechanical in time. Remember that. Everything you do consciously is preserved for you: everything you do mechanically, since *you* did not do it, is lost. So efforts must be conscious. Actually, there are no such things as mechanical efforts in the Work. They belong to life. There is a class of efforts called

95

in the Work efforts to avoid effort. This means that people make all sorts of useless and unnecessary efforts and avoid making the effort that is required. You remember the clown at the circus. He rushes about doing all sorts of useless things. This clown is ourselves. But we will speak of useless efforts next time.

Birdlip, January 3, 1942

COMMENTARY ON EFFORT

Part II.—All through this Work, on every side of it, the *effort of remembering* must be made. Memory lies in all three centres. Let us suppose a man reaches a state in the Work in which he feels the necessity of making an aim, based on what he has observed in himself. He makes an aim and then decides to keep to it. But in order to keep it, he must *remember*. He must not merely remember what his aim is, but he must remember why he made it, and what led him to decide to keep it. If he merely remembers his aim as words, as a sentence—namely, that his aim is not to do this or that, not to react in this or that way—for our aims should at first be *not to do*—it is not enough. He is only remembering in a very small part of the Intellectual Centre. To remember in a real way he must go back and re-create the situation where he made his aim, and think of its meaning and re-feel the circumstances when he decided to keep it, etc. Full memory is a question of all three centres working together and an *aim* includes all three. For if a man is going to work against something in himself, the thing, whatever it is, will be represented in the Intellectual Centre, and in the Emotional Centre and in the Moving Centre, and keeping the aim will involve all three; and remembering it will also involve all three centres.

In making effort on some side of oneself, such as some particular form of being negative, remember that *everything* goes in cycles in oneself—that is, everything comes round at certain intervals. It is not that these intervals are regular, but that things recur or return, internally, sometimes sooner, sometimes later. The point is that by observation, a person may notice and remember that this is so, and in this way he may gain some foresight and give himself a shock before some mood, some state in himself has properly begun. This belongs to the idea of making *effort at the right time*. Once a characteristic state or mood, etc., has gained enough strength, it is difficult or impossible to stop it—i.e. it is too late. But if self-observation has developed that special memory of oneself that results from it (and can only result from it) then if this new memory is strong enough it will give you a point of vantage from where you can make effort upon some useless state, when it is beginning to return. That is, you recognize it. If you really have begun to dislike it, then you will

96

have an emotion to help your memory and thought. This will help and it will also help you to observe more—namely, that the state starts up earlier than you thought, in little trifling things that you had not connected with it before, such as beginning to use certain phrases or in a slight change of feeling to others, and so on.

Fuller observation can help us to recognize states of depression and to distinguish them from negative states. Depression is different from being negative. Try to see the truth of this for yourselves. Observe that it is so. This distinction was particularly emphasized in the last paper, and if you have not observed that depression is different from being negative, then you cannot see what is meant. Being depressed often happens to people who like to think that they are always bright, cheerful and happy. In any case, it is not the same as being negative. Self-observation and memory of one's state of depression are most important, because unless one recognizes depression for what it is one may make the wrong kind of effort. It is only by understanding such states that one can work on them in the right way. Depression is often a result of illness, or rather, when one is ill the possibility of being depressed is present. Being ill lowers the vitality. This is not really depression but is due to the fact that when the Instinctive Centre, which attends to the inner work of the organism and its chemistry, has to meet illness, it borrows from other centres, just as in war money is taken from all kinds of sources. You have all heard that Instinctive Centre borrows usually from the "Bank" of Moving Centre first, then from the Emotional Centre and then from the Intellectual Centre. But this is not necessarily itself *depression* ; it is a depressed vitality, and if one is careful to be passive to it and *does not identify with it* when it begins, if one does not expect anything and is quiet and small in oneself, there need be no depression —i.e. loss of hope, and so on—but only a state in which one must not think and has to remain quite still, and silent in oneself. There are, of course, rhythmical alterations in the body which lead to depression. One must learn in illness and in such states of altered vitality to see where one is in oneself and what one can do, what is closed, and what is open. To expect to be as usual when one is ill will make one depressed. This is wrong attitude. To be internally quiet, to stop imagining, to stop complaining, to relax, to realize one is ill and has little available force, is the right approach.

Unlike depression, negative emotion is caused *always* by another person. The other person need not be present. One has something called imagination which acts instead. Imagination makes us negative —memory makes us negative—but it is always imagination or memory of a *person*. When the negative emotion arises from imagination or memory it is generally a repetition of what one has felt before about the person in question and after a time it is possible to observe it when it first begins, in which case it can sometimes be separated from before it reaches its full strength. When you are "violently negative", as someone said, it is not possible to do much. Why? Because you do not wish to, and most of us like being violently negative at the moment. You must realize that people love being negative, feeling they suffer, and so on. That is all that can be said. But you have to see it. A great struggle is needed over a long period to begin to *dislike* being negative. It is so easy to be negative—that is the trouble. Only you yourself, in your deepest thought and understanding and feeling, can extricate yourself from the pit of negative states, by the light of consciousness and aim. One of the most serious negative states can be the result of long-standing self-pity, which especially can lead to loss of the power to make effort. Even the mildest self-pity is negative in colour. It may turn into romance with oneself, but it is negative and has the colour and taste of negative emotion, if one tries to observe it. When my wife and I were in France, G. said : "If you will not pity yourself, I will pity you." A dog, when it is washed, pities itself sometimes. What does it do? It takes advantage—jumps on your bed when it knows it must not. There was a dog in France called "Kakvas"—that is, "like yourself". The thing to realize is that everyone tends to pity himself—rich or poor, married or single, successful or a failure. When a man pities himself, he feels he is owed—like the dog. If you feel that you are owed, you will never begin truly to work on yourself. How could you? You must feel you owe. To make the effort to work on yourself you must actually feel something is *wrong with you*. It usually takes years and years before a person can even begin to see this with any conviction. The Work has to pass through layer after layer of pride, vanity, ignorance, self-complacency, self-indulgence, self-love, self-merit, and so on. Yet it can penetrate eventually. But before it can, the first sign is usually that a person suddenly begins to realize the Work is talking about something real and shews some sign of thinking about the ideas. The first change is in the mind—i.e. to think differently. This is *metanoia*—in the Gospels wrongly translated as "repentance". It is called "Driver awakening" in the Work. It begins with realizing one's situation. You must understand that this is not very common. People seldom really think of the Work from themselves—I mean, as if their life depended on it. This is because they do not very often feel that anything is wrong with them, although they are certain others are wrong. It is like the man who became short-sighted and refused to wear glasses, saying there was nothing wrong with him, but that the trouble was that the recent papers were so badly printed. I am speaking of a step people must take.

As long as one thinks in the same way and feels in the same way one is mechanical. One is a machine, you know—but one imagines otherwise. Our life is not action as we imagine, but *reaction*; and we react to things in the same mechanical way over and over again. It is only by seeing one is a *machine*, first in this *small* respect, then in that *small* respect, that one can get the right emotion to help one to change. Fortunately there is something in us that hates mechanicalness but this is lulled to sleep by our imagination that we are quite conscious and always act from will, and consciousness, and one permanent "I", and always know what we are doing and saying and thinking and so on. It is only by *conscious effort* that one can realize one's mechanicalness, and this effort must be made towards a definite thing, a definite reaction, something practical and clear and distinct. To take it as a theory is worse than useless. When one realizes one is mechanical in some definite respect, it gives a shock—actually, it is a moment of self-remembering. To work against mechanicalness requires the effort of self-observation. The reason why we react to things in the same mechanical way over and over again is because of the connections and associations in and between our centres. But we are not conscious of this until we observe our centres. In order to change it is necessary to make centres work in a new way. Let us take an example: let us suppose you always get upset when you cannot find something. Is this mechanical or not? Yes, it is a mechanical reaction that will regularly recur unless you put the light of consciousness into it. It is consciousness that changes us. First the effort of self-observation is needed. Suppose you observe that you react by being negative if you cannot find a thing. This is the first effort and this belongs to the general effort of self-observation—that is, of becoming more conscious, of noticing oneself and not always taking oneself for granted. Next, observe your thoughts. What thought comes to you always when you have lost something? Then observe the emotion; notice it, its taste. Then notice your movements, your expression, etc. Next time it will not be so easy to react mechanically when you lose something. What will help you? The work you have done previously on this mechanical reaction—namely, the effort to be more conscious. Everything we do consciously remains for us: everything we do mechanically is lost to us.

★   ★   ★

Since we are going to speak about the cosmological side of this Work, I must say something now in preparation about *the relationship of conscious effort, or effort in the Work, to mechanical effort, or effort in life.* Work is *vertical* to life. All Work-effort is to lift a man to a higher level, and a higher level is vertical to him—that is, *above* him. Let us take this symbol, which gives one meaning of the Cross.

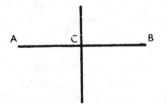

The vertical line is a line representing different levels of being, not only of Man, but of the Universe itself. A horizontal line, drawn at right angles, such as AB, and cutting the vertical line at C, will represent a person's life in Time at the level of being represented by the point C. The efforts we make from Cause and Effect in Time—that is, mechanical effort—lie along AB. The vertical line represents a direction of effort different from those made in Time. You have heard that higher states of consciousness are timeless—i.e. without any sense of Time. Movement on the vertical line is timeless. A higher state of a man does not lie along the line AB, but *above* the man—namely, on the vertical line. This line is what gives *meaning* to all things. It represents the eternal scale of meaning.

In approaching the cosmological side of this teaching, we have to understand that it is an essential part of the mental apparatus of this system and without it the teaching cannot be rightly formed and connected in the different parts of the mind as an instrument for the reception of the influences coming from higher centres. But I intend to give as much help as possible, in the form of comments, to bring the cosmological side nearer to you so that some of its meaning can begin to influence you. The cosmological side is a very powerful thing, but if no attempt is made to think of it, its force will not affect a person and so he will not feel the Work much beyond his limited self-interests.

Now try to think of this vertical side. We can understand Cause and Effect in Time. In Time Cause always comes before Effect. But *Cause* is not only in past Time. Cause can be above and below us. In illustration let us take the Table of Cosmoses, from the Earth downwards:

Cosmos of Earth
Cosmos of Organic Life
Cosmos of Man
Cosmos of Cells
Cosmos of Molecules
Cosmos of Atoms

You see how *Man* is not free, because he is a minute part of the Cosmos of Organic Life and he is composed of minute parts belonging to the Cosmos of Cells, which in turn are composed of minute parts —namely, molecules—and so on.

Man is composed of cells, which belong to their own cosmos. But Man is part of Organic Life. If Organic Life dies, Man, who is a part, would die. And if the cosmos below Man—the myriads of cells—dies, Man would cease to exist.

Now this *vertical* arrangement is permanent. It is, as it were, vertical Cause and Effect. Or you can call it permanent order, or permanent relationship, or the inter-fitting of all things. Whether you say order, permanent arrangement or relationship, etc., does not matter at present. What you have to see is that such a thing as order is not in Time, but that Time moves through order.

Now let me try to shew you how "vertical" Cause can be thought of. If you really begin to think of "vertical" Cause, you will see that there are two sorts and two origins of what we call "Cause". Take, for example, a brick. What is the vertical Cause of a brick?

Builder
|
House
|
Brick

Bricks would not be made unless there were the idea of a house, therefore, in the vertical meaning, the house is the cause of the brick. But in the temporal meaning (horizontal in Time) the brick-kiln is the cause. So it can be represented thus:

Builder
|
House
|
Brick-kiln—science——————— Brick ————————————— Time
of brick-making, etc.

The bricks make the house in Time. But the house makes the bricks in the vertical scale of meaning.

Man, as was said, stands like this, in the centre of the Cross. He has vertical meaning and temporal meaning. The temporal cause of Man is the past in Time: vertical cause is his meaning, and his meaning will be the level of being to which he belongs.

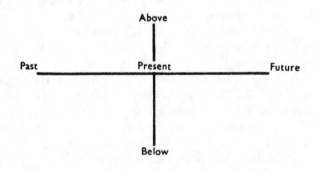

You have heard that your level of being attracts your life. This means your life will be according to your level of being. Levels of being can be represented as points in the vertical line and form life by the horizontal line. If your level of being changes, the horizontal line will pass through another point in the vertical line. I want you to take hold of the general principle involved in these illustrations, not to compare them, but to see the idea behind them. We will continue this subject next time.

COMMENTARY ON EFFORT

Part III.—The diagram of the Cross as given represents a single moment in a man's life. In this single moment the vertical line is cut across by the horizontal line of Time.

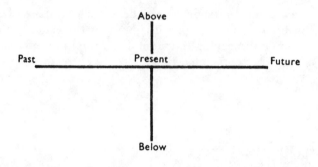

Every moment of a man's life can be represented in this way. The point of intersection of the vertical with the horizontal line is *now*. But this point only becomes *now* in its full meaning if a man is conscious. When a man is identified there is no *now* for him. If he is asleep in Time, being hurried on from past to future, identified with everything, there is no *now* in his life. There is not even a present moment. On the contrary, everything is running, everything is changing, everything is turning into something else; and even the moment so looked-forward to, so eagerly anticipated, when it comes is already in the past.

It is only this feeling of the existence and meaning of the direction represented by the vertical line that gives a man a sense of *now*. This feeling is sometimes called the *feeling of Eternity*. It is the beginning of the feeling of real 'I', for real 'I' stands above us, not ahead of us in Time. Eternity and Time are incommensurable. That means that no quantity of Time will make Eternity, just as no quantity of length will make breadth. They belong to different dimensions. But Eternity and Time meet in Man, at the point called *now*.

In this vertical line there is no past or future. What takes the place of Time, of past, present and future? What takes the place of Time is *state* or *level* or *quality*. The vertical line represents position, not in Time, as, say, the year 1942, or age, such as being aged 20 or 50, but position in the scale of states of being, in the level of understanding and the *quality* of knowledge. Everything in the Universe, visible and invisible, known and unknown, is at some point in this vertical line. Everything is *inevitably* at some point in this vertical scale, for everything finds its own level in it, according, as it were, to its density, like objects floating in the sea. All evolution, in a real sense, is to pass from one point to a higher point in this scale. Scale means *ladder*. In all the diagrams we are going to study, this idea of the Universe as a ladder or scale is found, and that is why it is so necessary to gain some preliminary conception of the significance of this *vertical direction*, that does not lie ahead of us, in the future of Time, in next year or the next century, that does not lie either in Space or in Time, but lies in another dimension—namely, *above* us. In a limited way, we all know of the existence of this vertical line, for we all know better and worse states of ourselves. This is particularly the case once a man has begun to work on himself and to know what it means to separate from bad states and what it means to be asleep.

Now there are two kinds of influences that can reach us at any particular moment. One comes from the horizontal line, the line representing Time. These are the influences of the past that enter at every moment into our lives and also the influences coming from the future—that is, the future represented in the line of Time we are moving along. But there are also other influences. When a man remembers himself he lifts himself in the vertical line upwards and tastes for a moment a new state. This happens when a man no longer merely thinks about self-remembering, but actually does it—when he no longer tries to escape from negative states by thinking himself out of them, but stops all his thoughts and lifts himself up into self-remembering. And it is only by this inner movement that new influences can reach him. As you know it has been repeatedly said that "help" can only reach a man if he remembers himself—i.e. it can only reach the third state of consciousness.

In most of the ancient, mediaeval and later books, such as those of the 17th century, which contain traces of esoteric ideas—that is, that contain "B" influences—you will find this *vertical* direction represented. In the Old Testament—in the first few books or the Pentateuch, as it is called, where all the stories are allegorical and contain a hidden meaning—we find the example of Jacob's Ladder. This represents the Universe seen in its vertical height and depth—as above and below. Jacob represents Man asleep at the bottom of the possible scale of development existing in him.

It is related in Genesis that Jacob lay down in a certain place to sleep:
"And he dreamed, and behold a ladder set up on the earth, and the top of it reached to heaven: and behold the angels of God ascending and descending on it."

Let us take a similar example from this system. You know that Man in this system is taken in scale. There are different kinds of men—different in scale or level.

No. 7 Man ⎫
No. 6 Man ⎬ Conscious Man—Man awake.
No. 5 Man ⎭

No. 4 Man   Balanced Man (awaking).

No. 3 Man ⎫
No. 2 Man ⎬ Mechanical Man—Man asleep.
No. 1 Man ⎭

Man is born as a self-evolving organism. He can rise from one level to another in this vertical scale. And that is why there is such a thing as esoteric teaching. All the knowledge belonging to this system is about the possibility of man's undergoing an inner transformation and rising in the scale of being. In the Christian and Mahometan religions, for example, this is called union with God. To pass from one point in the vertical line to a higher point, a thing must be *transformed*—become different from what it was at a lower level. From the standpoint of this teaching, man is not a *fixed point* in the Universe seen in this vertical manner, as is an animal, which cannot change and is born what it is and what it must remain. Man is capable of inner change. He is an experiment; but he is of no importance in the total Universe unless he begins to fulfil the experiment that he represents. Perhaps you will see what is meant when I say that unless the Universe were invisibly a vertical scale of ascending and descending values, there would be no meaning in it. The Universe is a series of stages, of levels, of degrees, extending vertically from the highest to the lowest, and everything is at a certain point in the Universe. The chair you are sitting on is at a different point in the Universe from yourself. Yet if you take the Universe as space, existing only in the three dimensions of space, you might think that you and the chair were at the same point in the Universe. Man as a child of the Universe, as a product of it, bears in himself the stamp of the Universe—that is to say, Man has scale in him.

Birdlip, January 17, 1942

COMMENTARY ON EFFORT

Part IV

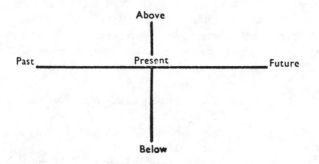

(1) Work-aim has to do with the vertical line. Life-aim has to do with the horizontal line. A man can reach his life-aim. (When he does so he usually is at a loss and does not know what to do.) The supreme formulation of Work-aim is found in the Gospels where it is said: "Seek ye first the Kingdom of God and his righteousness; and all these things shall be added unto you." (*Matthew* VI *xxxiii*). The Kingdom of Heaven is above a man, not in the future of Time, but *now*. It is a state of man, reached internally, and so is said to be "within you".

All the teaching in the Gospels is about the Kingdom of Heaven—that is, aim is to ascend the vertical line. Here lies the possibility of a man's becoming a conscious man and this is his hidden meaning—i.e. man can rise in the vertical scale. He is where he is in the vertical line and so has one life, but he can change his position in the Universe. Life does not contain inexhaustible meaning, but the vertical line represents inexhaustible meaning—hence "vertical aim" can never be fulfilled as "life-aim" may be.

(2) The vertical line represents the line of *transformation*, and this line cuts at right angles the horizontal line of Time, which is the line of *change*. This requires to be explained. The line of transformation is at right angles to the line of change. You are all aware that Time is change. Nothing in Time remains the same—even the mountains are changing. But this change, that belongs to Time, is not transformation. The passage of Time does not *transform* a thing. It changes it, alters it, makes it, for example, decay or wear out. All things get older in Time. But this is not transformation. Transformation does not lie along the horizontal line, but is a necessity in the vertical line.

In this Work, the term *change of Being* ultimately means *transformation of Being*. But many changes must take place in Time before any degree of transformation can occur. The inner arrangement of a man must change—i.e. the lower centres in a man must be prepared by work before the transforming influences from higher centres can begin to reach him. The forces of transformation act from the vertical line. They act upon "substances" lying in the horizontal line in Time. If these substances are in a fit state—that is, if their qualities and quantities and arrangement are right, transformation will result. Let us find an example. You know that in the cosmos below Man, the world of living cells, certain of these cells are incomplete in their inner structure because they are capable of developing into human beings. This is *transformation*. Strictly speaking, transformation is the real meaning of evolution. These cells have, by union, the necessary substances, and under certain conditions undergo transformation. Through the union of these cells, a human being results. But this takes a certain *time* as well, first in the internal arrangement of the minute world of the two cells after union, where certain substances are selected and others are actually expelled from the united cells, and then in regard to their division and multiplication and miraculous ordering subsequently. But all these changes in Time are controlled by the vertically acting forces of transformation and the result is a passage of a living thing from one cosmos to another cosmos—from the cell-cosmos to the cosmos of Man. And, as you know, similar and even more extraordinary transformation occurs in the insect world, where it would seem many experiments in transformation have been made.

But a human being, a man, is again incomplete, and so feels the desire for union. Those cells in him which are incomplete communicate their desire for completeness and this forms one desire for union. But a man is not merely the reflection of the cell-cosmos. He feels incomplete in other ways, if he possesses magnetic centre. Now, you will understand that in this vertical line, if we could move a thing upwards, it would at once become transformed. Whereas if we could move a thing in Time, it would merely change—get younger or older according to the direction in which we moved it.

(3) In this horizontal line representing our lives we live and move. But where this horizontal line cuts the vertical line marks the point of our level of Being, and what we experience in Time is the result of our level of Being. Being is vertical to Time, and is a man's "stature". There is an interesting phrase used in the Acts about this idea. Paul says that God is not far from each one of us: "For", he says, "in Him we live, and move, and have our being." We live and move in Time but we have our Being in this vertical line which descends from the highest to the lowest. But ordinarily we think that our origin lies in the horizontal line in Time—namely, the past—and we do not understand that our origin is also vertical to this line. You have heard the expression that essence comes from the stars and when we come to talk about the Ray of Creation you will see plainly that the stars signify an order of worlds far above the earth in vertical scale. That is to say, essence in its origin —and you must remember that at birth we are essence—lies above us. The point where it enters into Time is the moment of our birth. The point where it leaves Time is the moment of our death. In between these two points lies our life in Time, where a development of essence is possible, and where, apart from this, personality is formed inevitably. That is, personality is formed in Time, and belongs to Time, whereas essence enters Time and leaves Time. Essence is beyond Time. The quality of essence belongs to the vertical line drawn at right angles to Time—that is to say, essential being belongs here. Speaking in general, a man's being is made up of everything in him, but a man's essential being depends on the development of his essence—what is real in him. This is what he is. In the phrase quoted above, from the Acts, when it is said "in Him we have our *being*", the Greek ἐσμέν means *we are*— i.e. "in Him we are." Being is what we are and, as I said last time, the vertical line represents where a thing is in the total Universe of meaning. A thing is where it is essentially. Being is from the verb *to be* which signifies *being*. It is what you are. God is defined in the Old Testament

as "I am that I am". When Moses asked the name of God, the reply was: "I am that I am". In life we try to be *like* something; we are always trying to be like something, always trying to imitate, always pretending to be something we are not. If a man were to find real 'I' in himself, which lies vertically above him in the scale of being, he would no longer be *like* anything but would be himself, what he is. In this vertical scale the being of everything lies, the being of a stone, the being of a tree, the being of a dog, the being of organic life, the being of the earth, the being of the sun, the being of the starry galaxy. This is nothing to do with Time. But to each level of being there is a scale in Time allotted, for the perfection of being lies in Time. We have our allotted span of life in Time appropriate to changing our being. For, as you know, from the standpoint of this Work, the whole Universe, on every scale and in every degree, is evolving. This Work does not teach that we live in a dying Universe, but in an evolving one, and everything in it, in every different world or cosmos, is seeking its evolution—that is to say, it is seeking to rise higher and higher in the level of being. And in every cosmos something is working. We know directly that in the cosmos of Man to which we belong, in this cosmos, something is working. This Work itself is a sign of it. The whole idea of esotericism is a sign of it. You are taught that Man is a self-evolving organism, that there is and always has been a special kind of teaching that deals with this inner evolution, and you are taught that there are conscious men who have attained this possible inner evolution.

Now let us turn to the Cosmos of Cells which is below Man in order to see whether there is anything similar here. Three kinds of cells with very distinct differences exist in Man:

(1) Brain-cells,
(2) Sex-cells,
(3) Body-cells—namely, the cells composing the organs, the skin, the muscles, which are all different but in a sense similar.

(1) *Brain-cells* are shut off from the body in a special way with bony coverings (skull and vertebrae), they are cushioned by water-jackets from shock, they are completely isolated from the bodily organs, they get the best nourishment and in starvation shew the least changes. Brain-cells live for the life-period of Man—i.e. they are immortal in respect to the ordinary period of cell-life which is very roughly in the order of 24 hours. That is, they live 80 years of Man's time, which is 2,400,000 years of their own time. They can be compared with the circle of conscious humanity, with those who have reached *immortality*.

(2) *Sex-cells* are incomplete internally in a certain way and they have a destiny quite different from that of the Body-cells.

(3) *Body-cells*, the cells composing the liver, the stomach, etc. are constantly dividing in periods shorter and longer than 24 hours— maybe months—yet of that order of period of Time. These cells can be compared with mechanical humanity, which is under certain laws and must submit to them in one way or another.

We can arrange these cells in vertical order:

Brain-cells
|
Sex-cells
|
Body-cells

just as we arranged Man in vertical order, Conscious Man, Balanced Man, and Mechanical Man. At present I only wish to draw attention to this correspondence between the cosmos of Man and the cosmos of Cells. We will speak of the cosmos of Atoms and special kinds of Atoms later. What I wish to indicate is that "something is working" in each cosmos, or, if you prefer, that what exists in the cosmos of Man must in some corresponding way exist in the cosmoses below him, for *every cosmos is under the same laws*.

Birdlip, January 25, 1942

THE LAW OF THREE

Part I.—To what ultimate principles, to what fundamental laws, can the Universe and all its manifestations and processes be reduced? According to the teaching of this Work there are behind all things two ultimate laws called respectively the *Law of Three* and the *Law of Seven*. These two laws are fundamental.

From the standpoint of this teaching the Universe is created: we live in firstly a *created* and secondly an *ordered* Universe. If the Universe were chaos, there would be no order and no laws. *Cosmos* literally means *order* as distinct from *chaos*. If the world were chaos, the study of the laws of matter and so on would be impossible. Science could not exist.

The *Law of Three* is the Law of the Three Forces of *Creation*. This law states that *three forces must enter into every manifestation*. But creation is governed by another law—the *Law of Seven* or the *Law of Order of Manifestation*. Creative forces could not work unless they created in some order and this order of manifestation or order of creation is due to the Law of Seven. But at present we have to speak only of the Law of Three.

Every manifestation in the Universe is a result of the combination of three forces. These forces are called Active Force, Passive Force and Neutralizing Force.

Active Force is called 1st Force,
Passive Force is called 2nd Force,
Neutralizing Force is called 3rd Force.

1st Force can be defined as initiating force, 2nd Force as force of resistance or reaction, and 3rd Force as balancing or relating principle or connecting force or point of application.

These three forces are found both in Nature and in Man. Throughout the Universe, on every plane, these three forces are at work. They are the creative forces. Nothing is produced without the conjunction of these three forces.

The conjunction of these three forces constitutes a triad. One triad creates another triad, both in the vertical scale and in the horizontal scale of Time. In Time, what we call the chain of events is a chain of triads.

Every manifestation, every creation, results from the meeting together of these three forces, Active, Passive and Neutralizing. Active Force, or 1st Force, cannot create anything by itself. Passive Force, or 2nd Force, cannot create anything by itself. Neutralizing Force, or 3rd Force, cannot create anything by itself. Nor can any two of the three forces produce a manifestation. It is necessary that all the three forces meet together for any manifestation or creation to take place. This can be represented in this way.

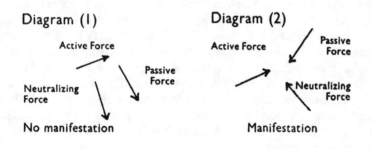

The three forces are only creative *at the point of their conjunction* and here a manifestation, a creation, an event, takes place, but not otherwise. Out of all the infinite number of things that could happen, only a few actually take place—namely, when these three forces meet in conjunction. If they do not all meet, then nothing can take place. For example, if Active Force and Passive Force meet, nothing can happen, no event will take place. But if Neutralizing Force appears, then there will be three forces at work, and something will take place. A triad will be present—that is, a triad composed of the three forces— and wherever the three forces meet in conjunction as a triad a manifestation must result. Every triad, every conjunction of three forces, can give rise to another triad and under right conditions a chain of triads results. It is always from the Neutralizing Force—that is, the 3rd Force —that a new triad springs.

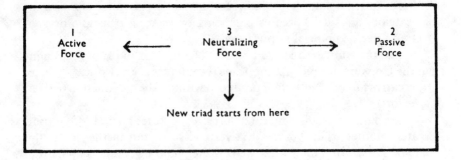

| 1
Active
Force | ⟵ | 3
Neutralizing
Force | ⟶ | 2
Passive
Force |

New triad starts from here

In the next triad, the Neutralizing Force of the prior triad becomes Active or Passive Force. We will speak another time of this.

The Neutralizing Force or 3rd Force in a triad brings the Active Force and the Passive Force into relationship. It connects them together somewhat in the same way as the fulcrum brings the two sides of a balance into relation. Without the Neutralizing Force, the Active and Passive Forces would cancel each other out, because they are opposed to one another. They are opposites. A connecting or relating force is necessary. Neutralizing Force is *intermediary* between Active and Passive Forces. When the right neutralizing force is present, an active and a passive force no longer oppose one another uselessly, but are brought into a working relationship that creates a manifestation. For example, a machine can be sometimes regarded as Neutralizing Force. A rough example is a windmill. The Active or originating Force is the wind. The Passive or resisting Force is the building. The turning sails make a relation between the pressure of the wind and the resistance of the building and a manifestation takes place. If there are no sails, or if the building collapses, or if there is no wind, there is no manifestation. This is only a very rough illustration.

The idea of Three Forces is found in religion in the conception of the Trinity. In science the idea of different forces exists, as in positive and negative electrical charges of which matter is ultimately composed. But in science the idea of a third or relating force is not yet distinct.

The fact that *three* forces create means that *three wills* create. The First Order of Creation is therefore subject to three wills or three laws, and it follows that subsequent orders of creation proceeding from the first order are under more and more laws.

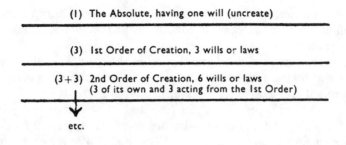

(1) The Absolute, having one will (uncreate)

(3) 1st Order of Creation, 3 wills or laws

(3 + 3) 2nd Order of Creation, 6 wills or laws
(3 of its own and 3 acting from the 1st Order)

↓

etc.

The three Forces are said to proceed from Unity. This Unity is termed the Absolute which means that which is not conditioned or limited in any way and so under no laws save its own will. Since Three Forces are necessary for any manifestation, the Absolute is Unmanifest or Uncreate.

The Absolute is beyond all human thought.

Creation proceeds vertically downwards into increasing density of laws, and further and further away from the Absolute. As we shall see, in the Ray of Creation the Earth comes at a very low level in the vertical scale of the Universe.

★   ★   ★

Part II.—Change in the quality of the Neutralizing Force will not only alter the relation of forces in a triad but may *reverse* the Active and Passive Forces. When life is Neutralizing Force, personality is active in a man and essence is passive.

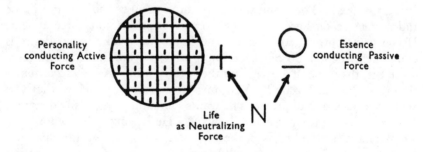

Personality conducting Active Force

Essence conducting Passive Force

Life as Neutralizing Force

When the Work is Neutralizing Force the position is reversed—namely, essence, or the real part, becomes active, and personality, or the acquired part, passive.

In this case we have to consider again the significance of the vertical and horizontal lines of the Cross. We can conceive the Neutralizing Force of life acting along the horizontal line and the Neutralizing Force of the Work entering at every moment from the vertical direction and only felt when a man ceases to identify with the things of Time and remembers himself.

Let us now speak of the Three Forces in their psychological aspect.

The study of the Three Forces begins with the study of them in oneself. As was said, Three Forces exist in Nature and in Man. It is very difficult to see the Three Forces. They must be studied at first *psychologically*— that is, as they exist in oneself—by means of self-observation. Active Force or 1st Force can be taken as *what one wants*. Passive Force or 2nd Force can be taken as what resists or prevents what one wants. This is as far as one must go to begin with. *It is impossible to see 3rd Force until one sees 1st Force and 2nd Force.*

The 2nd Force or force of resistance exists in everything. That is, to what we want there is inevitably a force of resistance. If people realize this they will not blame so much as they do, nor will they feel that their difficulties are unique. I will speak briefly of one or two points in connection with the study of the Three Forces on the psychological side.

In making *aim*, 2nd Force must be calculated, otherwise the aim will be unpractical. If you make an aim, you must count the cost of keeping it. When you do so, you will probably make your aim more practical. Aim must not be too difficult. Everything that prevents you from keeping your aim is 2nd Force, provided you wish to keep your aim. Let us suppose you make an artificial temporary aim—that you will not sit down all day. Then you will notice 2nd Force in yourself in connection with this aim—namely, what resists you, what opposes your keeping this aim, all the different "I"'s, the different arguments, etc. The nature of the 2nd Force will of course be determined by the nature of the 1st Force—in this case the aim you want to keep.

Do not attempt to try to see 3rd Force. It is quite useless at first. But try to see 1st Force and then 2nd Force. You cannot see 2nd Force unless you see 1st Force. It is 1st Force that makes 2nd Force appear. If you want nothing, there is no 2nd Force, in so far as your desire is concerned. People do not even know what 1st Force is in themselves —that is, they do not know what they really want. Ask yourself sometimes: "What do I want?" You must be sincere in noticing what you really want. If a man pretends he wants something, and really does not, his Active Force is what he really wants. He is lying to himself.

We have spoken briefly of the Law of Three Forces in their psychological aspect. Next time we will begin to speak of the Ray of Creation in the light of the Three Forces of Creation—that is, we will consider the Law of Three in its cosmological application.

* * *

Part III.—Let us take the phrase already used—namely: "The fact that three *forces* create means that three *wills* create." It may be asked if these three wills which proceed from the Absolute are identical when in conjunction with the Will of the Absolute Itself. This cannot be assumed, for it reverses the order of creation by making three pass into one. Three cannot pass into one save by the Will of the Absolute and this would mean the *indrawing* of all creation. (Notice that if you divide 3 into 1 you get 3 repeating to infinity.) The created Universe proceeds from the Absolute by reason of the three forces which no longer, as such, belong to the Uncreate Absolute. (Compare the Christian cosmology, where in the Athanasian Creed it is said: "There are not three Uncreate, but One Uncreate.") The Absolute is uncreate, unmanifest, unconditioned, and this is beyond all human thought. The three forces proceeding from the Absolute in the first act of creation are already conditioned (1) by the single Will of the Absolute and (2) by their mutual *relation* to one another as 'Active, Passive and Neutralizing'. These forces at their primal level are all conscious, but already limited, and as their reduplication proceeds in the outbreathing or descending order of creation of all things, they become increasingly mechanical and limited, the further they are in the *vertical* scale from the Absolute. If we were to say that the sum total of the primal three forces in conjunction together made the single Will of the Absolute, we would imply that the primal three forces would pass into the Absolute on conjunction with each other, in which case there would be no creation. Three would pass into One. But it is the Will of the Absolute to create, and the three forces or separate wills of creation proceed in consequence from the Absolute and cannot return unless it is the Will of the Absolute Itself to draw in all creation. The three primal forces unite to create the Universe in successive stages. They do not unite to form the single Will of the Absolute, which is uncreate, for if their conjunction made a unity identical with the Will of the Absolute, there would be no creative process.

ON THE STUDY OF THREE FORCES IN ONESELF

Part IV.—We have greater opportunities of observing ourselves than of observing the external world. We live very little in the external world, which is foreign to us. We are intermittently aware of it, but notice very little about it. We can pass the same house a thousand times and be unable to describe it. Actually, we are far more permanent even for ourselves than is the world. This is one reason why the study of Three Forces begins with self-observation. Also you must remember that a force is invisible and our more direct contact with what is invisible is by means of self-observation.

You must understand that in trying to study this question of forces you are not studying things. A desire is a force, not a thing, for example. A train of thought is a force and is not a thing. An idea is a force, not a thing.

One reason why we have so much difficulty in understanding three forces is that we tend to see in everything *one* force. We think of force as *one*, and in everything that happens, in any manifestation, in any event, we tend to see merely one force. We attribute it to one force. We see one action in one event. This is partly due to our inability to think of more than one thing at a time as a rule. Sometimes we think in terms of two things, but to think in terms of three things is beyond us—i.e. it is beyond formatory thought. An event, for instance, must always be good *or* bad, right or wrong for us. We see only one action in it, and further, we do not even think of events being due to forces. We see an apple falling from the tree and merely see the apple now lying on the ground. We see a magnet attracting or repulsing one pole of a compass. We see it all, but scarcely think of forces—in this case obviously different kinds of forces. Nor do we notice how forces change for us. At one moment we are attracted by a thing and next moment repelled by the same thing. Or we are repelled and then an idea comes to us and we feel attracted. We do not realize that the thing at one time conducts one force and at another time an opposite one. In the same way, our relationship to a person changes. That is, the person undergoes a change of sign for us, and this means that in the triad of forces that produce the relationship there has been a change of forces—e.g. mechanical love can turn to hate, mechanical trust to suspicion, and so on. All such ordinary manifestations in human life are due to forces and changes in these forces. I am not asking you to designate in such cases the forces, but to notice them.

The Three Forces cannot be studied theoretically. The only practical way of studying three forces in ourselves is by doing something. By this is meant imitating or personifying in ourselves one of the three forces, in relation to some other force either (1) acting in ourselves or (2) in external events.

Example: (1) Struggle with habits,
Struggle with suffering,
Struggle with ignorance, etc.

(2) Struggle with expression of unpleasant emotions towards someone one mechanically dislikes,
Struggle to carry out some difficult task.

In this way we can begin to realize what second force is for us in each case, and from this can begin to catch a glimpse of 3rd force.

Example.—A sudden accession of force that assists one's struggle with a particular task means a change in the quality of the neutralizing force —e.g. encouragement may have this effect. The active force in the triad is thus increased and the task (the 2nd force) *may* be more easily gone on with. On the other hand it may *weaken* active force (by creating the imagination that one is able to do the task) so that the task becomes active—i.e. the resisting force becomes the strongest.

THE LAW OF THREE

Part V.—In speaking of the Ray of Creation, I wish to connect it with your thoughts in some way. Everyone can admit that the Universe is created and many believe that it is. They say, if they are, for example, religious, that God created the Universe. Also they have heard of the Trinity, if they are Christians, and may or may not have thought about it. In any case, the idea of the creation of the world by God and some vague notion of the Trinity may exist in their minds. But no connection is made. For example, even if they have thought that creation is in some way connected with the Trinity, they do not see the inevitable consequence of Three Wills at work in creation. They merely think that God created everything, as it were, all round Him, like a lot of toys, and that no laws were at work, and although in the allegorical account of creation in Genesis they are told that the Universe was created on successive days, they do not think that any scale is meant here, and that creation is not all at the same level but descends in order of degrees lower and lower. Consequently, they are inclined to think that God's Will is directly in touch with and in charge of everything created. They omit to think of the meaning of the Trinity—that is, the primal Three Forces or Three Wills that bring about creation, and so think that the Will of God reaches directly every created thing. Some religions teach only the Unity of God, such as the Mohammedan religion. The Christian religion teaches the Trinity. The *psychological* consequences are very great. If people believe only in God, they think that God's Will is done everywhere and in everything, and so tend to fanaticism, persecution, and so on. Not that Christianity can shew anything much different, but at the same time this religion contains the idea of the Trinity, which comes between God and the world. The connection of "God"—or the Absolute—and the process of creation can only be understood through the Trinity or Primal Triad of Three Forces and the derivation of subsequent triads. As an ancient saying puts it: "God is difficult to understand for He is first One, then Three, and then Seven."

To return to the Ray of Creation: the first triad of three forces proceeds from the Absolute and creates the First Order of Worlds, which is under three laws—that is, the three wills of the Primal Triad.

(I) Absolute

(3) First Order of Created Worlds or World 3

This is the first act of creation represented diagrammatically. Actually, it is a living process, inconceivable and eternal. By the term World 3 is meant the first level of creation, subject to three laws or wills. This world creates in turn another order of worlds below it which has 3 forces of its own. This is called World 6, because it is under 3 wills or laws acting on it from World 3. This process of creation continues. The next order of worlds therefore is World 12, having 3 forces of its own, 6 derived from World 6 and 3 derived directly from World 3.

In a similar way, three further worlds are created, making in all six orders of worlds or six descending levels of creation below the Absolute, all knit together by laws.

(1)	Absolute
(3)	World 3 under 3 laws
(6)	World 6 under 6 laws
(12)	World 12 under 12 laws
(24)	World 24 under 24 laws
Position of the Earth in the Ray ⟶ (48)	World 48 under 48 laws
(96)	World 96 under 96 laws

The process of creation halts at World 96, for a reason that will be explained when the Law of 7—or Law of *Order* of Creation—is given.

World 96, at the termination of the Ray of Creation, is under 96 laws. This world (or this order of worlds) is furthest from the Absolute and under the greatest density of laws. The further the process of creation proceeds from the Absolute, the greater the number of laws.

What it is necessary to grasp is that *creation* necessarily implies *laws*, and this arises from the very fact that *three forces* are necessary for any manifestation. There can be no creation without laws and this means that every created thing is inevitably under laws—that is, *nothing created is free.*

Now if we consider this vertical line of Creation, we can see that if we could ascend it, we would pass under fewer and fewer laws—that is, we would gain more and more freedom. Whereas if we were to descend, we would pass under more and more restrictions and so be less and less free. If a creature, a being, is created at the level of World 12, it finds itself under 12 laws, or orders of laws. If it falls to the level of World 48 it is under 48 laws. Man as he is is at a certain level in the Ray. But he is created in such a way that he can change his level upwards or downwards and so pass under fewer laws or more laws.

The next point to consider is that the laws, or forces, or wills, or *influences*, coming down the Ray have different sources. If we take World 48, we can see that certain laws reach World 48 directly from World 3, some directly from World 6, and so on. That is to say, a being born in World 48 is under 48 laws, or orders of laws, but these laws are not of the same quality—some come from higher levels and some from lower levels.

A man, if he knows how, can put himself under one kind of influences or another kind.

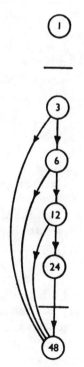

Earth

The next point is that creation is *forcible*—that is, it is brought about by force. It begins with the work of the Primal Triad of Three Forces derived from the Absolute and continues by the reduplication again and again of further triads of 3 forces. The ultimate or last point of Creation —World 96—is under many forces. This means enormous forces are locked up in creation. Through the action of the Law of Three the Universe is *wound up*. Sometimes in nature we can see these forces *unwinding* themselves, as, for instance, in the element radium.

* * *

Part VI.—We must now view the visible Universe from the standpoint of the Principle of the Ray of Creation. We know that the visible Universe in its greatest magnitude is made up of a vast number of immense star systems of which the Milky Way is one. We must conceive that the first act of Creation is comparable with making a general tenuous formation of all possible systems which are filled in by increasing condensation. This we call World 3: "All possible systems of worlds." Since we wish to find the position of our Earth in creation, we will take next our system of worlds which has separated from the primal mass —namely, our Starry Galaxy or Milky Way: World 6. Out of this we will take our Solar System or Sun: World 12. The Planetary mass formed from the Sun will then be World 24 of which we take our separated Planet or Earth (World 48) from which our Moon is derived (World 96). This is *our* Ray of Creation. Our Moon is the terminal point of that branch of the total tree of the Universe in which our Earth appears. But as you will notice so far there is no appearance of Man in the Ray.

The whole Ray is evolving. Every part of it seeks to rise higher in the scale of creation. The Moon is not a dead planet, but the youngest point in our Ray.

* * *

Part VII.—Let us try to find some simple illustrations. Any organism or organization reflects to some extent the Principle of the Ray of Creation. Let us take any organized body of people—say, the Army. Let us suppose that the General is at the head, the Colonel next, the Captain next, the Sergeant next, and the soldier last. How many laws is the soldier under? He is under the laws of the Sergeant, who is under the laws of the Captain, who is under the laws of the Colonel, who is under the laws of the General. But the laws of the General can reach the soldier *directly*; also the laws of the Colonel can reach the soldier directly, and so on. From all this we can see (1) that the *part* is always under more laws than the *whole*, and (2) that the laws the part is under come from different sources of origin. Let us continue this brief analogy. The soldier is under the laws of the Sergeant but he may attract the attention of the Captain; he will then pass under the laws of the Captain. He may even attract the attention of the General. In such a case he may pass out of the laws of the Sergeant.

Now let us take the analogy of the Body. The Body is again constructed on the principle of the Ray of Creation. It is an organization or organism and all organisms obey the Law of Creation. Now the Body as a whole is *one* thing. It is then divided into many systems— vascular, digestive, lymphatic, nervous, etc. Each again is sub-divided into groups of parts, until the smallest parts of the Body are reached. This is reaching a part *via* the principle of the Ray of Creation—namely, of increasing laws. For a rough example, take the muscles of your little finger: they are under their own laws, and then under the laws of the hand, and the hand is under the laws of the arm, the arm is under the laws of the muscular system in general and the muscular system is a part of many other systems which form finally the Body as a whole. This rough illustration is to shew how from the top downwards increasing laws exist, and in this respect it shews the principle of the Ray of Creation—namely, the principle of increasing laws from above downwards. And this, it must be grasped, is in the nature of things—i.e. *it is a fundamental law of creation.*

Birdlip, February 14, 1942

THE LAW OF SEVEN

INTRODUCTION

You all find you have little force for thinking about the cosmological ideas of this Work. A person lives in his or her own very small cosmos which is his or her world and this very small world is governed mainly by self-interests. People do not yet live even in this world—this small planet called the Earth. This is due to a lack of development of consciousness, as are also so many of the troubles on this Earth. Consciousness, in the majority of people, is confined to the very small world of themselves and their own interests. We have scarcely any proper consciousness of one another. We can only take in what we are interested in and if a person is only interested in himself and those belonging to his own self-interests, everything said about the Cosmos has little or no meaning, for it demands a form of thinking *beyond oneself*. A person is glued to his life —thus, he has, as a rule, very little free force in him to think beyond his immediate life-interests. In that case, only the most external sides of his centres are working, and they absorb his energies. This is the *sensual* man (of the New Testament), the man alive only in those parts of him turned towards the outer senses, towards life. But in everyone who has *magnetic centre*, there remains something *behind*, something *inner*, that wishes to understand *more*—for actually a man has far more *inner* senses than *outer* senses. But these inner senses require to be developed and this begins with self-observation which is one of the inner senses not ordinarily used. The real or essential part of a man (to which this Work is addressed) lies behind the external sense-controlled side. It is only reached by the inner senses. When a person begins to value this Work, it is a sign that behind the false personality of the man, which the life of the senses has created in him, there is some real thing, unspoiled by life: and that is *Essence*. Thoughts from personality may seem far cleverer than thoughts from Essence, which are thoughts from the most simple and genuine side of us. But the quality of thought from Essence is of a far higher order than that from personality. Therefore in trying to think of the created and ordered Universe, it is the simplest thoughts that can begin to make contact with its meaning.

Take a very simple thought: Has it occurred to you in any real, vivid, private way that you are staying on the Earth for a short time? Again, have you had a quite simple thought that the Earth is a part of the Solar System—a part of the Sun? It is such simple, vivid, strange thoughts that begin to connect us with the Ray of Creation.

The cosmological ideas of the Work must first fall on the most external parts of the Intellectual Centre and be *registered* by them. That is, you must learn the diagrams through paying attention. This must be done by everyone. It is a task the Work sets. But the diagrams can be *understood* only when they reach higher or emotional parts of the Intellectual Centre to begin with, and then pass to the Emotional Centre itself. When a man takes in something that his formatory side has registered and wonders about it because he *wants* emotionally to do so, then the diagrams begin to work in him and make him think for himself about the cosmological side. This is the first object of the Work: to connect a man with higher parts of ordinary centres, and finally with Higher Centres themselves. And this gradual process is called *awakening*. If a man denies all meaning in the Universe, his higher parts of centres are blocked by his attitude. The Universe is then what he thinks it is—that is, exactly as his attitude is to it—and then the man himself is what he thinks. But this Work is to make a man think in a new way. For unless a man begins to think in a new way, he cannot change. This is obvious enough if you look at people. But to think in a new way, a man must have new ideas, new conceptions, and take them in, and think from them.

THE LAW OF SEVEN

Part I.—The process of creation by means of the Three Forces proceeding from the Absolute has been traced as far as World 96. It has been explained that as creation proceeds by the action of the multiplication of the Three Forces on every plane or level of creation the density or laws increases. That is, the further the process of creation proceeds from the Absolute, the more restrictions appear until, in World 96, which in our particular Ray of Creation is our Moon and is the terminal point of the Ray, the number of laws or restrictions reaches its maximum.

We have now to consider a further law that restricts creation: the Law of Seven. Creation proceeds through increasing restrictions. The law of Three necessarily produces increasing restrictions but the Law of Seven adds further limitations. It has already been seen that the Earth comes very far down in the Ray of Creation and is under 48 orders of laws and that only one degree or level of creation exists below it, represented by the Moon. This means that the position of the Earth in the creative process is very bad, and only one worse position exists, where there are double the number of restrictions. But, regarded from the standpoint of the second fundamental law behind all things, namely, the Law of Seven, the position of the Earth is still more un-enviable. Let us try to understand what this means. The Law of Seven applies to the order of the manifestation of creation and it is in this word *order* that we shall find its supreme meaning. It is necessary to understand clearly that there is a law of *order* apart from a law of *creation*. Creation *is arranged in order* and it is ordered in a certain way. At certain points in this order difficulties appear and the Earth is situated at one of the points where difficulties in the ordering of the stages of creation inevitably arise. It has already been seen that the primal Three Forces of creation proceed from the Absolute as their Source and in turn create further forces. We might imagine that these forces proceed downwards without check. But this is not the case. They are checked *at two points* by reason of the Law of Seven.

Let us try to understand these points of check by means of a visual representation. Let us imagine a tube composed of some elastic sub-stance with two constrictions in it and let us suppose that water is poured into this tube at the top. We can represent the tube as follows :

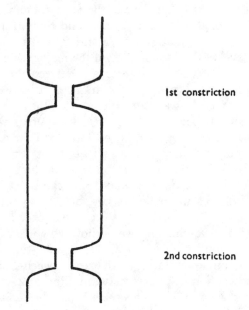

1st constriction

2nd constriction

You will see that the passage of the water, which we can take as representing force, is held up at two places in its descent in the tube.

Now let us apply this image to the Ray of Creation as given so far in the following way, at the same time adding the Notes: *Do, Si, La,* etc.

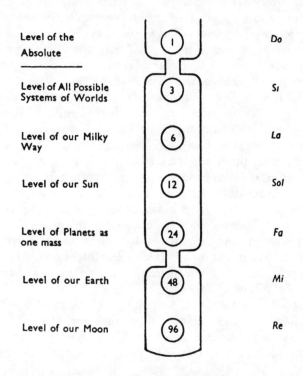

Level of the Absolute	1	*Do*
Level of All Possible Systems of Worlds	3	*Si*
Level of our Milky Way	6	*La*
Level of our Sun	12	*Sol*
Level of Planets as one mass	24	*Fa*
Level of our Earth	48	*Mi*
Level of our Moon	96	*Re*

You will notice that the first tone of the scale, namely, *Do,* has been placed at the level of the Absolute, the second tone *Si* at the level of World 3, the tone *La* at the level of World 6, and so on, until *Re* is reached, at the level of the Moon. Now if the major scale be taken two points are formed in it where the intervals between the notes are not full tones, but *semi-tones.* These points correspond to *Do–Si* and *Fa–Mi.* Actually the major scale was constructed to illustrate the Ray of Creation by unknown people belonging to some unknown school. It was constructed to illustrate the Law of Seven or Law of the Octave. In terms of the musical scale, we can speak of the interval between *Do* and *Si* as the place of a missing semi-tone and in the same way of the interval between *Fa* and *Mi.* The whole Ray can be called an octave in which the Absolute sounds the first *Do,* but we do not know of the existence of the lower *Do.* The Moon always turns exactly the same side to us, although it is revolving and we do not know what lies behind it. The first "constriction" or place of a missing semi-tone appears then between the Absolute and World 3—that is, between *Do* and *Si*—and the second "constriction" appears between World 24 and World 48 —that is, between *Fa* and *Mi.* This means that the passage of force is held up at these two places owing to the nature of the Law of Seven and here a *shock* is necessary. Between *Si* and *Fa* force passes freely and again between *Mi* and *Re*, but between *Do* and *Si* a check occurs, and between *Fa* and *Mi* a second check occurs. This is in the nature of things—that is, it arises from one of the two fundamental laws behind all things. It is not a question of *why*: it is so. For a fundamental law means a law that cannot be reduced further and so cannot be explained further, in terms of everything else. It is like saying that there are positive and negative charges of electricity. It is not a question of *why*. It is so, and nothing more can be said save that the Law of Three and the Law of Seven *are so*. You must understand that if ultimately nothing were so nothing would exist. Something must fundamentally *be so* for things to exist at all. You can explain the chair you are sitting on in terms of wood, and wood in terms of cells, and cells in terms of molecules, and molecules in terms of atoms, and atoms, finally, in terms of positive and negative charges of electricity. But you cannot go further for here you are reaching down to two of the forces belonging to the Law of Three Forces and that Law is *fundamental*. It is so, and there is nothing beyond, save the Absolute, which is beyond human understanding. To reduce the Universe to one law, which is the dream of science, would be to understand the mind of the Absolute. The Work reduces the Universe to two laws, at the same time indicating the existence of one law.

The Law of Seven inevitably brings about the order of created things and produces at the same time two points of constriction or checks in that order to the forces passing down the Ray. How are these places of check surmounted? The first check, between the Absolute and World 3, is overcome by the *shock* of the *Will of the Absolute*. For that reason it was said that creation is *by* the Will of the Absolute *through* the primal Three Forces. But in the case of the second place of check in the Ray the matter is different. The Will of the Absolute does not reach this point and therefore something must be *created* at this point to act as a shock. It is here that Man appears.

It has already been said that *Man* does not appear in the Ray of Creation as given so far in gigantic scale. Only the Earth appears. But in order to enable the forces coming down the Ray to pass easily to the Earth and moon an apparatus must be created between the Notes *Fa* and *Mi*—that is, between the Planets taken as one whole, and the Earth taken as a part. For this purpose a small octave is created from that level of creation externally represented by the *Sun*. At the level of the Sun this octave sounds the Note *Do*, or rather, the Sun sounds the Note *Do*. At the level of the Planets it sounds the Note *Si*. Between the Planets and the Earth it sounds the three Notes : *La, Sol, Fa*. It then passes into the Earth as the Note *Mi* and reaches the Moon as the Note *Re*. The three Notes *La, Sol, Fa* that are sounded between the Planets and the Earth form Organic *Life*. Organic Life is a sensitive living film that lies over the surface of the Earth and acts as a transmitter of the forces passing between the upper and lower parts of the Ray. Man is a part of Organic Life and it is in this specially created apparatus for transmission that he appears in the Ray itself. By Organic Life is meant every form of life on the Earth—the human race, all animals, birds, reptiles, insects, fishes, all trees, plants, every form of vegetation down to the most minute living cells. This sensitive film, which collects influences from the upper part of the Ray and transmits them to the Earth and the Moon, is created from the level of the Sun and its appearance in the great Ray of Creation is due to the point of check where a shock is needed between the Notes *Fa* and *Mi*, arising from the nature of the Law of Seven.

* * *

Part II.—When this system is presented in a purely formal way, the Ray of Creation is given in terms of the external Universe. But the Ray is a principle that when applied to the external Universe gives the different levels of the starry masses, the sun, planets and moons, in their descending order. It can be understood in this way. When, for example, it is said that the Sun creates a small octave which forms Organic Life on Earth, it can be understood literally. But the Ray represents levels of Being, and is internal as well as *external*. That is, the Sun represents in the external meaning of the Ray the actual Sun. In the internal meaning it *represents* Beings at that level in the vertical scale of being. But you can understand it as you like to begin with—that is, literally or psycho-logically—for the two correspond—that is, different levels in the external Universe are representations of different levels of intelligence which are internal or psychological. If we speak of the Intelligence of the Sun we can understand that it is higher than the Intelligence of the Earth simply from external representation, for the Sun has infinitely more energies and radiance than the Earth. But the Ray should be actually under-stood in both senses for outer and inner correspond and everything internal has something corresponding externally. We can notice this in our use of a language. We speak of internal or psychological things in terms of external or visible things. We call a cunning man a fox or a brave man a lion, and so on. Because outer and inner have a similar source they therefore can represent each other, for, as was said, the fundamental laws, the Law of 3 and the Law of 7, are found *in Nature* and *in Man*. For this reason complex psychological ideas can be repre-sented in visual imagery, drawn from outer objects, as in the case of the parable. And for the same reason to take Man apart from the Universe in which he is born is an error. The Universe is macrocosmos and Man is microcosmos. Man is in the Universe and the Universe is in Man. To say, then, that the Universe is dying and Man is evolving is an absurdity from the standpoint of this Work.

* * *

Part III.—The Ray of Creation represents a descending octave. It descends into greater and greater obscurity and complexity and restrictions the further it proceeds from the Absolute. The idea of an *ascending* octave from the Absolute is impossible for the Absolute is all goodness and all perfection and an ascending octave would imply increasing perfection.

Let us now speak briefly of the Law of Seven or the Law of the Octave from the psychological side. One can observe octaves in oneself —or rather, one can observe the beginnings of octaves. Everything you set out to do can be called the beginning of an octave. When you decide to do something, you sound *Do*. If this *Do* is weakly sounded, nothing will happen. But if it is sounded more strongly you may reach the Note *Re* and even the Note *Mi*. But here you reach the "place of missing semi-tone" and here a shock is necessary to enable you to reach the Note *Fa*. This rarely happens. It may happen accidentally. But as a rule it does not happen. That is why in this Work it is said that life is full of broken octaves. People start something and give it up. But you must remember that Man is created a self-developing organism and that means he only develops by efforts, for all evolution of Man is conscious—that is, by conscious effort. There is no mechanical evolution. And we need not be surprised to find many difficulties. The Law of 7 makes things difficult by its very nature. But we will speak more of this next time.

Birdlip, February 21, 1942

THE LAW OF SEVEN

THE SUN OCTAVE

Part IV.—To-day we will speak of the small octave between the Sun and the Moon. This octave created by the Intelligence of the Sun sounds three notes on the Earth, *La, Sol, Fa*, which represent the living machine called Organic Life on Earth, of which Man is a part. At present we will not speak of the meaning of the different notes of this small octave. What must be first understood is that Man does not appear in the great octave of creation but in the little side octave pro-ceeding from the Sun. *Man is a special creation within the Ray.* Let us now try to grasp why Man appears and why the small octave is necessary.

The reason why the Intelligence of the Sun creates this small octave is to fill the gap or place of "missing semi-tone" between *Fa* and *Mi* in the Great Ray, due to the nature of the Law of Seven. Unless something were created at this point the force passing down the Ray from the Absolute could not pass freely to the Earth and Moon. A shock is necessary at this point *owing to the nature of the Law of Seven.* This Law governs the order of creation and brings about conditions at certain points where something must be added in the nature of a *shock*. The Law of Seven is therefore sometimes referred to as the *Law of the Shocks*. Understand this clearly: certain shocks are required at certain points in the unfolding or progress or evolution of anything.

The Intelligence of the Earth or the Planets is not great enough to create anything to act as a shock at this point. The Intelligence of the Sun is needed. But the Sun, in creating the small octave, has two objects which it is essential to grasp and distinguish between very clearly.

One object is to create a sensitive transmitting machine between the great Notes *Fa* and *Mi* in the Great Ray to enable the force to pass to the Earth and Moon at the termination of the Ray. From this point of view Organic Life, including Man, exists only for the purposes of the Ray and its creation is due to the nature of the Law of Seven, which causes certain difficult or narrow places to appear in the order of creation. If this were the only object Man's situation would be one in which as a part of this transmitting machine he must always serve the Ray and its evolution, which takes place over immense periods of time.

The other object is connected with the Sun itself. In creating the small octave, the Sun is not merely creating on behalf of the Ray itself to fill a missing place, but is also acting for itself. *The Sun wants something* apart from the needs of the Ray of Creation. It is here that the *possibilities* of Man are found. Let us now think of this idea which it is of such fundamental importance to understand in this Work. *The Intelligence of the Sun wants something for itself in creating Man on Earth*, quite apart from the necessities of the Great Ray. What does it want? It wants Man to ascend from the level of the Earth to the level of the Sun. For this reason it creates Man as something *incomplete*, as an unfinished being. In what sense incomplete?

In regard to being a part of Organic Life, serving the purposes of the Ray of Creation he is *complete* and nothing more is required of him than the life he ordinarily leads. He is capable of living on Earth as he is. He is then said (in the Work) *to serve Nature*. But in regard to his real origin from the Octave from the Sun he has another destiny locked up in him. In regard to this destiny Man is unfinished, incomplete, because the Intelligence of the Sun has created him for another reason and has put in him, apart from what is necessary to serve Nature, other powers and possibilities. That is, *Man has in him far more than is necessary for the purposes of serving Nature*. In speaking of *Nature* here what is meant is all Life on Earth—all that we see around us on the Earth, the life of plants, animals, trees, fishes, and also the life of mankind, with all its struggles, all the killing, pain, birth and death, which, all together, make up this perpetual-motion machine called *Organic Life* created by the Sun to transmit influences from the upper to the lower part of the Ray of Creation.

In regard to the second object of the Sun, Man is created on the Earth as incomplete in order that he may develop up to the level of being represented by the Sun. It is in this sense that Man is said in the Work to be a *self-developing organism*. Man is thus an experiment of the

Sun, placed on the Earth. He can remain asleep and serve Organic Life: or he can awake and serve the Sun. If he had been created with the same being and intelligence as the Sun he would not be on Earth. Man has therefore two explanations. He is created to serve Nature—that is, to be part of Organic Life—and in this sense it is not in the interests of Nature that Man should develop and so cease to serve Nature. But Man is also created to develop himself, until he reaches the level of the Sun. If you will make the effort to think, if you will really try to understand the meaning of the Ray of Creation and the Octave from the Sun, many inexplicable and apparently irreconcilable things will become clear to your mind. That is, you will be able to begin to think rightly about life on Earth, and of Man's situation—that is, of your own situation.

$$\star \quad \star \quad \star$$

Part V.—Speaking in an external way about the Ray of Creation, it is quite obvious that physical life on Earth depends on the physical Sun. But for the physical light and heat of the Sun no life on Earth could exist. Every green leaf, every blade of grass, every form of the algae floating in the sea, is a minute solar machine, that receives energy from the Sun and by its means manufactures from air, water and minerals, food-substances upon which all animal creation feeds. But when we speak of the Intelligence of the Sun we are speaking of another light seen only internally by the mind—the light of Intelligence—and so we are speaking of the Ray of Creation in an internal sense as a vertical scale of intelligence and being of increasing excellence as we ascend it. In this respect, the Intelligence of the Sun is divine in relation to the Intelligence of the Earth. In the vast evolution of the Ray itself, on inconceivable scales of time, the Intelligence of the Earth may reach the level of the Sun. This is not necessarily guaranteed. The Earth may die having attained nothing. In the same way the Moon may or may not reach to the Intelligence of the Earth. We cannot see the Sun or Earth or Moon as beings, as intelligences. One reason is that we see them as cross-sections of themselves, as mere circles in the sky, just as two-dimensional beings whose world was limited to a large sheet of paper would see a man only where he cut their plane—namely, as a circle, as a slice of the man, such as we see in a book of Anatomy. But from the standpoint of this system the Moon is a growing and developing being and in time may attain to the same level of being as the Earth. Then, near it, a new Moon will appear and the Earth will become its Sun. At one time the Sun was like the Earth and the Earth like the Moon. And earlier still the Sun was like the Moon. The Work teaches that the whole Universe is evolving, and this means that our Ray, with our Moon, our Earth, Planets and Sun, is evolving, as well as all the infinite number of other Rays. But parts of our Ray may fail, at the allotted period of time, to have reached the necessary stage of development and so will be destroyed. As was said, if the evolution of Man depended on the evolution of the total Ray of Creation itself that reaches us, his chances would be remote. In so far as Man is part of Organic Life and Organic Life serves the purposes of our Ray, his evolution would be held back until all the processes of the cosmic evolution of the Moon and Earth, and of the Planets and the Sun above us, had been fulfilled. But Man has other chances—special chances—which are due to the small octave from the Sun in which he is created, for Man is specially created. In this small octave he can rise or fall. He can reach the level of the Sun or fall to the level of the Moon. Fully developed Man—that is, Man No. 7—has reached the Intelligence of the Sun. He has attained his full development and is under only 12 laws, so for him there is freedom. For all freedom is gained by rising in the vertical scale of creation and so passing under fewer laws. And at the same time No. 7 Man has attained immortality on the scale of the life of the Sun. You have heard already many times that there are different levels of Man. To speak of Man is not enough. Which Man do you mean? People living on Earth can belong to very different levels. Just as there are different levels of Man so are there different levels in the Universe regarded as a vertical scale of being or scale of intelligence. The Intelligence of the Sun is divine to us on the Earth. The influences of the Sun reaching us through the small octave are of a higher order than are those of the Planetary World which are again higher than those at the level of the Earth or those coming from the Moon beneath us. A man can be under the influences of the Sun or the influences of the Planets, or the Earth or the Moon. And for Man there is a certain possibility of making a choice of influences —in other words, of passing from one influence to another. For example, if a man begins to struggle with negative emotions, he begins to pass out of one of the influences of the Moon. If a man remembers himself, he begins to pass first under Planetary influences and eventually under the influences of the Sun. But he must learn to make an inner choice and to do so he must know a great deal about himself and about different "I"'s in him and about parts of centres. The influence of the Sun reaches Higher Centres. But when a man lives in mechanical parts of centres he is under far lower influences. You must understand one thing: it is impossible to become free from one influence without becoming subject to another. All work on oneself consists in choosing the influence to which you want to subject yourself, and actually falling under this influence. And here, by long observation, you must know *what you want in this respect.*

*   *   *

Part VI.—The machine called Organic Life on Earth not only transmits forces down the Ray of Creation, but creates within itself certain forces which pass to the growing Moon and assist in its development. The Moon feeds on Organic Life, apart from receiving forces passing down the Ray. For example, all useless suffering on Earth is food for the Moon, such as negative emotions. Pain is food for the Moon and for this reason it is sometimes said that Organic Life is a pain-factory. Pain and death feed the Moon and a certain quantity is required. For this reason sacrifices were initiated in past ages by those who understood. Many things could be said here, taking Organic Life only from the point of view of a machine inserted at a particular point in the Ray for a particular purpose—namely, to serve the Ray. For you must understand that Man has no significance in the Ray itself save as a part of Organic Life. But in regard to the Sun, which creates him, Man has the greatest significance if he chooses to find it. Here there is a door open to him—not leading up the gigantic Ray itself, but up a separate ladder beside it. This is one meaning of the parable of the Prodigal Son: Man can return to the Father.

Many other significant things are said in the New Testament that are connected with the Sun-Octave. You have already seen that the Sun wants something for itself in creating Man on Earth. Man is not created only for the purpose of the Ray, but is created for the purposes of the Sun—*as an experiment in self-evolution*. Unless this self-evolution of Man is fulfilled in sufficient numbers the Sun will not receive what it wants and will not be satisfied. Let us take one out of the many parables in this connection in the Gospels:

"A certain man had a fig-tree planted in his vineyard; and he came seeking fruit thereon, and found none. And he said unto the vinedresser, Behold, these three years I come seeking fruit on this fig-tree, and find none: cut it down; why doth it also cumber the ground? And he answering saith unto him, Lord, let it alone this year also, till I shall dig about it and dung it: and if it bear fruit thenceforth, well; but if not, thou shalt cut it down."

(*Luke*: XIII *vi-ix*)

Do not try to understand this parable literally. Understand it psychologically and you will see that it means that Man has certain possibilities which can come to fruition and, unless some fruit is produced, Man will be cut off.

★ ★ ★

Part VII.—All that has been said so far, however briefly, about the creation of the Universe, through the action of the Law of 3 and the Law of 7, and about the octave from the Sun, should make it impossible now for any of you to say: "If there is a God, why does he allow things to happen on the Earth as they do?". But you will have to make your own effort of thought in connection with all that has been said about creation, and the tremendous ideas and massive diagrams given, to answer that question clearly and strongly from your new understanding. For unless you can arrange your thoughts on this question which is so baffling and such a stumbling-block to the vast majority of people, the right connections in your mind—in your Intellectual Centre—will not be made. According to an ancient saying "God must be justified." Looking round on life you will find this difficult if you do not understand creation. You will not see the difficulties and restrictions involved in

129

creation inevitably, nor the doors left open, and so you will secretly harbour a feeling difficult to define but negative in character that is capable of shutting you from every higher development of the understanding. You must get things the right way up in your mind and you cannot do so unless you realize the conditions and limitations of creation. The difficulty is that even when people come in contact with esoteric teaching they will not listen to it, or if they do, they do not understand it or really see what it means and take hold of it themselves, as one takes hold of a rope. We have only to look sincerely at ourselves to realize how difficult it is to work and how much we sleep. Yet the real, most intense meaning of Man on Earth lies in this Octave from the Sun into which he can grow internally and come under other influences. In our case we must subject ourselves to the influences of the Work and obey them. Once mankind loses all connection with the Intelligence of the Sun, it will inevitably be destroyed, and that is perhaps especially the danger to-day. And it is the same thing on the scale of an individual man. Once he loses contact with the better 'I's in himself, once he loses all faith, all meaning, all affirmation, all deeper understanding, he destroys himself. And when life assumes evil forms a man easily weakens. But if the Work is built up in his mind so that he thinks from it about all things in life, nothing can weaken him.

Birdlip, March 2, 1941

THE LAW OF SEVEN

THE LAW OF SEVEN AND THE IDEA OF SHOCK

Part VIII.—In life many things are started which turn out quite differently from what was expected of them. The starting of anything can be represented by this Note *Do*. The next stage of its development can be represented by the Note *Re*, and the next stage by the Note *Mi*. Now if the development of things were easy there would be no reason why any particular development should not proceed successfully to its fullest stage. That is, the octave would be completed. But two factors prevent this. First, the passage between the Notes *Do* and *Re* and *Re* and *Mi* requires effort to keep the direction of the development in right alignment with the starting-point. Let us take an example. When something is started, let us say an international society for preserving peace, or something of that kind, this starting-point sounds the Note *Do*. But as the development of this society proceeds, owing to misunderstandings and disagreements and many other factors, the original line is not quite adhered to. It begins to deviate to one side or the other of the original direction. Instead of developing in a straight line (Fig. 1), it starts turning its direction as in (Fig. 2).

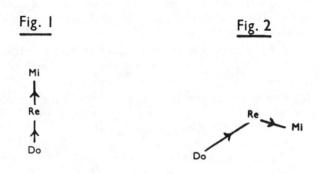

Fig. 1   Fig. 2

The result is that things in life started with one object may turn out to give completely contradictory results—e.g. a peace society may become the source of war. The second factor in preventing the full and successful development of things is the check, constriction or slowing-down point between the Notes *Mi* and *Fa*. When anything develops up to the stage *Mi*, the place of obstruction is encountered inevitably and unless a shock comes here from outside, the octave will not proceed. That is, the further developmental stages of that thing will not be reached. So apart from the tendency to deviation, there is also the point where a retardation or check appears, called the *place of shock*. Everything develops by stages, but it can only develop rightly by fulfilling the Law of Seven. Deviation is not proceeding by the Law, and to halt at the place of shock is failure. Each note must be sounded fully at each stage. For example, to speak and read and write a child must learn his letters before he learns his words. He must learn his words before he learns his phrases, and then he will get a shock from life because he is surrounded by people who are speaking and writing and reading. Then he will pass to *Fa*. But if he has not sounded *Do* properly —that is, if he has never learnt his letters—or if he has not sounded *Re* strongly—that is, if he has never learnt his words from his letters properly, and so on, his powers of speaking, reading or writing will be limited accordingly. You all know the amateur, who never has learnt his subject properly, and on the other hand, we can all understand what is meant by a man who is well-grounded. When a man develops his craft by proper stages, and passes, by the shock given by his master, to full craftsmanship, then you have a development proceeding in harmony with the Law of Seven and rightly knit together.

In the case of the marvellous development of a man from a single cell, shocks are given at certain points in the progressive evolution of the various parts and of the body as a whole. One cell, by dividing into two and the two into four, and the four into sixteen, until 50 stages of division are reached, in nine months, produces 100,000,000,000,000 living cells. The dividing process is due to the Law of Three. The ordering and arranging and integration of the whole developing man of living cells with the shocks given at certain points is controlled by the Law of Seven. The first shock in the first octave in the whole process is of course given by fertilization.

There are many ways of seeing how things reach a certain stage and cannot get further without help from outside—that is, without a shock. Have you ever thought that nature brings things to a point and stops? But Man can give a shock and take them further in their development. Think of wheat, for instance. Loaves do not grow in a wheat-field. Think of the uses Man makes of raw materials.

★　　★　　★

SCALES

Part IX.—Let us speak for a moment about diagrams. A diagram is only a means of understanding. It is like a map. A map is a diagram of a country which gives the position and relation of things. The whole Ray of Creation including the Octave from the Sun is a map. But it is a very strange map. Ordinary maps are either on one scale or another. You can have a map of the town you live in, shewing the position of your house. Or you can have a map of the county you live in, shewing only your town but not your house. Or you can have a map of the world which shews neither your town nor your house. Or you can have a map of the solar system, in which the world appears as a mere dot. This is what is meant by different scales. But the Ray of Creation is an extraordinary map because it is not on one scale but on many different scales. Take the Note *Si* (which stands for *Si*dera or stars) in the Great Ray. This note is called: "All possible systems of starry worlds." If we take the Ray in its physical or external meaning this Note *Si* represents a map shewing all starry systems. The diameter of the physical Universe as shewn by the 100 in. telescope is 600 million light-years and in this vast incredible space 100 million enormous stellar systems exist each containing a hundred thousand million suns. The next Note *La* in *our* Ray is only one of these stellar systems—our Milky Way (La = Lacteal Way or Galaxy). This Note is on a far smaller scale. The next Note *Sol* represents only one of the thousands of million suns in our Galaxy—namely, our Sun—and so on, till our minute Moon is reached. Every Note represents a map on a different scale and this ordering of scales, at different levels, is due to the Law of Seven, which enables us to find the position of our Earth in the Universe. For this reason the Law of Seven or the Law of the Octave can be said to be the law that gives the relation of the part to the whole. But for this law the creative activities of the Three Forces would not be bound into any fixed and firm relationship and order—that is, they would not be organized but merely a heap. It must be understood that the Universe is a vast living co-ordinated Organism. And everything created is created at a certain point and on a certain scale in this vast organism, in which everything is connected and nothing is independent and isolated.

Everything is created and knit together from the heights to the depths of the Universe by the double action of the Law of Three and the Law of Seven.

This brings us to what is meant in this Work by *relative understanding*. In order to understand anything rightly you must know something about the whole before you can understand the part. For example, you cannot understand the Earth by taking the Earth by itself. You must understand something of the Solar System, and then again of the Galaxy, and so on, in order to have any right understanding of the Earth. In the same way you cannot understand the town you live in, unless you know something of the country you live in, and again about the continent and finally of the world you live in. To try to understand a thing by itself, as something isolated, is impossible, for everything is connected with and depends on something else, for the whole Universe is connected. This is the basis of what is called *relative understanding* in the Work. You may have to know only very little about the whole in order to understand the part, about which you can know far more, but unless you think *relatively* your understanding will be wrong. It would be useless, for instance, to try to understand a sparking-plug unless you understood something about the car as a whole and again about electricity and about Man and his needs and so on. And this is what science is finding to-day— namely, that every domain of science is connected, and nothing can be understood separately, and this is especially the case in medicine, for every part of the body depends on another part and everything is connected to form the whole bodily Man. And when we have reached that point, we have to understand about Man himself and his significance and meaning on Earth.

The Ray of Creation with the Sun-Octave gives us a *relative understanding* of Man. It is a relative diagram and must be understood in that light. I have noticed that some of you seem to think there is only one Ray of Creation. This is of course quite wrong. There are an infinite number. We speak of *Our Ray of Creation*—the Ray we find ourselves in. By it we find our position in relation to the whole Universe. Imagine a vast tree. The undivided trunk is the Absolute. The first great branches are the Note *Si*—"all possible systems". You would have to conceive 100 million great branches at least. We then take our great branch—our Galaxy. Each great branch divides into 10,000 million lesser branches. These are suns. We take our Sun and so finally come to the twig where we dwell in this gigantic Tree of the World and at the end of our twig is a bud called our Moon. But you surely cannot imagine this is the only twig and bud, and that the Absolute terminates creation in our solitary Moon.

* * *

THE SUN-OCTAVE—*(continued)*

Part X.—It is necessary that everyone should form some distinct conceptions in regard to the Octave from the Sun. This octave represents in the form of a diagram Man's possibilities of development. We can understand this octave literally, in physical terms, or psychologically.

133

Physically, we can see for ourselves that life on the Earth depends on the heat and light of the Sun and we can, I suppose, believe that in some manner the physical visible Sun created Organic Life on Earth. We can take the three Notes *La, Sol, Fa*, sounded by the Sun on Earth and forming the sensitive matter on its surface, as representing perhaps mankind, animal life and vegetable life. We can take the Note *Mi* which passes into the Earth as the mineral débris of once living forms —the dead bodies interred in the Earth, the deposits of coal, the chalk cliffs, the coral-barriers, and so on, which were all once living things. And we can take the Note *Re* sounded on the Moon as some interchange of very fine energy-matters—electrons, atoms and molecules—passing between the Earth and Moon, for we know that in the case of the Earth hundreds of tons of very fine energy-matters fall on its surface from all parts of the Universe every day. But there is, apart from this literal understanding, another form of understanding called in this system *psychological understanding*. When it is said that Man is in the Universe and the Universe is in Man, the first phrase means that Man actually stands in the literal, external, visible Universe. And if we take the Ray in this sense we take it externally, in terms of the senses, that is, in terms of visible objects seen by the telescope. But the second phrase —the Universe is in Man—can only be understood *psychologically*. Just as the Universe externally is on different levels—for it is obvious that the Galaxy taken as one whole physical organism of suns stands on a higher level than any single Sun which is merely an infinitesimally small part of it—so is the Universe taken internally, as within Man, on different levels. That is, Man, having the Universe in him (approximately), has in him different levels, and these levels in him are levels of being, levels of knowledge, levels of understanding—that is, psychological things, attained only within him. A man who reaches the level of the Sun in this sense reaches to a level represented externally by the physical Sun and internally by the Intelligence belonging to this level. That is, he reaches a divine level, for the Intelligence of the Sun is divine for us. It is, for us, the Absolute, relatively speaking. At this level we must put Conscious Man—Man No. 7. At this level we must put the central theme of the Gospels—the Kingdom of Heaven—that is, Man fully evolved. And from this level we must understand that all esoteric teaching descends to Man on this Earth. For the object of all esoteric teaching is to raise Man to a higher level of himself and Man is created for this purpose. If we think of the Sun-Octave in this way—that is, psychologically—we can then understand how every note in this octave represents a possible state of Man. A man may fall or rise in this ladder reaching from the Sun to the Moon. He can be under more laws or less laws. He can sink, psychologically, to the level of the Moon, and find himself in a prison far worse than the Earth—a prison under 96 orders of laws. He can rise until he passes under 24 orders of laws, and finally under 12 orders of laws. If he is a Good Householder on Earth, he will be under 48 orders of laws. If he overcomes personality, he will be under planetary laws, that is, 24 orders of laws, for essence is under 24 laws. If essence develops, he will pass under 12 orders of laws and be at that level of Power, Intelligence and Being represented as the Sun.

Birdlip, May 18, 1942

PSYCHOLOGICAL TALK

We will now speak of the observation of connections between centres in the form of 'I's. As you know, this Work begins with self-observation because the subject of it is this invisible thing called "oneself" which we usually take for granted and which can only be observed by each person individually. The first thing is to realize that you are not one and the same person either at different moments or at the same moment. In the first practice of *self-observation* you are told to observe that you have quite different centres or minds in you which work simultaneously. You have *thoughts, emotions* and *movements,* taking only these three centres, namely, the Intellectual Centre, the Emotional Centre and the Moving Centre. They are three utterly different things. Now every person is a meeting-house of 'I's. The different 'I's in you have their representation in all these three centres in more or less degree. That is, every 'I' in you has its representation in these three different minds or centres, and so appears quite differently in each centre—in fact, so differently that it takes a long time before we can trace the manifestation of an 'I' in all these three forms of it.

Although other centres exist, let us speak of the Intellectual, Emotional and Moving Centres. Every 'I' in a man is represented in these three centres.

The Human Machine as Three Centres

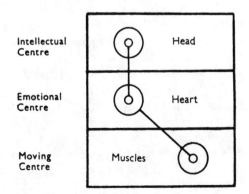

Intellectual Centre — Head

Emotional Centre — Heart

Moving Centre — Muscles

Representation of an 'I' as having a "Head" and a "Heart" and certain muscles.

In trying to control an observed 'I', you must remember that it is something that *thinks*, and *feels* and *moves*—that is, each representation of it in each centre is different. The control of the human machine is difficult therefore because everything that is formed in it psychologically —namely, as an 'I'—is represented in three entirely different ways, that seem at first sight unconnected. For example, you frown. This is in Moving Centre. But this frowning is represented in the Emotional Centre as a feeling, and it is represented in the Intellectual Centre as a thought or a gramophone record—that is, a series of thoughts going round and round mechanically. Full observation of an 'I' is the observation of it in all the three centres of its origin simultaneously.

Let us now find an example for general discussion. Let us take "Worrying".

QUESTION: What is worry? Does the Work say anything about worrying? How can it be stopped?

ANSWER: Worry is a form of identifying. Literally, the word has the meaning of tearing and twisting, or choking and strangling; it was originally connected with the word 'wring', which is still used in the expression 'wringing one's hands', one of the outward signs of worry. You will remember that every psychological or inner state finds some outer representation via the moving centre—that is, it is represented in some particular muscular movements or contractions, etc. You may have noticed that a state of worry is often reflected by a contracted wrinkling of the forehead or a twisting of the hands. States of joy never have this representation. Negative states, states of worry, or fear, or anxiety, or depression, represent themselves in the muscles by contraction, flexion, being bowed down, etc. (and often, also, by weakness in the muscles), whereas opposite emotional states are reflected into the moving centre as expansion, as standing upright, as extension of the limbs, relaxing of tension, and usually by a feeling of strength. *To stop worry*, people who worry and thereby frown too much or pucker up and corrugate their foreheads, clench their fists, almost cease breathing, etc., should begin here—*by relaxing the muscles* expressing the emotional state, and freeing the breath. Relaxing in general has behind it, esoterically speaking, the idea of *preventing* negative states. Negative states are less able to come when a person is in a state of relaxation. That is why it is said so often that it is necessary to practise relaxing every day, by passing the attention over the body and deliberately relaxing all tense muscles.

Control of the emotional centre is difficult directly, partly because it works so quickly—30,000 times more quickly than the formatory part of the intellectual centre, so that a man gets worried or negative before he knows it. But the emotional centre is sometimes in the Work compared with an uncontrolled rogue elephant with two controlled elephants on either side of it—namely, the intellectual centre and the moving centre. Wrong emotional states, habitual bad states of worry, crossness, etc. must first be noticed as existing in one. As a rule people do not see their states but are them. Next, one of the controlled elephants must be used. Let us consider what it means to use the intellectual centre in this respect. This means that you must notice the thoughts that are going on when you are worrying. We have a certain amount of will over the intellectual centre—that we can control thought to a small extent. By stopping, or not going with, not believing in, not consenting to, the thought-part of worrying, one elephant, so to speak, is brought alongside the uncontrolled emotional centre. The other controllable elephant is the moving centre, over which we have will if we direct attention to it. We can relax muscles and so on. As you know, in the directions given in the Work about relaxing, it is said first that the small muscles must be relaxed—the small muscles of the face, the muscles of expression, particularly. This includes the eye-muscles, the muscles round the mouth and chin, the tongue and throat and scalp muscles, and so on.

To return to worrying. Worrying is the wrong work of centres. It is always useless. It is a form of inner considering—i.e. of identifying. It is a continual mixing up of negative imagination with a few facts and so makes only wrong connections in centres. It is a sort of lying, among the many other kinds of lying that go on in us and mess up the centres. It is always easy to worry, as it gives a relief and is, as it were, a form of justifying oneself. It is close to self-pity and violence. Worrying is not thinking. The mind is driven by the worry, by the emotional state, and is obscured. Attention to anything always helps, for directed attention puts us into more conscious parts of centres. Worrying is not thinking of others. It is not external considering. It is mixed up with oneself and this takes a long time to observe distinctly. In learning how to live from the Work point of view, so that we live more consciously in life, or live in the Work in life and not just in life without anything between us and life, worrying is one of the things that shew us something about ourselves if we notice it uncritically and over a long enough period. But you must not think that the opposite of worrying is indifference. You can and should feel 'anxiety' about another person in danger—a mixture of hope and fear—but worrying is quite different, for then the imagination comes in. It becomes a habit, just as do so many other negative states, and people even imagine they are better than others by having them and feel merit in worrying. People even think it is right to worry about everything, about the past and the future, about themselves, about others, and so on. This is simply nothing but a serious negative illness, difficult to cure, for once a person has become nothing but an inverted machine for worrying, all sorts of wrong connections have been established and everything works in the wrong way, and since the only thing he enjoys is worrying, to deprive him of this, were it possible, would be to destroy his chief interest. In this connection, you will remember one of the Work sayings—that you are asked above all to do one thing, to give up your particular form of suffering. This sounds easy. Try it. The reason why it is so difficult is because to do so is to destroy whole systems of 'I's in yourself that enjoy making you suffer and that you think you are.

To return to the question: what is worrying? Since it is a form of identifying, it means that it brings about a continual loss of force. People who worry a great deal exhaust themselves, drain themselves of force. If you will notice yourself when you are worrying, you will see that it really is like tearing and twisting and strangling oneself inside, corresponding with the outer muscular movements which have already been described. There is no centre of gravity. There is no direction, no clear aim; everything is in disorder; everything is, as it were, running about in oneself in every direction. It is as if all the different 'I's in oneself got up and rushed about wringing their hands and saying anything that the negative imagination, which dominates the scene, suggests to them. I am not saying that it is possible never to worry. There are situations, especially to-day, where it is well-nigh impossible to stop it at times. I am speaking more of habitual tendencies to worry about everything and take every event as a source of worry. To formulate clearly what one is going to do—to have some direction—helps to prevent this state of disorder, which is, as said, a form of internal considering and is not external considering. Internal considering is always mechanical. External considering is always conscious—it is *consciously* putting yourself in another person's position and since this requires directed attention, it takes you out of worrying. If you notice, you will see that little forms of worrying start very early in the morning. It is a very good thing, which is worth doing, to work on oneself in the early morning, before, as it were, descending into life and duty. A little conscious work at that time, noticing the small beginnings of worrying or negative thoughts or self-pity, etc., etc. and saying *no* to them—lifting oneself out of them— not taking them as *you*—all this work on non-identifying with certain machines, certain 'I's, in the early morning, can alter the whole day. And to this, of course, belongs the idea of cancelling debts, letting go all inner accounts—if possible. Then something fresh and new begins the day, and the staleness of life is prevented which is really the staleness of *oneself* always reacting in the same way to everything, always having the same views, always taking others in the same way, and so on. Work on yourself can have marvellous results—if you remember you are in life *in the Work* and not in life without anything between you and it. The Work is to transform your relations to life. All the practical things said in it have this object. This is to *work on oneself*. That is, it is to be in the Work, in life—not in life. What is your task? Why are you down here? What is it that you have to change? What is it that you have to learn about yourself, this thing you take for granted, this thing that is your apparatus for living? Does your apparatus for living give you the results you wish for? Yourself, your personality, is the apparatus you are using for living life. It is good to begin to see that your way of taking life is your life—and that you can begin to work on your way of taking it— and that means working on yourself and your mechanical reactions to all that happens. For your mechanical reactions to life are *yourself* and that makes your unhappiness and happiness and this thing called yourself is the apparatus for living life that you have made and which has been made in you by thousands of forgotten causes. This is the thing we wheel out every morning to face the day with. And this is the thing the Work speaks of in all its stages—the thing that you can work upon and alter. Try to think that it is not life you can change, but yourself in your reaction to life. This is where the first idea of what it means to work on oneself lies. Once you see the idea, then, whatever the conditions of life, you have a power in your grasp whose value is beyond price. You have begun to grasp the pearl, to see what life on earth really means.

For a long time we absorb every kind of negative emotion, identifying with it and taking it as ourselves, as necessary, as true, and try to work on it once it has formed itself. But the time comes when it cannot form itself. Now the effect of not going with some mechanical reaction in yourself and feeling you are free in respect of it is quite magical. You will notice what happens. It is very interesting, but it is a matter of your own experience. You will perhaps grasp that the Work is not mere dull labour. It is self-freeing through a peculiar inner effort, which is called *work on oneself.*

During the months of March and April, 1942, *Dr. Nicoll was writing a series of Papers on the Gospels.*

Birdlip, May 21, 1942

PSYCHOLOGICAL COMMENTARY

I

This Work is psychological. It consists in making a number of specifically defined psychological efforts designed for a particular end. Everyone has a psychology as well as a body. The object of the Work is to lift a person off the psychological basis he rests upon. Let us try to speak about this.

Everyone admits he has a body, which may be in a better or worse condition. The body is an object of the senses and as you know we are all inclined to take only what the senses shew us as real. But everyone has also a *psychology.* This people do not so easily admit, for they cannot see or touch their own or another person's psychology via the outer senses. Moreover a person is usually especially unwilling to admit that he himself has a definite kind of psychology. A definite kind of body— yes. A psychology—no. He will agree that his body may be in a wrong state—but not his psychology. One result of this is that it not infrequently occurs that a person in the Work does not know where or in what direction to make any efforts. If the Work consisted in a number of physical exercises, everyone would know where and in what direction efforts had to be made and if anyone did an exercise wrongly, he would be seen doing it wrongly and corrected. A person would then know how he was progressing by the number of physical exercises he could perform correctly, and he could also feel the satisfaction of being able to do more than others could do, and so on. As you know, there are schools of teaching that deal only with the body. They are the schools belonging to the First Way—the Way of Number I Man. The control of the body by the development of will over the body is the object. The Fakir who sits with outstretched arms for years and years is an example. He develops will over the body. But by itself this is useless. In some cases, he may be taken into a school of another kind, and his arms broken down if possible and be given teaching to develop him psychologically. He has will over the body, but no understanding, and will without understanding is useless or even worse than useless. And such a man, quite ignorant and stupid, may "crystallize out" by his incredible efforts —that is, nothing can be altered in him and he will remain permanently ignorant and stupid, whether he is taken into another school or not. But such examples shew us one thing. They shew us the extent of *effort on oneself* that is possible among Eastern people and this may help us to understand why esoteric teaching has always come from the East. Now this teaching that we are beginning to try to understand here does not belong to the First Way, the Way of the Fakir, nor to the Second Way, which is the Way of the Monk, nor to the Third or Yogi Way. It is called the Fourth Way, and I will mention one of the great character- istics of the Fourth Way soon, but will say here that one of its general objects is to unite the Wisdom of the East with the Science of the West. But its individual starting-point is *psychological*, not physical, and as said, its object is to lift a person off the psychological basis he rests upon. That is, its object is to change a person, not physically, but psychologically. The efforts that it demands in personal work are not, primarily, physical efforts, although these come in in their place, but psychological efforts, the first of which is *self-observation*. To observe oneself is a psychological effort, and it is only by self-observation that you become aware that you have a psychology. You all know that this is not an easy effort to make. It is far more difficult than making a physical effort, such as doing some exercises, or cleaning pots and pans, or mixing concrete, or working a typewriter, or indeed doing anything connected with the outer visible world, which lies in space, and to which we must first make a relationship. But remember that each of us lives in two worlds, one outer and visible and lying in space and the other inner and invisible and not lying in space. Our bodies are in space but not our psychology. But, as distinct from animals, we are so made that we can look out, into the visible world in space where our bodies are standing, and in, into the invisible world, where our psychology is standing. And just as we are always somewhere in the outer world, so we are always somewhere in the inner world. Now the idea in the Work is that just as we can change our position in the outer world by physical effort, so we can change our position in the inner world by psychological effort. And just as a man can be in a better or worse place in the outer world, so can he be in a better or worse place in the inner world. But because it is difficult to look into the inner world and see where one is standing in it, people let themselves, as it were, be *anywhere* inside, although they would not think for a moment of letting themselves be *anywhere* outside.

Let us try to conceive what it means that each of us has a *psychology* and that it is necessary to observe it. Our psychology is, from one point of view, where we are and what we frequent in this inner world. Just as we live somewhere and tend to frequent certain places in the outer world, so we live in and tend to frequent certain places in the inner world. The difference is that in this inner world we are not dealing with *places in space*, but with *psychological states*. Now just as it is your body that brings you into contact with a physical place, so is it your psychology that brings you into contact with a psychological state. At any moment you are somewhere physically and somewhere psychologically. Outer observation shews you where you are physically; inner observation— that is, self-observation—shews you where you are psychologically. To be in a bad state psychologically is as if you might be in a dark corner of a room, sitting there, morose and gloomy, when you might shift your position easily and stand in the light. Now the practice of self-observation in the Work is to make us aware of where we are *psychologically* at any moment and eventually to shift our position. It leads to *self-awareness* which belongs to the third state of consciousness, the state where help can reach us. *Where we are* psychologically at any moment is *what we are* at that moment, unless we are aware of it and separate internally from it. If you identify with all your inner states, with your negative emotions and dreary thoughts and so on, as people do in life if they are quite asleep, then *where* you are psychologically will be *what* you are at that moment. You will be your state at that time. Now self-observation is not a monotonous exercise that one is supposed to perform because told to do so. It is an act of practical intelligence. It is just as practically intelligent as to notice where you are driving a car to. If you never observe anything in yourself, not only will you never avoid anything in yourself and so repeat your life day by day and always run into the same states, but you will think that your inner states are normal and natural and the only ones possible and take them for granted. You will only expect life to change, not yourself. In this way, you will not be willing to think you have a *psychology* at all, in any sense of the word, though you will admit that you have a body, which has its own peculiarities. You know what this Work teaches about life —how it happens—what a dark spot in the Universe we live in, and so on. Yet I suppose you all think what is happening now is exceptional.

Nothing is more useful or more interesting than to pull yourself up suddenly and notice *where you are inside* and *where* you are going. If you do this, you will begin to see what sort of psychology you have and what tendencies belong to it and what it keeps on connecting you with. You will begin to notice what you are always up to, inside. When you can see all this not as yourself—not as 'I'—but as your *psychology*, you can begin to separate from it and so change it. But if you cannot admit that you have a *psychology* at all and say 'I' to every state it leads you into you can get nowhere.

Now let us change the point of view a little. Let us imagine a conversation in the following terms. Let us suppose someone in the Work says to you: "I find it difficult to observe myself and I cannot quite see in what sense I have a psychology." You say to him: "Well, you dislike X, don't you?" He replies: "Yes, of course I do. He is very unfair." You say: "Some people like him." He replies: "I can't help that. I dislike him." You say: "Well, that is a part of your psychology, you know, something to do with your mechanical dislikes." He replies: "I cannot agree with you. I dislike X and that's the end of the matter. It has nothing to do with my psychology. It is a fact." You say: "Well, to speak frankly, some people think you are unfair." He replies: "But that is absurd. If there is anything I can be perfectly certain of, it is that I am always fair. And I always have been." You say: "Perhaps there is, all the same, something to observe here." He replies: "I don't see what there is to observe. It is all as clear as daylight to me. And I think you are very unfair to suggest that I am unfair. In fact, to tell you the truth, I think *you* are very often unfair." You say: "I am not unfair. It is the last thing I ever am or wish to be. In fact, people often say how fair I am. I can see that you do not understand me." He replies: "And I can see that you do not understand me." At this point we had better terminate this imaginary conversation. Do you believe that there is no "psychology" here? Both the imaginary persons are becoming indignant and neither of them apparently sees that any personal *psychology* enters into the situation that has arisen between them and caused it. Neither of them observes he has a cherished picture of himself as being fair. Neither of them sees he is speaking from false personality, and neither of them sees how he is lying. Let us notice one thing at this point: *when we know a thing is true about ourselves, and acknowledge it internally, accusation can never make us indignant.* It can make us sad perhaps. Indignation is mainly derived from false personality, imaginary 'I' and pictures of oneself—I refer to being indignant about oneself and how people treat one and what they say to one. It comes from ascribing to ourselves what we have not got, of imagining ourselves to be what we actually are not. And in this connection is not the fact that we are so sensitive to criticism or censure of any kind clear evidence that we have a *psychology* apart from merely having physical bodies? And is not this invisible psychology of ours more real to us and a greater source of suffering than are our visible bodies, save when the latter suffer considerable pain?

Let us now trace some results of this typical conversation we have imagined. Both of the people involved are indignant at being called unfair. They have, in fact, reacted just as we would ourselves. We are supposing them to be in the Work, and that both are now negative.

142

What will now happen *psychologically*? They will both begin to justify themselves. You know that one of the specific efforts we are taught to make in our personal work is the effort against self-justifying. Self-justifying is a complicated and very interesting process of inner and outer lying whereby we put ourselves in the right. It belongs to our psycho-logical level—to our level of being—and it is one of the things that keep us at that level. Negative emotions, self-justifying, identifying, and all the great central things taught in the Work in connection with practical effort on oneself are the things that keep us where we are. They keep us on the psychological basis we rest upon. They prevent any change, any evolution of ourselves. This is why they are specially mentioned and defined as things to be struggled and fought with. You must not think it *wrong* to self-justify just because the Work says so. It is not wrong in a moral sense, but of no *use* in work on oneself, just as it is no *use* mixing bread with concrete. It takes, certainly, some time before we can begin to see for ourselves why the Work mentions certain special things against which efforts must be made. But if you say: "I must not justify myself because the Work says I must not," you will again get nowhere, for you will not be doing anything from yourself, from your understanding—and *to work from one's understanding is one of the great characteristics of the Fourth Way*. When you see clearly from your own self-observation that self-justifying keeps you where you are and is a process that has this as its object, so that you may always be in the right, at the expense of any change or evolution of yourself, and if at the same time your aim is to change, you will have far greater power to stop it, for then *you* will understand and want to do so from your own understanding. You will see the *good* of doing this for yourself. It is then possible to begin to make right effort. For if you are always going to be right, you will never be in the wrong, and if you are never in the wrong, you will never change. To feel one is always right is to block the way to any self-change.

Let us now suppose that the two imaginary people allow the mechanical processes of self-justifying to go on unchecked and that neither of them observes it at work in them, but that both are fully identified with it, fully engaged in it, in fact, fully liking and enjoying it, without a trace of insight into themselves. They will begin to con-struct what can be called *negative systems* in themselves, against one another. Once this seriously starts between two people it is very difficult to get matters right again. They will remember only unpleasant things about one another, for when a person feels negative against another, his memory, working by association, calls up only unpleasant things, which the activity of self-justifying makes eager use of. And so it will go on, just as it does in life, quite unchecked internally but checked by outer things, such as the fear of the law, the fear of libel or slander, the fear of losing one's reputation or being laughed at, etc.—in short, by the external restraints that control people and which, if removed, would turn them into quite other kinds of people. You know what happens in war. You know what people can become if external restraints are removed.

Now suppose these two imaginary people have already got some inner checks and inner restraints developed in them by the Work and that each of them, at a certain moment, comes, as it were, to his senses —I mean, wakens a little, becomes more conscious, and passes into Work 'I's and begins to observe himself from the feeling of the Work and its influences, which are quite different from the influences of life. He notices that he is justifying himself. He notices that he is recalling only unpleasant things of the other person and nothing pleasant which, to say the least, is unfair. He thinks of what was said to him and what he said. He searches in that special memory formed in a man by conscious self-observation for examples of himself being unfair in the past and finds several that he has noticed. Suddenly all his indignation falls away from him. He is no longer defending his false idea of himself, his false pictures of himself. He sees the truth—that he is often unfair. Now self-justifying cannot work in the presence of acknowledged truth. It is a process of lying that keeps the great central lie in us alive and well— that is, the false personality. Now let us suppose that these two people meet next day. They will instantly know that each has worked on himself, without saying a word to one another, and the whole thing is over. It is not in the past any more. It is cancelled. They are both free.

All that we have been speaking about is *psychology* and *psychological work* on *oneself* from the point of view of this teaching and its psychological method in regard to the application of it to oneself.

Birdlip, May 28, 1942

PSYCHOLOGICAL COMMENTARY

II.—On Being

Part I.—To-night we will speak again about Knowledge and Being. Can you remember anything that was said before about Knowledge and Being? Let me remind you that this teaching that we are studying says that there are two sides in a man that must develop in the gradual course of his transformation: the side of his Knowledge and the side of his Being. You have heard many times that you must first of all *know* this system and this takes time and effort. But it leads to a definite development of knowledge and at the same time should lead to a development of self-knowledge if a man works. Now it is not difficult to understand that there are different levels of knowledge. But it is not so easy to understand that there are different levels of being. Let us try to understand once more what *being* is. Usually people confuse *existence*

144

with *being*. A stone exists, a plant exists, a man exists; but they exist quite differently. It is here that the idea of being comes in. For example, the being of a stone, the being of a plant, the being of an animal, the being of a man, and the Divine Being, are all on different levels. The being of a thing is from its origin, but its existence is from its birth, and conception takes place before birth. Let us take the being of animals. All animals have existence from birth. A horse exists, a dog exists, a cow exists. They have a common existence. But the being of a horse, the being of a dog, and the being of a cow are quite different and are not from birth but from conception.

Now let us turn to Man. Man is different from the animals. His being is capable of a definite development. He is born as a self-developing organism and so is incomplete, at a lower level of being than he is destined for by his creation. Animals are complete. Also, as distinct from animals, Man's upbringing extends over a very long period, during which he *acquires* many things in his being—by education, by imitation, by custom. This is one reason why the being of one man is not similar to the being of another man. We can understand that the knowledge of one man may not be on the same level as the knowledge of another man. But we do not so clearly see that the level of being can be different. Now from the standpoint of this teaching mankind is not taken as one and the same. Men are not the same in regard to their being. The concept of *Man* in this teaching is divided into seven categories to begin with: No. 1 Man, whose centre of gravity is in his instincts and movements, in his physical life, then No. 2 Man, whose centre of gravity is in his emotional life, then No. 3 Man whose centre of gravity is in his intellectual life. These three categories form mechanical humanity, the outer circle of mankind, who do not understand one another. As you know, this is called the circle of the confusion of tongues, the circle of Babel. Then there is No. 4 Man whose centre of gravity is not in the Instinctive-Moving Centre nor in the Emotional Centre nor in the Intellectual Centre but as it were distributed among them. This is the *balanced man*, in whom development is no longer one-sided and in whom awakening has begun. Then there is the circle of conscious humanity: No. 5, No. 6 and No. 7 Man, and these are men who have undergone different degrees of transformation or re-birth or development—in short, who have had a new conception. Now these seven divisions of the general idea of *Man* mean seven degrees or categories of being. Let us take No. 1, No. 2 and No. 3 Man. They belong to the circle of mechanical humanity, to "mankind asleep", but they shew many differences in regard to their being. All three may live only under life-influences—that is, A influences, namely, influences created in life from history, from the past, from custom, from the trend of things. But some may be affected both by influences A and influences B. I will remind you that B influences are not created by life but come from outside mechanical life, from the circle of conscious humanity, and I will remind you again that the Gospels are an example of B influences. Again, some men may be more under A than B influences, or more under B than A influences. Some may even have come in contact with C influences—namely, with some one belonging to the conscious circle of humanity, with someone who has been re-born, re-conceived, as the disciples came in contact with Christ. Some may even be already on the way to becoming No. 4 Man. All these different states mean different levels of being. Perhaps you have noticed that the idea of a man's level of being always entered into religious thought and it was regarded as more important than anything else. The level of being of a saint was different from that of a sinner. Good men, bad men, evil men, truthful men, liars, sincere men, patient men, hypocrites, self-righteous men, vain-glorious men, and so on, are all terms referring to the side of *being*, not to the side of *knowledge* in a man. Now-a-days people seem to be coming to think that *what a man is does not matter* in view of *what he knows*. They even think that a man with criminal being can be a great thinker or a great scientist or a great artist or a great writer.

*   *   *

Part II.—Let us now come to the *knowledge* of this Work and its relation to our being. This Work is given as knowledge and so must be learned, just as any other kind of knowledge must be learned. But this Work comes from Greater Mind. It is not ordinary knowledge. It is knowledge about transformation, just as the Gospels are knowledge about re-birth or being born anew, and whether we call it transformation or re-birth makes no difference. It is knowledge coming from those who attained full inner development and have reached, by a growth and transformation of their being, the state of consciousness called Objective Consciousness. Now the knowledge taught in this Work must gradually become your knowledge—i.e. you must *know* the knowledge the Work teaches, first of all, and this takes time and effort. But since this knowledge comes from a level of humanity far above our level of being, the full *understanding* of this knowledge will not be possible until our level of being corresponds with the level of knowledge that the Work teaches. As you know, a union between knowledge and being is necessary before *understanding* results. For this reason this knowledge that you are studying must be *applied* to your being—and you will certainly not apply it if you do not value the ideas of the Work. A parallel development of knowledge and being is necessary. That is, you must work on your being in accordance with the knowledge you are taught to raise your level of being. With the level of being you possess at present you will be able to *understand* the knowledge of the Work up to a point. If you have something *good* in your being, you will be able to *understand* something of this Work and not merely *know* it. There is a saying in the Work that you must have gold to get gold. This refers to the quality of being a person has. If there is good in him, he already has a little gold. No one can *understand* beyond the level of this being.

You will now see why a man with bad being, a degenerate man, a confirmed liar, a moral imbecile, a criminal, and so on, cannot *understand* this Work, and also you will see why it is said in regard to new people entering this Work that they must be at the level of Good Householders. But even so, they must be people who are looking for something, people who do not quite believe in life and who feel that there must be something else, some other meaning in their existence on this planet.

★   ★   ★

Part III.—So many things are said in this teaching about being that it is impossible to speak of them at one time. Let me mention one thing said about being which interested me very much when I first heard it. The saying was : *Your being attracts your life.* This saying made me see at once that there is a connection between what is *outer* and what is *inner*. For example, on a general scale, the level of being of mankind attracts war. If the being of mankind were on even a slightly higher level, war as it is now would be impossible. On an individual scale, a person's being attracts his life. It will always attract the same kind of things, the same situations, the same kind of friends, the same sort of people, the same difficulties, and so on, no matter where the person is or where he goes. To change being is to change one's life, but to change one's form of life is not to change one's being. By altering your outside condition you will not change your life, because your being will continue to attract a certain kind of life. A horse attracts to itself a certain kind of life different from that of a cow or a dog, and you can understand that this is due to their difference in being. By changing its form of life, a cow will not change. You would not like a cow to sit with you by the fireside or be on your bed, not merely because it would be inconvenient, but because its being is so different from that of a dog. In general you can see that the being of animals connects them with a certain kind of life. A weasel is attracted to the life of a weasel, a snake to the life of a snake, and so on. But we do not see in a similar way that the law that "the being attracts the life" holds for the small difference of being in people. Of course you have to study your being, to see that you have a certain kind of being, and study your life, to see that you have a certain kind of life. People do not easily see that they have very distinct and limited outlines. They think they are boundless and free. They think they can be anything they please and *do* anything they wish and *live* how they choose. But if one begins to study one's being—and at the same time one's life—one discovers that one has a certain kind of being. This is a very long task. This Work says that *the study of our being is absolutely necessary*.

★   ★   ★

You know this Work says that we are machines driven by external impressions. Now as long as a man has no knowledge of his being, he is

147

certainly a machine. For a machine cannot know itself. If it did it would not be a machine. But a man-machine *can* know itself. When a man begins to know himself he is no longer a machine. He may, indeed, even become a *man*. But this takes a long time and great effort. It takes a different kind of effort, of course, from that required to learn the knowledge of the Work. That is, work on the line of knowledge, and work on the line of being, require different efforts. A man cannot get to know himself unless he observes himself with his internal attention, and he cannot observe himself intelligently unless he has been taught definite knowledge of what to observe and sees a reason for it. There are certain special factors in our being that prevent its development. One, for example, is negative emotion, such as self-pity, and so on. These special factors must be known first of all as a matter of knowledge. So you learn first the knowledge of the Work. But then you must apply it so as to gain actual knowledge of your being in the light of the teaching. Knowledge of your being is self-knowledge. But in this teaching it is a particular kind of self-knowledge because this teaching points to certain things in one's being that must be observed and ultimately changed, through an increasing willingness to change them. Merely to *know* that negative emotions are bad and keep us at our level of being is not enough. But it often happens that people do not observe themselves along the lines taught them; or do not connect what they observe with what they are taught; or they take everything they think and feel and imagine and do and say for granted and cannot see there is anything to observe. But how, then, can one expect to change oneself if one takes everything in oneself for granted? One is then a machine, not a man. It is strange not to be able to observe anything in oneself. A shock is necessary. But this often makes a person negative. Yet then he notices something.

*　*　*

Part IV.—Everyone acts from the sense of good, from what he thinks good. No one acts from evil. But a man acts from good according to his level of being—that is, from what appears to him as good. A thief steals because he feels it is good to steal. A revolutionist shoots people because he thinks it is good to shoot them. So good struggles with good. Just as knowledge is relative, so is good relative. Now good is relative to the level of being. What people regard as good is different in different cases. Perhaps you have noticed that what you thought good formerly you do not think good now. This means a change in the level of being. If the level of being changes only a little, you have at once a new perception of good. For example, perhaps you do not like to be as negative as you once were. This is due to a slight change in the level of being.

The knowledge of this Work is about reaching a higher level and so is about another life, here. But it must be learned and verified by application to one's being through self-observation and through personal thought about it. When its truth begins to be seen *by you, for yourself,*

148

the driver or mind *in you* is beginning to wake up from its life-sleep. When you begin to see the good of doing and living the Work, your *being* begins to change. When you see it is good to remember yourself, good to stop internal considering, good to step aside from ridiculous illusions and pictures of yourself and from the vanity and self-conceit of false personality, good to dislike your negative states, good to realize your own nothingness at times, good to struggle with identifying always, good to think of all the teachings of the Work, good to value it—all these and a thousand and one other things—then you are getting a new perception of good, and that means the level of your being is changing, and good of a higher or inner level is replacing the former level of good.

Birdlip, June 4, 1942

PSYCHOLOGICAL COMMENTARY

III.—On Being—(*continued*)

Part I.—Everyone who has taken up this Work seriously and reflected upon its meaning, by means of that faculty which we all possess but rarely use—namely, *thinking for oneself*—should eventually be capable of entering consciously into and understanding the position of others. This is a development of *being* essential for us in the Work. No one can develop alone. Now relationship is possible only through the contact of inner worlds. We meet through our inner worlds. To understand another you must enter into his inner world, but this is not possible if you have not entered your own inner world. The first step therefore towards entering consciously into and understanding the position of another is attained through entering into and understanding the position of *oneself* and unless this step is taken, to as full a degree as is possible, there is little or no possibility of entering into and understanding the position of another person. The entry into oneself begins with self-observation and the understanding of oneself comes through long self-study in the light and knowledge of this teaching, whose ultimate aim is the gradual but definite *transformation* of oneself. For this reason, merely to think that one is capable of entering into and understanding the position of another person, and even giving help, *as one is*—and this illusion is very common—is to misunderstand entirely the nature of human contact and the universal difficulties that attend this impulse, which so frequently ends in disaster or some sort of compromise which, as often as not, is the breeding-ground of bitterness, mutual criticism, hostility and even worse emotional states and trains of thought. No one as he is mechanically—that is, as formed by life and its influences —can enter into and understand another, and, from that, give help,

149

unless he already knows from his own self-observation, self-study and insight and work on himself, what is in the other person. Only through self-knowledge is knowledge of others practically possible. Only by seeing, knowing and understanding what is in yourself can you see, know and understand what is in another person. One of the greatest evils of human relationship is that people make no attempt to enter into one another's position but merely criticize one another without any restraint and do not possess any inner check to this mechanical criticism owing to the absence of any insight into themselves and their own glaring crudities, faults and shortcomings. As a result not only do they not help each other, but the normal balance of things is upset, and by this I mean that an accumulation of wrong or evil psychic material is formed daily in human relationships and, in fact, in everyone's life, which should never exist if people saw themselves and others simultaneously, and in this way could neutralize the effects of their conduct day by day. This lack of psychological responsibility, both to oneself and to others, is perhaps especially characteristic of modern times and is the source of one part of the widespread modern unhappiness that marks the present age, in which, amongst other things, there is a decline in even ordinary human kindness, with a resulting hardness which is among the most dangerous factors in regard to the future, and which effectually stops all possibility of the right development of the emotional life.

People in this Work, who have a chance of emotional development, should particularly observe silent or expressed criticism of others as a continual wrong factor in themselves, which continually is making wrong psychic material in them, and sincerely reflect upon what they are doing. In many cases, stupidity, thick-headedness and ignorance are underlying causes, but many causes exist, as an unusual degree of vanity and self-complacency, of feeling that one is in the right, or self-meritoriousness, feelings of virtue and superiority, and other factors of this kind, which of course bar the way to any inner self-change. I mention here particularly in connection with the mechanical feeling of merit and self-excellence those who expect others to change and do not start from themselves, and who even judge of the Work by its effects on others without apparently realizing that they have very much work to do on themselves before they can pass judgment on others, and also that other people are judging them in precisely the same way as they judge others —a fact which always surprises them. Mechanical criticism of others produces a great many psychological difficulties in the person who criticizes—that is, wrong 'I's which hinder their own inner development and freedom. Perhaps this is not clear. What is meant is that if you allow critical and negative 'I's to develop freely in yourself, they will turn on you in the Work and hinder your own understanding and your own development. What you do to others, you do to yourself. Everything is arranged in this way. Everything wrong gradually reacts on yourself in the Work. After a time you will learn that you cannot *afford* to sleep too much and to talk and act mechanically and let your life be in the hands of wrong 'I's. You will begin to see for yourself that you must really live more consciously in regard to your inner world in which all past accounts must eventually be cancelled. And to live more consciously in your inner world is not to go with bad 'I's, to begin with. Remember that if you are in the Work you are putting yourself under *more* laws than others—namely, under the laws of the Work. You are putting yourself in a position in which you must *obey* what the Work teaches.

⋆   ⋆   ⋆

Part II.—The purification of the emotional life in this Work can perhaps artificially be divided into two sides for the purposes of practical self-observation. We will deal first with the emotions arising from *False Personality* or Imaginary 'I', this imaginary *oneself* to which this Work is constantly calling your attention and which should be a matter of daily self-study and work, in view of the fact that it is the source of so much daily misunderstanding and unhappiness and offence. This thing, formed by ourselves and by the environmental influences of our upbringing, and resting, as it were, like a coloured bubble on the surface of our psychic life, confuses and distorts the whole of our inner world. It forms a part of our *acquired being*. The fundamental causes of almost all the misunderstandings arising in the inner world of Man, as well as in the sphere of the common life of people and any possible human relationship between them, is this psychic factor called the False Personality, which is formed in the preparatory period of life. The stimulation of this psychic factor in a person, both before and during the period of responsible life, gives rise to the emotions of *vanity* and *self-conceit*. These emotions, arising from the stimulation of the False Personality, stand in the way of the normal development of the Emotional Centre. And it can be said that they stand in the way of any development of consciousness as well. They prevent the Third State of Consciousness—the State of Self-Awareness. That degree of happiness and of self-consciousness which should exist in a real person, a real man, as well as in a peaceful common human existence, depends almost entirely on the absence in one of *vanity* and *self-conceit*. But these emotions can take very subtle forms and require long and sincere inner observation and a great deal of insight and gradual self-realization. But often people even imagine they have not got them, and although they are constantly being offended and upset by what others say or by the way they are treated, they do not see that this has any connection with their vanity or self-conceit. After a time, when buried conscience begins to awaken, these emotions can be felt by *inner taste*. They are *impure* emotions. This, indeed, is what is chiefly meant in religious writings, by *impurity*, and what in the Gospels is so much attacked as in the case of the Pharisees, who do everything to "be seen of men"—that is, out of vanity and self-conceit. You know that when you are doing good to others and feel merit, it is your self-love that you are doing good to. This is impurity in the emotions. But if you do a thing out of the love of it, it is pure. Unfortunately, this happens as a rule only in connection with satisfying our appetites. The second factor, in regard to the purification of the emotional life, is, as you all know, the factor of *negative emotions*. I will not speak of them now except to remind you that they take many subtle forms. After a time they can be recognized through *inner taste*. They all smell badly. Remember also that at birth there is no False Personality. But, born amongst sleeping people, who enjoy their negative emotions, the child acquires them, as by infection. The pleasure people take in being negative is imitated by the child, and at the same time the formation of False Personality in the child assists the process because through the emotions of vanity and self-conceit the means of being easily offended are formed in all their endless diversity.

Now our level of being is characterized by the impure state of the emotional life described above. Work on being, in regard to the Emotional Centre, demands therefore, among other things, efforts to observe and realize the existence of these emotions in oneself, noticing their origin, and the course they take, and the effects they give rise to. When we are properly conscious of something in ourselves, we are on the way to changing it. The consciousness of it, alone, if it is full enough, will begin to change it. Once you have seen something in yourself, in your being, clearly, it will lead to your seeing something else. Understand that being must change and change definitely in everyone without exception and it must change *now* and *here*. Religious people often suppose they will be changed in some hereafter: or they imagine that, just as they are, with the level of being they have, and all their negative emotions, vanity, self-conceit, malicious talking, jealousies, unpleasant curiosities, and so on, they can reach *God*. And there are many other similar illusions, all of which are due to *not seeing one's level of being*, which actually determines where we are situated in the scale or ladder of all kinds of being, reaching up to the Divine Being. Everyone is at some place in this ladder. Now in this Work, on the psychological side, you are given *knowledge* about how to change being, and this knowledge must be applied to *your own being* through observing yourself in accordance with what that knowledge tells you to observe. From this, you get *knowledge of your being* and can begin to work on your being. If you begin to possess some real knowledge of your own being and have worked on it, then you will be able to enter into and understand the position of another person and so help him—but only in so far as your own knowledge of yourself and your own difficulties goes. And among other things, you will be able to know when you are speaking from vanity or a sense of superiority, or from a negative feeling, from the desire to hurt, or merely criticize, and so on. In short, you will be able to distinguish between the pure and impure in yourself better and from this be able to speak more purely to one another. If while you are speaking, you are seeing in yourself what you are seeing in the other, you will speak purely or more purely, and what is pure in this sense cannot hurt another or offend him but will help him. And if you do not know at the time when you are speaking to another whether you spoke rightly, yet you have spoken with the *double consciousness* of yourself and the other person, which is speaking in a State of Self-Remembering, namely, looking in and out simultaneously, then you will know later by *after-taste*. That is, the Work will shew you, for everything done sincerely, from the feeling of the Work, will be preserved for you and shewn you in its right light, if you listen and do not fall asleep.

*　　*　　*

Part III.—In the paper that was read last time, it was said that in religious writings many things are said about *being*. People are divided according to their state of being—into saints and sinners, bad and good men, and so on. Many things are said in the Gospels that refer to being. In the Parable of the Sower sowing the Seed of the Word of God in mankind, the different categories of men mentioned are divided according to their being in relation to the Seed of the Word, to their reception of it. In another place, men with wrong being are called "thorns" or "thistles", in the passage where Christ says: "Do men gather grapes of thorns or figs of thistles?" Men are then compared by Christ, in regard to their level of being, with trees, and it is said: "Every good tree bringeth forth good fruit, but the corrupt tree bringeth forth evil fruit." All this means that the level of being of a man is of the greatest importance. As you know, it is necessary to think about a person's level of being before you bring him into this Work. Something very serious is meant here and by now you will begin to understand what it is. The tendency to-day to make criminals heroes is entirely wrong. There are two signs of being in regard to people that you might wish to bring into the Work. They must be responsible people and they must have some *magnetic centre*. Other things have been said in the past on this question and I will try to recall some of them now. Apart from the idea of Good Householder and magnetic centre, a person entering the Work should have a natural sense of shame. You know that many so-called "moral defectives" have no sense of shame, and this is a very bad sign. And notice here that by being hard and never feeling shame you arrest the development of your own being. Again people entering the Work should have some sense of religion, some trace in their lives of a religious impulse—that is, of course, connected with magnetic centre, and with past influences and education. Then they should feel something of mortality, have some awareness of their own mortality. All these factors and several others form starting-points in their being from which ideas and teachings of the Work can develop.

NOTE ON PRAYER

Response and Request

In the paper that was read last time about the idea of Prayer as given in the Gospels (which is not included in this volume) it was said that the Universe can be taken as *response to request*. Man requests, and the Universe in all its full and total reality, outer and inner, responds according to the request. In regard to what was said last time, I wish to draw your attention to this fact: many people are getting responses to requests which they do not understand they are making. If the Universe, visible and invisible, material and psychological, gross and fine, as apprehended externally by the senses and internally by the mind and heart, is response to request, then you will see how important it is to realize what kind of *requests* you are making in order to understand why you get the response, from any side of life, that you are actually getting. The Work says: "Your being attracts your life". Do you see the connection? Without knowing it, a man or a woman may be making request and so getting a response from the total Universe that he or she does not like. They see the response but do not see what excites the response, what it is in themselves that attracts it. People, in other words, may be asking for trouble without being aware that they are. They only see the result—that is, the response. They see only effects, not causes. To think only from effects is one thing. It is how mechanical people think. To think from causes is another thing. It belongs to more conscious thinking. Now the level of your being enters into request as much or more than your knowledge. You may *ask* intellectually for happiness but not see how factors that govern your being, as love of your negative states, your grievances, your secret jealousies, your laziness, your dislikes, and so on, are asking for something quite different, and that the Universe is responding to these factors in your being that you are secretly willing and affirming without seeing that you are. Understand that *full request* must contain both thought and will—formulation and emotional desire. The side of knowledge is the side of thought and a man can only think from his knowledge. The side of being wills, and a man only *wills* what he desires. If you love negative states, then your will is of this quality. Your love is your will; it will attract the response belonging to it. Only self-knowledge will make you aware of your state of being and this begins with self-observation. Enough has been said here on this subject—namely, that a person may be getting *responses* he does not expect or desire, without seeing that he is attracting them because he is making *requests* for them that he is not aware of.

*   *   *

We will now speak of some things said in the Work, directly and indirectly, about Prayer.

THE TEACHING ABOUT PRAYER IN THE WORK

Part I.—In the teaching of the Work the idea of *Prayer* and the idea of Self-Remembering are so closely connected that the one cannot be separated from the other. Without Self-Remembering, Prayer is impossible. Let us look at what this means. A man as he is cannot pray. That is, a man in his ordinary daily state cannot pray. In order to pray a man must be in a state of Self-Remembering. To pray as one is, in one's ordinary state, is to pray in a state of sleep, and to pray in a state of sleep is useless. Nothing can happen. Such Prayer cannot be answered, because it does not get anywhere. Let us recall what is said about states of consciousness in the Work. Four states of consciousness are possible, but ordinarily Man knows and lives in only two, and both are called in the Work *states of sleep*. The first state of consciousness or the lowest is that of bodily sleep, which is a passive state in which a person lies in bed almost without movement. In this state a man spends a third or even more of his life. The second state of consciousness is the state in which people spend the remaining part of their lives, in which they move their limbs and walk about and talk and also write books and take part in politics and kill one another, and this state they regard as active and call it "clear consciousness or the waking state of consciousness". It is not too much to say that the terms clear consciousness or waking state of consciousness seem to have been given in jest especially when, through your own self-observation, you begin to realize what clear consciousness ought in reality to be, and what the state in which a man lives and acts really is. For in this so-called waking state a man is neither conscious of himself nor conscious of another. He lives and dies in darkness. And it would be better for him in one way if he remained passive in the first state of consciousness for then he could not move about and kill his neighbour.

The third state of consciousness is Self-Remembering or Self-Consciousness or the state of Self-Awareness. It is usual to consider that we have this state already and are always aware of ourselves and that we act, think and feel with full consciousness of what we are doing. But Western science has overlooked the fact that we do not possess this state of consciousness. And we cannot create it in ourselves by immediate desire alone, or decide that we will henceforth always live in a state of Self-Consciousness. But this third state constitutes the natural right of *Man as he is* and if Man does not possess it, it is because of the wrong conditions of his life. To-day this state of consciousness occurs only in the form of rare flashes and it is only by long practice, by trial and error, that a man can begin to re-establish a state of Self-Remembering in himself.

STATES OF CONSCIOUSNESS

Help Possible *Man Awake*	4th State	Objective Consciousness (where a man can see things as they really are).
LIGHT	3rd State	Self-Consciousness, Awareness of 'I', Self-Remembering.

No Help Possible *Man Asleep*	2nd State	So-called clear Consciousness or Waking State. Body-active-Man as walking and talking machine, not properly conscious. Man as sleep-walker. Man active to his dreams.
DARKNESS	1st State	Sleep with Dreams. Man dreaming. Body quiescent. Man as passive machine passive to dreams.

Now help only reaches to the third state of consciousness. It cannot reach down to the darkness that people live their daily lives in and in which they are so often content to exist. Therefore to pray from the state of sleep—to pray from the so-called waking state—is like dreaming that one is praying, for in this second state of consciousness we are also dreaming and everything is unreal, only we do not notice that we are doing everything in a dream unless we experience a moment of consciousness belonging to the 3rd and 4th states of consciousness and see the contrast. So when a man prays he must remember himself. He must be conscious of himself and of what he is praying for. He must feel the meaning of everything he says and feel himself saying it. He must feel it is really 'I' in him that prays and not a set of frightened little 'I's or a set of mechanical 'I's formed by habit. And finally a man can neither pray nor remember himself unless he feels there is both a higher state of himself and something higher than he is.

We must now consider the 4th state of consciousness in connection with all that class of praying which can be called *praying for enlightenment*. When a man prays for enlightenment he prays that he may see things as they really are, apart from his imagination and his subjective ideas. In the religions of all nations there are indications of the possibility of such a state of consciousness, which is called "Enlightenment" and other names, but which cannot be described in words for it transcends all words. When a man prays for enlightenment he prays for Objective Consciousness. But he must first be in the 3rd state of consciousness for it is only this 3rd state that can be touched and can retain the meaning of any experience or help coming from those who are at the level of the 4th state of consciousness. But you must realize that if a man prays for enlightenment, say about himself, he is praying to awaken and if a man fully awoke to himself and saw himself as he really is, that is, objectively, he would go mad. It is better to think of praying for more understanding. But of course this is useless if you make no effort to understand better for yourself. If a man in the Work works neither on the Line of Knowledge nor the Line of Being and merely prays for more understanding, his view of the Universe is very naive. He must realize the harshness of things and the price that must be paid and get rid of childish and sentimental views. I must repeat that to pray for something you should work for and can, if you try, is quite idle. But people take idle views and cannot wake up to their own danger. You must fight for the Work and fight to keep it, and you will not keep it unless you jump and catch hold of its rope and insist on holding on to it.

★　　★　　★

THE THREE BROTHERS IN A MAN

Part II.—The next thing that the Work says of Prayer is that all three centres in a man must pray. To begin with, if only the mind prays and the heart does not, there can be no response. The whole man must pray and the whole man is first of all three men—three brothers who do not agree. If these three centres, in the three-storey house that Man is, worked in harmony, Man would already be in the 3rd state of consciousness. He would be sufficiently awake to receive help, to obtain a response to his requests. But these three brothers in a man do not co-operate and especially to-day is this the case. For this reason, let us glance briefly at some of the teaching given in the Work about the state of our centres nowadays.

You know that the study of the multiplicity of our being which characterizes our *level of being* begins with the observation of centres. The three centres work independently owing to the abnormal conditions of modern life, which produce one-sided developments. Every conscious perception and every manifestation of a man, everything taken in and given out, should be the result of the co-ordinated working of the three centres, each of which should furnish its own share of associations and knowledge and experiences. In place of this, the working of these different centres is almost entirely disconnected nowadays. In consequence of this the intellectual, emotional and instinct-moving centres do not co-operate with one another and so correct and complement one another, but, as it were, travel along different roads which rarely meet. For this reason Man is very rarely *conscious*, and again, for the same reason, Man is, to begin with, not one individual, but three distinct people that are not in harmony. The first thinks in total isolation from the rest; the second feels in the same way; and the third acts mechanically, according to long-established habits. If development were normal these three men in a man, the intellectual man, the emotional man and the instinct-moving man, would form one single man, in harmony with all the different sides of himself. As it is, Man is, in himself, in a condition of disharmony. He is first of all three men, three brothers, who rarely agree, and who indeed spend their time in frustrating one another, quarrelling with one another and each dominating the other in turn. Any general result of their combined action, in which each of them is in agreement and each signs his name, so to speak, to the agreement, is thus very rare, but when this does happen, the man is at that moment in another state of *consciousness*. He is, in fact, conscious, in the sense of the Work teaching, for he is in simultaneous possession of all his faculties and conscious of each. His consciousness embraces all the centres at the same time, instead of being confined to one or another centre, or a small part of it, at a time. This extension or expansion of consciousness to include at the same time all the centres is not supernormal but is actually what a normal man should possess. This is the 3rd state of consciousness—the state of Self-Remembering or Self-Awareness—which is a man's right and into which he is born, but which he loses very soon owing to the effect of the sleeping people by whom he is surrounded. It is through wrong influences, wrong education, and the wrong conditions of modern life that Man has fallen away from this state of consciousness, which is his natural right, and which, if he possessed it, would make it impossible for him to act as he does to-day.

★　★　★

Part III.—I will now speak of one or two things that the Work says which *indirectly* bear on the subject of Prayer. The Work says that in the Lord's Prayer, as in the parables and sayings in the Gospels, there is meaning within meaning. This is why it is said in the Work that the Gospels are a test for a man's level of understanding, and also that as a man changes, so do the Gospels for him. In the Lord's Prayer there are innumerable ideas. Each phrase has inner octaves. There are so many things in it to a man who has formed the ideas of the Work in his mind that to speak at all fully about the Lord's Prayer is to speak about every side and every single thing in the Work itself. To read the Prayer at times and think of all its connections, beginning with the octave from the Divine Intelligence of the Sun in which Man is created and of all the Work says of Man and his inner state and what he must do to awaken, is to use the Prayer in its real sense. To repeat the words is useless.

Now I will refer to one of the sayings of Christ quoted in the past paper on Prayer, where it is said that a man must pray for a thing and have faith that he has it, and he will get it. "All things whatsoever ye pray for and ask for, have faith that ye *have* received them, and ye *shall have* them." (*Mark* XI *xxiv*). Now it is said in the Work that a man must not wait until he has the force to do something but must act, if it is his aim, as if he had it already, and then he will *attract it*. To wait until you have the strength and understanding to do something—I am speaking of the Work—makes it impossible to do it. But you must each think of this for yourselves.

Now I will add a few things. All prayer from self-pity is, of course useless. Prayer for others is only possible through understanding their difficulties and so through understanding yourself, for you understand others only so far as you understand yourself. All work is the preparation of lower centres for the reception of the influences coming from higher centres. Man has two centres fully developed in him and belonging to higher levels of intelligence. But though they are working all the time in him, he cannot hear them. Their influences touch the state of Self-Remembering, but go no further. So all work is prayer: for all real prayer is to connect Man with Heaven, and all work on oneself is to purify lower centres and make right order in the mind through being taught right knowledge, so that the influences of higher centres can be heard.

We can speak of different sorts of prayer:

(1) Prayer for Enlightenment or Understanding.

(2) Prayer about Temptation.

(3) Prayer about oneself and about others.

As regards (2), Prayer about Temptation, this refers to temptation about the Work. It is not necessarily answered, because the Work will answer it if you fight to hold to its teaching and apply it and use it. Remember that temptation in the Work and about it is necessary in order to change a man, and it follows that if you pray in this connection your prayer will not be answered, but if you work instead you will get a response. As I said, to pray when you should work, to expect help when you should make effort, is idle.

As regards prayer about oneself, it must be about others first and oneself last. Remember there are three levels of Work—Work for the Work, Work with others, Work on oneself. To pray only for oneself, to work only with regard to oneself and those connected by self-interests with one cannot give any result. Three forces must enter prayer, and this is too difficult to speak of at present, but you will find them in the Lord's Prayer if you think long enough about it.

During the month of July, 1942, Dr. Nicoll continued the writing of his Papers on the Gospels.

NOTE ON NEGATIVE EMOTIONS

Let us speak to-night of the Work. Let us speak of what work on one-self means in connection with negative emotions. The Work says: "You have a right not to be negative." Notice that the Work does not say: "You have no right to be negative." One of the signs whereby you can distinguish between a false and a true teaching is that a false teaching insists upon or makes a rule about your doing something you cannot do. It is the sign of a false teaching, for example, to make you promise something, or swear to it, or take an oath of silence and so on. A man —an ordinary man—cannot keep a promise under all circumstances, because he is not one person, but many persons. One person, one 'I' in him, may promise or even bind itself by an oath. But other 'I's in him will know nothing about this. To assume that a man can promise is to assume that he is already *one*, a unity—that is, a man having only one real, permanent 'I' controlling him and so only one will. But a man has many 'I's and as many different wills. Suppose the Work made a rule to this effect: "You *must* not be negative. You must swear never to be negative. If you break this promise, you must leave the Work." If the Work said that, it would mean that it took it for granted that *Man can do.* But the Work says that Man as he is *cannot do* and that this is one of the things you have to become aware of through self-observation. If you still imagine you *can do*, if you still think you can always remember and keep your aim, then you will make no room for the Work in your-self and the Work will not be able to help you. You will not feel your inner helplessness. If you begin to feel your inner helplessness in a right way, you will feel the need of the Work to help you. How can the Work help you? It can help you only if you begin to obey it. To feel the need of the Work is to feel you need something to guide you. If you are going to let something guide you, you must obey it. You must try to obey the Work. Of course, if you understand nothing, you cannot obey the Work. So you have to think what it is that the Work teaches and get it clearly into your mind. You have to think, you yourself, in your most private and real thoughts, what this Work is saying to you all the time. If you have thought in this deeper, intimate, private way, you will see that the Work tells you more about *what not to do* than about *what to do.* Now people often ask: "What am I to do?" On that side the Work says only two definite things: "Remember yourself" and "Observe or notice yourself." That is what you must try to do. But on the other side the Work says many things about what you must not do. It says, for example, that you must try to struggle against being identi-fied, try to struggle with mechanicalness, with mechanical and wrong talking, with every kind of internal considering, with every kind of self-justifying, with all the different pictures of yourself, with your special forms of imagination, with mechanical disliking, with all varieties of your self-pity and self-esteem, with your jealousy, with your hatreds, with your vanity, your inner falseness, with your lying, with your self-conceit, with your attitudes, prejudices, and so on. And it expressly speaks of struggling with your negative emotions taken as a whole. Sometimes you meet a person in the Work who is very eager and wishes to know exactly *what to do*. It is especially people who only have external attention and no internal attention who ask this. As you know, the Work begins with internal attention. Self-observation is internal attention. A person must begin to see for himself what he is like and what goes on in him—for example, he must begin to see through internal attention his own negative emotions instead of only seeing other people's with his external attention. He must see what it means to identify with his negative emotions and what it means not to identify with them. Once he sees this, he has got a key to the Work on the practical side in his hands. The first stages of the Work are sometimes called "cleaning the machine." A person who constantly says: "What should I do?", after hearing the practical teaching of the Work over and over again, is like a man who has a garden full of weeds and says eagerly: "What should I plant in it? What should I grow in it? " He must first clean the garden. So the Work lays great emphasis on *what not to do* —that is, on what must be stopped, what must no longer be indulged in, what is to be prevented, what is no longer to be nourished, what must be cleaned away from the human machine. For none of us have nice new machines when we enter this Work, but rusty, dirty machines that need a daily and indeed a life-long cleaning, to begin with. And one of the greatest forms of dirt is negative emotions and habitual indulgence in them. The greatest filth in a man is negative emotion. An habitually negative person is a filthy person, in the Work sense. A person who is always thinking unpleasant things about others, saying unpleasant things, disliking everyone, being jealous, always having some grievance, or some form of self-pity, always feeling that he or she is not rightly treated and so on—such a person has a filthy mind in the most real and practical sense, because all these things are forms of negative emotion and all negative emotions are dirt. Now the Work says *you have a right not to be negative*. As was pointed out, it does not say *you have no right to be negative*. If you will think of the difference, you will see how great it is. To feel that you have a right not to be negative means that you are well on your way to real inner work on yourself in regard to negative states. To be able to feel this draws down force to help you. You stand upright, as it were, in yourself, among all the mess of your negativeness, and you feel and know that it is not necessary to lie down in that mess. To say this phrase in the right way to yourself, to feel the meaning of the words: "I have a right not to be negative," is actually a form of self-remembering, of feeling a trace of real 'I', that lifts you up above the level of your negative 'I's which are all the time telling you without a pause that *you have every right to be negative*.

*　　*　　*

Part II.—You have all heard of levels, but some may not understand what a higher level means in a practical sense. What is a lower and what is a higher level in yourself? The Work is to make us live on a higher level of ourselves. For example, suppose you begin to internally consider. You start making accounts, making out that others owe you, thinking that you are badly treated, worrying about what others think of you, and so on. This is an activity of a *lower level* of yourself. That is, you cannot live on a better level of yourself if you are going to indulge all the time in internal considering. Now suppose you begin to dislike the inner taste of considering. Then when internal considering starts in you and you notice it you will feel uncomfortable. Why? Because you have already begun to feel what a higher level is like. You feel uncomfortable by reason of the contrast. You have seen something better. You are now in a position to make an inner choice. Or again, if you are in a negative state, are you on a lower or higher level of yourself? You are on a lower level and you will not be able to taste what a higher level is like as long as you indulge unchecked in your negative states. It is always a question of inner decision, of inner choice. If you begin to be interested in your *better states* and study what spoils them, you will begin to work practically on yourself. Better states belong to higher levels of yourself. They are in you, as different levels. You can live in the basement or higher up. But you have to see all this for yourself and get to know *where you are in yourself*. Ask yourself: "Where am I?" With what thoughts and emotions are you going, with what moods, with what 'I's? One has to learn not only *whom to live with* in oneself but *where to live* in oneself.

*   *   *

One note more. In dealing with a negative state, look at the 'I' in you and not at the person with whom you are negative. The real cause of the negative state is the 'I' that is speaking in you and to you and to which you are listening. If you let this 'I' go on talking and listen to it, you will become more and more negative. Its only object is to make you negative and absorb as much of your force as it can. Every negative 'I' has only one purpose—to get hold of you and feed upon you and strengthen itself at your expense. The real cause of negative states is in yourself—in negative 'I's that live only to persuade you with their half-truths and lies and to rule over you and spoil your lives. All negative 'I's only wish to destroy you, to ruin your lives. This is a very good exercise to practise.

INTRODUCTORY NOTE
TO CHAPTER ON GOOD AND TRUTH

All esoteric teaching regards Man as between two levels, sometimes called "Earth and Heaven". All esoteric teaching also says that if Man on earth is cut off from all influences coming from a higher level, mankind will perish. Just as physical nature, as we behold it in the external visible world, depends for its life on the influence of the sun, so Man, in his inner world, depends on influences from a higher level. If these influences are received by no one on earth, Man is cut off and perishes. One of the problems, therefore, of esotericism is how to keep alive this contact or connection. At different times in history different ways have been tried, but all with the same end in view. For example, different kinds of schools or " churches " have existed, which for a time have maintained this connection. But sooner or later any particular school or "church" or focus created for the reception and transmission of these higher influences, has died. But a new focus always appears. The death of a "church", if we use this term, is sometimes called a flood in the language of parables. The new church is the ark that survives it and contains representations of all forms of knowledge and good necessary for a new beginning. There have been many stages of Man, in regard to his contact with influences from a higher level, and, from the esoteric standpoint, Man has degenerated, psychologically, in this respect. To speak in the language of the Work, Man no longer lives in the 3rd State of Consciousness, he no longer remembers himself, and so is out of contact with the higher centres in him and their influences on him. In the Old Testament, many references are made to different forms of teaching in "churches" in ancient times. For instance, many of those long tables of references to so and so who begat so and so and lived for so many hundred years are records of different "schools" or branches of "churches". Again, there was a school or church called "Noah". Another existed also in Mesopotamia and was called when it was dying Babel or Babylon. The Jewish Church began much later. In fact, the Old Testament is a secret record of the history of esotericism.

One of the problems of esotericism is how to raise the *level of being* of a man apart from his level of knowledge—that is, to raise him on the side of *good*, for goodness is of being and knowledge is of mind. Man can no longer see good directly or be taught directly from good. His mind must alter first, so he must be taught knowledge or truth about a higher level of being first. But the object of the knowledge is to raise the man's level of being.

During the month of September, 1942, Dr. Nicoll continued the writing of his papers on the Gospels.

FURTHER NOTE ON KNOWLEDGE AND BEING

I

We will begin our talk to-night with further thoughts about the two sides of a man called in the Work the side of Knowledge and the side of Being. Since I notice that these two sides of the Work are not sufficiently thought about I will ask you this question: Suppose you have some person who is very primitive, very undeveloped in the ordinary sense, very superstitious, and, let us say, more like an animal than a human being. Now let us suppose that your task is to raise this person to a better state. How are you going to begin to do so? Now if you think over the subject you will realize that you have two tasks confronting you—and, in fact, you will begin to realize why the Work says that a man has two sides, Knowledge and Being. You will begin to understand that what the Work says about the *two* sides of a person that must be developed is quite true. Now this person whom you have to deal with knows nothing: and also this person lies and steals and behaves dishonestly and so on. Which side are you going to begin with? You must think for yourselves as to where you would begin. Would you begin by teaching him some Knowledge or by acting on his Being, with, say, a big stick? Do you now realize more distinctly that these two sides, the state of his Knowledge and the state of his Being, represent the man in a psychological sense—and that if we ourselves wish to grow it is only possible along these two lines?

*　　*　　*

II

Now let us speak of levels of Being. What are the signs of the level of Being in a man in the Work-sense? How can we understand what it means that each man is at a higher or at a lower level of Being? We can all understand, at least to some extent, what a man on a higher level of Knowledge is. That is, we can understand the Relativity of Knowledge. We can realize that a man *knows more* or *knows less* about some subject than we do. I say here, on purpose, that we can understand this to a *certain extent*. And by this I mean that we are not speaking of the *quality* of knowledge, but simply in a general sense of all knowledge. To-day, by the method of examinations, a man is tested as to his degree of knowledge, whether scientific or commercial, mathematical, classical, and so on. We are all prepared to admit that this or that man's knowledge of, say, astronomy, or finance, or the French language, or motor-cars, or literature, and so on, may be on a higher level than is our own. And this *standard of knowledge*, verified by examinations, is to-day the main standard *in practice* that people are judged by. But in the Work the case is different. People in the Work are not estimated from the side of Knowledge only, but from the side of *Being*. In the Work, the question is not merely *what a man knows* but *what a man is*. What a man *knows* belongs to the side of his Knowledge: what a man *is* belongs to the side of his Being. And just as Knowledge is relative, so is Being—that is, one man's being may be relatively on a higher level than another's. And in this respect, as you know, the Work says that a man must be at that level of Being called *Good Householder* before he is really regarded as being in the Work. Therefore on the side of Being, we begin with a man who is at that level called *Good Householder*. Notice the word *good*, because Being has to do with *goodness*. You cannot apply this word to Knowledge. Knowledge is either right or wrong Knowledge, true or false Knowledge. You can learn the truth about how to make a motor-car. This is knowledge that is truth. But you can also have false or wrong Knowledge. So the terms *truth* and *falsity* belong to the side of Knowledge. But in the case of Being these words cannot be used in quite the same way. A man is a *good* Householder or a *bad* Householder. A good man and a bad man are terms quite distinct from right or wrong as applied to Knowledge, or Knowledge that is true and Knowledge that is false. A man can be, in quite an ordinary sense, a good man, and have quite a wrong Knowledge, say, of how to make a motor-car. On the other hand, he can be, in an ordinary sense, a bad man, even a criminal, and have a very good Knowledge of how to make a motor-car. In other words, it is not *Knowledge* alone that defines a man in the Work. He is defined in terms of his *Being* as well—and, in fact, as a starting-point in the Work, he is taken first of all in terms of his Being. That is, he is not taken in terms of his level of Knowledge at the starting-point, but in terms of his level of Being. This does not mean that a man's Knowledge is useless in the Work. In the Fourth Way, which we are studying, a man's Knowledge can prove to be very useful. But what is first of all taken into consideration is his *level of Being*—the kind of man he is. He must be, or be near to, the level of *Good Householder*, and if he is not, no matter what he knows, he is of no use to the Work. But since we have already spoken many times of what *Good Householder* means, to-night we are going to speak of *levels of Being* and what they mean. I will begin with this Work phrase: "A man on first hearing this Work, understands it, and can only understand it, *on his level of Being*." This Work comes in to you as Knowledge. But Knowledge and Understanding are two different things. You may *know* a lot and *understand* nothing of what you know. Now this Work, coming into you as new Knowledge, will be *understood* exactly according to your level of Being, and that will depend upon whether you have *Magnetic Centre* or not. This is the second sign of *Being* in the Work.

Now let us go slowly and re-capitulate, in order that the teaching about Being can be grasped. First, in regard to Being, a man must be at the average level of Good Householder. He must be a responsible and decent person. He must not be a *tramp* or a *lunatic*—and of the meaning of these technical terms we have spoken enough elsewhere. The second sign of Being, at the start, is the possession of Magnetic Centre. In ordinary language, this means that a candidate for the teaching must be a man who has pondered about life and wondered about the meaning of himself on earth and had many private thoughts of his own, which have led him to feel dimly that there must be something else, some other sense in things than he has been taught, some other meaning in life than he was taught, as it were, at school. Putting the matter roughly, without using technical language, he must be a man who is not quite satisfied with position, money, possessions, success and so on, and has caught sight of something behind the world of the senses, behind the world of appearances. Or put more technically, a man with Magnetic Centre in his Being is a man who has had moments when he has felt that life cannot be interpreted and so cannot be understood simply in terms of itself. Sometimes in the country, in the woods, in the fields, we have seen something that has made us feel we were far away not only from ourselves but from all real meaning. Or it may have been that some words read from the Gospels in the School Chapel have made us catch our breath. Or the sudden sight of someone has awakened some strange feeling that we have forgotten something that we should have always remembered. Or we have touched a thought in some book that seemed filled with a meaning we could not reach and yet recognized. Now when a man is convinced in his inner and most hidden thoughts —the thoughts that he cannot easily put into words—that there must be *something else* behind life, and yet at the same time he fulfils his task in life and does his job and becomes what he must become—soldier, sailor, doctor, priest, lawyer, and so on—he is both a *Good Householder* and a man who has traces of Magnetic Centre. But—to put it as brutally as possible—if a man believes in nothing but getting on in life and sees life as the fulfilment of all he needs and cares nothing for anything else, then he has no Magnetic Centre. He may be a Good Householder but not quite in the Work-sense. For in the full Work-sense a Good Householder is a man who has fulfilled his duties in life in a responsible way and *no longer believes in life.* He no longer believes that life by itself leads anywhere, but believes that, under the circumstances, he must do his duty. Now no longer to believe in life as being capable of fulfilling all we seek is one thing: and to believe that there is something else that we must seek is another thing, for this latter means that a man has Magnetic Centre—something in him that points in a certain direction that does not obey the ordinary laws of a compass.

Let us again re-capitulate the teaching about Being. First, a man must be in life and have dealt with life and reached some adequate position in life and knowledge of life and so be a Good Householder, capable of dealing with the ordinary difficulties and problems of human existence—that is, the Work is not for people who seek to escape from the normal burdens of life. It is for *normal decent people* and starts from that level of Being. It is very important that everyone should understand this. Second, a man's Being must have some trace of Magnetic Centre in it. This means that in the Work-teaching of what *Being* means, a man who has no Magnetic Centre, whoever he is and whatever he is in life, is at a lower *level* of Being than a man who has Magnetic Centre. Here, you will all see, the Work-teaching about Being breaks away entirely from any ordinary conception of Being. A man who is on the general level of Being called Good Householder and *has* Magnetic Centre is at a higher level of Being than the man who is in a broad sense simply a Good Householder. And further, a man who has Magnetic Centre but is *not* at the general level of Good Householder but belongs to the category called "tramp" or "lunatic" is at a *lower level* of Being than is the Good Householder with *no* Magnetic Centre. Once more I emphasize how important it is to understand this first teaching of the Work about Being.

Many things could be added here, in this connection, but we will now go on to consider what this Work says about the signs of Being in its development.

Now the next technical thing said in regard to the quality or level of a man's Being, apart from the possession of Magnetic Centre, is that it is characterized by the fact that it is *multiple*. And it is exactly by means of the *multiplicity of Man's Being* that its development can be understood. Man has many different 'I's in him and this feature is a characteristic of his Being. The *highest Being* a man can reach is when only one permanent 'I' reigns in him. That is, all development of Being lies in the direction of increasing union and is finally attained by *unity of Being* in place of multiplicity of Being. The whole of a man should form *one* man. But as we are, we are not *one* but *many*. A man resembles an assembly in which now one person, now another, gets up and speaks and there is no agreement between these different persons. A man is like a house full of servants who quarrel and use the single telephone and all speak in the name of the master. A man is a house in disorder. A man is legion. Yet above him, at a higher level of himself, there is *real 'I'*, that sometimes he feels the existence of, especially in conditions of great danger or great fatigue. This one permanent and real 'I' is the highest Being of the man and every man has this in him. So all *development of Being*, in the Work-sense, is defined by the approach to this real 'I' which unites all that is in him and is concealed in everyone, in the depths of himself, and behind all the tedious things he does and says with his other side, which only begins to become realized through self-observation. Now people in the Work, who begin to feel it, have already more unity of Being. Why is this? It is because they are following something that unites them. If a number of people are thinking and practising the same thing they are more in union, and not only this, they are more in union in themselves. Only a teaching having the quality of the Work in it, can effect any sort of union, either in oneself or in connection with others. If you see the truth of one or another of the teachings of the Work you will be brought internally into the *beginning of unity* in yourselves, for this Work leads to union with real 'I' and is designed to. And you will begin to see for yourselves what you cannot go with—i.e. negative states—for real 'I' will never approach you if you are not tested in regard to all self-emotions.

Therefore we have a clear definition of what a higher level of Being means. A higher level of Being means an approach to unity or oneness of Being. If there were nothing above us, no goal that can be reached, there would be no definable development of Being. But there is a goal. But to attain this goal it is necessary to follow distinct directions —that is, a teaching—about how to reach it. The Work in every aspect and detail of it, is about reaching this goal. No higher level of Being is possible apart from that acquired in life, save through an extra force acting upon one. Unity of Being is not attainable through the influence of life. It is only attainable through influences coming from those who have attained this supreme development of Being. That is, *special Knowledge is necessary which must be applied to Being.* Now if you reflect on this teaching, and see what it is about for yourselves, you will see that both on the psychological and the cosmological side, it is all about raising the level of Being to unity. All the cosmological diagrams lead to unity. It is impossible in this conversation to go into everything said about this. You know that one of the great handicaps to the development of Being lies in *buffers* which prevent us from seeing inner contradictions, and that only long observation, and sincere desire to be different, can make you see inner contradictions. Do you suppose that a man full of buffers and so full of inner contradictions can reach any further stage in unity of Being? Do you suppose that a man who has no insight into himself can reach any further stage of unity in his Being? The continued action of the Work through noticing oneself begins to break up many contra-dictions in one's Being and to make many wrong expressions of Being less and less possible. For example, one sign of Being is the capacity to bear the unpleasant manifestations of others. Why is this a sign of greater Being? The answer is that you cannot do this unless you have seen in yourself what you dislike in others. Another sign of greater Being is to be able to remember and keep your aim. Why is this a sign of greater Being? It means that you are more in your conscious 'I's that are moving towards real 'I' in you. If you have not yet learned to distrust and so not to identify with 'I's that you already know always mislead you, how can you expect to feel more strength of Being in yourself? You are allowing your Being to be taken charge of by the worst 'I's in you. You have not begun to *select*—to separate—to throw away the bad and put the good into vessels. If you want to change your level of Being you have got to see what your level of Being is—that is, what kind of a person you are over a period—or, more strictly, what kind of 'I's you allow to take charge of you at different moments, over a period, and remember what you observed. If any 'I' in you can jump up and speak through your mouth then your state of Being is mechanical and cannot change. You have nothing conscious at work in you. You are not working on yourself and this Work therefore is not acting on you and you do not really exist.

IDENTIFYING

We speak to-night about identifying. At this time we all have to think very much about the state of being identified. We all have to struggle against being identified and we all have to resist life. Let me begin by asking this question of each of you: "Where do you place your feeling of 'I'?" It is like placing the voice. Now where you place the feeling of 'I' most mechanically is where you will most identify. If you could place the feeling of 'I' fully in *self-remembering*, and all that it means, you would not identify. But this is conscious placing, because no one can self-remember mechanically. To remember oneself is a conscious act, a conscious placing of 'I', requiring *attention* to begin with.

So let us consider *attention*. When you are paying attention, are you identified? Begin with *inner identifying*. A man may be fully identified with his inner state; he may be depressed or afraid or hurt or angry, etc.—and simply *be* his state. Then his feeling of 'I' and his state are one and the same. This is inner identifying. The man is identified with himself. His feeling of 'I' is placed in his mood. Now supposing he observes his state. This requires attention. As you know, attention puts us in more conscious parts of centres. Understand clearly that no one can observe himself mechanically. He may imagine he is observing himself, but he is not, and he is learning nothing new about himself but merely revolving in a circle. In fact, mechanical self-observation is one of the mental habits to be observed. Now, to ask this question again: When you are paying attention are you identified? To answer this question in connection with inner identifying, it means: "When you are identified with your inner state and observe it, are you still fully identified?" How can you be?

In the Work we all have a very powerful instrument in us called non-identifying. But how long it takes for any of us to see what it means and to use it. If a man is always identified with his inner state of the moment, with his thoughts and his moods, etc. then he cannot change. For a man to shift from the position he is in, he must first divide himself into two. That is, he must be able to observe his state. If he is his state, then nothing can take place. If he divides himself into an observing side and an observed side—that is, becomes *two*—then he begins to be able to shift his position, to change internally. Do you understand the depth of this idea? It is the way out of the prison of oneself.

Now, as regards being identified with life, take a first example like this: If you are paying careful attention to the horses in a race, one of which you have backed, are you identified? The answer is: Yes and No. In so far as you are paying attention you are not identified. In so far that you are anxious your horse should win, you are identified and cannot pay attention. So the two states—the state of attention and the state of being identified—struggle with each other. Take a second example like this: If you are in a great hurry to get an important letter finished, then you are identified. But if after many abortive attempts you find it necessary to attend carefully to what you are writing, you are not identified *while in this state of attention,* although you may remain identified as it were, in the background—that is, in mechanical parts of centres you may still be identified, but since you have had to move into more conscious parts of centres to write the letter properly, while in them you are not identified. In these examples, the man is conscious within mechanicalness. Let us note that it is also possible to be mechanical within consciousness.

Now let us speak in general of the state of being identified with life. What is life? I do not mean to ask this question in a philosophical or theoretical sense, but in a practical sense. *Life is a series of events on different scales.* It is not things, people, objects, but events that bring these things and people and objects into different relations with you at different times. The pen on your table is not an event itself but becomes part of a small event when you pick it up to sign a cheque. In this event, the pen, the cheque-book, the table, the ink, and yourself and the person to whom you make out the cheque, etc. are all suddenly connected together. This is an event. Next moment, the pen, the cheque-book and so on, fall, as it were, apart, and lie silent and motionless. Your water-tap is not an event to you except when you have a bath or unless it leaks. Your bed is not an event unless you go to bed. A nail may lie on your mantelpiece. This is not an event. Suddenly, you want to hang a picture. Then the nail gets caught up into an event. Your neighbour next door may be a person unknown to you. He is not an event. But you hear he has called you a fool and suddenly an event between you and your neighbour takes place. The leaves lie motionless on the road in autumn and suddenly a whirlwind comes and they are in an event. An event gathers things together, moves them about, and passes. Consider the world-event of the war. This is an event on the scale of humanity. The countries Great Britain, France, Germany, Italy, etc. are not events in themselves, but when war suddenly descends like a whirlwind and whirls them round and round, bringing them violently into a certain relationship with each other, then this is an event. The war gathers people together, moves them about, and when it has passed, the objects, the things of war, the people, will fall apart, and everyone will go home.

Now if you can begin to study life as events, what you are really studying is the Law of Three Forces, which says that every manifestation is the result of three forces. A *thing* is not an event unless it conducts one of the three forces in a triad: and any thing or person can conduct one or another of the three forces at different times and so be differently related to a particular *event*. Do you understand what this means? There is a stick and two people. There is no event. There are merely three things. Then the two people quarrel and one hits the other with the stick. All are now conducting the forces of a triad and a manifestation takes place—i.e. an event. You open an old cupboard and see an old rag-doll. It was once involved in many small events. Now it is simply a thing. You shut the cupboard-door: it remains a thing, involved in no event.

Now to talk briefly: Life can and should be seen as a series of events, not as things and people, as merely visible objects. If you can see what you are caught up by as a particular sort of event, it is an act of attention to do so, and makes it possible not to identify with it so much. All events recur. There are only a certain number. All possible events on earth were, so to speak, created with Man. Man was created with his life—with all the events possible to happen to him. Events are on different scales. Now ask yourself: "What event am I in? and am I totally identified with it?" This puts you in attention. This prevents you from being so identified with the event. Life keeps Man asleep and draws all his force from him, by a number of well-worn events with which he is always identified. But everyone must enter as if afresh and should pass through as many as possible of these different shows and side-shows of the great circus on earth called life, so as to have plenty of material on rolls in centres, plenty of experiences, for otherwise the necessary contrast between life and this Work is not possible—i.e. a person who knows nothing of life sees little difference between it and the Work and so has no basis of contrast or tension of opposites in him. That is, he takes life and the Work on the same scale. If you can draw back internally from whatever event you are identifying with in life, and try to formulate the event—like this: "This is called being blamed for something I did not do," "This is called losing one's temper," "This is called being insulted," "This is called being overlooked," "This is called losing something," "This is called being disappointed," "This is called being in a mess," "This is called being late," etc. etc.—then you will not identify so much.

Birdlip, October 26, 1942

PERSONAL AIM

We can all understand what aim means in life. It gives us a direction. Without aim we are aimless—going nowhere. Even without having aim in life perhaps we simply want to keep alive as long as possible or keep our money, comforts, etc. This is a kind of aim, but very poor. We are not going anywhere but simply clinging to what we have. But we may want a definite job or to pass an examination, and then we have definite aim and direction in life. We then find we have to make sacrifices to attain it—to discard what is useless and concentrate on what is useful to attain this aim in life.

Now aim in the Work has some similarities to aim in life. But it is different in many ways. A comparison can be made up to a point. But actually aim in the Work is not really the same, because it is aim in a different direction from life, and in a way is against life.

Now we speak to-night of Personal Aim, in the Work-sense, on Being.

The most general definition of what aim means in the Work-sense is that it is to *hear* what the Work teaches and to *do* what it says.

Aim in the Work is always connected with the act of self-remembering. This is because in the state of self-remembering a man can receive help, which cannot reach him in his ordinary states of consciousness. Certain influences in the Universe can only penetrate as far as the third state of consciousness, where a man is conscious *to* himself or self-conscious. If at the same time as he remembers himself he remembers his aim, he may get help. For example, he may understand his aim better.

Aim may be too general, or contain an inner contradiction, or be too difficult; or it may be too complicated and must be broken up into simpler parts; or it may have no sense in it. In making aim people usually try to run before they can walk.

In regard to Work on Being, the first aim in this Work is self-knowledge—Knowledge of one's Being. This applies to everyone. Knowledge of the Work is one thing: self-knowledge is another thing. Without self-knowledge you cannot make any aim about yourself. Real self-knowledge as distinct from imaginary ideas and illusions about oneself can only come from direct and long-continued personal observation of the different sides of oneself. That is why this Work begins with *self-observation*. You must see how you act, how you speak, and what things are in you, in this thing called "yourself" which you take for granted. This Work gives you careful instructions as to what you must observe; these instructions should be followed not for themselves but for what they lead to. They are a means, not an end: they tell you what things keep you asleep. All the many things you are told *not* to do, and the few things you are told to do, in the Work, are connected with the idea that Man can awaken from sleep and come under better influences. This is the grand aim of the Work. You must never forget this because personal aim must agree with the whole aim of the Work, which is awakening. It must lie in the same direction and not in some other or opposite one, because otherwise a contradiction appears. If you are studying a system about awaking from sleep, you cannot make a personal aim that causes you to sleep more deeply than ever.

Personal aim can only begin after some real self-knowledge is gained through direct observation in the light of the instructions of the Work. In order to work on your Being, you must see something in your Being to work on. You cannot work on nothing. At first all is in darkness and you can see nothing in yourself. Conscious objective self-observation begins to let in a ray of light and you begin to see some things dimly. This light, created by the friction of self-observation, should gradually get stronger by practice until you catch sight of something in you clearly and beyond any doubt. You will probably be startled. If so, you are now in a position to make a personal aim—namely, to work against this thing you have seen in yourself. Suppose it to be some bad negative emotion, some really evil ill-will. Hitherto you have identified with it and so you have been it and it has been you. You have been for years under its power. Your task will be to *separate yourself* internally from it; and not, as it were, touch it internally more than you can help. This will be a personal aim on the side of work upon your Being. But most people are satisfied with themselves, although not with their circumstances. So when they are told they must work on their Being, they either do not understand what it means or do not see why they should. Now if a man in the Work is capable of observing himself sincerely, he cannot remain satisfied with himself for long *in the light of the Work*. From a life-point-of-view a man may see no reason to work on himself. But the Work-point-of-view is different from the life-point-of-view. The Work is about awakening: whereas life puts Man to sleep and tries to prevent him from awakening and makes him do things that keep him asleep.

So you must distinguish between life and the Work. There may be no reason why you should not do something in life, but every reason why you should not do it in the Work. Unless you make this distinction you will be in a confusion about the meaning of aim in the Work. For example, in life you can dislike everyone if you want to, and hate people and talk scandal and enjoy your negative emotions. But in the Work you cannot do this because you are destroying yourself inside—you are simply poisoning yourself. If you are in this Work you are under more laws than the ordinary person. This means you have to do additional things. You have to *work*. But the laws you put yourself under lead to your own inner evolution and eventual freedom from the laws of the earth.

Many people in the Work find difficulty in understanding what personal aim means, in regard to work on the side of their Being—that is, on the kind of people they mechanically are. Here is a definite stage in the Work. They cannot see what to work on in themselves. One reason is that they do not apply the ideas of the Work to themselves and do not try to do *what the Work tells them to do*. They do not observe themselves from this angle. Being satisfied with themselves in life, they do not see the *place*, so to speak, where Work on themselves begins. They are not estimating themselves from what the Work says but from life-standards. But the Work-standards are quite different from life-standards. You may be all right in life but all wrong in the Work. That is why it is necessary to realize that the Work is *a new way of thinking*. It is a new standard, a new thing altogether, from which you can begin to estimate yourself in quite another light—not in the light of external life but in the light of the Work. The Work is to make you think differently—it is to change your mind, change your ways of thinking, so that you begin to look at yourself in a new way. (This is *metánoia*). Imagine a collection of monkeys. They may be perfectly good monkeys and satisfied with themselves. But if they have to become responsible human beings, they must follow a new way of thinking, a new conception of what they must be. And, from the standpoint of conscious humanity —that is, fully developed men who have reached the level of the divine Intelligence of the Sun and its laws—we are nothing but monkeys and of really no importance. We are nothing but an experiment in self-evolution.

All personal aim on a small scale is a means, not an end. It is to make you think and awaken, to keep you awake. Aim is on different scales. Aim on a great scale is to be awakened from sleep, to attain inner liberation. But to say that this is one's aim is not enough. You may see something in the far distance as your aim but in order to get to it you find that many lesser aims are necessary. You may say you want to go to China. But to get there, you must do many things in between and you must have enough money to buy a ticket. Mr. Ouspensky said that aim is like this: You see far off a light that you wish to reach. But on approaching it, you find many lesser lights, like lamp-posts along a road, that you must pass one by one, before you attain the final aim. Let us suppose a man aims at becoming a conscious man, and escaping from the circle of mechanical humanity. He does not, of course, understand what this means—that is, he does not understand his aim. To become No. 5 or 6 or 7 Man, a man must first become No. 4 man—that is, Balanced Man, a man in whom all his centres work rightly—Intellectual, Emotional, Instinctive-Moving. Now to become *balanced* a man must begin to notice what centre in him predominates and interferes with the proper development of his other centres. An instinctive man, for instance, a man who consults his own comfort first, who loves agreeable bodily sensations before anything else, cannot become *Balanced Man*, because all his psychic energy is used up in his agreeable bodily sensations. His aim then must be to work against the predominance of one centre in him, which causes him to be lop-sided and prevents the other centres from developing. But if you have under-stood what has been said so far, you will see that in such a case it is only by seeing himself and estimating his inner state *in the light of the Work* that he will become dissatisfied with himself. Viewing himself from life, there is no reason why he should attempt to be different from what he is. Or let us take a man whose centre of gravity is in the Intellectual Centre. He is only interested in theories and abstractions. In life, there is no reason why he should be dissatisfied with himself. But observing himself in the light of the teaching of the Work, he will begin to be dissatisfied with his state of being.

It is only through understanding the ideas of the Work that a man can make Work aim. It is only by beginning to think in a new way and viewing himself in that light that he can make a Work aim. You cannot make a Work aim if you think as you always did. By seeing himself in the light of the Work view of him a man can see what is wrong with him *in a Work sense*. In a life-sense he will see nothing wrong with him. Life will not judge him, but the Work will judge him; and exactly in terms of his valuation and understanding of it—that is, he will begin to judge himself. For the Work judges no one. The man himself will begin to judge himself, and when this once begins, the man has a *point in the Work* in himself.

Now as regards the often-asked question: "Can you give me examples of what personal aim means?" On the side of knowledge, personal aim means to become familiar with the ideas of the Work. On the side of Being, personal aim means to observe yourself in the light of the knowledge of the Work and apply it to yourself. Personal work on your own Being begins when you notice something that the Work tells you about in yourself. Have you noticed in yourself when you are negative? Have you noticed in yourself where you are too identified? Have you noticed day-dreaming? Have you noticed wrong talking? Have you noticed what false personality means in yourself? Have you noticed where you justify yourself? Have you noticed lying in yourself? Have you noticed what sleep means? Have you noticed what making accounts means?—and so on. Start with one single thing that you have noticed and begin to watch it and try to work against it. But start with something you have no doubt about. Start with something clear and distinct and try for a time to observe it and not consent to it internally. Once you start, the way opens out. But you must actually start from something definite and you must do this in the light of the meaning of the Work and its great aim. If you find you cannot keep your aim as first intended, because it is too difficult, modify your aim, and then you may find that a better aim is suggested to you, especially if you remember your aim whenever you try to remember yourself.

Everything taught in this Work on its practical side shews more than one aim to you. You must begin with one thing. But after a time you must include all the rest. For example, you cannot confine yourself simply to working, say, on one form of irritation or one form of negative emotion and not do anything else. If you really start to work on your being, from one thing in the Work, you will find that it is necessary to do all the other things in order to keep your aim. You must understand that if you hold too long to one small aim exclusively and neglect everything else in the Work, it is useless. Your aim, whatever it starts with, must eventually regard all other things you are taught in the Work. Otherwise you simply make your aim ineffective, if not worse, because it is unsupported. But you must start with one definite thing that you have observed in yourself and then you will find that everything else taught you is necessary as well, if you wish to keep the aim that you began with. Every side of the practical teaching of the Work must become your aim. And then, if you cannot work in one way, you will find you can work in another way. The whole teaching is necessary to effect any change in Being.

Here are some suggestions of aim:

Anything anti-mechanical is a temporary aim and helps us to awaken. All making of effort against mechanicalness is aim. Efforts made when you are tired are useful, if you yourself make them—not otherwise.

Aim must be made by everyone about wrong talking, negative talking, scandal, gossiping, which destroys the force of the Work in you. It is a form of lying—and lying can destroy essence itself. Try to notice what you say. If you cannot at the time, go through it afterwards. Try to see what you are like in your talking and think about this.

Find out what helps and what hinders you in working and *what stops you from working.*

By keeping to Work aim we create will. You should weigh your aim and see what you are prepared to give up for it. *Aim requires effort.*

Notice what you regard as a nuisance and make yourself passive for a time.

Notice your inner doubts and try occasionally to answer them clearly from the Work-ideas. This is a very good occasional aim and makes you think.

Observe your boredom and your tendency to speak of your life as dreary and so on. This is very important, as it prevents a lot of self-poisoning.

When you have just criticized someone, go over what you said carefully and apply it to yourself. This neutralizes poison in you.

When you are alone, do not let yourself think you are quite alone, and out of the Work. People allow themselves to change too much in this respect—they let go, so to speak.

Remember in regard to making aim about negative emotions that emotions are much quicker than time. You may not be able to check them at first, but you can remember them afterwards and realize what has happened. This makes it possible to know them *beforehand.*

Aim must be made from Work 'I's, not mechanical 'I's. You cannot make aim suddenly. People in life swear they will not do this or that again. In the Work you must not "swear" like this. It leads to nothing. Aim must be made consciously, with insight, after long observation, in view of realizing what is putting you to sleep and what helps you to keep awake.

Finally, you must all remember that in this Work the development of all parts of centres is an aim. This means that you must overcome ignorance and get to know as many as possible of the branches of knowledge and study that exist in life because each one develops some particular part of a centre. If you do this in the light of the meaning of the Work, understanding why it is necessary, it will help you to awaken.

But if you do it from a life-point-of-view in order to be superior to other people, to out-rival others, you will be doing it in a useless way. And do not think that because others know more than you do about any particular subject or craft that you can learn that it is not worth while. The point of this Work is self-development, development of *yourself* on every side, and whether other people do anything better than you makes not the slightest difference. Remember that to take up anything new requires effort. Wherever you find yourself in life if you are in this Work you should be able to " make good "—to take it as Work. This aspect of the Work can give you many different kinds of aims.

This can be generalized under the Work phrase: "*Struggle against ignorance.*"

Birdlip, October 31, 1942

THE PLACE OF AIM

INTRODUCTION

Last time we spoke about the necessity of aim. To-night we will try to speak about the *place* where aim comes from. Last time it was said that to find any real aim in the Work-sense it is necessary to think of oneself in the light of the knowledge taught by the Work. This can only begin after a long period of self-observation, so that one can actually see what one is like in view of the Work. It was also said that a person may be all right in life but all wrong in the Work. For example, a person can enjoy being negative in life if he wants to, but not in the Work. That is, the Work changes our view of ourselves and makes us think in a new way about ourselves. To-night we speak of aim in regard to where it comes from in oneself.

*   *   *

Part I.—Aim can come from right or wrong places in us. Aim may be right and come from a wrong place, and aim may be wrong and yet come from a right place. In order to understand what this means, we have to turn back to centres and parts of centres and also speak a little about Attention once more. Aim comes from a wrong place when it comes from small mechanical divisions of centres, where attention is at a minimum or passes from one trifle to another—where, in fact, there is zero-attention, or only a number of separate small attentions, and no comprehensive attention. Aim cannot come from these small scattered

177

attentions, which belong to mechanical divisions of centres. It must be formed and must come from higher divisions where the *quality* of attention is different. Ordinary attention is not sufficient. Some time ago, Mr. Ouspensky, in speaking about attention, said that ordinary attention, which goes here and there all the time, is not really attention. He said that only attention that could keep its direction for some time could be called attention. And I remember that he began here to speak of how people gave so much attention to small things and were constantly distracted by them and remarked that if we wasted all the force of our attention on small things we had no attention for bigger things. In that case, it would be a long time before we could increase our attention. He said it was necessary to struggle against giving too much attention to small things. Small things did not need much attention. The moving parts of centres could perform their small daily tasks with little attention. Now unless we have some power of free attention we cannot expect to keep aim or indeed learn what the Work is about because we will be occupied with small things and the Work can never be understood if it is taken either as a small thing or on the level of small things. The reason is that the mind is not one and the same, but has smaller and bigger parts, and the Work belongs to its bigger part and cannot fit into and so cannot be grasped by its smaller parts. Each centre has first of all three divisions corresponding to the three centres themselves, Intellectual, Emotional and Instinct-Moving Centre. Now it is in the moving parts of centres that small things lie, and here, let us notice, in these parts, nothing belongs to us and so we cannot make aim from these parts. This is interesting to think about. What lies in the mechanical or moving parts of your Intellectual Centre, for example, does not belong to you. These small mechanical parts are filled with conversations you have heard, newspapers you have read, all sorts of tittle-tattle, phrases, pictures and words, etc. and these things do not belong to you at all. They come and go. But aim must not come and go. It must belong to you. Now when we take in anything in *Emotional* or *Intellectual* parts of centres, then it begins to belong to us and can even create something. And it is here that the ideas of the Work, and all similar ideas, such as those found in the Gospels, must fall, for here they can breathe and live and become one's own. But people in whom only the moving parts of centres are working find it impossible to make aim in the right place in themselves.

We have parts of centres for life and parts of centres for other things. The same thing, passed through different parts of centres, will look quite different. The same idea or the same phrase received in Moving, in Emotional and in Intellectual parts of centres becomes quite different. The ideas of the Work are too big for small parts of centres to take in. They will only see a small bit and will not understand what it means and so will distort it. Only bigger divisions of centres can catch sight of the whole conception of the teaching of this Work. Moving parts of centres which are turned towards external life, towards the senses, cannot grasp it, because it is not their function to do so. Not only is each distinct centre in us for a distinct purpose, but every part and sub-division. We have not one mind, but three: and in each are many minds. If we could use the particular right mind for a particular thing —that is, the right centre or part of it—we should be *balanced* in our centres. But we are nearly always out of our right mind and use the wrong centre or part. And to take this Work with mechanical parts of centres and to let it fall there is exactly an example of being out of one's right mind. To chat about the Work and then about the latest rumour, scandal, etc. is to let the Work fall on and so get mixed up with small mechanical parts of centres and with the small 'I's dwelling in these little uninteresting villas. To listen to the Work without valuation or attention is to take it with these little mechanical life 'I's. That is why the Work says that everything begins with evaluation. Certainly at first we listen to the Work as best we can. But if we have magnetic centre—that is, ears to hear—it begins to fall on emotional parts of centres.

★ ★ ★

Part II.—Once you understand that *mind*, in this teaching, is regarded as being on different levels, just as is the Universe, and the lowest level is called the moving or mechanical part of a centre, you will understand the *psychological* reason for many things. You will understand, for example, why you must not talk too much of this Work, because it tends to put it into moving parts of centres. It is better for people in the Work to talk of other things rather than do this—or if they have spoken seriously of the Work, to get into some other kind of talk as soon as possible and notice the difference. You will also understand in quite a practical way why it is said you must not take the name of God in vain. Things belonging to higher and so more conscious parts of centres must not be allowed to mix themselves up with what belongs to lower mechanical parts. This is the real meaning of *profanity*. Profanity is mixing higher and lower. It destroys the proper order of parts of centres. It messes up and destroys the very complex and delicate machine in a man, each of whose parts has a definite and distinct function. You will also understand why so much importance is attached to the possession of magnetic centre. In life there are two kinds of influences, called A and B in this system. A influences belong to life and are created by life—by politics, war, sport, money, and so on. B influences are of a different order and come from outside life. The Gospels are an example. They come from conscious mankind, not mechanical humanity. Now notice this carefully: Moving parts of centres can only take in A influences and are only meant to do so; B influences fall on emotional parts of centres; and C influences, if you meet with them, which come directly from Conscious Man, fall on intellectual parts.

179

By treating the matter in this way, you see how things all fall into their right places.

To get into higher—that is, more conscious—parts of centres, the act of attention is necessary. It is easier to remain in moving or mechanical parts and it is interesting to notice how we avoid the effort. To become more conscious of our lives and of what we are like, it is necessary to be in more conscious parts of centres—that is, in those parts that can see several things together and not only one at a time. Self-observation leads to an increase of the consciousness of oneself, of one's life, and from this aim becomes clearer. You begin to see what is wrong, not just at the moment, but what runs through your life. This is not possible to see from moving parts of centres. Here the life cannot be seen but only the moment. So to make aim from mechanical 'I's in moving parts of centres is quite wrong. They only see through narrow chinks. So it becomes important to think of *where* you make aim from, as well as *what* your aim is. You cannot, of course, make a permanent aim suddenly. You cannot exclaim suddenly: "I swear I will never identify again, or never be negative," and so on. Larger and more permanent aim in the Work must be based on self-knowledge gained through practical self-observation. Take negative emotions. They are a big question. You cannot suddenly make an aim about them. You can and should begin by making the temporary aim of not expressing them, as the Work suggests. This helps you to observe them better. Then you can see gradually that if you waste so much force on being negative you have no force for anything else, such as happiness, for instance. Then you may see you cannot get into attention and so cannot get into better parts of centres if all your force is drawn into this useless direction. After you have seen all this for yourself and many other things, then you may begin to make a more permanent and real aim about some of your negative states, and one that comes *from the right place* in you. For you will understand better what you are doing and so will be doing it more from yourself, and what belongs to you. But if, hearing that one must struggle against negative states, you make an aim from a little imitative 'I', in the moving part of a centre, just because you heard it was the thing to do, and jotted it down in your note-book like a good scholar, you will not understand anything about your aim. It will not belong to you. Aim will be perhaps right, but will come from an utterly wrong place. So it is important to think of *where* aim comes from and not only *what* your aim is. Or to take another example, suppose you aim at getting over your unwanted associations about people. If you do this simply from moving parts of centres—from small mechanical 'I's—these 'I's will see no reason why you should, because these unwanted mechanical associations are their special work. You are telling a factory not to do its special job. The unwanted associations lie in mechanical parts, in mechanical 'I's. But if in this case you think about the people in connection with the Work, you will be lifted out of mechanical parts of centres and mechanical associations.

You will take them on another level. All the chances we have depend on the existence of another level. Your aim will then come from the right place and may have results. That is, you may be able to get quite a new way of taking people whom mechanically you dislike, and so on, and you may see their mechanicalness in terms of what you see in your own mechanicalness. So you see again that aim may be right, but it is *where* it comes from in you that is so important. You can do many things quite easily or more easily from the level of the Work, which are impossible if you try to do them from the level of life. The explanation lies in these different parts of centres and from what part your aim comes. For this reason it is necessary to know, by observation, where you are in yourself—in what part of the large psychological house you are, and not to try to do things when you are in the basement that belong to another floor, and vice versa. It is quite a practical question to ask yourself: "Where am I?" You may be close to a very bad and narrow and evil 'I' or in very small parts of centres, where your powers of attention are zero. Then you must not expect to make important decisions successfully, or, if you are looking forward to something, expect it to go very well. You will spoil it without doubt. The mere act of attention, due to self-observation, may change your position in yourself, and get you into a better place. You know you can be in a place in outer space and not be in the right place in inner space. We know a lot about being in the wrong or right place externally, in space, but very little about being in the wrong or right place internally, in ourselves—and the latter is far more important. Of course, as long as you take yourself as *one*, you cannot understand what this means. But once, by observation, you see you are *many* and that you have many *places* in you, it becomes easier to grasp. And bear in mind that the Work teaches, as a practical thing, that by means of directed attention we can change our inner position.

Birdlip, November 14, 1942

ON HYDROGENS

I

After a long interval we are going to speak again to-night about the cosmological side of the Work. This is so great a subject that I suppose it can never be exhausted by us. It is all about the fact that Man is in the Universe and the Universe in Man, so you cannot expect it to be easily explained. For this reason there exists in this Work a Psychological and a Cosmological side, which interconnect and which are gradually understood. Otherwise there could be no *real* Psychology. The Work says Man cannot be taken apart from the Universe, or Cosmos, in which he exists, nor can the Cosmos be taken apart from Man. The *Great World* in which Man appears is the *Macrocosmos* and Man in it *should be* a *Microcosmos*, or little Universe—that is, he has in him the possibilities of reflecting the Universe in himself and being in harmony with it.

We have already spoken of the small side-octave from the Sun in the Great Ray of Creation, in which *Man* finds his place and at this point we stopped, in our study of the cosmological side of the Work, and began to study the ideas in the parables of the Gospels from this standpoint. Man does not appear in the Great Ray itself. Man is an experiment of the Sun in self-evolution. As a part of Organic Life on Earth, he serves nature. He serves the evolution of the Earth and its Moon. But he is created by the Sun with the possibility of another fate, if he tries to awaken. That is why the Work and all similar teaching exists on Earth—to awaken Man, who is only in the service of nature as long as he is asleep, so that he can awaken and come under more intelligent influences and finally return to his source of origin. This is the double aspect of Man, and this is why *Man* in the Work is divided into Man asleep or *mechanical Man*, and Man awakening or partly awakened or fully awakened—that is, *conscious Man.*

Now in what follows I am going to speak very briefly and give a mere outline of all the many different ideas which are derived in this Work from the first great cosmological diagram, the Ray of Creation. This diagram starts from the Absolute and descends in stages to the smallest and most undeveloped parts of the Universe, in a scale of descending order. Our Ray of Creation descends to our Moon. To-night we are going to connect with this diagram the idea of different *matters* or *energies* at different levels of the Ray. Matter and energy in this system are spoken of together, as being different sides of the same thing. The first thing you must understand in this respect is that at the top of the Ray the very finest matter exists and at the bottom of the Ray the coarsest or grossest matters exist. This gives you the idea of *different materialities* belonging to each stage of creation. As the creative process, following the Law of Three Forces, and manifesting itself in successive stages according to the Law of Seven or the Law of the Octave—as the creative process descends, the *materiality* of each level of creation becomes *denser*. With the highest level, the Absolute itself, we must associate the *finest* matter and so the *greatest* energy. With the Moon at the bottom of the Ray we must associate the coarsest matter and so the least free energy. There are matters belonging to the level of the Absolute, there are matters belonging to the level of the Starry Galaxy, to the level of the Sun, to the level of the Earth, and to the level of the Moon. Once you grasp that the Universe is a Descending Scale of Creation, becoming further away from the Absolute and, as it were, colder and denser, you will realize something of what it means when the Work speaks of a *point in the Universe.* A point in the Universe occurs where a particular form of matter is found—or let us call it *matter-energy.* Visibly, we can understand that the materiality of the incandescent Sun is finer than the materiality of the chairs and tables on the Earth—or indeed the materiality of Earth as a substance—which could not exist in the Sun. If then we only grasp at present that the act of creation is a series of successive *condensations* we shall not be far wrong. Seen in this light the Universe, as a Scale of Descent proceeding from the Absolute, is a series of energies or *matter-energies.* Or, in brief, a series of *different materialities.* In this system these different points in the Universe or different matters are called *Hydrogens.* For the present you must accept this term without explanation. The Universe is a series of *Hydrogens* or matters, starting from the top and descending to the bottom. These "Hydrogens" or matter-energies increase in density as they go downwards. They become coarser, thicker, or heavier, so to speak.

Here is a diagram shewing how the Universe is turned into a series of Matter-Energies. First, four points are taken in the Ray of Creation —Absolute, Sun, Earth and Moon. They are connected by 3 octaves, and the result is called the 3 Octaves of Radiation. The first 3 notes *Do, Si, La,* form the first energy-matter or Hydrogen, and so on. All this will be explained in full detail at some other time. My object here is to give you an idea of what *Hydrogen* means so that I can go on to several other diagrams. As long as you gain the conception that these Hydrogens or Energies are formed at different *levels* of the Ray as it descends, it will be sufficient. Now the Hydrogens are scaled down, as you see in the last column. This is because *in Man* only certain Hydrogens are or can be present. Man has not *all* the matters or energies that compose the Universe in him. He has not, for example, the matter of the Absolute. The third column gives the Hydrogens found in Man, or rather, that Man can have in him. Study this diagram for a little. You will see that the Universe in order of descent has been turned now into a Universe of energies of different qualities and densities coming from different *points* in the Ray of Creation. The first four Hydrogens, *6, 12, 24* and *48* are *Psychic.* That is, they are the energies that are "psychological". They are the energies that the centres in Man work with. The fifth Hydrogen—*96*—is called "Animal Magnetism". The sixth—*192*—is called "air". Then comes *384* "water", *768* "Food," then *1536*, which includes substances like wood, fibres, grass, then *3072*, called minerals. All these Hydrogens occur *in Man.* And because he has these matters in him, he represents the cosmos (up to a point) in himself. Notice that at a certain point, these Hydrogens become "visible." The Psychic Hydrogens are "invisible."

Now let us apply these Hydrogens to Man, regarded as a 3-storey Factory. Three Foods enter Man—which in terms of Hydrogens are Hydrogens *48, 192* and *768.*

Diagram (1)

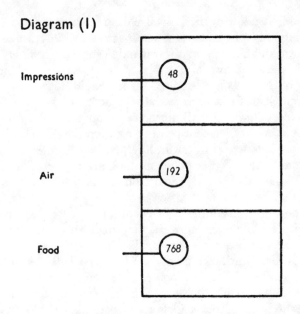

Man is fed by the Universe from three points in it. These Hydrogens become *digested*. Let us trace the Digestion of *768*. Digestion is *Transformation*. The Body transforms lower Hydrogens into higher Hydrogens by the law of octaves. Speaking briefly, *768* is transformed into *384*, etc. until Hydrogen *12* is reached.

Diagram (2)

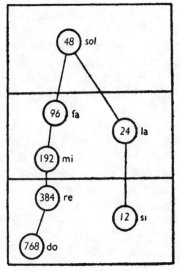

Now, since we are speaking briefly, we will leave out the air octave, and speak about the transformation of Impressions *48*. This does not proceed by itself save in small quantities. Yet this is the most important octave of *digestion* in the Body.

Diagram (3)

Food of impressions

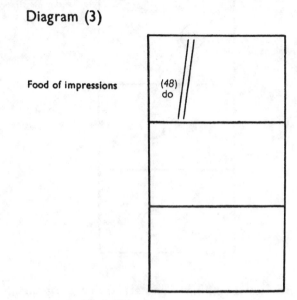

This energy stops unless something is brought up to it to *digest* it. If the octave is started it forms *extra Hydrogens* in the Body.

Diagram (4)

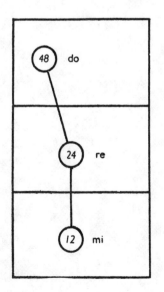

The First Conscious Shock must be given, however, to effect this. As thus:

Diagram (5)

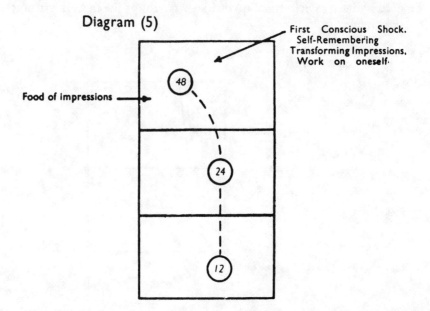

First Conscious Shock.
Self-Remembering
Transforming Impressions.
Work on oneself.

Food of Impressions

48

24

12

When a man *works* on himself he starts the octave going and creates new *energies* in himself. This is when the Work starts in a man as regards the creation of new forces in him. I want you all merely to understand the general idea. All details can be left until later.

Our Ray of Creation	Law of Seven	Three Octaves of Radiation	Law of Three	Hydro-gens	First Scaling down	Second Scaling down	
Absolute	Do	Absolute	Do				
			Si	H 6			
			La				
All Worlds	Si		Sol	H 12	H 6		
			Fa				
Galaxy	La		▭	H 24	H 12	H 6	Absolute for Man
			Mi				
			Re	H 48	H 24	H 12	
Sun	Sol	☀	Do				
			Si	H 96	H 48	H 24	Psychic Energies
			La				
			Sol	H 192	H 96	H 48	
Planets	Fa		Fa				
			▭	H 384	H 192	H 96	Animal Magnetism
			Mi				
			Re	H 768	H 384	H 192	"Air"
Earth	Mi	◯	Do				
			Si	H 1536	H 768	H 384	"Water"
			La				
			Sol	H 3072	H 1536	H 768	"Food for Man"
			Fa				
			▭	H 6144	H 3072	H 1536	"Wood"
			Mi				
			Re	H 12288	H 6144	H 3072	"Stone"
Moon	Re	☾	Do				

ON HYDROGENS

II

THE FOOD OCTAVE

To-night we speak only of the Food Octave.

Regarded as an octave, the Ray of Creation, starting with the note *Do* at the upper level of the Absolute and reaching the note *Re* below at the level of the Moon, is a *descending* octave: *Do-Si-La-Sol-Fa-Mi-Re*. You will see that it could not be an ascending octave once you grasp the conception of the Hydrogens or energy-levels, which are formed at different points in the descending scale of creation. The Absolute is composed of the finest possible matter. It is the Highest Energy-Level. No higher, no finer matter, or no finer, subtler, more penetrative energy, is possible. The act of creation, therefore, cannot be in the form of an *ascending* octave, for that would imply the creation of finer and finer matters than those belonging to the starting-point—i.e. the Absolute would be creating something finer than itself, which is impossible. But Man has the possibility of creating finer matters in himself. He is created as a self-developing being. That is, he can create something finer than himself and so *ascend* in the ladder of creation. Just where he can create finer energies belongs to a further talk.

The Ray of Creation is, then, necessarily a descending octave and the energy-matters belonging to. it at different points in its descent necessarily increase in density or coarseness. They become coarser and coarser the further removed they are from the source of the Ray—the Absolute itself. This is shewn by the numbers connected with the Hydrogens: *H 6*, *H 12*, *H 24*, and so on. Each number denotes a denser or coarser energy. So the Hydrogens get denser or coarser as we pass down the Ray and this is shewn clearly in the Diagrams where the relation of the Hydrogens to their positions in the Ray of Creation is given.

Now although the Octave of Creation itself is a descending octave, the octaves in the human machine are all *ascending* octaves. They go in the reverse way. The three Hydrogens in the Universe used by Man for his life enter him from outside and form starting-points or *Do's* for ascending octaves and this is *life* for Man. That is, Man as a living being *transforms* lower energy-matters into higher energy-matters. This is life. Life is transformation. Man transforms lower Hydrogens into finer Hydrogens.

To-night we take only the Food Octave, starting from the *Hydrogen 768* which is called "Food for Man". It is transformed into *Hydrogen 12* ultimately in a series of successive steps, which constitute an *ascending* octave: *Do 768* becomes by transformation *Re 384*, *Re 384* becomes *Mi 192* and so on by transformation.

Ascending Octave of Food in Man
regarded as a Three-Storey Factory.

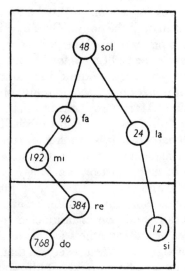

The Food taken in at
the lowest storey
H 768 "Food for Man"

As was pointed out last time, I am giving these diagrams in as simple
and abbreviated form as possible. Now the whole of this ascending
octave of *Food* represents successive stages in the *digestion* of ordinary
food taken by the mouth into the body, from the standpoint of the Work.
Many stages and steps in its digestion exist. The first digestion or transformation occurs in the mouth, stomach, etc. and this can be understood
easily enough. It is what we call "digestion of food". The food we eat
is first transformed into a finer form and as such can begin to pass
inwards through the walls of the stomach into the lymph and blood-
stream. At this stage it is called (in the Work) *Hydrogen 384* or "Water"
at the note or stage *Re*. We should make a great mistake however, in
thinking that this is the end of the process of the "digestion of food" in
the human machine. It has only begun. It is the first step in full digestion in the Work sense. *Hydrogen 384* passes to *Hydrogen 192* called
"Air", at the stage or note *Mi*. All I will say here is that just as wrong or
faulty digestion may occur in the passage of *Hydrogen 768* to *Hydrogen
384* in the stomach, etc., which is ordinary digestion, so again another
kind of wrong digestion can occur in the passage of *Hydrogen 384* into
Hydrogen 192, and this has to do with the air we breathe. That is to
say, digestion at this stage cannot go on without air. But this subject
cannot properly be included here in this simple explanation and so will
come later on. *Hydrogen 192* then passes into *Hydrogen 96* at the
note *Fa*. This is a further stage of digestion. *Hydrogen 96* at the note
Fa, or *Fa 96* is called "Animal Magnetism". Other names are given

to it. The point is that its *materiality* is intermediate between the coarser visible Hydrogens and finer invisible or psychic Hydrogens. Notice that it is made in the middle compartment of the 3-storey factory comprising the human machine.

Let us look for a moment at this *Hydrogen 96*, which appears here under the sign or at the note of *Fa*. *Fa 96* is called "Animal Magnetism" for want of a better term. If we call it simply *vitality* or *health*, we may not be using quite the right term for it. But it is connected with vitality or health and yet it is not quite the same. Physical vitality or health depends as much on proper amounts of *Hydrogen 384* and *192*. The term "Animal Magnetism" means something "animal" and so in a way something "physical", some sort of vitality or health: the term "magnetism" denotes that it is at a higher level. A man may not enjoy very good physical health, in the ordinary sense, and yet possess the resiliency and strength that comes from having *Fa 96*. A person, indeed, may be ill physically and yet possess sufficient quantities of the substance called *Fa 96* to make him transcend illness, and on the other hand he may be well physically and possess insufficient quantities of *Fa 96* and have little power of making others feel better. Long ago someone asked G. what *Fa 96* signified: the answer was that if you had sufficient quantities of this Hydrogen "fleas would not bite you." Of course, naturally, some people who heard this answer were shocked and considered it irrelevant and crude. But the idea is exactly expressed in this answer. *Fa 96* is something that protects us, as it were, like an "envelope" surrounding us. Now let us look at its position. As was said, it is manufactured in the second storey. As you know, in the diagram of the centres in Man, the *emotional centre* comes in the second storey. It dominates it. Therefore the formation of *Fa 96* is interfered with if the emotional state is wrong. Negative emotion, despair, nervous fear, wrong imagination, jealousy, depression, anxiety, chronic dislike, constant worrying, and so on, are all negative states of the emotional centre. Such states occurring in the second compartment of the human machine may prevent the formation of *Fa 96* in sufficient quantities and so deplete a man of this important substance. He is then robbed of his "Animal Magnetism". That is, this step in the digestion of food is interfered with and so he suffers a particular form of "indigestion" at this point which prevents the octave of food from developing further in its right way. Sometimes very negative people, or some kinds of sick people, can drain a person of *Fa 96*—but only if one identifies with them. Then one feels drained, although one may be quite well otherwise, whereas contact with a person with *Fa 96* gives one energy. People who are habitually negative and especially perhaps those who are evil in their long-developed jealousies and hatreds and so on feed on *Fa 96* in others and actually have a delight in exhausting them, especially in the case of young people. They are the real vampires, so to speak, who suck that aspect of the blood called *Fa 96*. One should always avoid contact with them. Again, simply dull, depressed people, who make no effort in life can without any evil intention sometimes drain another person in the same way of this very important force. But remember only for the time being that all negative states of oneself can prevent the proper formation of *Fa 96*, which is a very important energy in the human machine and protects us from many ills, both physical and psychic.

The next stage (in the full digestion of food from the Work point of view) is the passage of *Fa 96* into *Sol 48*. This *Hydrogen 48* is the first mental or psychic Hydrogen. It is the lowest energy-matter used for thinking. It is used by the formatory side of the Intellectual Centre— the ordinary thinking part in life. If the formation of *Fa 96* is being interfered with—say, by negative states, by internal considering, by self-pity, or any other cause—then very little *Sol 48* is made. So the person cannot concentrate, cannot think clearly, cannot make any effort of *mind*. And this is often the first sign of nervous breakdown.

The next stage in "digestion"—that is, transformation—consists in the passage of *Sol 48* to *La 24*. *Hydrogen 24* is the energy (or "petrol") that works the Emotional Centre. This "petrol" can be used up entirely in negative emotions, in which case the final stage of the digestion of food—namely, the passage of *La 24* into *Si 12*—is interfered with. *Hydrogen 12* is the energy that works the sex centre. This centre rarely works with its own energy.

Now all this is very brief and you will see that many things could be said. What you should grasp, as a principle, is that the *full* digestion of food in the human machine (in the Work teaching) consists of six stages. It goes far beyond the ordinary scientific idea of "digestion". And you will see that at every stage mal-transformation or "indigestion" may occur.

Now in a balanced man all the different energies or Hydrogens or "Petrols" are used in proper amounts at their different points of manufacture. But suppose, let us say, a man is engaged in formatory work. Say he studies day and night. He uses *Hydrogen 48*—that is, *Sol 48*— for this purpose. If he uses too much, then none, or very little, is available for the further passage of it to *La 24* and *Si 12*. His emotional and his sex life are starved. In other words, there is a *use* and *mis-use* of every Hydrogen in the body. For if a man does not use *Hydrogen 48* enough—that is, never tries to think, never applies his mind to anything —there is then a wrong accumulation of *H 48* in the centre in which it should be used. It then *poisons* the centre. But of all this we will speak more fully at another time. Remember at present that not a single activity, physical or psychic, is possible save with the appropriate and right amount of energy—that is, the necessary Hydrogen. You cannot think or feel or have sensation or move without the particular and necessary Hydrogen for the purpose present in your human machine. You all know how, if you are seriously ill, it is impossible to think or feel or move very much. This is because the Octave of Food with all the different energies or Hydrogens that are derived from it is working at very low intensity. But you may eat wrong food. That is at the beginning

—768. You start wrongly. Next, you may not have enough air—that belongs to *192*, as will be explained. Then you may be negative—that interferes with *96* and *24* and this is very serious. Or you may not think enough, or too much—that implicates *48* and so *24* and *12*. But all this is too complex to talk of save in a general outline. What you should get hold of is simply the general principle. Simply grasp that our wrong function, our wrong thinking, may interfere with everything.

Birdlip, November 30, 1942

ON HYDROGENS

III

Part I.—You must understand that the Diagram of the Centres in Man and the Diagram of Man as a Three-Storey Factory are not the same. In each, three compartments appear, upper, middle and lower, and these correspond *roughly* with the Head, with the Lungs and Heart, and with the Belly and Organs of Sex. The diagrams represent, roughly, Man in profile.

Last time we spoke of the six stages of digestion of ordinary food, which is taken into the lowest factory, as *Hydrogen 768*, and is transformed in the stomach into *Hydrogen 384*, which passes into the lymph and blood-stream and is transformed into *Hydrogen 192*, and so on by successive stages of transformation until the finest matter or energy, made mechanically in the body, is reached, namely, *Hydrogen 12*, at the note *Si*. This energy, you will notice, cannot proceed further by transformation without beginning a new octave.

It was also said that since the Emotional Centre lies in the middle compartment, all unpleasant emotional states can disturb the chemical processes of tranformation taking place in the middle compartment or laboratory. If a person is thoroughly identified with his negative emotions, or depressed, or sad, or without hope, and so on, the work of the Food Octave may be disturbed both in its up-going and down-going. That is, the formation both of *Fa 96* and *La 24* may be interfered with, and you will see plainly that if the formation of *Fa 96* is disturbed, then the formation of *Sol 48* from it will be disturbed and *Sol 48* is the first *psychic* Hydrogen, being the energy ordinarily used for thinking by the Intellectual Centre. That is, the power of thought, of concentration, will be disturbed. Remember that every human activity, whether of thought, feeling, movement, pleasure, self-love, self-satisfaction, sensation, and so on, is due to the presence of some requisite Hydrogen or Energy-Matter. For example, you cannot *think* without a supply of *Hydrogen 48* any more than you can drive a car

192

without petrol. Nor can you *move*, feel, and so on, without the appropriate energy-substance or Hydrogen being present in you in sufficient amount. Nor can you admire yourself without becoming depressed afterwards. We have a common idea that the body works with *one* energy. Actually it works with *six* energies, on different levels of intensity, and these energies or *Hydrogens*, from *384* to *12*, are derived from different levels of the created Universe, as shewn in the Ray of Creation and Three Octaves of Radiation. Notice here that *768* is not an energy *in* the body. Perhaps we do not realize that *to think* or *to feel* takes energy. To think or to feel one must have food. One cannot, of course, *think* with a beefsteak, but a beefsteak when eaten is transformed successively by stages and passes into *Hydrogen 48* and then *24* etc. and without these higher energies thinking and feeling are impossible.

*　　*　　*

Part II.—Now we have to speak of the place of shock in the Food Octave. Between *Mi 192* and *Fa 96* in the Food Octave at the "place of the missing semi-tone" a shock is necessary and this comes from Air, which enters the body as *Hydrogen 192* at the note *Do*. I will explain this later on in more detail. At present we are speaking as simply as possible about the Hydrogens made in the Body. The shock given by the air we breathe is essential to the further development of the digestion of Food. It is essential to the Food Octave at the place between *Mi* and *Fa*. If not given sufficiently, as when people breathe bad air, or do not breathe air properly owing to some nervous tension or depressed state, or for whatever reason, then the transformation of food at the stage *192* into *96* is interfered with, and in consequence the formation of the further *Hydrogens 24* and *12* is interfered with. And here, once more, the state of the Emotional Centre comes in, for the emotions influence the breathing *via* the muscular walls of the tiny air tubes in the lungs. Everyone should notice through self-observation when the breathing is easy or difficult, and what relaxation and tension mean in this respect. The *shock of air* is called a *mechanical shock*.

*　　*　　*

We must speak briefly of Air and Impressions. Air or *Hydrogen 192* entering the body as *Do* passes by itself to the stage *Mi 48*. Here this octave, the Octave of Air, reaches the "place of shock". A shock is required at this stage for the Air Octave to pass on. But this shock is not supplied by nature. The food of *Impressions* enters the Body as *Do 48* and does not proceed by transformation any further. The diagram, then, represents the Hydrogens made in Man naturally—that is, by nature. As you know, it is not in the interests of nature that Man should evolve beyond a certain point. If he did, he would no longer serve nature.

193

We have, then, in this Diagram, a picture of the energies or Hydrogens made in Man naturally. But we can easily see from it that there are two places where further energies might be made. *Do 48*—that is, impressions coming into the upper compartment of the three-storey factory—could proceed further. And also the Air Octave, which only goes by itself as far as the stage *Mi 48*, could, were a shock given it, obviously proceed further. You will notice that *Do 48* and *Mi 48* lie close together in this upper compartment. Now if *Do 48* could in some way be activated it would give a shock, or reinforce, *Mi 48*, just as *Do 192*, or Air, reinforces the Food Octave at the note *Mi 192* in the middle compartment. The activation of *Do 48* or impressions is possible, but it can only be done consciously. That is, a *conscious shock* must be given at the point of incoming impressions. This means that something must be *created* here which nature does not create for us. Nature creates for us a stomach with gastric juices, etc. into which Food, *Do 768*, passes, and in which it is digested. But nature does not create anything similar for the Food of Impressions, *Do 48*. The transformation of *Do 48* into *Re 24* is only possible through a conscious act. For this reason it is called the *First Conscious Shock*. For the ordinary purposes of life this shock is quite unnecessary. Man asleep living in a world of sleeping people and serving nature and the purposes of the Ray of Creation does not require to give himself the First Conscious Shock. Yet Man is so created that this possibility exists in him. There is a definite place where he can begin. This is the place of the First Conscious Shock, which is the act of *Remembering Oneself* or *Self-Remembering*. But this is a very concentrated definition and can only be understood gradually. The technical definition of Self-Remembering is expressed by two arrows, thus

$$\longleftarrow \hspace{-1em} \longrightarrow$$

It means that a man looks out and looks in simultaneously. He observes, say, the person, and observes his own reaction to the person, at the same time. He "sees" the impression coming from the person and "sees" his own reaction to it together. This increased state of consciousness is Self-Remembering. But I will speak of the First Conscious Shock next time and try to explain further what Self-Remembering means. What has to be understood is that unless the shock of Self-Remembering is given, no further Hydrogens are created in the Body, and if a man seeks growth of Being *extra* Hydrogens must be made in him.

Birdlip, December 5, 1942

ON HYDROGENS

IV

THE FIRST CONSCIOUS SHOCK

Introduction

To-night we will speak of the First Conscious Shock, by means of which extra Hydrogens are created in the Body. The point at which the First Conscious Shock is given is at the place of incoming impressions reaching consciousness where *Do 48* enters the upper storey of the factory and where the *Hydrogen Mi 48*, coming from the beginning of the Air Octave, is present. The Air Octave, at the stage *Mi 48*, cannot proceed to *Fa 24* unless a shock is given it, and the Octave of Impressions, starting from *Do 48*, does not even begin to develop unless it is activated by a shock. The shock that is required at this place in the upper storey is called in general the shock of Self-Remembering. But before we proceed, it must be clearly understood that this shock does not happen mechanically, as does the shock of breathing. It is a shock that must be given deliberately, by certain kinds of efforts, all connected with awakening, and these efforts are in general called *Remembering Oneself*. If this shock is successfully given, Impressions coming in to the upper storey as *Do 48*, and reaching consciousness, are transformed into *Re 24* and later into *Mi 12*. At the same time the Air Octave can pass from *Mi 48* to *Fa 24* and later to *Sol 12*. The result therefore of giving the First Conscious Shock is to create the *extra* Hydrogens *Re 24*, *Mi 12* and *Fa 24* and *Sol 12*. You will notice that there are now, in the lower storey, three *Hydrogens 12*, where there was formerly only one—namely, *Mi 12*, *Sol 12* and *Si 12*. Here is then a picture in the form of a Diagram shewing what extra energies can be created in Man when he begins to live more *consciously* and work on himself and remember himself—that is, when he begins to give himself the First Conscious Shock.

195

Diagram of Extra Hydrogens created by First Conscious Shock

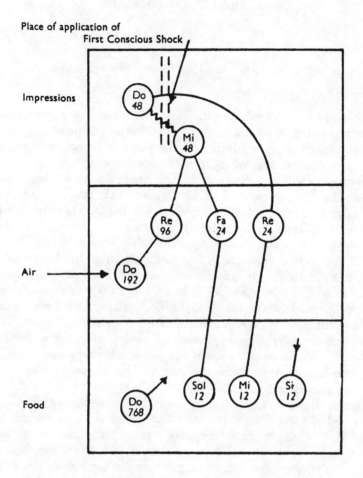

The Hydrogens made from the Food Octave are omitted save *Si 12*

Self-Remembering

For most people, even for educated and thinking people, the chief obstacle to their attaining the state of consciousness called *Self-Remembering* lies in the fact that they think they possess it already. They think that they remember themselves in everything they do and in everything they say, and they not only think that they are conscious at every moment and aware of themselves but believe that they are conscious of their inner lives also and fully aware of all the thoughts and emotions that pass through them in a continuous stream. And because they think they always remember themselves and act and speak with full consciousness and are fully aware of everything they say and do, they believe that they have real *will* and a permanent unchanging '*I*' and that they have the ability to *do*—as, for example, that they can change themselves if they really wish to, or change their lives, or change other people, or do just as they like. But of course they cannot change themselves or their lives or other people or do just as they like, because they do not possess any real will, but many contradictory wills, nor have they any permanent 'I' but many changing 'I's and when they are doing something it is not from conscious will and conscious choice but from what only can happen at that moment to them. For just as in life everything happens in the only way in which it can possibly happen, and no one really *does* anything at all, although it looks as if people do, so is it in the case of a single man. Everything in his life takes place in the only way in which it can possibly take place, and as long as the man remains the same, everything else will be the same.

It is evident that a man will not be interested if you tell him about a state of consciousness that he thinks he already possesses. And this is one reason why people find it so difficult to understand anything about the meaning of *Remembering Oneself* or the state of *Self-Awareness* or *Self-Consciousness*. They ascribe this state to themselves as they are and really believe they pass their existence in a full state of consciousness. They do not realize that they cannot help doing what they are doing. They believe that all their actions are controlled by their will, that they do everything deliberately, and so on. Yet a man's ordinary state of consciousness is almost the reverse of all this. A man ordinarily does not remember himself, he is not aware of himself, he is not properly conscious of what he does nor of what he says. Nor does he make the decisions he imagines he makes. Nor is he properly conscious of his inner life, which is actually very obscure to him. Of all the thoughts and feelings that pass through him mechanically he is scarcely conscious of a millionth part. Yet actually the state of consciousness called "Self-Remembering" in which a man is aware of himself and of all he sees round him, and at the same time aware of all the thoughts and feelings passing through him—this state of consciousness is Man's right. And if Man does not possess it, it is only because of the wrong conditions of his life. It can be said without exaggeration that at the present time, the state of consciousness called Self-Remembering (or the Third State of Consciousness) occurs in Man only in the form of rare flashes and it can only be made more permanent in him by a long and special training.

This special training begins with *self-observation*. It is only by means of observing himself uncritically and over a considerable period that a man begins to understand that he does not remember himself. He realizes that most of the time he lives in dreams. He realizes that he forgets himself, forgets his aims, forgets what he was doing or thinking and so on. But this is not all that he begins to understand. He begins to realize what it means to awaken to some extent and what it means to be asleep. Through self-observation he begins to feel the taste of what it might be to be more awake, more conscious of himself. Self-Observation is not Self-Remembering, but it enables a man to realize he does not remember himself and that most of the time he has no distinct and separate feeling of himself, no proper sense of 'I', no real consciousness of himself. From this he realizes that he lives his life in a state of sleep which people call *full consciousness*, almost as if in mockery, it might be thought, for it is in this so-called state of full consciousness that people behave as they do to one another and even kill each other without realizing what they are doing. Look at to-day. What is the real explanation of what is happening in the world? The real explanation is that people are not conscious. They are asleep and acting in their sleep. And even if they feel something of this, they do not know how to awaken from the sleep or what they must do. Yet since the creation of the world men have been told they are asleep and must awaken. How many times is this said in the Gospels: "Awake, watch, sleep not!" But people do not understand it or they think it is a metaphor whereas it is literally true. If people awakened from sleep, if they began to remember themselves, the whole of life would change. And nothing can change in life unless people begin to awaken.

It is necessary to say all this before coming to the practical side of Self-Remembering because everyone who wishes to understand this Work must have, as it were, a background of principles from which he can think about details. This Work teaches as a principle that Man is asleep and that his greatest and most important task is to awaken.

*   *   *

A man must first come to the realization that he is asleep and that he does not remember himself, before anything else can happen. And he can only gain this realization by means of observing himself uncritically at all times and over a long period. But in this system he is taught to observe certain particular things in himself which especially prevent a man from beginning to awaken. Awakening, you must understand, takes a very long time and all the first stages of the Work are to do with gradually awakening. One of the most important things to observe in oneself is the state of being identified. A man cannot remember himself if he is identified. And the more he is identified with himself, the less can he remember himself. A man is identified with pictures of himself, he is identified with his dreams, he is identified with every 'I' that for a moment takes the stage, he is identified with every mood, he is identified with every emotion, he is identified especially with his negative emotions, and he is identified with his suffering. And it must be mentioned here that this latter form of identifying must be struggled against from the very first moment of practical work on oneself. A man must give up his suffering from the very beginning. All the thousand and one forms of identifying must become subjects of self-study through self-observation. Now if a man observes that he is about to identify with, say, some negative state and at the same time remembers the Work and his aim not to identify, he may separate from this state completely. He will then probably experience a moment of Self-Remembering either then or later on. What has happened? I will try to explain. When you have practised self-observation for a certain time, you are more conscious of your inner state and in consequence you have, as it were, a moment of choice. You can see what is going to happen before it takes place. Self-Observation clears a space in your mind so that you can see things coming in and going out. If the energy which was about to go into a negative emotion is prevented from doing so, it may pass on and may create a moment of Self-Remembering. All this means that you have brought the Work up to the point of incoming impressions. Ordinarily impressions do not pass on because at the point where impressions enter the human machine, they fall on a network of long-established associations. After a time, at a certain age, people no longer experience new impressions. This is not because impressions are not new, for they are always new every moment but because they always "ring up", as it were, the same associations and produce the same reactions. People then live only in their associations and this makes their inner life almost empty, almost dead. If you wish to keep young in yourself you must take in the food of new impressions. That means, you must actually work on impressions as they enter and prevent certain of them from falling on the old places. Life is impressions coming in. You cannot change life. But you can change the way impressions fall on you. Take, for example, the question of *aim*. Everyone must have aim in this Work. He must think about it. Aim can be smaller and greater. But a man should know what his aim is, great or small, at any one moment. It gives shape and meaning to his inner life. Now if he brings his aim into consciousness—that is, does not forget it—at the point where life is acting on him through incoming impressions and prevents himself from reacting to any of these impressions in a way that is contrary to his aim, he is then in a state of Self-Awareness. His *mechanical* reaction is prevented by his conscious act. This action belongs to the First Conscious Shock. It is, so to speak, the beginning of it. The energy which would have gone into a mechanical reaction, through mechanical associations, can now pass on and become transformed first into *Hydrogen Re 24*. This is *emotional*. The result will be that either then or later he will "see something" or he will understand something in a new way—behind the network of associations. Impressions will, in fact, begin to fall directly on centres.

Impressions that are taken in in a state of Self-Remembering become emotional. Even the simplest thing can become interesting or beautiful and reflect some meaning you had never perceived.

Now as regards the question: "Which self must I remember when I try to remember myself?" First, remember the self or 'I' that knows what your aim is. This brings all the 'I's in you that wish to awaken into consciousness. Second, there is such a thing as real 'I' in us. But we are always being what we are not, substituting one 'I' after another in place of the trace of real 'I' that we have access to. Trying to feel the pure feeling of 'I' doing this, 'I' saying this, 'I' sitting here, 'I' being negative, and so on, can become sometimes a form of Self-Remembering. Full Self-Remembering is consciousness of real 'I' which stands above all the 'I's artificially created by life in us.

Finally, no one can remember himself unless he feels that there is something higher than himself. Unless he feels this, his Self-Remembering will always lead him into False Personality.

Many other things could be said about the First Conscious Shock, which has many sides to it, but enough has been given for discussion and questions. But you must all keep to the paper in your discussion and this will be an exercise in Self-Remembering for you.

Birdlip, December 14, 1942

ON HYDROGENS

V

First Conscious Shock—(*continued*)

Part I.—It has already been said that when a man tries to remember himself he must also remember his aim. When a man remembers the Work within him and his aim in it and at the same time looks out at life, this act of Self-Remembering brings the Work up to the point of entry of impressions—that is, it enables a man to take incoming life from a Work point of view and notice the reations he is about to make and prevent impressions from falling on their customary places in him and producing their habitual reactions. All this involves a struggle between "Yes" and "No". A man in such a state can see an impression about to produce a typical response in him and say "Yes" to it, or "No". If the response the impression is about to cause is contrary to the man's aim and the man says "No" to it, then he is keeping his aim. He is working on himself and *in that moment* he has sacrificed something. What has he sacrificed? The satisfaction of reacting as usual—that is, mechanically—the satisfaction, let us say, of feeling aggrieved, or the satisfaction of some unpleasant thought or some unpleasant manifestation, and so on. All this involves a struggle which is very quick and does not shew itself externally. It takes place *within* a man and has to do with his *inner* assent or *inner* refusal. It takes place *where* a man should be conscious, *where* he should be awake—and where, actually, he is asleep. *This place can be found.* It is the place where the *First Conscious Shock* is given.

*   *   *

Part II.—As was said, a man should always remember his aim when he remembers himself. A man cannot develop unless he remembers himself, for his point of development is at the point *where he remembers himself*. And here is the point where a man can struggle consciously. For a man to develop, a struggle must be set up in him—a struggle between "Yes" and "No", a struggle between aim and not-aim. But everything will depend on the nature of this struggle—that is, upon *what a man struggles for* and what he remembers as *Yes* and what as *No*. Upon this the *result* of the struggle will depend.

As a rule, there is no struggle in a man's inner life. In a mechanical man, a man who does not remember himself, a man of routine who reacts mechanically to his surroundings, in his own acquired way, who goes with his acquired habits, there is no inner struggle. A struggle only begins when he goes against his routine, his mechanicalness, which he imagines he follows from his will. But if a struggle does begin in him, especially if there is a continued and definite line in this struggle, then gradually more and more permanent traits begin to form in him as a result. But what kind of permanent traits begin to form in him will depend on the nature of the struggle and upon what is "Yes" and what is "No". A man may have a hard life, he may have to deny himself, to struggle with great adversity and hardship and so on, and as a result permanent traits may begin to form in him. But it does not follow that these permanent traits are desirable or useful to his right development in the Work—they may indeed very easily stand in the way of his real inner development. That is, before the man can develop aright, these permanent traits may have to be dissolved and a new starting-point made, and this may be impossible. A fanatical belief may cause permanent traits to form in a man so strongly that what is called in this system *crystallization* takes place in him. Something *crystallizes* out in a man—something hard in the sense of its being unyielding, permanent, fixed. This word crystallization is the term used in the Work to describe some degree of inner *fusion* of qualities.

One meaning of the saying of Christ: "Except ye *turn* and become as little children ye shall in no wise enter into the kingdom of heaven" (*Matt.* XVIII 3) is that a man meeting this Work must always turn back and *begin again*, owing to the wrong ideas and attitudes and the wrong development life has given him. And this is all the more difficult if there is some degree of crystallization in him. That is so when more or less permanent traits have been formed. Crystallization can take place for different reasons. For example, *fear* can set up a struggle in a man. He may struggle in order to overcome fear, in order to shew he is not afraid, or he may struggle because he is terrified of failure: or he may struggle because of some punishment he dreads such as fear of sin or fear of hell. In the latter case he may struggle with himself with the greatest violence and as a result *"crystallizes out"*. What is the basis of his crystallization? The basis is fear. The fear of sin, of hell, can evoke a terrible internal struggle between "Yes" and "No"; but if a man crystallizes out on this foundation, he crystallizes *in a wrong way*. Fear is not a right basis for crystallization. It is not only a wrong, but an *incomplete* crystallization, for in right crystallization all that is useful and capable of growth in a man must be included. Fear is negative. Such a man will not possess any further possibility of development as he is. For a further development to take place, he must first of all be *melted down* and this can only be accomplished by terrible suffering. All this basis of fear must be removed. What is the result of wrong crystallization? It means that something so permanent and so resistant is formed in a man that *it may survive death* and may once more enter into the world in *another* body. This is because a certain inner fusion has taken place, through the friction of the struggle between "Yes" and "No". But, as was said, friction through the struggle between "Yes" and "No" can easily take place on a wrong foundation, and result in a wrong, incomplete crystallization. In other words crystallization is possible *on any foundation good or bad*, the result being a certain "psychic" permanence capable of resisting and surviving death *for a certain time* and even of finding another physical body and entering life. For example, a man may crystallize out on the basis of revenge or hatred, and through denying himself everything that does not aid his possibilities of revenge and hatred, he may form something permanent in him that can exist after the death of the physical body—something evil.

Speaking of this possibility of psychic crystallization *on any foundation*, G. once said: "Take for example a brigand, a really good, genuine brigand. I knew such brigands in the Caucasus. He will stand with a rifle behind a stone by the roadside for eight hours without stirring. Could you do this? All the time, mind you, a struggle is going on in him. He is thirsty and hot, flies are biting him; but he stands still. Another is a monk; he is afraid of the devil; all night long he beats his head on the floor and prays. Thus crystallization is achieved. In such ways people can generate in themselves an enormous inner strength; they can endure torture; they can get what they want. This means that there is now in them something solid, something permanent. Such people can become immortal. But what is the good of it? A man of this kind becomes an 'immortal thing', although a certain amount of consciousness is sometimes preserved in him. But even this, it must be remembered, occurs very rarely."

In the above two examples given by G. you will see how in the first case a man can crystallize *wrongly* with an ordinary life-aim, and in the second, with a so-called "religious" aim. For right crystallization to take place, the struggle between "Yes" and "No" must be *on a higher level of understanding*. A man must not crystallize in small parts of centres, or in negative parts. He must first gain possession of right knowledge and then must begin to *understand* it and apply it to himself. Unless he is given right knowledge and begins to *understand* and apply it, he will not know *what* he must struggle with; and he may indeed start to struggle with something that will only do him harm. In this connection, it is interesting to notice what the Work teaches us to begin to observe and struggle with.

You will see that what it is here important to grasp is the quality of the struggle of *Yes* and *No*. What quality, what kind, of *Yes* and *No* does a man remember when he remembers himself? If a man remembers all he understands of the Work and its teaching, then the quality of his Yes and No, in his inner struggle with himself, will be right, and if crystallization begins in him on the *foundation* of the Work, it will be a right crystallization.

FURTHER NOTE ON HYDROGENS

Note on the question: Is to be conscious in a Hydrogen a Work phrase?

The question is formatory but at the same time interesting. It is necessary to think what consciousness means and what Hydrogen means. Literally, consciousness means 'knowing together'. Self-knowledge means to become more conscious, first of the different contradictory 'I's, different moods, etc., and to know them together. This signifies increase of consciousness in the sense of knowing together. Change of being can only take place through this method—namely, an increase of consciousness in this sense.

The First Conscious Shock is the transformation of *Hydrogen 48* into *Hydrogen 24* by means of *Hydrogen 12*. This has to be brought to the place of incoming impressions where it acts as Carbon. Aim, if it is really emotional and can be remembered in a moment of difficulty, brings this Carbon 12 into position. In a sense, this Carbon is the entire emotional feeling and valuation that a man has towards the Work itself. If the power to work is so great in a man that he does not forget it, and feels that his whole life and all its meaning is connected with it, then this Carbon 12 begins to assume its right position, but if he is merely a creature of the senses, etc., this transformation cannot be effected and his life is, as it were, a manifestation of *Hydrogen 48*. If one can know together one's mechanical reactions (through Self-Observation) and at the same time feel the presence of the Work, then one's consciousness is increased in the sense that one knows together far more—that is to say, one knows and sees one's mechanicalness in the light of the Work and what it indicates, namely, one becomes conscious in the Work in reference to how one acts in life and so it can be said that one is conscious in a higher Hydrogen.

It is then necessary to think about what a Hydrogen means. A Hydrogen is a point in the universe regarded as a qualitative scale— namely, a scale of degrees of excellence. The lower Hydrogens are manifested to our external senses as objects, as 'stones', as 'grass', as 'meat', as 'water', etc. But when that point in the universe called *Hydrogen 48* is reached, its manifestation is only internal and so has to do with states of consciousness. *Hydrogen 48* is the lowest of the so-called psychic Hydrogens. Our ordinary consciousness uses, as it were,

Hydrogen 48. It then sees everything in terms of opposites. As you know, the formatory part of the Intellectual Centre which works with *Hydrogen 48* is called 'Third Force Blind'. The range of knowledge given by this Hydrogen determines the world of opposites for us and so we see things as either 'yes' or 'no' and are really incapable of relative thinking and incapable of seeing as 'yes' *and* 'no'. Higher centres which work with *Hydrogen 12* and *Hydrogen 6* contain no contradictions. This is because the degree of illumination is such that we see all sides of a question simultaneously and not divided into irreconcilable opposites. Sometimes consciousness is compared in this system with *light*. Our inner life is said to be darkness and this is what is meant in the Gospels by the words: 'People who live in darkness'. The idea of Self-Observation is to let a ray of light into this darkness. We must imagine that to be conscious in a higher Hydrogen or by means of a higher Hydrogen is similar to having a greatly increased light shed on everything. Whereas the ray of a candle illuminates feebly the surroundings, the light of an arc-lamp lights up what were mere shadows before and makes us see everything in an entirely different relation: that is to say, to be conscious in a higher Hydrogen is to see entirely new relations, and this moment of seeing new relations sometimes occurs to us in times of trouble and distress when suddenly everything becomes transformed and we see things in an entirely different light. When we are fixed in our negative states, when we are full of self-pity and only conscious of injured self-love, etc., we see everything very darkly. We are, in fact, conscious in *Hydrogen 48*, let us say. But when we have a moment of awakening and are lifted out of that state by the action of the Work, all our thoughts and emotions in that state now seem to be trivial. We cannot understand why we said this thing or thought that thing. This is a moment of illumination, of increased light, and so increased consciousness, in the sense that we are 'knowing together' far more than we do in our contracted state. Everything falls into its right proportion, as it were, in the light of this increased consciousness, so we can say that at that moment we were conscious in a higher Hydrogen. Actually, at such a moment we are conscious at a higher point in the universe regarded as a scale of qualities represented by Hydrogens. Quite simply, we rise above ourselves for a moment and see things in a new light. Everyone must notice that he is in a worse state or a better state at different times and it is really upon the basis of this perfectly incontrovertible experience that we can become certain of the existence of higher degrees of consciousness.

I think it is a mistake to try to connect the four given states of consciousness with Hydrogens. The two ideas should be given separately, although obviously they are connected. The third state of consciousness —namely, Self-Awareness or Self-Remembering—always arises from a higher Hydrogen, but it may be *Hydrogen 24*, or *Hydrogen 12* or even, very rarely, *Hydrogen 6*. We spoke at the meeting here of the effects of dental gas when people suddenly have a marvellous experience and cannot remember it afterwards. That is to say, they are for a moment put into a higher Hydrogen. G. once said to me that opium has a higher Hydrogen in it which people can become conscious in sometimes. He said it is like becoming conscious *in the plant*; but you know a man must create higher Hydrogens in himself by trying to give himself first of all the First Conscious Shock, and, if he can, the Second Conscious Shock, which set going new octaves in the development of all Hydrogens in his body.

I would like it if you would try to grasp in some way and get some vision of the universe as a scale of Hydrogens. It has to do with intensities of meaning and use—that is to say, it is qualitative, not quantitative. Think now, all of you, look round the room you are in. You see different things—things made of wood, things made of stone, perhaps some food on the table, water, air, etc. Have you ever thought what relation all these different things have towards one another? If you have, you may see why, when Mr. O. first heard of the Table of Hydrogens, he said this was knowledge from higher centres.

You will remember that everything is defined by what it eats, what eats it, etc. The cow can eat the flowers in the vase on the table, but you cannot; but you can eat the cow. Insects can eat the wood of the chair you are sitting on. The wood of the chair you are sitting on is a certain point in the universe. Meat is more highly organized and is a different point in the universe; its functions, its properties, its uses, its possibilities, are entirely different. Now let us take thought, based on *Hydrogen 48*; its uses, its properties, its functions, are entirely different from those of meat, and yet it has its properties. Meat is cleverer, as it is said, than wood, and thought is cleverer than meat. A cooked potato is cleverer than a raw potato because it is *768* and can be eaten by man. Emotional perception, if it is really based on *Hydrogen 24*, is far more clever than perception based on *Hydrogen 48*.

Try to think from this point of view and if you will send me some definite questions I will try to answer them.

ADDED NOTE

Dr. Nicoll added this note as the result of a conversation. He said: "Have any of you ever thought of the difference between a quantitative view of the universe and a qualitative view of the universe? It is quite simple. Mathematics cannot deal with qualities, but only with quantities. Let us take first mere quantities. Will any quantities of coppers make one golden sovereign? No. But by human agreement—that is, by establishing an artificial transforming system—240 coppers theoretically can be turned into a golden sovereign. But unless such a human arrangement—that is, such an artificially agreed upon transforming system—existed, this could never happen through the mere factor of quantities alone. A man might accumulate millions of coppers, but no gold would result from any effort of that sort alone, unless the Bank agreed to transform each 240 coppers into a gold sovereign. Now if we lived in a merely quantitative universe, no transformation would be possible, because transformation is a question of *qualities*—that is, of qualitative differences, of one thing turning into something else. This work teaches that we live in a world of real qualitative differences, and this is its meaning. Transformation is possible in the very nature of things. We see a seed transforming itself into a tree, but scarcely think of the miracle. We eat meat and from it the substances necessary for *thought, feeling* and *love* are created by the transformation of a lower Hydrogen into the higher Hydrogens. This is the inherent nature of the universe. What we call *life* is based on the power of transforming, in a universe that is, itself, based on transformation—that is, of lower and higher, and so of endless qualitative differences. Life is transformation, in a universe having this nature or significance. Transformation means the turning of something lower into something higher. The octave of food in the body shews this. All this connects itself with the *basic idea* of the Work—that we live in a *growing, evolving,* and so *transforming universe*—that is, a living and so transforming universe or universe of transformation. And actually, unless this is understood and felt, more and more deeply, the emotional centre in man cannot awaken and develop, and soon deteriorates. As you know, science teaches that we live in a dying universe. This system, this Work, teaches quite the contrary. You must think for yourselves of the psychological difference and emotional value of these two views and judge between their power for good or bad. Although 'religion' in the broadest sense has taught something *positive*—perhaps in terms of a 'hereafter' and so on—if we consider for a moment the psychological difference, we can decide which is the more valuable. And we can see for ourselves that transformation exists on all sides. All life exists physically by transforming a lower into a higher Hydrogen—that is to say, we eat *meat (H 768)* and so are able to *think (H 48).* All these ideas are in a way obvious, once we really think for ourselves—that is, once the '*driver*' in us awakens and climbs on to the box. But unless we begin to think for ourselves through the help of this work, we remain asleep, and life then exerts a force over us that is not necessary and is contrary to our real destiny. The idea that all life is based on transformation is so obvious, physically, that really not to see it is due to mental blindness or to a deliberate dislike of seeing any meaning in anything—and this is a common modern disease that leads to negative emotion by itself."

Dr. Nicoll later added the following: "In speaking of efforts in the Work—is it not obvious that the mere quantity of efforts is useless in comparison with the quality of the efforts? Mere lip-service, mere imitation of work, mere pretending to work or trying to attract merit —all such efforts, however great in quantity, lead to nothing, because such efforts are insincere. They are of bad quality, however great their quantity may be. The Work is based on inner sincerity. One effort arising out of inner sincerity and unshakeable valuation of the Work will produce a change of being and shift a man's position in the universe

206

because it is *qualitative*, different from any quantity of external, insincere or weak efforts. That is why in this Work people are brought to a point of decision. This means that everything external, at a certain point, will go against them and so they will find plenty of complaints and criticism and other external reasons and plenty of reasons for finding fault with others and so on—and, in fact, this point may be artificially created, if it does not inevitably arise, as usually happens. Then everything depends on whether the Work has become born in them and is truly internal: and if so, the effort made at such a moment actually leads to change of being—that is, to a new growth of essence—because then the necessary effort must be at the expense of personality. 'We have', G. once said to us, 'to reach a point in the work when however we are turned and twisted we never lose sight of our aim.' Here our attitude to the Work comes in—to this *eternal* Work. Is it not obvious that such a moment demands the most *qualitative* sincere effort? If our attitude is shallow, how shall we meet it? Let us think for ourselves what this means and on what this Work is based—namely, on inner change, and all that it means, even if we have not thought of it before. Change is not addition, but actual change of the kind of person one is, and so, painful. And only the sincerest moments are of use here. Nothing false in the way of effort is any good. The very fact that the universe is a scale of qualities shews everyone that what is intrinsically false cannot lead to any change, but must necessarily—by law—find its own level and remain there because it is what it is. And whatever a thing is, it is where it is in the universe, regarded as a scale of qualities, and must remain where it is by reason of actual laws, which determine the position of everything according to its quality. This is what a qualitative view of the universe means. This is the meaning of the *Table of Hydrogens*."

Birdlip, December 27, 1942

KNOWLEDGE

Introduction

To-night I wish first to speak of the "Work Octave". This sounds *Do* as Evaluation of the Work. This means that nothing can begin unless there is valuation. And this is not anything mysterious. You will not begin anything unless you think it worth while, and the worth of a thing is its value for you. If you regard a thing as worthless you do not value it. Now this note *Do* is not necessarily sounded just when you come in contact with the Work. It may be. That is, when you hear the ideas of the Work they may fall on some ready-prepared place in you— that is, on Magnetic Centre. You may feel that here is what you have wanted. This valuation is due to the action of the kind of *Magnetic*

Centre in you. And in different people Magnetic Centre is different. But it lies in emotional parts of centres—that is, it lies in the places where you feel worth, where you feel valuation, for valuation is emotional. But this, so to speak, first-love will not last. It may be a very beautiful feeling, yet it passes away, having fulfilled its task, and you are left to the task of re-valuation. For Magnetic Centre may bring a person into the Work but it will not keep him in it. No doubt everyone has known the first feelings of love, those extraordinary and unearthly feelings that come in early life, which are not physical but rather devotional, and which seem to be touched by influences coming from the Higher Emotional Centre. And then, later, comes quite a different task—that of practical relationship. It is just the same in regard to the Work. And I have often thought that we repeat the history of our life of love in the Work itself. In my own case I know that when I first met the Work I felt again the same wonder, the same sense of mystery, of the miraculous, that I had felt in my earliest youth—feelings indeed that seemed self-sustaining and only slightly connected with an outer object, a person. But whatever early emotions we may have felt in connection with the ideas of the Work and the discovery that such a thing really exists, whatever extraordinary feelings we may have experienced, they are not enough. Even if we have right Magnetic Centre, the feelings and emotions that spring from it will not last. We must get to know the object of our love and relate ourselves to it practically. This note is called *Re* in the Work Octave. The note *Re* is sounded when a person begins to study the ideas of the Work and its teaching, and, begins to apply the Work to himself. This note *Re* is called "Application of the Work to Oneself". And if the note *Do*, sounded first by Magnetic Centre, does not change its quality, but remains simply as a feeling of the miraculous, the note *Re* will not sound strongly. Yet no one will pass into the Work unless there is some initial feeling of the miraculous. That is, a man must feel the difference between life and the Work. Otherwise the Work will fall on the places life falls on in him—that is, on those parts of centres that cannot receive and are not meant to receive the Work. Man has parts of centres for life and parts of centres for the Work. He is constructed for life and for the Work. And, not possessing Magnetic Centre, he will take in the ideas of the Work on his life-parts-of-centres. He will try to add the Work directly to life as if it were the same thing. He will pour new wine into old bottles, patch his old coat with new cloth. It is the function of *Magnetic Centre* to prevent this. Magentic Centre is sometimes defined as the capacity of distinguishing between A and B influences, between life-influences, influences created in mechanical life, and influences that come from outside life and are sown into mechanical life. Unless Magnetic Centre existed, nothing would be possible as regards inner evolution. No transformation of the feeling of life or of the feeling of oneself would be possible. Yet, as was said, Magnetic Centre, once its part is played, is *no longer of use*. It introduces you to a new world. And you must then find your way. That is, it may bring a man to the Work and make it possible for him to value the Work, but that is all. A man must then revalue the Work for himself by the application of the ideas of the Work to himself and to his whole standpoint, and this will strengthen *Do* in him. That is, the note *Re* will strengthen the note *Do* in him, and change its quality to a *conscious evaluation*. Seeing the truth of the Work, a man will value it in a more and more conscious way, and this re-valuation will strengthen *Do* and make it a real *Do*. For we must consider whether a *Do* sounded by Magnetic Centre is really a *consciously* sounded *Do*.

The third note in the Work Octave, the note *Mi*, is called "Realization of Personal Difficulties". You can easily understand that this has many sides to it, many different meanings for each person. There are, for example, personal difficulties that appear in regard to one's *being*. And there are personal difficulties connected with one's *knowledge*—that is, in accepting certain sides of the Work as knowledge. For there are many strange ideas that relate to the *knowledge* side of the Work—ideas that we have heard many times, but have not yet begun to acknowledge. In this Work we have to *think in a new way*. And this is possible only through new knowledge, for you will always think *in the same way* unless you have new knowledge. New thinking demands new knowledge, but new knowledge will not make you think in a new way unless it is acknowledged. Yet, you must be able to think in a new way, for otherwise you will never see your life and never see the meaning of the Work. Work on knowledge is as difficult as Work on being. And it is even more difficult. All this belongs to realization of personal difficulties—the note *Mi*.

There are many difficult things said in the Work. This means that many things are said that strike against *our usual forms of knowledge*. You will meet with this in every form of esoteric teaching. For instance, Christ many times said to his disciples: "If you can bear it." And this means that knowledge—great knowledge—knowledge about Man and his situation on earth and his possibilities—is not something that you can take in an everyday way, or join up with ordinary knowledge or think about as being foolish because it does not correspond with your opinion. Great knowledge demands great sacrifice and a long struggle with oneself. Now to-night I want to give you the Work teaching on *knowledge* itself, which is not at all easy to accept and must be thought of for a long time to become part of one's mind.

KNOWLEDGE

Mr. Ouspensky is speaking:

"During one conversation with G. in our Group, which was beginning to become permanent, I asked: why, if ancient knowledge has been preserved and if, speaking in general, there always existed a knowledge distinct from our science and philosophy or even surpassing it, is it so carefully concealed? Why is it not made common property? Why are the men who possess this special knowledge unwilling to let it pass into general circulation, for the sake of a better and more successful struggle with deceit, evil and ignorance?

This is, I think a question which usually arises in everyone's mind on first acquaintance with the ideas of esotericism.

There are two answers to that, said G. In the first place this knowledge is not concealed; and in the second place it cannot, from its very nature, become common property. We will consider the second of these statements first. I will prove to you afterwards that *knowledge* (he emphasized the word) is far more accessible to those capable of assimilating it than is usually supposed; and that the whole trouble is that people either do not want it or cannot receive it. But first of all another thing must be understood, namely, that knowledge cannot belong to all, cannot even belong to many. Such is the law. You do not understand this because you do not understand that knowledge, like everything else in the world, is *material*. It is material, and this means that it possesses all the characteristics of materiality. One of the first characteristics of materiality is that matter in a given place and under given conditions is limited. Even the sand of the desert and the water of the sea is a definite and unchangeable quantity. So that, if knowledge is material, then it means that there is a definite quantity of it at a given time. It may be said that, in the course of a certain period of time, say a century, humanity has a definite amount of knowledge at its disposal. But we know, even from an ordinary observation of life, that the *matter of knowledge* possesses entirely different qualities according to whether it is taken in small or large quantities. Taken in a large quantity in a given place, that is, by one man, let us say, or by a small group of men, it produces very good results; taken in a small quantity (that is, by every one of a large number of people), it gives no results at all; or it may give even negative results, contrary to those expected. Thus, if a certain definite quantity of knowledge is distributed among millions of people, each individual will receive very little, and this small amount of knowledge will change nothing either in his life or in his understanding of things. And however large the number of people who receive this small amount of knowledge, it will change nothing in their lives, except, perhaps, to make them still more difficult.

But if, on the contrary, large quantities of knowledge are concentrated in a small number of people, then this knowledge will give very great results. From this point of view it is far more advantageous that knowledge should be preserved among a small number of people and not dispersed among the masses.

If we take a certain quantity of gold and decide to gild a number of objects with it, we must know, or calculate, exactly what number of objects can be gilded with this quantity of gold. If we try to gild a greater number, they will be covered with gold unevenly, in patches, and will look much worse than if they had no gold at all; in fact, we shall lose our gold.

The distribution of knowledge is based upon exactly the same principle. If knowledge is given to all, nobody will get any. If it is preserved among a few, each will receive not only enough to keep, but to increase, what he receives.

At the first glance this theory seems very unjust, since the position of those who are, so to speak, denied knowledge in order that others may receive a greater share, appears to be very sad and undeservedly harder than it ought to be. Actually, however, this is not so at all; and in the distribution of knowledge there is not the slightest injustice.

The fact is that the enormous majority of people do not want any knowledge whatever; they refuse their share of it, and do not even take the ration allotted to them in the general distribution for the purposes of life. This is particularly evident in times of mass madness such as wars, revolutions and so on, when men suddenly seem to lose even the small amount of common sense they had and turn into complete automatons, giving themselves over to wholesale destruction in vast numbers—in other words, even losing the instinct of self-preservation. Owing to this, enormous quantities of knowledge remain, so to speak, unclaimed and can be distributed among those who realize its value.

There is nothing unjust in this, because those who receive knowledge take nothing that belongs to others, deprive others of nothing; they take only what others have rejected as useless and what would in any case be lost if they did not take it.

The collecting of knowledge by some depends upon the rejection of knowledge by others.

There are periods in the life of humanity, which generally coincide with the beginning of the fall of cultures and civilizations, when the masses irretrievably lose their reason and begin to destroy everything that has been created by centuries and millenniums of culture. Such periods of mass-madness, often coinciding with geological cataclysms, climatic changes and similar phenomena of a planetary character, release a very great quantity of the matter of knowledge. This, in its turn, necessitates the work of collecting this matter of knowledge which would otherwise be lost. Thus the work of collecting scattered matter of knowledge frequently coincides with the beginning of the destruction and fall of cultures and civilizations.

This aspect of the question is clear. The crowd neither wants nor seeks knowledge, and the leaders of the crowd, in their own interests, try to strengthen its fear and dislike of everything new and unknown.

The slavery in which mankind lives is based upon this fear. It is even difficult to imagine all the horror of this slavery. We do not understand *what* people are losing. But in order to understand the cause of this slavery it is enough to see how people live, what constitutes the aim of their existence, the object of their desires, passions and aspirations, of what they think, of what they talk, what they serve and what they worship. Consider what the cultured humanity of our time spends money on, what commands the highest price, where the biggest crowds are. If we think for a moment about these questions it becomes clearer that humanity, as it is now, with the interests it lives by, cannot expect to have anything different from what it has. But, as I have already said, it cannot be otherwise. Imagine that for the whole of mankind half a pound of knowledge is allotted a year. If this knowledge is distributed among everyone, each will receive so little that he will remain the fool he was. But, thanks to the fact that very few want to have this knowledge, those who take it are able to get, let us say, a grain each, and acquire the possibility of becoming more intelligent. All cannot become intelligent even if they wish. And if they did become intelligent it would not help matters. There exists a general equilibrium which cannot be upset.

That is one aspect. The other, as I have already said, consists in the fact that no one is concealing anything; there is no mystery whatever. But the acquisition or transmission of true knowledge demands great labour and great effort both from him who receives and from him who gives. And those who possess this knowledge are doing everything they can to transmit and communicate it to the greatest possible number of people, to facilitate people's approach to it and enable them to prepare themselves to receive the truth. But knowledge cannot be given by force to anyone and, as I have already said, an unprejudiced survey of the average man's life, of what fills his day, and of the things he is interested in, will at once shew whether it is possible to accuse men who possess knowledge of concealing it, of not wishing to give it to people or of not wishing to teach people what they know themselves.

He who wants knowledge must himself make the initial effort to find the source of knowledge and to approach it, taking advantage of the help and indications which are given to all, but which people as a rule do not want to see or recognize. Knowledge cannot come to people without effort on their own part. They understand this very well in connection with ordinary knowledge, but in the case of *great knowledge*, when they admit the possibility of its existence, they find it possible to expect something different. Everyone knows very well that if, for instance, a man wants to learn Chinese, it will take several years of intense work; everyone knows that five years are needed to grasp the principles of medicine, and perhaps twice as many years for the study of painting or music. And yet there are theories which affirm that knowledge can come to people without any effort on their part, that they can acquire it *even in sleep*. The very existence of such theories constitutes an additional explanation of why knowledge cannot come to people. At the same time it is essential to understand that Man's *independent* effort to attain anything in this direction can also give no results. A man can only attain knowledge with the help of those who possess it. This must be understood from the very beginning. *One must learn from him who knows*."

SELF-OBSERVATION

There are many things that can be said about self-observation and what it is and what it is not. The whole of the Work starts from a man beginning to observe himself. Self-observation is a means of self-change. Serious and continuous self-observation, if done aright, leads to definite inner changes in a man.

Let us, first of all, consider self-observation in connection with a mistake often made about it. The mistake is the confusing of self-observation with *knowing*. To know and to observe are not the same thing. Speaking superficially, you may *know* you are sitting in a chair in your room, but can you say that you actually *observe* it? Speaking more deeply, you may *know* you are in a negative state, but that does not mean that you are *observing* it. A person in the Work said to me that he disliked somebody intensely. I said: "Try to observe it." He replied: "Why should I observe it? I don't need to. I *know* it already." In such a case, the person is confusing *knowing* with *observing*—that is, he does not understand what self-observation is. Moreover he has not grasped that *self-observation*, which is active, is a means of self-change, whereas merely knowing, which is passive, is not. Knowing is not an act of attention. Self-observation is an act of attention directed inwards —to what is going on in you. The attention must be active—that is, directed. In the case of a person you dislike, you notice what thoughts crowd into your mind, the chorus of voices speaking in you, what they are saying, what unpleasant emotions surge up, and so on. You notice also that you are treating the person you dislike very badly inside. Nothing is too bad to think of him or feel about him. But to see all this requires *directed attention*, not passive attention. The attention comes from the *observing side*, whereas the thoughts and emotions belong to the *observed* side in yourself. This is dividing yourself into two. There is a saying: "A man is first one, then two, and then one." The observing side, or Observing 'I', stands interior to, or above, the observed side, but its power of independent consciousness varies, because it may be submerged at any moment. Then you are completely identified with the negative state. You do not observe the state but you are the state. You can then say that you know you are negative, but that is not to observe it. If the Observing 'I' is supported by other 'I's which value the Work and recall it and wish to become more conscious, then it is not so easily submerged by the flood of negative things. It is then helped by—and is a part of—Deputy-Steward. All this is quite different from merely *knowing* one is negative. Passive knowing can be said to be mechanical in contrast to self-observation which is a *conscious act* and cannot become mechanical. Mechanical self-observation has nothing to do with Work self-observation.

People not only confuse knowing with the continuous act of self-observation but they mistake *thinking* for observing. To think is quite different from observing oneself. A man may think about himself all day and never observe himself once. The observation of one's thoughts is not the same as thinking. It should be clear now that *knowing* and *thinking* are not the same as observation.

The question is often asked: "What must I observe?" First, the Work explains carefully what you must begin to observe. But later a man must attain to fuller observation of himself—for a whole day—or a week—and see himself as an outside person. He must think what he would think if he met himself. He would, of course, cordially dislike this man who is himself. A man must observe *everything* in himself and always as if it were not himself but IT. This means that he must say: "What is IT doing?" not "What am I doing?" He then sees now these thoughts going on in him, now these emotions, now these private plays and self-dramas, now these elaborate lies, now these speeches, excuses and inventions, and so on, passing through him, one after the other. Next moment, of course, he goes to sleep again and takes part in them all. That is, he acts in the play he has composed and thinks it is real. He thinks he is the part he invented.

Let us consider this viewpoint further. A man must be able to say: "This is not me" to all his set pieces and his songs, to all the performances going on in him, to all the voices that he takes as his own. You know how sometimes just before going to sleep at night, you hear loud voices in your head. These are 'I's speaking. During the day, they are speaking all the time, only you take them as '*I*'—as yourself. But just before sleep, a separation takes place naturally, for connections are being broken between centres and between 'I's in order that sleep may be possible. Two or more 'I's can keep you from sleeping. So you hear them, as it were, as voices talking, just for a moment, because they are being separated by natural processes from you.

Inner separation means the power of not merely saying: "This is not I", but ultimately of actually perceiving it for oneself—*perceiving that it is true*, that "this is not I", not merely thinking it is so or trying to persuade oneself it is, or saying this is what the Work says.

When you are in an unpleasant state, if you observe yourself over some considerable time, you will notice that all sorts of different groups of unpleasant 'I's try to deal with it in succession and make something out of it. This is because negative 'I's live by being negative. Their life consists in negative thinking or negative feeling—that is, in providing you with unpleasant thoughts and feelings. It is their delight to do so for it is their life. In the Work, the enjoyment of negative states must be observed sincerely, especially the secret enjoyment of them. The reason is that if a man enjoys being negative, in whatever forms, and they are legion, he can never separate from them. You cannot separate yourself from what you have a secret affection for. The case actually is that you identify with the negative 'I's through secret affection and so feel *their enjoyment*, for whatever you identify with you become. A man in himself is constantly transforming himself into different 'I's. He has nothing permanent, but by separation he can make something permanent. The line of separation is between what likes and what hates the Work.

Now we speak once more of observing *talking*. All rules are about talking, practically speaking, and how to deal with wrong talking. It is necessary to observe *inner talking* and from where it is coming. Wrong inner talking is the breeding-ground not only of many future unpleasant states but also of wrong outer talking. You know that there is in the Work what is called the practice of *inner silence*. The practice and meaning of inner silence is like this: first, it must be about something quite distinct and definite; and second, it is like not touching it. That is, you cannot practise inner silence in any vague general way, save perhaps as an experiment for a time. But you can practise it rigidly in regard to some distinct and definite thing, something you know and see quite clearly. Someone once asked: "Is practising inner silence the same as not letting something come into your mind?" The answer is no. It is not the same. What you are practising inner silence about is already in the mind and you must be aware of it, but you must not *touch* it with your inner speech, your inner tongue. Your outer literal tongue likes to touch sore places, as when a tooth hurts. So does your inner tongue. But if it does, the sore thing in your mind flows into your inner speech and unwraps itself as *inner talking* in every direction. You have noticed of course that inner talking always goes on in negative states and that it coins many unpleasant phrases, which suddenly find expression in outer talking, perhaps long after. In the Work we are told that it is necessary to be careful about wrong outer talking at first, and, later on, about wrong inner talking. Actually, wrong outer talking is mostly due to wrong inner talking. Wrong inner talking, particularly venomous and evil inner talking, and so on, makes a mess within, like excrement. They are all different forms of lying and this is why they have such strength and persistence. Lies are always more powerful than truth because they can hurt. If you observe wrong inner talking you will notice it is only half-truths, or truths connected in the wrong order, or with something added or left out. In other words, it is simply lying to oneself. If you say: "Is this quite true?" it may stop it, but it will find another set of lies. Eventually you must dislike it. If you enjoy it, you will never lessen its power. It is not enough to dislike liking it: you must dislike *it*.

All this belongs to the purification of the emotional life. Mechanic- ally we only like ourselves, and so we dislike or hate those who do not like us. A development of being is not possible, and quite obviously so, unless the emotions cease to have only this basis of *self-liking*. External considering, in the Work, is putting oneself in the position of others. This is referred to in the Gospels: "All things . . . whatsoever ye would that men should do unto you, even so do ye also unto them" (*Matt.*: VII 12). This is one of the definite formulations in the Gospels of what in the Work is called External Considering. But a man must think very deeply what it says and perceive internally what it means, because it has an outer and an inner meaning. If you say: "I always think of others," then observe it. It is probably a buffer. You do not notice perhaps that you say things, or you write things, which, if you received, you would not tolerate for a moment. This is one very interesting form of self-observation and it includes observing "inner talking". In your- self everyone else is helpless. You can, as it were, drag a person into the cave of yourself and do what you like with her or him. You may be polite naturally, but in the Work, which is all about purifying or organ- izing the inner life, it is not enough. It is how you behave internally and invisibly to one another that really counts. This is very difficult to understand. You may think you know this already. But to *understand* —even to begin to *understand* it—takes many years of work. When the inner corresponds with the outer and when the outer obeys the inner, then a man possesses a "second body". As we are, our outer life does not correspond with our inner life, and our outer life controls our inner. The inner grows by seeing the good of something. Recently here we were talking of what the saint, Cassian, says about a man being able to do the same thing for different reasons. A man may act from fear— fear of law, fear of reputation, fear of opinion. Then he acts from outside. Or he may act from ambition—and many other similar forms of self- interest. Or he may act from good—from seeing the good of acting so. This develops the internal man. Now all this can be a subject of self- observation. But even the first stages of self-observation have a certain effect. They let in rays of light into the darkness of our psychic life. It is the psychic life we have to think of in the Work. All the instructions of the Work are about one's psychic life, which is in chaos. In this way, self-observation becomes deeper, and the valuation of the Work becomes more and more internal. So the Work begins to act on Essence—on what is the real part of a man.

Work on oneself is always the same. It does not matter *where* you are. You are always in contact with the Work if your inner attitude to it is right. If your inner attitude is right, the Work will teach you about what work on yourself means. If your inner attitude is wrong, it cannot, because you block the way. In all self-observation, if it is to become *full* self-observation, you must observe IT. That is, you must see all your reactions to life and circumstances as IT in you and not as 'I'. If you say 'I', then nothing can happen. The saying of 'I', the feeling of 'I', makes it impossible to change. If to every negative state you say 'I', then you cannot escape it. At first a man takes himself as *one* and says 'I' to all that happens in his psychic life. But in order to change he must become two. He must divide himself into IT and Observing 'I'—that is, into two. Then, later on, he may become one—a unity. The instrument of self-observation is like a knife that cuts us away from what is not us. If you begin to see what it means to say: "This is not I", then you begin to use this instrument.

When you can really say: "What is IT doing?" instead of "What am I doing?" you begin to understand the Work. The Work is to make a new set of reactions or rather new ways of taking things. As long as you are nothing but ordinary life-reactions, you cannot change. When you take ordinary things in a new way you begin to change. You cannot remain the same—and change. If you are always the same it means that you always react to life in the same way. You insist on your pound of flesh. The idea of *change* is not to be the *same*. The idea of the Work is to change oneself. The idea of self-observation is to separate from *what one was* by not going with what one observes. In this way self-observation is a means of self-change.

*   *   *

When you have begun to form in yourself the powerful mental instrument of this Work, you will find that wherever you turn it, you will catch new meanings. The Work forms in us a new instrument of reception, a new apparatus for receiving impressions, both from outside and from inside. The Work lies in parts that have to be joined together by means of *understanding*. Each part of the Work, each separate idea, each bit of the teaching, is exactly like the parts of, say, a radio-machine. The parts of a radio are, let us say, lying on a table and you can see them. If you know enough, if you understand what they are, you can put them together and then the instrument begins to work and you hear all sorts of invisible things that otherwise you could not hear. In the case of the Work, each part is not something physical, an outer object lying on a table, but is psychical—an idea, a thought, a direction, a formulation, a diagram, and so on. If all these parts are fitted together by understanding, and valuation, the Work forms a new and organized apparatus in you. That is, you are newly organized. You have a new psychic organism in you. The Work is actually a whole and complete *organism* which is given little by little, part by part, but all these parts are parts of a true *whole*. If the Work is thus formed in you, you have a new thing, a new organized instrument, in you. Even a single part of the Work, if taken in with valuation and understanding, will begin to work a change in you because it will transmit *new influences*. But the whole of the Work must be formed in a man. This can be thought of as *another body*—another organized thing in a man—if the man *lives* the Work. Then it will control the man he *was*.

Birdlip, January 2, 1943

THE FOUR BODIES OF MAN

Paper I

Part I.—As this subject is of so great and significant a nature, and requires presentation from so many points of view in order to make possible any living grasp of its meaning and to prevent it from being taken in in an indifferent or merely formatory way, I have thought it best, after long reflection, to begin by a gradual approach. The teaching, in brief, is that Man, living in the given body, by his first birth, is capable of developing *three* further bodies composed of finer matters. But what does this mean and what ideas will help us to comprehend it? What, for example, might it mean that Man can develop *another* body apart from three further bodies? In what way can we picture *another* or *second* body? Now, we can conceive it first in this way. Imagine one man standing behind another man and controlling him in everything he does or says. The man in front obeys the instructions of the man behind him. That is, the intelligence and will of the man behind controls the actions of the man in front. We can take the man in front as the first body and the man behind as another or *second* body—that is, we can gain the idea of the second body *controlling* the first. This is easy enough to understand, for in any organization in life, as a military or business organization, there must be some degree of control of one individual by another in a higher position. In the case of a single individual, it is more difficult to grasp.

What in a single individual is going to control *what* in him? Indeed, it is impossible to understand, as long as a man takes himself as *one* —that is, as long as he believes that that which thinks, speaks, acts, feels, loves and hates in him is always one and the same thing. Now you know that there is a phrase in the Work which says that *unless a man divides himself into two, into an observing and an observed side, he can never shift from where he is.* This is the starting-point of all else. It is actually the starting-point of *another body* in the sense that unless this division begins in a man, unless he can become the subject of his own observation, nothing can ever develop in him that can eventually control him internally and make the outer *man-machine* obey. That is, no second body can be organized in him. Let us note here that the position of Observing 'I' is always *internal* to what it observes. What is more external cannot observe what is more internal. This means that 'I's that live in small mechanical external parts of centres cannot observe 'I's that lie in more internal conscious parts of centres. As self-observation becomes *deeper*, more *emotional*, more *real* and more *necessary*, the position of Observing 'I' becomes more internal. Self-Observation ceases to be superficial. Now around Observing 'I' gather all those 'I's in a man that wish to work and bring about order in the house that a man is. This forms what is called *Deputy-Steward*. The position of Deputy-Steward is therefore *internal* to the superficial man, the man turned to life and driven by outer circumstances. And so it is therefore among other things *internal* to False Personality. Now if all that is more external, more mechanical, in a man, begins to obey what is more internal in him, the internal begins to develop control of the outer or *man-machine* and the result is that the order of things begins to be *reversed*. The man is no longer so easily driven by life, by external influences, by changing circumstances, and by characteristic reactions of his personality to life and by the habits of his body. He is no longer driven from outside so completely, he is no longer a slave of his body, but begins to be controlled from within, for brief moments. This can be expressed in the following way:

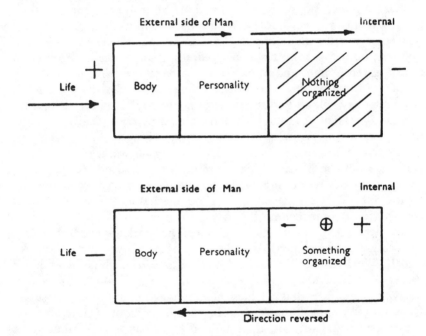

Now if you will take this idea as simply as possible, you will see to some extent that the possession of a *Second Body* means that a man is different from an ordinary man. He is different because an ordinary man—a man-machine—is a function of life. A man-machine is driven by life, and so always acted upon by and obedient to life. That is, he is driven from outside and from the more external parts of him. But a man who has begun to have something internally organized in him is no longer so easily driven by outer life but is at times controlled from something within himself. That is, at times *he works in a reverse direction*. We may all imagine that we work already in this reverse direction, but this is only imagination. A very little sincere self-observation will shew us that we are truly functions of life. We are driven by life and circumstances and have nothing or very little that is strong enough to resist being driven in this way. You must realize that each man, is, of course, driven by life in a different way from other men. But all ordinary men, all men belonging to the circle of mechanical humanity, all men No. 1, No. 2 and No. 3, are driven *from outside*, even though they believe that they are not. In this sense, they are *man-machines*. And this is because nothing internal in them has been developed to such an extent that they obey this internal thing and so resist the kaleidoscope of changing life. Nothing *in them* is strong enough to resist life—that is, strong enough to resist the reactions they ordinarily have to life. They certainly may notice they do not react to life as others do, and then they imagine they can resist life. This is mere illusion. Everyone reacts differently, in his or her own way. Where one person reacts, another may not. But it is all the same. It is all *mechanical* and life controls them through their particular special mechanical and habitual reactions to it. A good man fancies he is different from a bad man, an optimistic man feels he is different from a pessimistic man, a careful man thinks he is different from a careless man, and so on. Yet all are *mechanical*. All are driven by life. All cannot help being what they are. And if they try to be different, they will all find the same difficulties of changing themselves confronting them. And this means that all are, psychologically speaking, without anything *organized in them* to resist the particular mechanical effects that life has upon them. That is, they all work, or rather, are worked, from the life-side. They are all different kinds of machines, reacting or working in different ways, but all are driven by the impact of outer life. They are mechanically good, mechanically bad, mechanically optimistic, mechanically pessimistic, mechanically this and mechanically that. That is the teaching of the Work about Mechanicalness—about undeveloped Man, the *Man-Machine*, who serves Nature. But the Work teaches that Man can cease to be a machine by an inner development of individuality, consciousness and will—that is, of precisely those qualities that mechanical man imagines he already possesses. In a fully-developed man—that is, a man possessing individuality, consciousness and will—it is not life and changing outer circumstances that mechanically drive him. Such a man has something *organized* in him which can resist life, something from which he can act. Such a man in short, *can do*. And this is because he possesses more bodies than the one he received at birth.

*   *   *

Part II.—In this connection let us glance at the New Testament. In the Gospels Christ says that unless a man is *re-born*, he cannot enter the Kingdom of Heaven. Birth means a body and Re-birth a second body. To be re-born is to have a second body. We know that Christ was transfigured and appeared to his disciples *in another body*. Again, St.

Paul speaks about the *natural* and the *spiritual* bodies of Man. Speaking
of the resurrection of the dead, he says:

"But some man will say, How are the dead raised up? and with
what body do they come? Thou fool, that which thou sowest is
not quickened, except it die: and that which thou sowest, thou
sowest not that body that shall be, but bare grain, it may chance
of wheat, or of some other grain: But God giveth it a body as it
hath pleased him, and to every seed his own body. All flesh is not
the same flesh: but there is one kind of flesh of man, another flesh
of beasts, another of fishes, and another of birds. There are also
celestial bodies, and bodies terrestrial: but the glory of the celestial
is one, and the glory of the terrestrial is another. There is one glory
of the sun, and another glory of the moon, and another glory of
the stars: for one star differeth from another star in glory. So also
is the resurrection of the dead. It is sown in corruption; it is raised
in incorruption: it is sown in dishonour; it is raised in glory: it is
sown in weakness; it is raised in power: It is sown a natural body;
it is raised a spiritual body. There is a natural body, and there
is a spiritual body." (*I Corinthians*: XV 35-44)

In this passage you can dimly see outlined two great teachings of
the Work, one the Ray of Creation, spoken of here as the "glory of the
sun", the "glory of the moon", and so on, and the other the teaching
that Man has (or rather, let us say here, can have) more bodies than
the physical body. For Paul speaks of Man as if he had a second body
already, while Christ teaches that a man must be born again.

* * *

Part III.—The Work speaks almost from its starting-point of the Essence
in Man being undeveloped. It defines a growth of Essence as a change
in the level of Being: and it speaks very often about making Personality
passive so that Essence can develop. Especially does it speak of False
Personality or Imaginary 'I' and of the necessity of observing ourselves
in regard to these and separating from them. The object of this is to
allow something else to grow. Essence can develop. It is where a man
can grow from. And in connection with the development of Essence a
second body can grow. But it cannot do so as long as Personality is
active and controls the inner life.

Let us take the idea of *inner separation*. In my case I must observe
Nicoll and continually try to separate from the reactions and habits of
Nicoll. In your case, if your name is Smith, you must separate from
Smith. What is your name? Repeat it silently to yourself. Then understand you must observe and separate yourself internally from all that
your name stands for in yourself. Is this clear? Let us suppose that in
this Group, Miss Robinson, Mr. Smith, Mr. Black, Miss Browne, and
so on, are all sitting here. They are all the time being Miss Robinson,

Mr. Smith, Mr. Black, Miss Browne, in various ways, pleasant and unpleasant. Now in the work of inner separation lies the whole first task of practical work. Mr. Smith feels he is superior to Miss Browne and she in turn feels superior to Mr. Smith, and so on, endlessly. All this is very difficult to explain in words. You must have the intelligence to see what is meant. Now you know that *Personality is active* and *Essence is passive* in mechanical man and this is due to the action of Life that keeps this relationship between Personality and Essence. Life is the neutralizing force that keeps Personality active and Essence passive

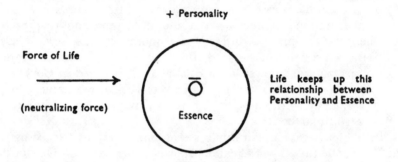

There is only one force that can change this relationship of Personality and Essence—a force coming from *outside life*. This is the Work, or, in general, *conscious influences*, coming from the Conscious Circle of Humanity, outside mechanical life.

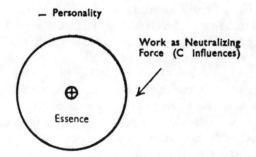

This new arrangement is a *reversal* of the former arrangement. A *reversal of sign* has taken place. It begins when Work in a man begins to become stronger than life. And this means that something organized has been made in a man that controls him. For the Work, coming from Conscious Influences, can form, in suitable soil, a receptive organ through which a man can receive force—that is, his "daily bread".

And since Essence is the most real part of a man and Personality *relatively* unreal, for this organ to form itself aright, it must eventually form itself out of what is *most real and sincere* in a man. It cannot form itself in the external man, nor in the hypocrite in a man which is the False Personality. So you will understand that many thoughts enter here concerning the relation of Personality and Essence, in connection with the idea of something new forming itself as a result of a development of Essence. For this reason let us consider once more what the Work says about the relation of Personality and Essence.

You all know how extraordinary the teaching of the Work is about Personality and Essence. It says that Personality must be properly formed first of all, and, unless it is, Essence cannot grow beyond a limited point. Essence grows a little and then Personality must form round it. Then Essence *can* grow by using the food of Personality, that is, by making Personality passive. So you see that Man, properly under-stood, is a series of experiments on himself. A badly-formed Personality, in conjunction with a childish Essence, handicaps a man. The idea is that a man must go *out* of himself into life, and, as it were, come back again—a movement similar to that of the prodigal son. Life must act on a man fully before Essence can grow beyond its natural point. What is extraordinary is that often people think that Essence can grow by itself. The Work says it cannot. It can grow to a certain point where it is still childish. And then it stops. Personality must now form the potential, eventual food for Essence and so Personality must be formed and become active. A man must learn all about the life he is born into on this earth. Later, if he has magnetic centre, and if he wishes, he may find the means of making his developed Personality passive by long inner work. By doing so, he feeds Essence, through inner struggle. So the Work, which is the right, *second* education, starts with making Personality passive by inner separation, non-identifying, self-remember-ing, and so on.

Now the formation of second body is connected with a growth of Essence, which is internal to Personality. The second body is not made of the matter composing Personality, which is *roughly H 48*, but of planetary matter, which is roughly $H\ 24$. But a man cannot start from Essence. Essence must be *taught* to develop. The Work does not start from Essence. It starts, in a man having magnetic centre, from those 'I's in him which wish to work, and they form "Deputy-Steward". This is the first point of Work made in a man. It can break up: or it can become stronger. These 'I's must *teach Essence*—that is, Personality must, at first, teach Essence. But as Essence grows—that is, as the Work becomes more and more real and essential in a man—the Work of Deputy-Steward passes into that of the Steward. This can be expressed in this diagram:

Diagram (1)

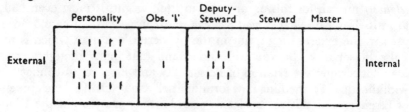

which is the same as the one you know as:

Diagram (2)

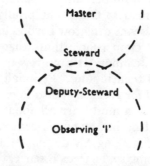

Notice that the *Higher* in Diagram II becomes in Diagram I the *inner*. What is higher is more internal in a man and what is lower is more external. Deputy-Steward must then struggle not only with wrong or ignorant 'I's in Personality, with wrong mental and emotional habits, with False Personality, with sleep, with imagination, with internal considering, with identifying, with lying, with negative emotion, with self-justifying, and so on, but also with undeveloped or childish Essence. For the evolution of the man himself depends on a development of his Essence: and a development of his Essence is connected with the formation in him of "second body".

*　　*　　*

Part IV.—Let us now look briefly at the diagram of the Four Bodies of Man, when they are fully developed:

	1	2	3	4	
Christian terminology	"Corporeal" Body	"Natural" Body	"Spiritual" Body	"Celestial" or "Divine" Body	
Outer					Inner
Work terminology	1st Body	2nd Body	3rd Body	4th Body	

Such a man, having these bodies developed in him, is in the *right order* internally. Internal things rule over outer things. To use the Christian terminology, the Celestial or Divine Body rules over the Spiritual Body: the Spiritual Body rules over the Natural Body: and the Natural Body rules over the Corporeal or Physical Body. Next time we will speak of these bodies.

Birdlip, January 17, 1943

THE FOUR BODIES OF MAN

PAPER II

We have already made a few approaches to the idea of further bodies in Man than the physical body. To-night you will hear what might be called the purely formal teaching about the Four Bodies of Man as it was originally given by G. But you must understand that the form in which it is given is, so to speak, highly compressed. It is, as it were, the first glance at the whole subject, and it was given on two occasions. But it was expressly said that very many other ideas enter into this first presentation and that many modifications are necessary in order to understand this very great subject. You will know that in giving a subject that is difficult to people who know nothing about it, a general outline of the conception of the whole matter may be first presented. For example, if a traveller is going to give a lecture upon an unknown country that he has visited himself he may first of all give a general sketch or outline. This lecture on the Four Bodies, given many years ago by G. and recorded by Mr. Ouspensky, must be taken as a general survey. Many additions were made subsequently and many modifications of the original presentation. These we will deal with later in subsequent papers but I think it best now for you to have a general survey concerning the Four Bodies of Man given to you in a purely formal way so that I can refer to this paper later on, knowing that you have already heard it.

Here I will remind you again that in the Gospels there is very definite evidence of the fact that a man must acquire a new body. It is expressed

225

in the terms that a man must be re-born before he can see the Kingdom of Heaven. A man is born once into his physical body but the man who lives in his physical body must acquire a second or psychological body. And when he acquires it he is re-born. You all understand that a man is not merely his physical body. What is really the man himself is the *psychological man* who lives in the physical body. The formation of further bodies refers to the psychological not to the physical man. They refer to the centres in Man which are psychological. The organization of the centres constitutes the basis of the formation of further bodies that can survive the death of the physical body. If a man is psychologically in chaos then nothing is organized in him apart from his physical body. If a man is nothing but a mass of contradictory 'I's, then he has no real permanent 'I' in him.

But I must warn you that in understanding this subject many difficulties have to be faced. Great knowledge is not easy to understand. But I will remind you here of what was said in the last paper—namely, that if this Work becomes real and living to a man and so well organized in him that he does act from the Work, and remembers himself in daily life, that he acts from the Work and no longer from himself, then there is something organized in him and this is *Second Body*. But for this to take place a man must never forget what he is doing in the Work. He must, as G. once said, reach a state such that, in whatever direction he is twisted and turned, however badly he is treated, he never forgets the Work, and never acts save through the medium of the Work.

You all know that this Work is to create something new in you, to give you new ways of taking things, new ways of thinking about life. This is the whole object of the Work. The whole object of the Work is to create something new in you—a *new man* in place of the *old man*. If you see what is meant then you will understand better what the creation of a *Second Body* means.

In the paper that follows you must understand that Mr. Ouspensky is speaking:

· ★ ★ ★

At a meeting of the group one of those present asked G.: "Can it be said that Man possesses immortality?"

"Immortality is one of the qualities we ascribe to people without having a sufficient understanding of their meaning," said G. "Other qualities of this kind are 'individuality', in the sense of an inner unity, a 'permanent and unchangeable 'I' ', 'consciousness' and 'will'. All these qualities *can* belong to Man (he emphasized the word 'can') but this certainly does not mean that they *do belong* to him or belong to each and everyone.

In order to understand *what* Man is at the present time—that is, at the present level of development—it is necessary to imagine to a certain extent what he can be—that is, what he can attain. Only by understanding the correct sequence of development possible will people cease to ascribe to themselves what, at present, they do not possess, and what, perhaps, they can only acquire after great effort and great labour.

According to an ancient teaching, traces of which may be found in many systems, old and new, a man who has attained the full development possible for Man, a man in the full sense of the word, *consists of four bodies*. These four bodies are composed of substances which are finer and finer, mutually interpenetrate one another and form four independent organisms, standing in a definite relationship to one another but capable of independent action.

The reason why it is possible for four bodies to exist is that the human organism, that is, the physical body, has such a complex organization that, under certain conditions, a new independent organism can grow in it, affording a much more convenient and responsive instrument for the activity of consciousness than the physical body. The consciousness manifested in this new body is capable of governing and having full power and control over the physical body. In this second body, under certain conditions, a third body can grow, again having characteristics of its own. The consciousness manifested in this third body has full power and control over the first two bodies; and the third body possesses the possibility of acquiring knowledge inaccessible either to the first or to the second body. In the third body, under certain conditions, a fourth can grow, which differs as much from the third as the third differs from the second and the second from the first. The consciousness manifested in the fourth body has full control over the first three bodies and itself.

These four bodies are defined in different teachings in various ways."

G. drew a diagram reproduced in Figure I and said:

"The first is the physical body, in Christian terminology the 'carnal' body; the second, in Christian terminology, is the 'natural' body; the third is the 'spiritual' body; and the fourth, in the terminology of *esoteric Christianity*, is the 'divine' body.

FIGURE I

1st body	2nd body	3rd body	4th body
Carnal body 'Carriage' (body)	Natural body 'Horse' (feelings, desires)	Spiritual body 'Driver' (mind)	Divine body 'Master' (consciousness and will)

In the terminology of certain Eastern teachings the first body is the *carriage* (body), the second body is the *horse* (feelings, desires), the third, the *driver* (mind) and the fourth, the *master* ('I', consciousness, will).

Such comparisons and parallels may be found in most systems and teachings which recognize something more in Man than the physical body. But almost all these teachings, while repeating in a more or less familiar form the definitions and divisions of the ancient teaching, have forgotten or omitted its most important feature which is that Man is not born with the finer bodies, and that they can only be artificially cultivated in him provided favourable conditions, both internal and external, are present.

The 'second body' is not an indispensable implement for Man. A man can live quite well without a second body. His physical body possesses all the functions necessary for life.

This applies still more, of course, to the 'third body' and the 'fourth body'. Ordinary man does not possess those bodies or their corresponding functions. The reasons for this are, first, the fact that the physical body works with the same substances of which the higher bodies are composed, only these substances are not crystallized in him, and so do not belong to him; and secondly, it has all the functions analogous to those of the higher bodies, though of course they differ from them considerably. The chief difference between a man possessing the physical body and the other functions undeveloped, and a man possessing the developed functions of all four bodies, is that, in the first case, the *physical body* governs all the other functions—in other words, everything is governed by the body which, in its turn, is governed by the external influences of life: such a man is governed by life. In the second case, the command or control emanates from the higher bodies and so a man is no longer governed by outer life.

The functions of the physical body may be represented as parallel to the developed and crystallized functions of the four bodies in the following manner."

G. drew another diagram (Fig. II) representing the parallel functions of a man of physical body and undeveloped functions, and a man of four bodies in whom all the functions are developed.

FIGURE II

UNDEVELOPED MAN OR MAN WORKED BY LIFE: "MAN-MACHINE"

Life $\longrightarrow$	Physical Body Automaton working by external impressions	Desires produced by automaton	Thoughts proceeding from desires	Different and contradictory 'wills' created by desires

DEVELOPED MAN OR MAN OBEYING WILL: CONSCIOUS MAN

Life $\longleftarrow$	Body obeying desires and emotions which are subject to intelligence	Emotional powers and ← desires obeying thought and intelligence	Thinking functions ← obeying consciousness and will	Master. 'I'. ← Ego. Consciousness. Will.
	1st Body	*2nd Body*	*3rd Body*	*4th Body*

"In the first case," said G., "that is, in relation to the undeveloped functions of a man of physical body only, the automaton or man-machine depends upon external influences, and the next three functions depend upon the physical body and the external influences it receives. Changing desires and aversions—'I want', 'I don't want', 'I like', 'I don't like'—that is, functions occupying the place of the second body, depend upon accidental shocks and influences. Thinking, which corresponds to the functions of the third body, is an entirely mechanical process. 'Will' is absent in ordinary mechanical man—he has desires only; and a greater or lesser *permanence* of desires and wishes is called a strong or a weak will."

In the second case—that is, in relation to the developed functions of the four bodies—the working of the physical body depends upon the influences of the other or higher bodies. Instead of the discordant and often contradictory activity of different desires, there is *one single 'I'*, whole, indivisible and permanent; there is *individuality*, dominating the physical body and its desires, and able to overcome both its reluctance and its resistance. Instead of the mechanical process of thinking there is *consciousness*. And there is *will*—that is, a power, not merely composed of various, often contradictory, desires belonging to different 'I's, but issuing from consciousness and governed by individuality or a single and permanent 'I'. Only such a will can be called 'free', for it is independent of accident and cannot be altered or directed from without.

An Eastern teaching describes the functions of the four bodies, their gradual growth and the conditions of this growth, in the following way:

Let us imagine a vessel or a retort filled with various metallic powders. The powders are not in any way connected with each other and every accidental change in the position of the retort or vessel, every accidental knock it receives, changes the relative position of the loose powders. If the retort be shaken or tapped with the finger, then the powder which was at the top may appear at the bottom or in the middle, while the one which was at the bottom may appear at the top. There is nothing permanent in the position of the powders and under such conditions there can be nothing permanent. This is an exact picture of our psychic life, which changes at every moment. Each succeeding moment new influences may change the position of the powder which is on the top and put in its place another which is absolutely its opposite. Science calls this state of the powders the state of mechanical mixture. The essential characteristic of the inter-relation of the powders to one another in this kind of mixture is the instability of these inter-relations and their variability.

It is impossible to stabilize the inter-relation of powders in a state of merely mechanical mixture. But the powders may be *fused*; the nature of the powders makes this possible. To do this a special kind of fire must be lighted under the retort which, by heating and melting the powders, finally fuses them together. Fused in this way the powders will be no longer a mechanical mixture but in a state of chemical union.

And now they can no longer be separated by those simple methods which separated them and made them change places when they were in a state of mechanical mixture. The contents of the retort have become indivisible, 'individual', by fusion. This is a picture of the formation of the second body. The fire by means of which fusion is attained is produced by friction, which, in its turn, is produced in a man by the struggle between 'yes' and 'no' within him. If a man gives way to himself at all times, if he gives way to all his desires and moods, to his changing thoughts, there will be no inner struggle in him, no friction, and so *no fire*. But if, for the sake of attaining a definite aim, he struggles with himself, if he struggles with the thoughts and desires that hinder him, he will then create a fire which will gradually transform his inner world into a single whole.

Let us return to our example. The chemical compound obtained by fusion of the powders in the retort possesses certain qualities, comparable to a certain specific gravity, a certain electrical conductivity and so on. These qualities constitute the characteristics of the substance in question. But by means of work upon it of a certain kind the number of these characteristics may be increased, that is, the fused alloy may be given new properties which did not primarily belong to it. It may be possible to create inner changes in it, to magnetize it, to make it radio-active, and so on.

The process of imparting new properties to the fused alloy corresponds to the process of the formation of the third body and of the acquisition of new knowledge and powers with the help of the third body.

When the third body has been formed and has acquired all the properties, powers and knowledge possible for it, there remains the problem of fixing and directing this knowledge and these powers, because, having been imparted to it by influences of a certain kind, they may be taken away by these same influences or by others. By means of a special kind of work the acquired properties may be made the permanent and inalienable possession of the third body. The process of fixing these acquired properties corresponds to the process of the formation of the fourth body, through which the 'Master' works.

Only the man who possesses four fully-developed bodies can be called a 'man' in the full sense of the word. This man possesses very many properties which ordinary man does not possess and *one of these properties is immortality*. All religions and all ancient teachings contain the idea that, by acquiring the fourth or divine body Man acquires immortality; and they all contain indications of the ways to acquire the fourth body—that is, immortality.

In this connection, certain teachings compare Man with a house of four rooms. Man lives in one room, the smallest and the poorest of all, and, until he is told of it, he does not suspect the existence of the other rooms which are full of treasures. When he does learn of this he begins to seek the keys of these rooms and especially of the fourth, the most important room of all. And when a man has found his way into this room he really becomes the master of his house, for only then does the house belong to him, wholly and for ever.

The fourth room gives Man true immortality and all religious teachings strive to shew the way to it. There are a great many ways, some shorter, some longer, some harder and some easier, but all, without exception, lead or strive to lead, in one direction, that is, to immortality."

Birdlip, January 23, 1943

THE FOUR BODIES OF MAN

PAPER III—THE FOUR WAYS

Mr. Ouspensky is speaking throughout this chapter.

At the next meeting G. began where he had left off the time before.

"I said last time," he said, "that *immortality* is not a property with which Man is born. But Man can acquire immortality. All existing and generally known ways to immortality can be divided into three categories:

1. *The way of the Fakir,*
2. *The way of the Monk,*
3. *The way of the Yogi.*

The way of the fakir is the way of struggle with the physical body, the way of work in the first room. This is a long, difficult and uncertain way. The fakir strives to develop physical will, power over the body. This is attained by means of terrible sufferings, by torturing the body. The whole way of the fakir consists of various incredibly difficult physical exercises. The fakir either stands motionless in the same position for hours, days, months or years; or sits with outstretched arms on a bare stone in sun, rain and snow; or tortures himself with fire, puts his legs into an ant-heap and so on. If he does not fall ill and die before what may be called physical will is developed in him, then he attains the fourth room or the possibility of forming the fourth body. But his other functions—emotional, intellectual and so forth—remain undeveloped. He has acquired will but he has nothing to which he can apply it; he cannot make use of it for gaining knowledge or for self-perfection. As a rule he is too old to begin new work.

But where there are schools of fakirs there are also schools of yogis. Yogis generally keep an eye on fakirs. If a fakir attains what he has aspired to before he is too old, they take him into a yogi school, where first they heal him and restore his power of movement, and then begin to teach him. A fakir has to learn to walk and to speak like a baby. But he now possesses a will which has overcome incredible difficulties on his way and this will may help him to overcome the

231

difficulties on the second part of the way, the difficulties, namely, of developing the intellectual and emotional functions.

You cannot imagine what hardships fakirs undergo. I do not know whether you have seen real fakirs or not. I have seen many: for instance I saw one in the inner court of a temple in India and I even slept near him. Day and night for twenty years he had been standing on the tips of his fingers and toes. He was no longer able to straighten himself. His pupils carried him from one place to another, took him to the river and washed him like some inanimate object. But this was not attained all at once. Think what he had to overcome, what torture he must have suffered in order to get to that stage.

And a man becomes a fakir not because he understands the possibilities and the results of this way, and not because of religious feeling. In all Eastern countries where fakirs exist there is a custom among the common people of promising to give to fakirs a child born after some happy event. Besides this, fakirs often adopt orphans, or simply buy little children from poor parents. These children become their pupils and imitate them, some only outwardly, but some afterwards become fakirs themselves.

In addition to these, other people become fakirs simply from being struck by some fakir they may have seen. Near every fakir in the temples people can be seen who imitate him, who sit or stand in the same posture—not for long of course, but still, occasionally for several hours. And sometimes it happens that a man who went into the temple accidentally on a feast-day, and began to imitate some fakir who particularly struck him, does not return home any more but joins the crowd of that fakir's disciples and later, in the course of time, becomes a fakir himself. You must understand that I take the word 'fakir' in inverted commas. In Persia *Fakir* simply means a beggar; and in India a great many jugglers call themselves *fakirs*. And Europeans, particularly learned Europeans, very often give the name of fakir to *yogis*, as well as to monks of various wandering orders. But in reality the way of fakir, the way of monk and the way of the yogi are entirely different. So far I have spoken of fakirs. *This is the First Way.*

The Second Way is the way of the monk. This is the way of devotion to faith, the way of religious feeling, religious sacrifices. Only a man with very strong religious emotions and a very strong religious imagination can become a 'monk' in the true sense of the word. The way of the monk also is very long and hard. A monk spends years and tens of years struggling with himself, but all his work is concentrated on the 'second room', on the second body, that is, on *feelings*. Subjecting all his other emotions to one emotion, that is, devotion to his faith, he develops *unity* in himself as will over the emotions, and in this way reaches the 'fourth room'. But his physical body and his thinking capacities may remain entirely undeveloped. In order to be able to make use of what he has attained, he must develop the use and control of his body and his capacity to think. This can only be achieved by means of fresh sacrifices, fresh hardships, fresh renunciations. That is, *a monk has to become a yogi and a fakir*: and very few get as far as this.

The Third Way is the way of the yogi. This is the way of knowledge, the way of mind. The way of the yogi consists in working in the 'third room' and in striving to enter the 'fourth room' by means of knowledge. The yogi reaches the 'fourth room' by developing his mind and the control of his thoughts, but his body and emotions may remain un-developed in a corresponding way and, like the fakir and the monk, he may be unable to make use of the results of his attainments. In his case, however, he has the advantage of understanding his position, of knowing what he lacks, what he must do and in what direction he must go.

But all the ways, the way of the fakir as well as the way of the monk and the way of the yogi, have one thing in common. They all begin with the most difficult thing, with a complete change of life, with a renuncia-tion of all wordly things. A man must give up his home, his family, his friends, renounce all the pleasures, attachments and duties of life and go out into the desert, or into a monastery or a yogi school. From the very first day, from the very first step on his way, he must die to the world; only thus can he hope to attain anything in one of these ways.

The Fourth Way is different from the three Ways already considered because the Fourth Way requires no retirement into the desert, nor does it require a man to give up and renounce everything by which he formerly lived. The Fourth Way begins much further on than does the way of the Yogi. This means that a man must be *prepared* for the Fourth Way and this preparation embraces many different sides and takes a long time. Furthermore a man must be living in conditions favourable for work in the Fourth Way, or, in any case, in conditions which do not render it impossible. It must be understood that both in the inner and in the external life of a man there may be conditions which create insuperable *barriers* to the Fourth Way. Furthermore, the Fourth Way has no definite forms like the ways of the fakir, the monk and the yogi. First of all, it has to *be found*. This is the first test. At the same time, the beginning of the Fourth Way is easier than the beginning of the ways of the fakir, the monk and the yogi. In the Fourth Way it is possible to work and to follow this way while remaining in the usual conditions of life, continuing to do the usual work, preserving former relations with people, and without renouncing or giving up anything. On the contrary, the conditions of life in which a man is placed at the beginning of his work, in which, so to speak, the Work finds him, are the *best possible* for him, at any rate at the beginning of the work. These conditions are natural for him. These conditions *are the man himself*, because a man's life and its conditions correspond to *what he is*. Any conditions different from those created by life would be artificial for a man and in such artificial conditions the Work would not be able to touch *every side* of his being at once.

Thanks to this the Fourth Way affects simultaneously every side of a man's being. It is work *in the three rooms at once*. The fakir works in the first room, the monk in the second, the yogi in the third. On reaching the fourth room the fakir, the monk and the yogi leave behind them many things unfinished, and they cannot make full use of what they have attained because they are not masters of all their functions. The fakir is master of his body but not of his emotions or his mind, which remain undeveloped; the monk is master of his emotions but not of his body or his mind; the yogi is master of his mind but not of his body or his emotions.

Then again the Fourth Way differs from the other ways in that *the principal demand made upon a man in it is the demand for understanding*. A man must do nothing that he does not understand, except as an experiment under the supervision and direction of a teacher. In the Fourth Way the more a man *understands* what he is doing the greater will be the results of his efforts. *This is a fundamental principle of the Fourth Way.* The results of work in it are in proportion to the consciousness and understanding of the Work. No 'faith' is required in the Fourth Way; on the contrary faith of any kind is opposed to the Fourth Way. In the Fourth Way a man must see for himself. He must satisfy himself of the truth of what he is told. And until he is satisfied he must do nothing.

The method of the Fourth Way consists in doing something in one room and simultaneously doing something corresponding to it in the other two rooms—that is to say, while working on the physical body to work simultaneously on the mind and the emotions, and while working on the mind to work on the physical body and the emotions, and while working on the emotions to work on the mind and the physical body. This can be achieved, thanks to the fact that in the Fourth Way it is possible to make use of certain knowledge inaccessible to the ways of the fakir, the monk and the yogi. This knowledge makes it possible to work in three directions simultaneously. A whole parallel series of physical, mental and emotional efforts and exercises serves this purpose. In addition, in the Fourth Way it is possible to individualize the work of each separate person—that is to say, each person can only do what is necessary and not what is useless *for him*. This is due to the fact that the Fourth Way dispenses with a great deal of what is superfluous and preserved simply through tradition in the other ways.

So that when a man attains will in the Fourth Way he can make use of it because he has acquired the necessary development and control of bodily, emotional and intellectual functions as well. And besides, he has saved a great deal of time by working on the three sides of his being in a parallel way and simultaneously.

The Fourth Way is sometimes called the *way of the sly man*. The 'sly man' knows some secret which the fakir, monk and yogi do not know. How the 'sly man' learned this secret—is his secret. Perhaps he found it in some old book, perhaps he inherited it, perhaps he bought it, perhaps he stole it from someone. It makes no difference. The 'sly man' knows the secret and with its help outstrips the fakir, the monk and the yogi.

Of the four the fakir acts in the crudest manner; he knows very little and understands very little. Let us suppose that by a whole month of intense torture he develops in himself a certain energy, a certain substance which produces certain changes in him. He does it absolutely blindly, with his eyes shut, knowing neither aim, methods nor results, simply in imitation of others.

The monk knows what he wants a little better; he is guided by religious feeling, by a desire for achievement, for salvation; he trusts his teacher who tells him what to do, and he believes that his efforts and sacrifices are 'pleasing to God'. Let us suppose that a week of fasting, continual prayer, privations and so on, enables him to attain what the fakir develops in himself by a month of self-torture.

The yogi knows considerably more. He knows what he wants, he knows why he needs it, he knows how it can be acquired. He knows, for instance, that it is necessary for his purpose to produce a certain substance in himself. He knows that this substance can be produced in one day by certain kinds of mental exercises, or concentration of consciousness. So he keeps his attention on these exercises for a whole day without allowing himself a single outside thought, and he obtains what he needs. In this way a Yogi spends on the same thing only one day compared with a month spent by the fakir and a week spent by the monk.

But in the Fourth Way knowledge is still more exact and perfect. A man who follows the Fourth Way knows quite definitely what substances he needs for his aims and he knows that these substances can be produced within the body by a month of physical suffering, by a week of emotional strain or by a day of mental exercises—and also, *that they can be introduced into the organism from without if it is known how to do it.* And so, instead of spending a whole day in exercises like the Yogi, a week in prayer like the monk, or a month in self-torture life the fakir, he simply prepares and swallows a little pill which contains all the substances he wants and, in this way, without loss of time, he obtains the required results.

It must be noted further," said G., "that in addition to these proper and *legitimate* Ways, there are also artificial ways which give temporary results only, and also *wrong* ways which may even give permanent results. In these ways a man also seeks the key to the fourth room and sometimes finds it. But what he finds in the fourth room is not yet known. It also happens that the door to the fourth room is opened artificially with a skeleton key. And in both these cases the room may prove to be empty."

With this G. stopped.

Birdlip, February 1, 1943

THINKING FROM LIFE
AND THINKING FROM THE WORK

PAPER I

The following paper was written after a conversation about thinking from the level of life and thinking from the level of the Work. The conversation started with something that was said about people who are possessive—that is, identified with their possessions—who say, for instance: "Where is *my* book?" or "I have not had *my* breakfast" or "*My* proper sleep," or "*My* right share" and so on. It is not merely the question of possessing things but of feeling a right to have things that was discussed. You all know the kind of working-man who puts his sacred rights before everything else—who says: "I must have *my* dinner," in the middle of some job of the utmost importance, and is completely put out and deeply offended for the rest of the day if he is told to give up his dinner for once. And the same man, if some one borrows some tool he is not using will make endless fuss—"*my* chisel, *my* hammer" and so on. The example is clear enough. But the point is to find in yourself this "working-man"—this 'I' that insists on its sacred rights and says *my* to everything and which is so stiff and rigid and unintelligent. Remember the sign of intelligence is the power of adaptation and that all strength in the Work means flexibility, not rigidity. Your "strong man" in life is usually, from the Work angle, merely a man crystallized in Personality —a one-track man, as it is called. From this conversation we passed to thinking from life and thinking from the Work. To think from the Work is to think from the ideas taught by the Work. If you try to do this Work *without* having taken in the ideas, and without thinking from them, then it is like trying to learn swimming while you are lying on the ground. The basis of your efforts is all wrong.

The Work ideas are to give us *a new way of thinking*. Thinking from life-ideas and yet trying to do the Work is to mix things. You have to learn to look at life and its events *through* the ideas of the Work—to re-interpret life. Unless you have pondered and assimilated the ideas of the Work, you will not have enough force to resist the action of life on you. So your personal work will keep on losing force. Everyone thinks from *his ordinary ideas* or opinions. But the Work gives us *new* ideas, new conceptions. If we think from the ideas of the Work we see life differently and our personal work will be assisted by the ideas of the Work. Then work on oneself will receive force from the ideas of the Work. Ideas have force. Ideas are the most powerful of all things. But to work on oneself with ordinary life-ideas is eventually impossible. The parables about this in the Gospels were mentioned in previous Papers —for instance, sewing a new piece of cloth on to an old garment, and putting new wine into old bottles, and so on.

Let us take to-night one of the ideas of the Work that can make us think in a new way about life. Let me first remind you that in the Gospels it is constantly said that a man must *think in a new way*—the word being wrongly translated as *repent*. To change your being, to raise its level, you must begin to think in a new way. And all the ideas given you again and again in the Work are to furnish you with the means of thinking in a *new* way.

The idea that *Man is asleep* is a new idea, as is the personal application of it—meaning that *you* are asleep. The whole general idea that a man can *evolve* in this life, and is created to do so, is again a new idea.

Have you grasped the *idea of evolution* as taught by the Work? Have you made it part of your thinking yet? Have you, in short, taken it seriously? Or is it merely something vague lying in your memory? Remember that this Work is taught for a certain time only. There is a time-limit.

There is evolution and there is not evolution. There is, for us as individuals, no *mechanical* evolution. But there is *conscious evolution*, and esoteric teaching throughout the ages refers to the possibility of *conscious individual evolution*. Conscious evolution only takes place by conscious effort. This is what the Work is about. A single individual *can* evolve. But mankind cannot evolve save in terms of the evolution of the planets. *You* can evolve now. But *everyone* cannot evolve. There is no collective evolution: but there is *individual* evolution. The emphasis is upon *you*, as an individual and a self-evolving organism. Do you grasp the Work-teaching on this subject? This is one, and only one, example of thinking from an *idea* of the Work. If you begin to think from this idea you will receive *force* for working on yourself. Whereas, if you have no clear ideas, or merely life-ideas, you will think wrongly. The ideas in your mind will be wrong and so, when you try to work on yourself, what you are doing will contradict your ordinary thoughts. And so your ordinary thoughts and ideas will run counter to your efforts. Whereas if you work on yourself in the presence of the Work—that is, in correspondence with the ideas of the Work—your efforts on yourself will be aided by the ideas of the Work in your mind. The ideas of the Work conduct very great force when they are taken in and become part of your inner thinking. But life-ideas drain you of force. They make you identify with life and all its events. Life drains people. The Work-ideas protect you from life and help you to create more force. They prevent life from "eating" you—that is, the Moon. They prevent life from "working you"—that is, as a machine driven by outer events. The Work-ideas re-interpret life for you. They tell you what life is like.

Now let us refer to the opening part of the Paper—to the man who says: "*My* book, *my* breakfast, *my* dinner," and so on, and who has so many ideas about his sacred rights. Such a man is in every man and this man in a man thinks from life. But in the Work we must gradually no longer think in such a way. These personal matters become of less importance in view of the ideas of the teaching. But if we cannot escape from this level of personal thinking, of personal self-love, personal grievances and personal advantages, how can we expect even to begin to think *beyond ourselves* and our requirements? When my wife and I went to the Institute in France, G. said: "Remember, Personality has scarcely any right to exist here." Think what that means! How difficult it is to speak to people in the Work who value themselves, people who have precious ideas of themselves. They have their feelings of themselves or their particular forms of self-love. And it is the basis of self-love, self-conceit and self-admiration that has to be shifted—and how difficult it is! And you will see that a man or a woman who really thinks well of himself or herself will not be able to hear the Work-ideas. A person who has a strong sense of his or her virtue will at the same time have a strong sense of *my* and *me*.

Why? Because such a person is thinking of *my* book, *my* breakfast, *my* dinner, *my*self, *my* personal value, all the time. This is *sleep*. This is one reason, one of many, why the ideas of the Work, which are designed to produce a *mental revolution*, a *change of mind*, in short, a *transformation*, cannot act on us as they should. A man in the Work must come to the realization that he is *nothing*. We look vaguely at the diagrams or write down notes. Or we say: "Oh, yes, I have heard that before," and go on thinking just as we always do, often thinking we are sure of our own worth and sure that we really know what is right or wrong. But this sleep, this deep infatuation with ourselves, this self-conceit, must later on cease. A man must begin to feel that there is nothing else for him but the Work, and that he must *for himself* think out and see the meaning of everything he hears day after day taught him in the Work. Then he begins, at last, to awaken. The *Driver* in him begins to climb on to the box and take hold of the reins. The Driver is the *mind*—not the ordinary mind but the mind beginning to *think* the ideas of the Work. This is the *awakening mind*. This is thinking in a new way. This is that thing so insisted on in the Gospels—μετάνοια—*thinking in a new way*—the first step in leading to change of being. This is what in the Gospels is called "hearing"—"*whosoever heareth . . .*" It is hearing the ideas with the mind, not with the ears, not with the memory. And only this kind of *hearing* will awaken the Driver. It is hearing, not the words, but the meaning of the words. This is *hearing*.

*　　*　　*

We know, from the teaching of this Work, that Man is sown on "Earth" by the "Sun", as a self-developing seed. Man is an experiment on the Earth, an experiment made in the laboratory of the Sun. Now this is a new idea. The level of Being and Intelligence, represented externally by the Sun and marked in the Ray of Creation by the note *Sol*, creates Man as an experiment on the Earth, represented by the lower note *Mi*.

Notice that Man is created from *above*, from a higher level. The note *Sol*, externally represented by the Sun, creates Man on earth with the object of his evolving in understanding up to the level of the note *Sol*. Man is therefore created incomplete, undeveloped, unevolved—but capable of evolution. Unless the level of Being and Intelligence represented by the note *Sol* in the Ray of Creation can receive a sufficient number of evolved human beings, passing upwards from the note *Mi*, then this small twig in the whole created Tree of the Universe—namely, our private Earth and Moon—may be destroyed as useless.

*   *   *

Two kinds of evolution are possible for Man. Man finds himself situated on a *Being* called the Earth whose period of evolution is very vast in comparison with Man's life. Before the Earth evolves to the state of the Sun, many millions of years of our time must pass. To the Earth it is merely its lifetime. The Earth may however fail to evolve, in which case it is broken up into a mass of small fragments that revolve round the Sun as minute "planets" or "asteroids". There are many of these between Mars and Jupiter.

Now the evolution of the Earth is held back by the evolution of its Moon. You must understand that the idea of a planet *evolving* is a Work-idea. It is not found in science. It alters our whole notion of the Universe. The period of time necessary according to the Work-teaching for a planet to evolve is something of the order of eighty thousand million years of Man's time. I will remind you of the *Table of Time*. To the planet itself it is a period of eighty years on the scale of its time. Since the Earth is in close relation to its Moon, the evolution of the former is held back by the state of the latter. Actually influences—vibrations and very fine matters—continually reach the Moon from the Earth and feed it just as the Sun feeds the Earth in a similar way. For example, all the useless human suffering, negative emotions and violence on Earth, feeds the Moon. Remember that everything is made use of in the Universe. If Man were to evolve quickly—that is, begin to awaken— useless suffering and violence would cease on Earth. But it is not in the interests of the Earth and Moon that Man should evolve *independently* of them. Man's evolution must go hand in hand with their evolution. This is only one of the two kinds of evolution possible for Man. You will see that it demands periods of time that are so prodigious that for practical purposes it is meaningless for us. It has no relation to our short lives. For this reason it is said in the Work that there is *no progress* in human affairs. The planets keep Man back—keep him asleep. I will quote here to you a conversation that G. had with Mr. Ouspensky, many years ago, before the latter had been shewn the diagram of the Ray of Creation. G. was giving some preliminary ideas leading up to the great conception of the Ray.

Mr. Ouspensky reports this conversation:

Somewhere about this time I was very much struck by a talk about the *sun*, the *planets* and the *moon*. I do not remember how this talk began. But I remember that G. drew a small diagram and tried to explain what he called the *correlation of forces in different worlds*. This was in connection with the previous talk—that is, in connection with the influences acting upon humanity. The idea was roughly this: humanity, or, more correctly, *organic life on earth*, is acted upon simultaneously by influences proceeding from various sources and different worlds: influences from the planets, influences from the moon, influences from the sun, influences from the stars. All these influences act simultaneously; one influence predominates at one moment and another influence at another moment. And for Man there is a certain possibility of making a *choice of influences*—in other words, of passing from one influence to another.

"To explain *how* would need a very long talk," said G., "so we will talk about this some other time. At this moment I want you to understand one thing: it is impossible to become free from one influence without becoming subject to another. The whole thing, all *work on oneself*, consists in choosing the influence to which you wish to subject yourself, and actually falling under this influence. And for this it is necessary to know before-hand which influence is the more profitable."

What interested me in this talk was that G. spoke of the planets and the moon as *living beings*, having definite ages, a definite period of life and possibilities of development and transition to other planes of *being*. From what he said it appeared that the moon was not a 'dead planet', as is usually accepted, but, on the contrary, a 'planet in birth', a planet at the very initial stages of its development which had not yet 'reached the degree of intelligence possessed by the earth' as he expressed it.

"But the moon is growing and developing," said G., "And some time, it will, possibly, attain the same level as the Earth. Then, near it, a new moon will appear and the Earth will become their sun. At one time the Sun was like the Earth. And earlier still the Sun was like the Moon."

This attracted my attention at once. Nothing had ever seemed to me more artificial, unreliable and dogmatic than all the usual theories of the origin of planets and solar systems, from the Kant-Laplace theory down to the very latest, with all their additions and variations. The 'general public' considers these theories, or, at any rate, the last one known to it, to be scientific or proven. But in actual fact there is of course nothing less scientific and less proven than these theories. Therefore the fact that G.'s system accepted an altogether different theory, an *organic* theory having its origin in entirely new principles and shewing a different universal order, appeared to me very interesting and important.

"In what relation does the intelligence of the Earth stand to the intelligence of the Sun?" I asked.

"The intelligence of the Sun is divine," said G., "But the Earth can become the same; only, of course, it is not guaranteed and the Earth may die having attained nothing".

"Upon what does this depend?" I asked.

G.'s answer was very vague. "There is a definite period," he said, "for a certain thing to be done. If, by a certain time, what ought to be done has not been done, the Earth may perish without having attained what it could have attained."

"Is this period known?" I asked.

"It is known," said G., "But it would be of no advantage whatever for people to know it. It would even be worse. Some would believe it, some would not believe it, others would demand proofs. Afterwards they would begin to break one another's heads. Everything ends this way."

On another occasion, in connection with the idea that the evolution of Man in general is held back by the evolution of the planets, G. was speaking of *progress*. The talk was then about the latest inventions of science and so of Man's apparent progress. G. said: "Yes, machines are making progress, but not Man." In answer to a question whether Man had not progressed far beyond what he used to be, even in historical time, G. said: "It is strange how you so easily believe in this word progress. It is as if this word hypnotized you, so that you cannot see the truth. *Man* does not progress. *There is no progress whatever.* Everything is just the same as it was thousands, and tens of thousands, of years ago. It is only the outward form that changes. The essence does not change. This is because Man remains essentially just the same. "Civilised" and "cultured" people live with exactly the same interests as the most ignorant savages. Modern civilisation is based on violence and slavery, but these take different outer forms. All these fine words about progress and civilisation are merely words. If Man is the same, life is the same."

This of course produced a particularly deep impression on us, because it was said in 1916, at the time when the latest manifestation of "progress" and of "civilisation", in the form of a war such as the world had not yet seen, was continuing to grow and develop, drawing more and more millions of people into its orbit.

I remembered that a few days before this talk I had seen two enormous lorries loaded to the height of the first floors of the houses with new unpainted wooden *crutches*. For some reason I was particularly struck by these lorries. In these mountains of crutches *for legs which were not yet torn off* there was a particularly cynical mockery of all the things with which people deceive themselves. Involuntarily I imagined that similar lorries were sure to be going about in Berlin, Paris, London, Vienna, Rome and Constantinople. And, as a result of all this horror, all these cities, almost all of which I knew so well and liked just because they supplemented and gave contrast to one another, had now become hostile both to me and to one another and separated by new walls of hatred and crime.

I spoke about these lorry-loads of crutches and of my thoughts about them.

"What do you expect?" said G., "People are machines. Machines have to be blind and unconscious; they cannot be otherwise, and all their actions have to correspond to their nature. *Everything happens.* No one does anything. "Progress" and "civilisation", in the real meaning of these words, can appear only as the result of *conscious* efforts. And only each single man can make *conscious* efforts. But no one wants to do so. Progress is only possible in each single man. It cannot appear as the result of unconscious mechanical actions. And what conscious effort can there be in machines? And if one machine is unconscious then a hundred machines are unconscious, and so are a thousand machines, or a hundred thousand, or a million. And the unconscious activity of a *million machines* must necessarily result in mass-destruction and mass-extermination. *It is precisely in unconscious involuntary personal manifestations that all evil begins.* This is the origin of evil. You do not yet understand and cannot imagine all the results of this accumulation of evil, from small sources. But the time will come when you will understand. If Man behaved consciously, all this evil would cease. But *Man is not conscious.*"

With this, so far as I remember, the talk ended.

★　　★　　★

But apart from the evolution of Man in terms of vast planetary time, there is another evolution possible for him. There has always been a special teaching about Man that has to do with this immediate evolution. The very few fragments of Christ's teaching presented in the Gospels refer to knowledge about this evolution. All the teaching about Man's possible *inner* growth and evolution can be called *esoteric* teaching. Esoteric means *inner.* Esoteric teaching is about inner evolution—about the inner man—not the outer life-side of a man. All the Work is about this possible immediate inner evolution that is open to Man. And here lies another great conception or idea taught by the Work, in connection with the Ray of Creation and the side-octave from the Sun. Man is sown on Earth from the note *Sol* with the possibility of inner development, and the existence of this Work, the existence of Christ's teaching and the existence of many other teachings, is due solely to this fact— that Man is created as an organism capable of undergoing an inner evolution, quite apart from the evolution of the planets.

Now if you can grasp these two great conceptions of Man—how mankind in general is held back for planetary reasons and how at the same time there is a way open for those who wish to awaken, you will begin to think in terms of the Work.

THINKING FROM LIFE
AND THINKING FROM THE WORK

PAPER II

There are two practical sides to this Work called the line of work on knowledge and the line of work on being. No one can work on the second line—the line of being—unless he has worked on the line of knowledge. That is, a man must *know* first what he has to work upon in his being.

Knowledge is a matter belonging to the Intellectual Centre. This must change first, before anything else can change. A man must absorb new knowledge before he can change. The knowledge of this Work needs to be *thought about.* Thinking is the function of the Intellectual Centre. If you do not think about the knowledge the Work is teaching you, then your *mind* cannot change. And if your mind does not change, *you* cannot change.

You may believe that it makes no difference how you think. But it is important, in the Work, not to think wrongly. Every time you think, you make a track in the mind. If you think wrongly, you make a wrong track and the mind becomes like a delicate electrical machine which is all wrongly connected. This certainly is the ordinary effect of life on the mind. But the ideas of the Work are to make right connections and so give you a new mind. The Work is rich in ideas and the Work as a whole can form a complete mental organism in the mind. Life does not do this. The ideas you learn from life are confused and contradictory. They cannot *form* the mind on all its sides. But the Work ideas can. They relate everything rightly in giving the right scale to things. This is because they come from Conscious Man.

Last time the first part of the paper on "Thinking from Life and Thinking from the Work" was read. This followed on the talks about the Four Bodies that exist in a fully conscious man. Now, although the subject is difficult to understand, as you were warned, it is not so difficult to understand the idea of a man being worked from outside or from inside. You remember the diagram with the arrows:

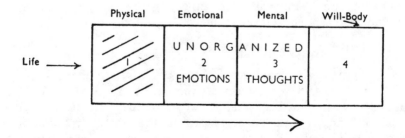

This is an ordinary man, having one organized body—the physical body, represented by the first room—and nothing organized in the second or third rooms, and no entry into the Fourth Room. Such a man is acted upon from outside, from life, from the body, from the senses, from what he sees, hears and touches. He is undeveloped Man, or Man-Machine, because he is driven like a cog-wheel by the great wheel of life.

Let us take the second diagram, representing a fully conscious man:

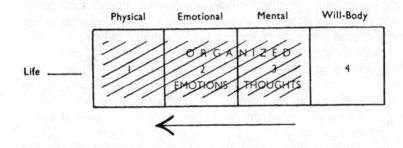

In his case Will controls him, acting through his developed bodies in the direction of the arrow. That is, he is not controlled from outside, by life, but from within. Notice the direction of the arrows, in the two cases. The diagrams represent a man controlled from outside and a man controlled from within. Let us simply take this general idea.

Now as long as we think from *life* we are controlled by life. To *create* anything mentally in ourselves that can resist life we must think *from the Work*. We are given in this Work a system of ideas which, if connected rightly, will relate us in a new way to every side of life. When the Work ideas are assimilated and lived they transform the way in which you take life and take yourself. But this cannot happen if you do not think from the Work. Until the Work ideas are rightly connected, the third room will never be properly furnished or organized. But if these ideas become connected rightly in you then your mind will become a receiver, an organized instrument, that can pick up the vibrations of Higher Centres, of finer and finer meaning, and then you will be taught from within. If you think from the Work you will think from *inside*. The mind, strengthened by receiving the ideas of the Work and thinking from them, will form something organized, something *within* and independent of outer life.

*　　*　　*

Let us continue to study one of the Work-ideas, in the light of what has just been said. We spoke last time of the Work-ideas about evolution. It was pointed out that the Work teaches that the general evolution of Man cannot be taken apart from the general evolution of the part of the Universe in which we live. We spoke of the evolution of the planets and the evolution of Mankind and the connection between them. It was said that the evolution of Mankind as a whole cannot go faster than the evolution of the earth with its attendant moon. That is, Mankind's evolution as distinct from *one* man's evolution is in terms of planetary time, which is prodigious time for us—thousands of millions of years. So for practical purposes, Mankind does not evolve mechanically, and there is no mechanical progress. If a person is told that in, say, a thousand million years, all Mankind may possibly be on a higher level of evolution, it cannot interest him in any genuine way or really alter anything for him in his daily life and his difficulties.

Now, in connection with "thinking from the Work", let us take the phrase: "Mankind on earth is an experiment of the Solar Laboratory". It may easily prove that this experiment will be useless and be set aside as a failure. That is, in a thousand million years, Mankind may not be in any higher state, but perhaps may have been made like the ants, discarded as being of no importance and made to follow a useless cycle of toil that leads in no direction, and from which there is no way out. But this can only happen if the *primary* reason for Man's creation on earth is not fulfilled. The primary reason is *individual evolution*. If the conditions for the individual evolution of an individual man are destroyed, then the experiment of Man on earth will prove a failure. And if Man tampers with himself, with his body, with his glands, and so on, as the ants appear to have done, then one of the conditions of evolution will be destroyed. If the experiment of Man on earth proves a failure, this will mean also that there will be no evolution for Mankind in general in terms of planetary time and planetary evolution. Everything depends upon the primary reason for Man's creation on earth—namely, *individual evolution*. Man is created a self-developing organism and if the conditions for his self-development are destroyed, then Mankind, as an experiment, becomes useless. The Sun sows Man on earth primarily as a being capable of a definite inner development and secondarily to serve nature, to serve the necessities of the Ray of Creation. That is, Man taken *individually* has quite a different meaning from Man taken *collectively*. Evolution is possible for *a man*: but it is not possible for *Mankind*. A single individual can come under the influences descending from the level of the Divine Intelligence of the Sun. But Mankind as a *mass* has a cosmic function and is under the influences of the earth and the moon. Mankind as a mass serves the Ray together with the rest of Organic Life at the point where a sensitive transmitter or *shock* is required between the notes *Fa* and *Mi*. This is the teaching of the Work about evolution. Unless the mind grasps it and thinks from it, a person will think wrongly —that is, he will not think *from the ideas of the Work*. Of course we are only taking one example here. But if a man does not think from the ideas of the Work, the Work will be faint and weak in him.

One difficulty in thinking in this way, in the above example, is due to the fact that people think that the *masses* do things. They do not realize that only *individuals* do anything. Cultures have been founded by individual men, never by the masses. Humanity, the masses, never do anything save that they *destroy* often enough what individual men have built. All progress in the sciences is the work of individual men, not of the masses. All art, architecture, music, is due to the work of individual men. The explanation is that a *mass* of people is on a *lower level* than a single individual and so, from this point of view, evolution is only possible for individuals and not for the masses.

*　　*　　*

Now if you are going to think from the Work, you must grasp the meaning of esoteric teaching. You have been told that unless the Sun receives a sufficient quantity of evolving beings rising from the earth, the primary object of Man's creation will not be fulfilled. The chief conditions under which an individual man can evolve depends upon the existence of *esoteric teaching on the earth* and its reception by those capable of understanding it. Esoteric teaching is about inner evolution. It comes from the level of the Sun. That is, it comes from the circle of Conscious Humanity. Fully-developed man, fully-evolved man, is at the level of the intelligence of the Sun. From this level, teaching is sown on the earth. If the conditions of life are such that esoteric teaching, whether in religious form or otherwise, cannot exist on the earth, then Man is doomed to failure, and another experiment will have to be made. Now since the evolution of Man depends on contact with the Conscious Circle of Humanity, let us try to understand what takes place when a teaching is sown on the earth. All real teaching begins with the formation of a *school*. A *school* is not open to life as is an ordinary school, but it has some similarities. For instance, no one can enter a real school without long preliminary training. Everyone has to reach a certain level of understanding, just as, to enter, let us say, a University, a man must be able to pass certain examinations. Speaking very briefly, a school only lasts for a certain time, just as does a religion. That is, it dies in so far as it no longer conducts any force. Everything on earth has its period of life. A religion can become mechanical and no longer capable of awaking the inner side of a man. Its inner meaning is lost, and ritual and outer form only remain. The meaning has been lost —that is, the force. But esoteric teaching does not die. When a particular school on earth, or a religion, dies, then there is always another school, another form of teaching arising. Esoteric teaching continues. It preserves itself. The Ark riding on the flood of evil refers to this idea. Christ's parables about the *vineyard* that might be destroyed refer to an esoteric school of teaching, not to esotericism itself. But all these matters must be spoken of later. The point is that if Man loses touch with esoteric teaching, he is cut off and must degenerate. We cannot speak fully about schools in this paper. The main thing to grasp is that any real teaching coming from the Conscious Circle of Humanity can only exist in a school and be transmitted orally. When it passes into life, when it is written down, it becomes changed. One reason for the change is that the mind of Conscious Man thinks in a way in which ordinary minds cannot think. Conscious Man thinks psychologically: mechanical man thinks logically. This change is expressed in the Work by the diagram of the three influences called C, B and A. C influences are directly from Conscious Humanity. When they enter the circle of mechanical life they are changed into B influences. A influences are the influences created in life, by wars, money, politics, science, business, and so on.

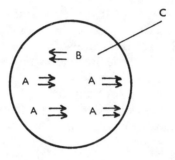

In the mechanical circle of life, A and B influences exist. A man who possesses Magnetic Centre is aware of this. But a man who does not, cannot perceive it. A influences drive life and produce the ordinary history of the world. Now the Conscious Circle of Humanity cannot communicate *directly* with the mechanical circle of humanity, for they would not be understood. .The Conscious Circle of Humanity understand one another, but mechanical men would understand in quite different ways and begin to quarrel and break one another's heads. And this actually does take place. If all Mankind were developing, if all were overcoming their violence, their state of sleep, their negative emotions, their internal considering—in fact—doing this Work—then it would be possible. But for this understanding to *begin* to be possible, men would have to speak a common language. But there is no common language, and so people do not and cannot possibly understand one another. Only the Conscious Circle of Humanity—that is, No. 5, No. 6 and No. 7 Man—can understand one another. No. 4 men begin to understand one another—that is, people developed in all 3 centres and so *balanced men*. But the circle of mechanical humanity—No. 1, No. 2 and No. 3 Man—cannot understand one another. They are respectively one-centre men, one-sided, and so unbalanced. In the study of this Work, we are learning a common language by means of which we can begin to understand one another. You have only to realize the difference between talking to a person who knows this Work and a person who knows nothing to realize a little what this means. It makes no difference whether you learn this Work in Russian or French or English. You are, just the same, learning a *common language*. And, in a sense, it can be said that we are studying the language of Conscious

Humanity. And that is why it is important to learn it and understand it and *think* in terms of it—that is, think from the Work. If everyone on earth began to study and speak a common language, in this respect, then it might be possible for Mankind to take a step forward. It would be possible for something universally agreed upon to develop. It would be possible for everyone to make the necessary sacrifices and efforts at the right time, when shocks were necessary, so as to fulfil the demands of the Law of the Octave. And the Work teaches that a step forward is now possible and that Man need not "serve the Moon" as formerly. But look what is happening. Is there any less servitude on earth even though there is less servitude needed by the moon?

Now if you will leave the world of *If*, the world of phantasy and imagination, and think practically, you will realize the difficulty of any step forward. You have only to notice how difficult it is for yourself to learn the common language of the Work and how difficult it is to keep awake and make the necessary efforts that this Work teaches. Habit is so strong. And do not blame the Conscious Circle of Humanity. Man has been given many things to ease his life, but he misuses them all. Look at to-day—all the world turning to making weapons as never before. Yet everything that can be done to make men evolve *individually* has been done and is done. But there can be no mass-evolution, no forced evolution, no evolution by command or by compulsion. For all evolution is a matter of the individual understanding—of a man seeing for himself. The right inner development of a man and his right crystallization depend upon *understanding*. And you know that from the esoteric point of view a man *is* his understanding: and a man's understanding is *what he is*. But you cannot *make* a man understand. You cannot *force him* to understand why he should not act as he does, or *compel* him to understand that he should not speak as he does. There can be no violence, no collective coercion and above all no physical *fear* used—for fear does not develop the understanding. You cannot make a dog understand what you want him to do by fear. You can only teach him what he must not do by that method and he will never *understand* why. Our case is the same. The Esoteric Circle of Humanity cannot force Man to understand. It cannot appear visibly in some supernatural or terrible way to Man—for then Man would be forced by the evidence of his senses and also forced by fear. He would be forced from *outside*. But that is not *understanding*, which depends on your seeing the meaning of something for yourself. And to see the meaning of something is *internal* and develops the internal side of a man, so that it becomes stronger than the outer, life-driven side. It is necessary to see the difference between seeing something with the senses and understanding something with the mind. A man's evolution is *inner*. His possibilities, as a created being, lie in a development of the mind and emotions—of his *knowledge* and *being*. And these form his *understanding*. Only through understanding is development possible. This is the basis of the Fourth Way—*understanding*.

THINKING FROM LIFE
AND THINKING FROM THE WORK

PAPER III—ON EFFORT IN THE WORK

This Work has sometimes been compared with a map and a compass. A man is given a map and a compass, neither of which he understands at first.

After a time he begins to realize one or two things, as, for example, that Personality must get less active. You know that whatever is done through Personality is done through the force of external circumstances. You think *you* are active, but it is Personality. If life alone makes you act, you are not free. External circumstances make great and small men. External circumstances drive men, as different kinds of machines, in this direction or in that. But the directions given by the map and compass of the Work are not derived from external circumstances because the Work is another force coming, not from life, but from outside life; the ideas of the Work are not new directions for life but new directions for *living in life*.

Let us take the Work-idea that a man must aim to become No. 4 man—that is, *Balanced Man*. No. 1 man is either moving or instinctive, No. 2 man is emotional and No. 3 man is intellectual. All these are one-sided. One centre predominates over the other centres. But in Balanced Man, all the centres have a requisite development. That is, No. 4 man is *all-sided*, and this means that all sides of life are known and understood by him to some extent. He is not a man who says, for example: "Oh, politics are all rot," or "Greek and Latin are silly," or "Emotion is hysteria," or "Sport should be abolished," or "Religion is rubbish," or "Science is bunk," or "What's the good of this or that?" and so on. A Balanced Man or a man aiming at balance knows that every aspect of life is necessary for development. He does not waste his time complaining of life and finding fault with it, because he realizes that life is a *school* and that is its real meaning, that life is a means and *not an end* in itself.

Now at this point people often say: "Yes, but the Work teaches that Man has no will, so how can he alter anything?" The Work says that Man has no real permanent will because he has no real permanent 'I'. But it says that Man has a small degree of will, comparable with the degree of freedom of movement a violin has in its case. But it will all depend *in what direction* he uses the small will that he naturally has. If he never uses it in connection with the *directions* given by the Work, he will not develop any further will. But it is impossible to get this point of view aright unless one has the possibility of viewing one's own life from the judgment of esoteric teaching—that is, unless one sees the necessity of inner development. A man, viewing himself, as the result of his personal self-observation, in the light of the directions given by the Work, will recognize sooner or later where he is deficient, and seek on purpose what in life will help him in this respect and will go to it willingly. He will not be following a life-direction but a direction in life, given him by the Work. It will not be done through Personality —that is, through the force of *external* circumstances, from life-ideas— but from his own insight into himself—that is, through *internal* circumstances, created in him by thinking from Work-ideas. Everyone, without exception, is *crossed* in life. But if a man in the Work begins to reach the point of understanding that he must bear the burden of his own life and begin to work on himself and change himself, then the whole situation is changed. His choice of will then will lie no longer in life—whether he smokes these or those cigarettes, etc. The small amount of will that we have must begin to turn in the direction given by the map and compass that the Work offers us. If people are still thinking from life, they say: "Why should we do this?" Yet exactly here lies the beginning of the Work in regard to effort. You can be the same person every day if you like: or you can wish to be different. You can go on submitting to negative emotions, identifying, being angry, justifying yourself from your life-ideas, and so on—or, on the other hand, you can think from the Work-ideas and *use a little choice*. If you sincerely evaluate the Work and desire to *make choice* for it, for its meaning and teaching, then the small amount of energy gained will pass into Deputy-Steward, or even towards the *essential you*, the real person in you, and strengthen you and perhaps open up for a moment a certain happiness that is internal and quiet.

Now let me give you an example of a man following the directions of the Work in life and not the directions of life only—that is, a man living and willing the Work in life. Let us take the example of a man so placed that he *cannot* change his outer circumstances. What can he change? He can change his *attitude*, his way of taking life. I am going to quote what Mr. Ouspensky writes about *Karma* Yoga in the "New Model of the Universe"—a passage that everyone should read at least once a year. Karma means roughly Fate, and the Yoga refers to those who by Fate cannot change their outer conditions. Everyone in this Work must to some extent practise this Yoga, which is that of *non-identifying*. This Work is not Karma Yoga: Karma Yoga is part of this Work, part of the Fourth Way. Remember that the passages that I quote here are written to illustrate what it means to follow *new directions* in life and not life-directions, not the hypnotism of life.

"Karma Yoga teaches right living. Karma Yoga is the Yoga of activity. Karma Yoga teaches the right relation towards people and the right action in the ordinary circumstances of life . . . Karma Yoga is always connected with the aim of inner development, of inner improvement. It helps man not to fall asleep inwardly amidst the entangling influences of life, especially in the midst of the *hypnotizing influence of activity*. It makes him remember that nothing external has any significance, that everything must be done without caring about results. Without Karma Yoga Man becomes absorbed in the nearest, the visible aims, and forgets the chief aim. Karma Yoga teaches Man to change his fate, to direct it at will. According to the fundamental idea of Karma Yoga this is attained only by altering the inner attitude of Man towards things and towards his own actions. The same action can be performed differently, one and the same event can be lived through differently. And if a man alters his attitude towards what happens to him, this will in the course of time inevitably change the character of the events which he encounters on his way. Karma Yoga teaches Man to understand that when it seems to him that he himself is acting, in reality it is not he who acts, but only a power passing through him. Karma Yoga asserts that a man is not at all what he thinks himself to be, and teaches Man to understand that only in very rare cases does he act of himself and independently, and that in most cases he acts only as a part of one or another great whole. This is the 'occult' side of Karma Yoga, the teaching concerning the forces and laws which govern Man. A man who understands the ideas of Karma Yoga feels all the time that he is but a tiny screw or a tiny wheel in the big machine, and that the success or unsuccess of what he thinks he is doing depends very little on his own actions. Acting and feeling in this way, a man can never meet with failure in anything, because the greatest failure, the greatest unsuccess, may further success in his inner work, in his struggle with himself, if he only finds the right attitude towards this unsuccess.

A life governed by the principles of Karma Yoga differs greatly from an ordinary life. In ordinary life, no matter what the conditions may be, the chief aim of Man consists in avoiding all unpleasantnesses, difficulties and discomforts, so far as this is possible. In a life governed by the principles of Karma Yoga, a man does not seek to avoid unpleasantnesses or discomforts. On the contrary, he welcomes them, for they afford him a chance of overcoming them. From the point of view of Karma Yoga, if life offered no difficulties it would be necessary to create them artificially. And therefore the difficulties which are met with in life are regarded not as something unpleasant which one must try to avoid, but as very useful conditions for the aims of inner work and inner development.

When a man realizes this and feels it constantly, life itself becomes his 'teacher.'

The chief principle of Karma Yoga is *non-attachment*. A man who follows the methods of Karma Yoga must practise non-attachment always and in everything, whether to good or to evil, to pleasure or to pain. Non-attachment does not mean indifference. It is a certain kind of separation of self from what happens or from what a man is doing. It is not coldness, nor is it the desire to shut oneself off from life. It is the recognition and the constant realization that everything is done according to certain laws and that everything in the world has its own fate. From an ordinary point of view the following of the principles of Karma

Yoga appears as fatalism. But it is not fatalism in the sense of the accepting of the exact and unalterable preordination of everything without the possibility of any change whatever. On the contrary, Karma Yoga teaches how to change the karma—how to influence the karma. But from the point of view of Karma Yoga this influencing is an entirely inner process. Karma Yoga teaches that a man may change the people and events around him by changing his attitude towards them.

The idea of this is very clear. Every man from his birth is surrounded by a certain karma, by certain people and certain events. And in accordance with his nature, education, tastes and habits he adopts a certain definite attitude towards things, people and events. So long as his attitude remains unchanged, people, things and events also remain unchanged—that is, corresponding to his karma. If he is not satisfied with his karma, if he wants something new and unknown he must change his attitude towards what he has and then the new events will come.

Karma Yoga is the only way possible for people who are tied to life, who are unable to free themselves from the external forms of life, for people who either through their birth or through their own powers and capacities are placed at the head of human communities or groups, for people who are connected with the progress of the life of humanity, for historical personages, for people whose personal life seems to be the expression of the life of an epoch or a nation. These people cannot change themselves visibly; they can change themselves only internally, while externally remaining the same as before, saying the same things, doing the same things, but *without attachment*, as actors on the stage. Having become such actors in relation to their life, they become *Yogis* in the midst of the most varied and intense activity. There can be peace in their soul whatever their troubles may be. Their thought can work without hindrance, independently of anything that may surround it. Karma Yoga gives freedom to the prisoner in a gaol and to the king on a throne, if only they can feel that they are actors playing their rôles."

This example has been given to shew how a man can follow *new directions* in life and so live his life under other laws while being in life. The Work is a set of new directions for living life. These directions come from a far source: they come from Conscious Humanity, from those at a level far above our level. In terms of the side-octave of the sun, they come from those who have reached the level of being and understanding and consciousness represented physically by the sun. All those who have evolved have left memorials behind them in teachings, parables, and other directions for those still in prison on earth. These constitute the map and compass, the chart, the secret instructions, and, in our case, the Work itself. If you follow these directions—that is, if you think from the ideas of the Work, you are no longer driven by life even though you may still be living in life.

INTERNAL CONSIDERING
AND EXTERNAL CONSIDERING

I

Amongst the many things that we have to observe in ourselves and work upon, according to this teaching that we are studying, there is the psychological state called *internal considering*. This refers to a process which takes a great deal of force from us and, like everything that takes energy from us uselessly, keeps us asleep.

Internal considering is a branch of identifying. As you know, the study of identifying in all its different branches is one of the most important forms of practical work on oneself. A man who identifies with everything is unable to remember himself. In order to remember oneself it is necessary not to identify. But in order to learn not to identify a man must first of all learn not to be identified with himself. One form of identifying is internal considering, of which there are several kinds, and some are forms of identifying with oneself. One of the most frequent forms of internal considering is *thinking what others think of us*, and how they treat us, and what attitude they shew towards us. A man may feel he is not valued enough and this torments him and makes him suspect others and causes him to lose an immense amount of energy and may develop in him a distrustful and hostile attitude.

Closely connected with this is that form of identifying called *making accounts*. A man begins to feel that people *owe* him, that he deserves better treatment, more rewards, more recognition, and he writes all this down in a psychological account-book, the pages of which he is continually turning over in his mind. And such a man begins to pity himself so much that it may be almost impossible to talk to him about anything without making him at once refer to all his sufferings. All accounts of this kind, all feelings that you are owed by other people *and that you owe nothing yourself*, are of very great psychological consequence to the inner development of a man.

A man in the Work can only grow through the forgiveness of others. That is, unless you cancel your debts, nothing in you can grow. It is said in the Lord's Prayer: "Forgive us our debts as we forgive our debtors." Feeling you are owed, feeling debts, stops everything. You hold back yourself and you hold back the other person. This is the inner meaning of Christ's remark that one should make peace with one's enemy. He says:

"Agree with thine adversary quickly, whiles thou art with him in the way; lest haply the adversary deliver thee to the judge, and the judge deliver thee to the officer, and thou be cast into prison. Verily, I say unto thee, thou shalt not come out until thou hast paid the last farthing." (*Matt.* V 25, 26)

253

If you are going to exact psychologically every pound of flesh or every "farthing" from a man who owes you—that is, if you are going to make everyone apologise and make amends and eat the dust, then you will be *under* the exacting law that Christ warns you to escape from. You will put yourself in prison—that is, under unnecessary laws—and you will not get out until you have paid on your side for all your *own* faults. But there is a *law of mercy*—that is, an influence higher than the literal law of an eye for an eye, which is the law of the man of violence. This is an example of "putting yourself under new influences". If you want to put yourself under better influences coming down the Ray of Creation, you must behave differently, take everything differently—that is, *work*. You must put yourself first under the influences of the Work and try to obey them. That means, you must hear and do the Work. In the Work, negative emotions, internal considering, making accounts, feeling violent, jealous, etc. are not encouraged. Now if you make inner accounts, then you feel always that someone *owes* you. Try to *think* what this means: and then try to *observe* what it means *in yourself* and then finally try *to do* what the Work says—i.e. separate. And do not imagine it is quite easy. The Work means *work—hard work—on yourself*. Remember that this Work is for those who really wish to work and change themselves. It is not for those who wish to change the world.

We now come to a fuller description of one form of internal considering, but you must understand that you must observe this form *in yourself*. No one can work on himself without observing what this Work tells him to observe in himself and seeing what it is he has to work on. You must be able to perceive your inner state at any particular time as distinct from your outer physical body and what it is doing. Once people can distinguish between their physical appearance and their inner states, they can begin to work. They see that they have a body which obeys orders, and a psychology. The Work is about what a person *is* psychologically. Let us speak to-day of that aspect of a person called in the Work *"Singing your Song"*. This is psychological, not physical, singing. It is based on internal considering—making inner accounts—that is, feeling what you are owed and recording it in memory. Everyone has a song to sing in this respect. If you really want to know what kinds of inner accounts you have made throughout your life, begin to notice the typical "songs you sing". When a person in the Work is called a "good singer", this refers to the songs he or she sings. Sometimes people sing their songs without any encouragement and sometimes, after a few glasses of wine, they begin to sing openly. They sing about how badly they have been treated, about how they never had a real chance, about their past glories, about how no one understood their difficulties, about how they married wrongly, about how their parents did not understand them, about how nice they really are, about how they have been un-appreciated, misunderstood, and so on, and all this means how everyone is to-blame except themselves. All this is making *inner accounts*, or rather it is the result of making accounts. This is one form of internal considering.

Now why do you think it is necessary in the Work to get rid as far as possible of songs? Why is it necessary to notice them, to starve them, to push them away, out of a central position in one's life, until they are sung only on rare occasions, in faint voice, and perhaps, finally, never? They cripple you inside. They take energy. You smile—bravely—you all know that brave smile—and it is all lies. A good singer in the Work cannot get beyond himself. He is a victim of his own account-making. As soon as anything is difficult he begins singing. This stops him: he cannot grow. He perhaps begins to weep. He cannot change his level of being. He cannot get beyond what he *is*—i.e. crippled by sad songs. It is a sign of being. Being is what you *are* and to change being one must not be what one is. Instead of working on himself in some difficult situation, he begins to sing at once, perhaps very nicely and quietly. If he is criticized or spoken to sharply, he begins to pity himself, or gets furious, and feels he is not understood, and so on. And then he begins to sing, either softly to himself or to others, especially to people who will listen to him—or, it may be, to her. Often a person makes friends with another person only because it is easy to sing his or her song to him or her, and if the latter suddenly tells him in so many words to "shut up", he or she is so deeply offended that he goes in search of a new friend— a person who will really *understand* him or her, as the expression goes —as if anyone could understand another person, just like that. 'If only', they say. To understand another, one must first understand oneself, and this only begins after long work on oneself and catching glimpses of what one is really like. A good singer certainly does not understand himself. He prefers to sing the song that he is misunderstood and so he dreams of a marvellous world in which everything is arranged so that he is the central figure in it. And this attitude and these dreams create a weakness and, in fact, a real, psychological sickness, for which a man may have to pay all through life.

He has, as it were, let life overcome him. But you must realize that this does not apply merely to people who make no effort, to people who are not adjusted. It applies also to people who do make ordinary efforts and who yet are sick in this sense because they feel life owes them things that they have never attained. They feel they should be happier and very often think that other people seem to be happier. And other people think the same thing of them. And although they do not sing their songs openly perhaps songs go on in them secretly. They feel an inner sadness, a sense of monotony, a kind of inner tiredness or frustration around which thoughts gather. It is about these *inner secret songs* that I wish to speak to-night. For they also stand in one's way, and very often they are not observed, although they are all the time secretly eating one's life. Only deeper self-observation will reveal them. All self-observation is to let light in—to oneself. Nothing can change in us unless it is brought into the light of self-observation—that is, into the light of consciousness —and all self-observation is to make us more conscious of what is going on *in us*.

You know, you must observe yourself when you are alone, just as much as when you are with people. Self-observation is inner attention. Do not think that when you are alone there is no need for inner attention. When you are alone, quite different 'I's, different forms of imagination, different thoughts, different moods, come forward. You must not think that you are necessarily in good company when you are alone. You may easily be in the worst company and yet not even think of observing where you are in yourself and what company you are keeping in yourself. Your most negative and most dangerous 'I's may come forward when you are alone. You may have quite well-written songs that only come when you are quite alone—when you feel no one is looking. Yes, but *you* must look. You must never feel no one is looking, simply because the door is shut. You must never feel that you can indulge yourself in your worst negative 'I's just because you are alone and that therefore you can behave as you like in yourself. You must cultivate quite a new idea of your responsibility to yourself in this respect. To think that you can go to sleep in yourself just because there is no one there and that you can enjoy all your inner negative talking for that reason is to have no proper conception of what this Work means. It means that you have no inner sincerity—and this Work demands inner sincerity as the first thing that is essential. In life we keep up outer appearances. But in the Work the case is quite different. It is about what goes on *in* you—inside yourself, in your thoughts and feelings. By *inner work* on ourselves when we are alone, we can often change a whole outer situation. But we cannot do that without inner sincerity and observing which 'I's in us are lying or twisting things and so on. We may make an aim not to be negative with some person, but if we are alone and let our negative 'I's say what they please and make no effort not to identify with them, then we are not working sincerely—and we can undo a week of work in a few moments. If we do not go with negative 'I's in public, but indulge them in private, what do we think we are doing? We certainly have not begun to understand what work means. We must handle a person we are working with as carefully and as consciously in our inner thoughts and feelings as we do externally from polite manners. If we cannot see what this means, then we do not see what self-observation means.

On one occasion I was sitting with Mr. Ouspensky. We had been silent. He looked up at me with a smile and asked me why I was so sad. I said I did not know that I was. He said: "It is a habit. You are listening to some 'I's that are singing some sad far-away song, perhaps a song without words or words you have forgotten. Try to observe it. It takes force from you and is quite useless." And he added: "This is an example of the Moon eating you."

I give this as an example of what I call in this commentary "inner secret songs". We know that the Work sometimes speaks of sacrifice —that we must sacrifice something in order to get anything. What does the Work say that we must sacrifice first of all? It says we must sacrifice *our suffering*. We express our suffering often in songs, articulate and inarticulate. I am calling attention here to these inner inarticulate songs that we should try to observe and which can make us easily lose force, without our knowing what is happening. They are, as it were, strange little sad private relationships we have with ourselves, that steal force from us and that we do not notice because they are habits.

Birdlip, March 1, 1943

INTERNAL CONSIDERING
AND EXTERNAL CONSIDERING

II

The more requirements you make, the more internal considering you will have. You will always be disappointed and feel that somebody else is to blame. People who make many requirements make life very difficult for themselves. Nothing is right: they are not surrounded by the right people, they are not treated properly, and so on. In this Work we must gradually feel our own nothingness by observation.

The opposite to internal considering is external considering. External considering is thinking of others. It is one of the few things in the Work that we are actually told to do. We are told *not* to internally consider and *not* to have negative emotions, and so on, but we are told to externally consider just as we are told to remember ourselves. When we are in a state of internal considering (and this is our usual state) we are really thinking only of ourselves. We regard ourselves as the centre of the Universe. Like Copernicus, we have to realize that we are not the centre of the Universe. To internally consider gives us only self-emotions and as these increase the character becomes more shut in. You all know people, surely, to whom you cannot speak for a moment without their beginning to tell you what troubles they have, what a hard life they lead, and so on. Such people are ruined. They are dead. You know that the Work says that it is negative emotions that govern the world, and not sex or power. Just think how many people are completely ruined by constantly indulging in negative emotions. Internal considering is a branch of identifying. It is closely connected with negative states in us. You must not think that the opposite to internal considering consists in a hearty, optimistic manner and loud laughter. This is not external considering.

*   *   *

I will now quote what Mr. Ouspensky once said about external considering:

257

"The opposite of internal considering, and what is in part a means of fighting against it, is 'external considering'. External considering is based upon an entirely different relationship towards people from internal considering. It is adaptation towards people, to their understanding, to *their* requirements. By considering externally a man does that which makes life easy for other people and for himself. External considering requires a knowledge of men, an understanding of their tastes, habits and superstitions. At the same time external considering requires a great power over oneself, a great control over oneself. Very often a man desires not to express or to shew to another man what he really thinks of him or feels about him. But if he is a weak man he will of course give way and say what he really thinks and afterwards justify himself and say that he did not want to lie, did not want to pretend, but he wanted to be sincere. Then he convinces himself that it was the other man's fault. He really wanted to externally consider him, even to give way to him, not to quarrel, and so on. But the *other man* did not at all want to consider him, so that nothing could be done with him. It very often happens that a man begins with a blessing and ends with a curse: he begins by deciding to externally consider, and afterwards blames other people for not externally considering him. This is an example of how *external* considering passes into *internal* considering. But if a man really remembers himself, he understands that another man is a *machine* just as he is himself, and then he will *enter into his position*, he will put himself in his place, and he will be really able to understand and feel what another man thinks and feels. If he can do this, his work becomes easier for him. But if he approaches a man with his own requirements nothing except new internal considering can ever be obtained from it.

Right external considering is very important *in the Work*. It often happens that people who understand very well the necessity of external considering in life do not understand the necessity of external considering in the Work. They even imagine that just because they are in the Work they have a right not to consider others: whereas in reality, in the Work—that is, for Man's successful work—ten times more external considering is necessary than in life, because only external considering on his part shews his valuation of the Work and his understanding of the Work—and success in the Work is always proportional to the valuation and understanding of it. Remember that work cannot begin and cannot proceed on a level lower than that of ordinary life—that is, it must begin on the level of Good Householder. This is a very important principle, which, for some reason or other, is usually forgotten. People must behave as Good Householders."

*   *   *

In the Work external considering is more necessary than in life. It does not make "self-emotions", but "others-emotions" The second one of the Work, Work in conjunction with others, brings in the necessity of external considering, of putting ourselves into another person's

*If you wish to receive a copy
of the latest Shambhala Publications catalogue of books
and to be placed on our mailing list
please send us this card.*

PLEASE PRINT

Book in which this card was found

NAME

ADDRESS

CITY & STATE

ZIP OR POSTAL CODE   COUNTRY

(IF OUTSIDE U.S.A.)

SHAMBHALA PUBLICATIONS, INC.

Mailing List
P.O. Box 308, Back Bay Annex
Boston, Massachusetts   02117

place, of realizing other people's difficulties. In the practice of external considering it is necessary to realize that other people are mirrors of ourselves. If you have taken an album of good photographs of yourself through long self-observation, then you will not have to look far in it to find in yourself what you object to so much in the other person and then you will be able to put yourself in the other person's position, to realize that he has also this thing that you have noticed in yourself, that he has his inner difficulties, just as much as you have, and so on. External considering can be practised when you are alone. I will give you one example: go over carefully what you said to someone and put yourself in his place by visualizing him saying the same things to you and using the same intonation. External considering is as vast and as varied in its range as is internal considering. There cannot be right development of the Emotional Centre without the practice of external considering: valuation of this Work, and the practice of external considering develop Emotional Centre. The more you value this Work the less can false personality govern you, the less vanity can you have, and the more you externally consider the less important will you think yourself.

*   *   *

In this Work there is no such thing as pretending to do good when you really *will* bad. It is no use pretending to be nice to other people when you hate them in your heart. All this Work depends on inner sincerity. External considering is not hypocrisy, it is not "good works," but it is a question of inner attitude. Remember that when you find the same thing in yourself that you are blaming in someone else it has the magical effect of cancelling the whole situation out. This is real "forgiving". You know that our natural state is to be very surprised that there is anything wrong with ourselves. Of course we often blame ourselves, as it were. We say, for example: "Yes, I am afraid I was very much to blame for that incident." "Yes, certainly you were," says the other person. Are you not then very startled? Why, you will be hurt and offended at once. All this is because it is very difficult to think that anything is wrong with us and it is all part of the sleep we are in, the deep sleep that covers all humanity. Now self-observation is very harsh and becomes more harsh. If it is done sincerely it will hurt. But it lets light in and stops all sorts of rank weeds from growing within, and amongst them all the strange growths due to internal considering and self-pity and song-singing. And then at last we begin to see what it means that a man must realize that he is nothing before he can expect to *be* something.

*   *   *

With regard to that form of internal considering which is based on feeling that life has cheated you, that you should be in a different situation, you must remember that the Work says very emphatically

259

that everyone starts from where he should be. It says that the conditions under which you encounter this Work are the right conditions for you. Nothing is more absurd than to think that one's life is being wasted in this Work. It is extraordinary that people have very narrow opinions as to what life should be like. They have as it were one or two prescriptions for life and if a person's life does not correspond to these prescriptions it is regarded as being wasted or useless and with such an outlook a person may internally consider a great deal and feel that everything is against him, even God and the whole Universe, and it is simply because he does not take his life in the right way. He makes requirements which cannot be satisfied. He is like a person who goes into a grocer's shop and asks for a top-hat or a sewing-machine and does not take what can be sold to him. The forces of hypnotism which keep Man asleep are the same for everyone. If *awakening* is your aim, then whatever your circumstances are, it should make no difference to you, unless perhaps you are forcibly deprived of the Work. You heard the section on Karma Yoga read out a week or two ago. No better formulation has been made as far as I know about how to avoid internal considering in connection with the ordinary circumstances of your life. Since internal considering is a form of identifying you will realize that the practice of non-identifying which Mr. Ouspensky outlined in terms of the word *detachment* is the cure for internal considering. If you realize that internal considering can become a real illness and can ruin you, if you can see it at work in yourselves, then you will do all in your power to try to escape from it. It is no good saying, for instance, "Oh, so and so has no idea what life is like for a person like me." It will only increase your internal considering. It is the internal considering in yourself that has to be stopped or else it will grow and grow and grow. It will spread a fire over everything young and growing in you.

Do not ask what is the remedy for internal considering please. You have got to study it in yourselves and notice what harm it does you and from that gain a real desire to free yourself from it. You have got to see it first in yourself and then you have to take it seriously, in conjunction with all the other things that you are told in this Work to practise. For the whole Work is necessary. The application of all the parts of the Work is necessary, for the whole Work is a living organism.

INTERNAL CONSIDERING
AND EXTERNAL CONSIDERING

III

Last time we spoke of the necessity for considering externally in the Work. External considering must begin from the start of the Work, as far as a person is capable of it. A person who is self-centred—that is, who only thinks of himself or herself and of others only in reference to himself or herself—cannot go far. Such a person works only along the first line of Work, the line of Work on oneself, and that only to a very limited extent. The second line of Work has to do with other people and one's attitude to them. This demands work on oneself also. It does not mean merely that you must endure the unpleasant manifestations of others—and remember that they have to endure yours—but it means rather *the practice of external considering in general.*

Everyone has a more or less fixed way of taking other people, due to attitudes and buffers. We see others through our attitudes and buffers. In general we do not like other people. Instinctively we are hostile. I remember G. once saying that when we pass someone in a lane we tend to tense our muscles. You know that it has been said that we should not pretend we like other people, but try to work on dislike. Dislike grows very early. You cannot externally consider another person, if you nourish dislike only. Everyone splits easily into like and dislike, and in relationships the dislikes must not be allowed to grow mechanically. By self-observation we notice we have two memories for a person. When we are negative we remember only unpleasant things: when not negative we forget them. We have some idea of what fair treatment means in regard to outer behaviour. But we have to be fair *in ourselves* to others and this really is work on oneself that takes the form of external considering. A cluster of unpleasant thoughts and feelings about another person, that you have allowed to enter consciousness *willingly*, can begin to grow. It is both for the sake of yourself and the other person that something must be done—that is, that you must work on yourself to neutralize, as it were, this unpleasant and powerful material in you. All your intelligence and sincerity and work-memory will be required probably to neutralize this poison, so that you can once more treat the other person fairly inside yourself. You will have to put yourself in the other person's place. You will have to drop all self-justifying, and above all you will have to remember what you have observed in yourself, and what you are like, before you criticize so easily this other person.

On the other hand, you need not do this. You can simply *internally consider*. You can make accounts—saying to yourself that the other person is wrong, that you have not been properly treated, that you are owed, that the other person is indebted to you—that is, in debt to you.

All this is the basis of so many relationships in life. The basis is internal considering. Have you also noticed that in a relationship between two people, one of them usually externally considers a little more and the other often only internally considers and complains about everything?

In the Work, external considering must go more deeply than in life. It really belongs to the purification of the Emotional Centre. One of the great objects of this Work is to awaken the Emotional Centre, which is drugged with negative emotions and all the small emotions of self, of vanity, of self-conceit, etc. External considering (in the Work-sense) requires *conscious effort*, whereas internal considering is mechanical —that is, it requires no effort but goes on by itself and grows by itself just as do negative emotions. In the Work, external considering does not spring from life-motives. That is why it requires conscious effort. You have to consider people whom, in life, you would probably not for a moment think of considering. It is this kind of external considering that can change the level of being. Let us take a person who practises external considering in life—for example, a head-waiter. He is perhaps very clever. He notices what people like, what their peculiarities are, what they expect from him, what forms of irritation they have, what food they prefer, and so on. He panders to all this. Like St. Paul he is "all things to all men" but not from the same motives. He is intelligent enough to adapt himself to people's requirements. He puts himself out for the sake of others. He is tactful, observant, he effaces himself, and so on. But he does all this because he is playing a game. And he is quite right. He is intelligent. But in the Work the case is different. External considering from a life point of view is not the same as external considering from a Work point of view. At the same time, a person who knows what external considering means in life and who is trained in studying the requirements of other people may perhaps learn better what external considering means in the Work.

What I want you to see to-night is that the kind of external considering done by the waiter is not the same as that which becomes eventually necessary for everyone in the Work. You come to the necessity and to the meaning of external considering in the Work from a different side which is certainly connected with yourself and your self-interest, but not in the same way. Our object is to try to awaken, not to be so identified with everything, not to be slaves to useless negative states and blank minds, and so on. If we continually make accounts against one another, by privately despising, by wrong talking, by psychologically murdering others and so on, all work on oneself is spoiled. In the process of awaking from sleep, one thing hangs on another thing. One leg cannot get out of bed. The whole of you must get out of bed, if you want to stand upright. After a time in the Work you come to that point of sincerity with your-self in which you realize that you simply cannot allow yourself to be in some particular state that you observe you are in. It is then that you will begin to see why you must externally consider—that is, that you must get things right *in yourself* with regard to other people. So you will see from this brief note that external considering, in the Work, is not something superficial, but something very deep. At first you must practise external considering quite externally, so to speak, but notice the quality of it. The more sincere it is, the better the quality. The more superficial and pretended, the worse the quality. All efforts in the Work, as has been often said, depend for their results on their quality. I suggest that for practical work each of you decides to externally consider a particular person during this next week. Observe your mechanical reactions to this person. Observe your mechanical criticisms. Observe where you feel superior. Try to find in yourself the same things that you complain of in the other person. Think how you would like the other person to think of you as you think of him or her. Put yourself in the other person's place. Try to see where the trouble lies in yourself as well as in the other person. Try not to identify. Notice your inner talking and what it is up to. Keep awake to what you are doing, which will be your aim for a week. Remember it every day on getting up. Think of it at night—where you failed, why you failed, where you began to internally consider instead of to externally consider. Then you will see better the meaning of externally considering and how it can change being.

Birdlip, March 15, 1943

INTERNAL CONSIDERING
AND EXTERNAL CONSIDERING

IV

When you feel that some one has not behaved rightly to you, you feel that you have not been estimated at your proper value. For example, to feel insulted is to feel that you are not estimated at your proper value. So people often say, when insulted: "Do you know who I am?" or something like that. They mean that they have a certain valuation of themselves, so they say: "Do you know who I am?" meaning that if the other person did know, he would not dare to behave as he does. Of course, if you have little or no picture of yourself as being valuable, you will not be so easily upset. A high estimate of yourself naturally will make it more easy for you to feel that others do not estimate you at your proper value. So you will internally consider more easily. A person may even be so pre-occupied with the question of others treating him rightly, and with suspicions about whether others are laughing at him, that his whole life may be said to be involved in internal considering. Or again, some persons may value themselves above others because of sufferings. People cling to their own suffering and come to regard themselves as worthy of special evaluation because they have had all kinds of hardships, miseries and sufferings. They are offended if another person begins to talk of his own suffering. They feel that the other person does not consider them enough and that he is selfish. It is difficult for them to realize that other people also have sufferings. Nor do they realize that to see selfishness in others is to see the reflection of one's own selfishness, for the more requirements you make from others, the more selfish will others appear to you.

What is it that causes us to begin to internally consider? Let us ask the question: "At what point, or where, do you start making accounts?" You start when you feel you are not estimated aright, when you feel you are undervalued. The waiter does not come when called. The shop-assistant serves another person first. Perhaps people do not look at you enough in the street, or, let us say, pay sufficient attention in general. Or one person seems persistently to ignore you. Or perhaps you hear what someone said of you: that is nearly always unpleasant. There are a thousand and one possible examples, less, and more, serious. Small incidents upset us easily—the waiter, the shop-assistant. These form short accounts and may eventually become a habit. But we have all sorts of long-standing accounts against others, some of them stored up in the past, unfortunately for ourselves. They all begin with this mysterious question of *one's own valuation of oneself*. A person with some self-observation might well exclaim: "What is this thing in me that is offended at this moment and has already begun to make accounts? Look, I can observe it at work in me collecting materials and beginning to remember unpleasant things and to find words and phrases to use against the other person so as to make him feel that he is underestimated by me—in fact, to make him realize he is so much dirt. Is it a picture of myself? Is it imaginary 'I'? Is it false personality? or what is it that is at the bottom of it all?" The answer is that what is at the bottom of it all is *where you identify with yourself*. All forms of internal considering, of which making accounts against another person is one form, belong to *identifying*. The Work says that we must study *identifying* down to its very roots. A man is only offended *where he is identified with himself*. And the Work also says that the study of identifying must begin with a study of where you are *identified with yourself*. It is here that you can be upset, hurt, offended, insulted. The being identified with oneself comes first, being upset and offended comes second, making inner accounts comes third.

INTERNAL CONSIDERING
AND EXTERNAL CONSIDERING

V

Some people find it difficult to understand what external considering means and others to understand what internal considering means. In this Work external considering must be done and internal considering stopped. To externally consider another person it is first necessary to put yourself in the other person's position. To do this you must think of yourself as being this other person, having to do the same things, having the same difficulties, the same handicaps, the same life. Now if you will begin to think of this preliminary step, you can hardly say that external considering has anything to do with being indifferent. To put yourself in another person's situation calls upon your whole understanding. It requires a directed effort of the mind and feelings and not merely·once but time and again. And you will certainly be quite incapable of doing this if you are always pre-occupied with your own personal problems and woes and with the way you are being treated—that is, if you are always taking your life from the standpoint of internal considering.

I remember the case of a man who was always internally considering, always suffering, who wrote on his wife's tombstone: "From your heart-broken husband." You see, even then he could only think of himself, of his own suffering. Now if you begin to externally consider another person over a considerable period, you must again and again put yourself in the other person's place. In this way you become more conscious. The object of the Work is to become more conscious. Self-observation makes you more conscious of yourself: external considering makes you more conscious also of others. Through externally considering, things you were not conscious of before are revealed to you. Let us take a simple example of revelations of this kind: you put yourself in another person's position and after a time you realize that you expect this person to do things you would not think of doing yourself—for example, you expect this person perhaps to put up with conditions that you would not put up with for a moment. Do you see that you have gained in consciousness? Now if you have a revelation of this kind it means that you are really beginning to externally consider, to understand what it means to put yourself in another person's position.

People who make a great many requirements expect a great deal from others and if they do not get what they expect, they are disappointed and they feel they are owed. That is, they begin to form a great background of internal considering to their lives. This makes them bitter. They feel they have scores to settle. For a person of this kind to externally consider becomes very difficult. But it should not be so difficult for you unless you are crystallized. To realize that you expect the other person to do things you would never think of doing yourself makes a very good starting-point from which to begin to externally consider another person. It is a practical starting-point and a Work starting-point. You realize then that you expect the other person not only to do things you would never think of doing but to be different from you, behave differently, put up with things differently, and so on. Let us suppose you have always compared yourself very favourably with other people and perhaps even are sure that none of the unpleasant things you notice in others exists in yourself. It will be very surprising, then, to have the revelation that you are unjust and that you expect others in the Work to do what you would not dream of doing yourself. It is always painful to realize that there is really anything wrong with oneself. As was said in an earlier paper, you may often say that you are to blame for something, but if someone agrees with you, it is startling and you feel offended. Yes, we easily *pretend* we are wrong.   But to *see* it, direct and unmistakable, in oneself, is *pain*. This is real and so, useful, suffering, for all real suffering purifies the emotions. It only lasts a brief time as real suffering and then gets infected by false personality and changes into some complicated negative state, some sort of unpleasant self-pity or endless self-justifying, which is useless suffering.

Now suppose you have to live with a person called yourself. I once read a story of a man who died and went into the next world where he met numbers of people some of whom he knew and liked and some he knew and disliked. But there was one person there whom he did not know and he could not bear him. Everything he said infuriated and disgusted him—his manner, his habits, his laziness, his insincere way of speaking, his facial expressions—and it seemed to him also that he could see into this man's thoughts and his feelings and all his secrets and, in fact, into all his life. He asked the others who this impossible man was. They answered: "Up here we have very special mirrors which are quite different from those in your world. This man is yourself." Let us suppose, then, that you have to live with a person who is you.   Perhaps this is what the other person has to do. Of course, if you have no self-observation you may actually imagine this would be charming and that if everyone were just like you, the world would indeed be a happy place. There are no limits to vanity and self-conceit. Now in putting yourself into another person's position you are also putting yourself into his point of view, into *how* he sees you, and hears you, and experiences you in your daily behaviour. You are seeing yourself through his eyes. If you have no self-observation you cannot do this, because you will simply take yourself for granted as being "quite all right" in everything. But if you have become sufficiently trained in self-observation to have begun to lose your former ideas of yourself and if you already have a collection not only of snapshots but of cabinet-size photographs of yourself in your most typical roles, the case will be quite different.   You will be able to see yourself to some extent as the other person sees you and so you will begin to realize practically what the other person's situation is and what some of his or her difficulties are and what it might mean if you had to live with yourself. Of course, the other person must do the same. Some of you may think, on hearing this, that it is quite right to say that the other person should try to see how difficult he or she is. But notice that we are beginning the other way round. It is you who have to see how difficult you are for the other person. Let me tell you that all this is not at all easy to grasp. You may think you know it all already. You may have heard it already, but a life-time at least is needed to see all that it implies.

In the Work, relationship is important. Work relationship is impossible without external considering. In general we must approach one another through the medium of the Work. The Work and its teachings must lie between you and the other person. You must look at one another through the common window of the Work. You must be related through the common valuation of the Work—but quite *practically*—by working. When two people in the Work quarrel, they have a great deal of work to do. They may not be ready for it, in which case sore places will be made, just as in life. They may refuse to work on themselves or in connection with one another: they then will both internally consider, both think they are owed, both think that the other should apologize. Of course if you do not work on yourself and just live and do nothing extra, the Work cannot become Third Force for you. Third Force is relating force. In this case life will be Third Force and life divides, whereas the Work should unite. Life divides because in life people do not understand one another. They have no common basis, no common language. But in the Work there is a common basis and people can begin to speak a common language and so to understand one another. But ten times more external considering is necessary in the Work than in life—and of quite a different quality, because the Work is the relating force. If two people in the Work quarrel, and are ready to work and wish to, then both of them will do so from themselves —not by meeting and talking it over—but simply as part of the Work itself. Each will put himself in the other's position and each see himself from the other person's viewpoint. External considering is very good work. It is not about whether you were right or the other person. It increases consciousness. It includes the first and second lines of work.

If you base your existence on internal considering, you will end your lives as most people do. Your lives, then, are all one-sided, undealt with, undigested, so many unhappy things just left lying about, and rotting, so to speak, in the past, so many violent or bitter feelings, so many places to which one has become glued down by past identifying. All this is certainly due to not giving oneself the First Conscious Shock, to not letting life fall on the Work in one. I think one can see so often how internal considering has spoiled life and what a terrible form of identifying it is. It is really like looking at life the wrong way round. And people who can only internally consider and feel that others should be different, take hold of one another so wrongly that they accumulate between one another, as it were, a mass of heavy, dense, negative material, to which they get fastened, and which they will not give up. But external considering is utterly different. It cleanses you. It frees you. It joins together what is missing by making you see the other side and realize the effect of what you do. It cancels all the feeling of being owed by bringing together the debit and credit sides of the accounts. An hour of external considering will free you from the effects of weeks of internal considering. And the more you can see yourself by observation, at the moment, and the more you can see the kind of person you have been all your life, the more will you be able to externally consider rightly. But remember that external considering can only begin, in its practical application, with putting yourself in the other person's place, and looking out, as it were, of the other person's mind and consciousness at yourself as he sees you. So do not think that external considering is merely doing something for the other person.

Birdlip, March 27, 1943

INTERNAL CONSIDERING
AND EXTERNAL CONSIDERING

VI

As long as you externally consider another person with a view to trying to change him or her—that is, as long as you think the other person should be different—you are not externally considering, but internally considering. The basis of internal considering is thinking that others should be different, and from this comes "making accounts" against others. It is necessary to understand this point clearly. You feel another person should not treat you as he does, or should not annoy you, or should not be as he is. Are you then making demands or not? Of course you are. Now in real external considering you cannot start from this point. You are starting from the idea that you are right and they are wrong. And because you think you are right and they are wrong, you feel that they owe you something. In what sense do they owe you something? You feel they should correspond to your ideas and because they do not you feel that something is lacking which they should do. So you feel they owe you right behaviour, according to your private standards of what is right and wrong. You see that all this means that you are putting yourself in the position of a judge. You are judging the other person from your own acquired ideas of what that person should be like. This is a source of internal considering in regard to that side of it called "making accounts". In short, you feel the other person owes you something. Now if you start by trying to externally consider another person from the basis of internal considering, from the basis of thinking the other person should be different, your external considering will be nothing but internal considering. You are making no attempt to start from the right basis of external considering, which is putting yourself in the other person's situation. On the contrary, you are starting from your own situation, not from the other person's. And in comparison with the real external considering, this is nothing but a form of hypocrisy and you will probably end only by shrugging your shoulders and saying: "Well, I have done my best for this person and I cannot do more." So you will wash your hands of him in your own feelings of merit and virtue. But I assure you that external considering in the Work-sense is nothing like that. Take an ordinary mechanical man—that is, an ordinary person. He is full of buffers, prejudices, negative attitudes, pictures of himself, vanity, typical gramophone records, and so on. Suppose he attempts, as he is, to externally consider, really to put himself in another person's life, into his situation, into his mind. Do you think he will be able to do so? Of course not. He does not see himself. So how can he see the other person? And if he does not see the other person, how can he put himself in the other person's position? That is why it is said that before you can begin to externally consider in a real way, you must have reached some degree of self-observation and it is only according to your degree of self-observation and self-knowledge that you can externally consider another person. In so far as you know yourself, you will know aright the other person: in so far as you can see yourself you can see others aright. Do you know, each one of you here now, how tiresome, how difficult, how unpleasant, how prejudiced, how exacting, you can be? Have you noticed it? If so, then you are in a better position to externally consider other people, for when you see their faults you will also see your own faults. But as we are made, looking out from our senses, and not looking in at ourselves, we only see other people's faults and to balance the account takes a life-time of work and insight. We all have pictures of ourselves; we are all, in one way or another, smug. Let me give you the dictionary definition of *smug*. The word is derived from a German word meaning to dress up; smock, smuggle, and so: "to be scrupulous in keeping up the appearance of respectability, to be absurdly self-satisfied and complacent." One thing is quite certain, and that is that the more sincerely we observe ourselves and what is in us, the less smug we shall be. And from this it follows that we shall be less satisfied to think that we know what the other person should be like. So we shall judge less and in consequence be able to put ourselves in another person's position more easily. You will remember the two examples of praying in the Gospels—the man who prayed thanking God he was not as other men, and the man who beat his breast and said he was a sinner. Which of these two men do you think would best be able to externally consider ? And which of those two men would you rather be judged by? There is a saying in the Work

269

that you must have heard more than once, that unless a man begins to realize his own *nothingness*, he cannot *do* this Work. He will not jump to catch the rope let down from above to save him. But all this takes time: and we must take the Work, stage by stage, in our gradual understanding of it. No one can outstrip himself—that is, his level of being. As being alters, so does understanding alter. Now external considering is work on being, as was said. Your being is roughly how you take things. In life, people do not really externally consider one another because of their level of being. If people really externally considered one another, war would be impossible. But war is possible because of Man's level of being, which is such that only internally considering, making accounts, thirsting for revenge, and so on, is understood. So you will understand that to externally consider in the Work-sense is to take a step beyond your ordinary level of being. Or, to put it in another way, if you can really externally consider, your level of being will be different.

Now all external considering, in the Work-sense, requires effort, whereas all internal considering is easy, mechanical, self-indulgent. The taste of the two is quite different. A conscious effort has quite a different taste from a mechanical automatic reaction. To be offended is extremely easy. It is a mechanical reaction. Not to be offended, or to *transform* being offended, is difficult. It requires conscious effort. It requires a lot of thought, a lot of inner adjustment, a lot of remembering what one is like oneself, and so on, to transform the first impact of being offended. But that is real work on oneself. Do you wish to belong to the terrific chain of cause and effect which makes up mechanical humanity or do you wish to get out of it? Then, if you do, you must work on your mechanical reactions. If you follow the law of "an eye for an eye, a tooth for a tooth", then you will always remain in the circle of mechanical humanity which leads nowhere. Esotericism brings a new law—the law of non-identifying, the law of self-observation—in fact, the application of the Work itself to daily life. This Work is esoteric Christianity. Christ said: "I bring you a new law". The Work says the same. Do you not see how the Work brings you new laws for behaviour, inner and outer? How then can you say you do not know what it means to think from the Work ideas?

*   *   *

Now you can make it your aim to externally consider a person in the Work or in life, as you like. I would add, you should practise external considering in the Work, because it is easier if the other person is working also, but if this is not possible—or, let us say, not too easy for the moment—then you must do the same in life. Life *can* become your teacher. It becomes your teacher as soon as you begin to work *from yourself*, from a genuine desire to work, which means an evaluation of the Work. Remember the Work can become very cold and distant if you do not keep it alive and you will not keep it alive if you do not love it. To externally consider a person in life is just the same as in the Work, only you will not be helped by the other person necessarily, and so it will be very easy for your attempts at external considering to turn into an increased form of internal considering. You must calculate *second force*—that is, the difficulties. It will be useless, of course, if you start off from a superior position and try to put the other person right. Remember that when you feel offended you are beginning to internally consider. You must be quite passive to the other person and work *on yourself* all the time, if you can, and not get offended. If you are sincere in your aim, you may be able to carry it out. You must *never* find fault, or shew that you are finding fault. You must be ready to bear false accusations And of course you must be ready to bear the unpleasant manifestations of the other person and not lose your temper and begin to chant: "Here am I doing my best to be nice", and so on. Once this begins, then it means you are internally considering. And if you do that, you are starting from a very shallow basis—that is, not from a real, matured aim. And in externally considering a person in life, which means that you must change yourself, you must have already got some idea of what it means to be "all things to all men". You must be able to eat and drink and joke and listen and talk without any trace of the Work being behind you. You *may* have an opportunity to say something, and you may not. That doesn't matter. A person in the Fourth Way of Work must be able to be quite ordinary in life. There must be no kind of superiority, no hinting, no persuasion, no dark remarks. But if you *work* on yourself, when the other person is difficult, *that* will make the other person aware that *you are different.* But you must not shew it openly. When life becomes one's teacher, then the highest work is reached. And then you are right in the track of the Fourth Way. But it is difficult—Oh, how difficult!—and requires much and long work on oneself and patient understanding. You must, as it were, be able to suffer all things at the hands of men and yet keep on working. But if you externally consider a person in life, feeling superior, and so feeling a constant judgment and shewing it openly, you are not working. That is not the way of the Fourth Way. To become *passive* in the Work sense to another person requires very great inner work, especially so to a person in life. In *some* ways, it is easier than becoming passive to a person in the Work. But you must realize what I mean for yourselves, by experience. You know how in life people are always trying to improve one another by reproving one another, always finding fault with one another. This is quite useless and leads to all the endless strife in life. But making oneself *passive* to a person and working on oneself therefrom—for to be passive requires constant inner work on yourself —this, I assure you, can effect a change in the other person, because your work makes *room* for him to alter. But if you react mechanically all the time it makes no room for the other person to turn about and change. By not reacting, you leave room. In regard to externally considering a person in life, remember that you must really *aim* at doing this. Do you really want to, or not? You must have a genuine matured conscious aim that starts in the light of the Work and to which you hold on every time you remember yourself and every time you think of what you are doing practically in this Work. Only then will the Work help you. If the basis of your aim is only a life-one, it will not conduct the force of the Work. It may be easier to work from a life-aim. We are told to make friends of the Mammon of Unrighteousness. In real relationship *in the Work* this is not enough. It is indeed far from enough. But in externally considering a person *in life*, what belongs to life-aim can enter, if it helps your Work-aim. I will give you an example: if you fear to lose some job, some position, and so on, your life-aim may help your Work-aim to be passive to unpleasant manifestations. This is allowed. But you must know *which is which*, and when genuine Work comes in, and realize what *you* are doing, and what life-considerations make you do. A different example is when a person may be so placed that his contact with the Work depends on his externally considering people in life. This *can* be done, only it requires intelligence and being passive to criticism. It especially requires the capacity of *inner silence*. Wrong talking will of course create difficulties. That is, a person in this Work, surrounded by people in life who have no magnetic centre, must behave in an ordinary way—he must be silent, not in an obvious or intriguing way, but really internally silent, so that others notice nothing unusual. This will be part of his work. His other work will consist in not reacting mechanically as he always did. We are speaking of those in the Work who are connected by ties with people not in the Work. Now we will speak of those in the Work who wish for a special reason to make relationship with those not in the Work. The whole question is then about magnetic centre. If you feel the Work emotionally, you will find it difficult to make contact with those who cannot feel it. After some conversations you will probably notice that a line of cleavage appears. Do not blame the Work for this fact. The Work guides you to certain people, or not. One has to listen to the Work, as it were, as best one can. You must also remember that the difference between a person who knows something of this Work and a person who does not is very considerable. In fact, a gulf lies between them. Socially you may like someone and be attracted and wish to bring him into the Work, but if there is no magnetic centre and the whole quality of conversation is limited to life, then you will feel that there is, as is actually the case, a gulf. There are quite nice people in life who cannot enter the Work. And this is as it must be. We can only meet through a common understanding, not through external appearances or physical bodies. Let us try to grasp this. A person who is beginning to understand the Work will find it not easy to unite with one who has no magnetic centre. Remember that the possession of magnetic centre is a sign of level of *being*. Some have it without knowing they have. But in general people of different levels of being do not unite. How can they? Understand that *magnetic centre* is a very big thing, in regard to the sign of a man's being. A man may be clever and a good scientist and so on, but have no sense of anything higher—no feeling of Greater Mind. A man in the highest position in life does not necessarily possess magnetic centre and usually does not. Life is not a standard for estimating a person in the Work valuation, save in regard to Good Householder. Neither Herod nor Pilate was fit for the esoteric teaching of Christ. All that is obvious enough surely. Life-values and Work-values are quite different: a big man in life is not a big man in the Work. You cannot talk to a highly successful man in life of this Work, thinking that he will understand you. I mean, you must never think that high position in life means a high understanding of this Work. In fact, as often as not, the case is quite the contrary. This idea takes a long time to sink into people.

Let me add one thing which is of the greatest importance in external considering. You cannot externally consider another person unless you can break him or her up into different 'I's. And you cannot do this unless you can see different 'I's in yourself. If you always think of yourself as 'I' then you will also always think of others as having one single permanent 'I'. Can you yet think of different 'I's in yourself and not say 'I' to everything in you? Then you will, in the same degree, be able to see different 'I's in another person. You will see his good and his bad 'I's. This will help you to externally consider the other person.

Birdlip, April 3,. 1943

INTERNAL CONSIDERING
AND EXTERNAL CONSIDERING

VII—On being Passive (1)

It was said last time, in connection with external considering, that it is necessary to be *passive* to another person. To-day we will begin to speak of the Work-meaning of *being passive*. What is the central theme of the Work in regard to its practical side—that is, in regard to work on oneself? And in this connection what does inner change mean? Practical work on oneself is directed towards making something passive in oneself which is at present active, and something active which is at present passive. Personality which is active must become passive so that essence which is passive can become active. This is the central idea of practical work on oneself. The Work is a *second* education. First of all life must develop personality so that it surrounds essence. This is the first education. Then, if a man wishes to go further in his development personality must become passive so that essence can grow and become active. So you see that a *reversal* must gradually take place. First of all, a child is born with only essence which is active. Then life forms

273

personality round essence, and personality is active. This situation will remain unchanged unless a man begins to work on himself. If he does so, personality will gradually become passive and essence active. There are thus three possible orientations: first, in the child, essence active, second, in the adult, personality active, and third, in the case of a man who works on himself, personality passive and essence active. The whole aim of the Work is to make acquired personality passive. In the Work-sense to become passive means inner work on personality. It means eventually separation from personality. By the action of life there has been formed in every one of you a very complex built-up thing called personality. This has been formed by imitation, by custom, by the influence of the period you grew up in, by example, by fantasies derived from novels, from drama, from the film, by attraction, hero-worship, and by a thousand and one other influences acting upon you from the outside and entering through the external senses, from outer life. All this forms the *acquired* side of you and is called, in general, the personality. Essence is what you are born with: personality is what you acquire. And what you are born with, or as, is changed by all these things that you acquire and accept and consent to and believe in and identify with. A new person therefore grows around the original essence. This is personality. And all this *must* take place because essence by itself cannot grow beyond a limited point. A man cannot grow straight up from essence. This is one of the strange things the Work teaches.

Now in consequence of the formation of personality your centre of gravity of consciousness shifts from essence (in childhood) outwards into the personality acquired from the particular circumstances you are brought up in and the particular things that have interested you on the one side or have attracted your vanity on the other side. In this way, you, as it were, lose your original basis and become something *acquired*, something invented. Your feeling of 'I' passes outwards into all sorts of feelings derived from life. A man feels no real inner stability when he derives his feeling of himself from life. That is, he is always afraid that something may happen to him, or to his fortune, or to his position, or his reputation. This is due to his identifying with everything that life has formed in him and this means that he only feels himself through personality. But other feelings of oneself are possible that are not derived from life and personality, and these feelings give a man a sense of stability that nothing outside him can take away. And it is from these feelings that a man begins to feel himself free, because they depend on nothing outside him, and so cannot be taken away from him. Such a man begins to be no longer so much a slave to outer things.

Now let us say that as a boy you get into the first team at school. Then you begin to feel yourself outwardly through this and you wear a cap that gives you this feeling. You become a man in the first team and this is now your greatest feeling of 'I'. Then you are thrown out of the team. What a tragedy! All this is necessary in regard to the first education. So you become this or you become that, in life, and you should and must. You have this or that success or triumph and so on, and you should. It is a sort of training. It is all necessary at first. All this forms feelings of yourself in personality, which, roughly speaking, lives by comparison with others. That is, you feel a loss of yourself in the presence of a person who wears a more distinguished cap and so on. I repeat, all this is necessary, but it gives a wrong centre of gravity. Let us suppose that you are a great actor or a great boxer. You will not easily listen to praise of another actor or boxer. Why? Because your feeling of 'I' is derived from personality and you will feel a loss of 'I', a loss of the very feeling of yourself, if someone else surpasses you. But all this is to train you in illusions about 'I'. For if you have any trace of real feeling of 'I', this is impossible. Real 'I' does not exist through *comparison*. Therefore you will understand that when it is said that personality roughly lives by comparison, you only have to study yourself or others in this light for a short time to see how easily everyone is upset or chagrined, and how brittle this feeling of 'I' is, in which people keep on trying to live—that is, in the feeling of 'I' derived from some aspect of personality.

Now let us keep for the time being to the great formulation of the Work concerning personality and essence. The third or neutralizing force of life makes, and must make, personality active and essence passive. So the Work says that if you come into the third force of the Work, which opposes life, personality must gradually become passive to let essence develop. All *individual* evolution, all real inner development of *yourself*, depends upon a *growth of essence*. If you are full of false feelings of 'I', of invented ideas of yourself, then there can be no growth of essence. Real inner change is a development of essence—that is, of what is the most real and the deepest part of you. For this to take place, personality must gradually become passive. This is the real meaning of *being passive* in the Work. It is becoming passive to personality in yourself. So when it is said that in real external considering you must be passive, the meaning is that you must become passive *to the reactions of your personality*. And this requires the most conscious and most concentrated work on oneself. That is, it requires a very active conscious inner state. And we must not suppose we are capable of reaching this state in a moment.

Owing to the formation of personality, you all have typical, habitual ways of reacting to circumstances and events, and to other people. If you cannot observe your typical reactions, your continual mechanical ways of taking things and people, your usual stereotyped behaviour, your ever-recurring unpleasant manifestations, your vexations and strictures, etc. then of course you have no idea that you even have an acquired *personality*. You take yourself for granted—as a kind of solid virtuous lump. But, although we take ourselves for granted so easily, we are not one and the same person at different moments, as we suppose. We are not solid. If we saw clearly that we are not one and the same solid person always, we would not take ourselves for granted as we do. Something of our vanity and self-conceit which binds personality together would begin to leave us. Remember that personality is *many*. It is composed of many different and contradictory 'I's that have been acquired. And it also contains all sorts of other things about which the Work often speaks: negative attitudes, buffers, pictures of oneself, mechanical associations, songs, gramophone records, typical forms of imagination, negative states, characteristic forms of lying, and, in short, all that the practical side of this Work teaches us to notice and observe in ourselves throughout life. Once the Work begins to act on a person genuinely, all these forms of feeling oneself, all these feelings of 'I' derived from personality, begin to dissolve away. But the action of the Work in this respect is very gradual, because the Work acts on people very gently and only in reference to what each of us can stand. When you really begin to see something in yourself, then it means that you can stand it. If you cannot see any 'I's it means that you are not ready. To see oneself as one really is would be intolerable. So the action of the Work is gradual. You *may* begin to see something—some 'I'—that you do not, let us say, quite like, but you will not be freed from it until you either see or know some better 'I' and prefer it, or until you can be freed from this 'I' without danger to yourself. But we will speak of this in the next paper.

Now let us come back to the meaning of *being passive*. In the full sense it means being passive to the personality, and this, in turn, means being passive to oneself. Can you be passive to your mechanically-arising objections for even five minutes? Well, I advise you to observe how your personality reacts every moment to everyone and everything. It is this constant mechanical reaction that must be worked on in order to begin to be passive to oneself. And this requires a constant conscious state of self-observation. No one can do it as yet for long. But you can practise *being passive* in this sense for a short time, say, five minutes. Notice when you begin to object inside—notice what reactions arise in you—and try to be passive *to them*, not to the people who cause them to arise. Is this clear? You must make yourself passive to your own re-actions, not to the people you are reacting to. To do this you must be awake inside yourself and capable of seeing different 'I's in you and what they want to say or how they want to act at the moment.

Let us try to get all this quite clear. Do you all understand that you have *acquired* many things in yourselves that you take as *you*? Can you agree by education, imitation, example, what you were taught, and so on, you have all sorts of ideas, ambitions, estimations, values, judgments, expectations, ways of shewing like and dislike, characteristic ways of speaking, and, in short, many typical *reactions* to life? And is it too much to say that all these built-up acquired reactions in you are usually taken by you as *yourself*? You think them necessary, do you not, or natural, because you think that they are *you*. But the real *you*, or rather, the real 'I' in you, is *not* all these things that you keep holding on to and taking as *yourself*. If you will start from this simple basis you will begin to understand what it means to be *passive*—that is, passive to yourself—or rather, passive to what you always have been taking as *yourself*. To be passive to oneself, one must not take oneself for granted. There is no such thing as 'I' in you. When a person, totally identified with his acquired personality, says, for example, "I think this," "I think that," the Work answer is "Which 'I' is speaking?" Do you see how powerful this idea is? And can you begin to apply the power of this Work-idea to yourself? Certainly not, if you do not begin to break yourself up into different 'I's. If you take yourself for granted as a solid, then there is no breaking up of yourself and so no change is possible. The word 'I' will come out of your mouth at every moment, but you will not see that it is a different 'I' speaking at every moment. One 'I' will shout, another 'I' will speak tenderly, and so on. Yet you do not see that each 'I' is utterly different. It is a great shock to self-conceit to realize that there is no such person as 'I'. But unless this begins to dawn on you, you will never be able to begin to be passive *to yourself*. You cannot begin to be passive to yourself unless you see yourself as *many* different people by inner observation and learn about your different 'I's and know especially which 'I's in you you must never allow to take full charge of you. Next time we will speak of *identifying with oneself* more fully, and the different forms of practising inner separation. Let me say here that 'I's that value this Work must never be allowed to lose their authority in you. Notice the 'I's you are consorting with. Do not keep company with wrong people in you. Remember you are a city, with slums and dangerous streets, and also better streets and good citizens. Remember you are a house full of servants under no control. Has not our first education partly to do with not going with wrong people outside us? Our second education is not to go with wrong 'I's inside us. Our first education is *external*: our second education is *internal*. Life does not give us the second education. Only esoteric teaching gives us the second education—that is, for those who are looking for something different from life.

Birdlip, April 20, 1943

INTERNAL CONSIDERING
AND EXTERNAL CONSIDERING

VIII—On being Passive (2)

This Work is to weaken personality. This is a disadvantage at first, because actually one feels weak when one can no longer react in the usual way. Let us suppose that you were always accustomed to fly into a temper over something, and now you cannot. You feel weak. You feel a loss. A loss of what? A loss of a part of personality. At the same time, you gain something and are really stronger.

Let us try, in these commentaries on internal and external considering, to understand better about what it means to make personality passive. The object is to allow essence to grow. Every time you go against personality consciously, you gain something. Of course, you must not take this arithmetically. You cannot expect that you have instantly some exact gain. It is rather more complex and subtle than that. Personality keeps you where you are. It is acquired. It has become *you*: or you have become *it*. *It* does, *it* acts, *it* says, *it* finds fault, *it* spoils a happy time, *it* takes charge of you at every moment. So *it* keeps you where you are and your life what it is. Now where are you? You are where you are in the sense of what you have in you that is active, and so what you experience, what you think you enjoy. You see life, just there, outside you, and perhaps want all sorts of things, but you cannot get into life and get things from it save in so far as your personality allows you. You go into life according to the shape of your personality. You encounter life, people, and so on, through your personality, not directly. Is this clear? Now you do not *see* your personality. It is not conscious to you. So perhaps you blame life or people, or feel disappointed, and so on. The trouble is that you have acquired a certain mechanical device for making contact with life called *personality* that renders life to you according to its shape, as it were. And so here you are, always carrying about with you your personality, your apparatus for experiencing life, and always hoping perhaps, if you had a new environment, new people, a new house, new clothes, etc. that everything would be utterly different. How can that be? You are carrying about your apparatus for contacting life—that is, your personality. You may pack your bags and fill them with new clothes and go to the Antipodes —but you carry your personality with you, with all its acquired *habits* of mind, *habits* of emotion, *habits* of behaviour, *habits* of talking, *habits* of finding fault, *habits* of movement, *habits* of health, and so on. Now this Work is about how to get away *from oneself*, not from life. You do not get away from yourself by changing your outer scene. For this reason it is necessary to observe oneself and see what one's personality is like and study it and see what one's apparatus is like. We all have all sorts of dreams about a new life—about ideal circumstances, marvellous people, etc. But such dreams are idle because even if we were placed in exceptional and beautiful conditions, such as are said to obtain in Paradise, we would react to them through our personalities and very soon be turned out as quite unsuitable, I fancy. The trouble really is that none of us knows how to live, because none of us sees that the trouble lies in the personality—that is, in the receptive-reactive machine we use to contact life. And we shall never learn how to live even a little aright if we do not work on *personality* in us, and see what it is in us in each case and what troubles arise from *ourselves* and not merely from others and from life.

All this Work is about imitating Conscious Man. But if we do not work on personality, we remain mechanical men. Then *it* will act.

The machine will speak. *It* will get angry. *It* will take charge of everything. And even if you begin to be aware that there is something else in you, something deeper, that does not want to act, to speak, to feel, to think, in the way that you do, you will not be able to alter anything—at least, for a long time. But even so, if you see this, you are in a far better position than that of a person who does not perceive that something is always taking charge of him and spoiling everything. In the Work we have to realize that we are at the mercy of something called personality in us and that this is a machine that controls us. You may lie in bed in the morning in a half-sleep state and see quite clearly what you should say or think or feel or do, but immediately you get up *something takes charge of you*. *It* takes charge of you and *it* begins to act and speak in a way quite contrary to what *you* perceived and planned. What takes charge of you? It is *personality*. And in a short time—in a moment—you are fully under its sway and everything you thought and planned when you were more awake, more free, that is, from personality, seems far away, or even nonsense. So you behave exactly in the same way as yesterday. Something grips you and you fall asleep in its grip. This is our tragedy, that we cannot change, and we even forget that we should change, for a whole day, or a week, or even more. Once we are in personality, everything goes by machinery. Only, once in the grip of personality, we do not see it as machinery. One thing leads to another by the easy paths of association and habit and so to-day is like yesterday and to-morrow like to-day. And it seems to us to be all logical, all reasonable, all justifiable, all natural. But when a man begins to awaken a little—that is, to be more free from personality —he has moments of seeing this *machine* to which he is attached, and under whose power he is. He sees he is in prison. He may even begin to be *afraid* of this smooth, powerful, self-acting machine, this Franken-stein-monster that insists on controlling him, which life has gradually created in him without his knowledge. And then he begins to understand what *work on himself* means and what his task is, and what he must struggle with for the rest of his life. This externally-created thing in him, this personality fashioned by outer life, this machine, whatever form it takes, is the dragon that is to be overcome, in the language of mythology. In the Fourth Way, which lies in life, you cannot go into a monastery or sit in a cave in the desert to free yourself from personality. Making personality passive is, in this Way that we are studying, continual work on oneself *in life*, by means of observation, by not identifying with oneself, by inner separation and so on. The whole work is about this.

Let me quote something that was recorded many years ago by Mr. Ouspensky, about the struggle with personality. It had been explained that a man must gradually learn to take photographs of himself as a whole, and not merely observe single details. He must begin to see himself *altogether*, in all centres, at any particular moment. "For this purpose," it was said, " a man must learn to take, so to speak, mental photographs of himself in different moments of his life, and in different emotional states, and not photographs merely of details, but photographs of the whole as he saw it. In other words these photographs must contain *simultaneously* everything that a man can see in himself at a given moment: his emotions, moods, thoughts, sensations, postures, his behaviour, his movements, his tones of voice, facial expressions, and so on. If a man succeeds in seizing interesting moments for taking these photographs, he will collect a whole album of portraits of himself which, taken together, will shew him quite clearly what he really is. But it is not so easy to take these photographs of oneself at the most interesting and characteristic moments. It takes time to learn how to do it. But if the photographs are taken successfully, and if there are a sufficient number of them, a man will see that his usual conception of himself with which he has lived from year to year is very far from reality.

Instead of the man he had supposed himself to be, he will see quite another man. This 'other' man is himself and at the same time not himself.

In this Work you must learn to know the real from the invented and later to separate them. And to begin self-observation and self-study it is necessary to divide oneself into a real and an invented side. That is, a man must realize that he indeed consists of *two men*. All this takes time. But so long as a man takes himself as *one person he will never move from where he is*. His work on himself starts from the moment he begins to feel *two men* in himself. One is passive and the most it can do is to register or observe what is happening to it. The other, which calls itself 'I', is active, and speaks of itself in the first person, is in reality only an invented unreal person. (Let us call this invented person in a man *A*.)

When a man understands his helplessness in the face of *A*, his attitude towards himself and towards *A* in him ceases to be either indifferent or unconcerned. Self-observation becomes observation of *A*. A man understands that he is not *A*, that *A* is nothing but the mask he wears, the part that he unconsciously plays and which unfortunately he cannot stop playing, a part which rules him, and makes him do and say a thousand stupid things, a thousand things which he would never do or say himself. If he is sincere with himself, he feels that he is in the power of *A* and at the same time he feels that he is not *A*.

He begins to be afraid of *A*, he begins to feel that *A* is his enemy. No matter what he would like to do, everything is altered and intercepted by *A*. *A* is his enemy. *A*'s desires, tastes, sympathies, thoughts, opinions, are either opposed to his own views, feelings and moods, or they have nothing in common with them. And at the same time, *A* is his master. He is the slave, he has no will of his own. He has no means of expressing his desires because whatever he would like to do or say is done for him by *A*.

When a man has reached this level of self-observation he must understand that his whole aim is to free himself from *A*. And since he

cannot in fact free himself from *A* because he is himself, he must therefore master *A* and make him do, not what the *A* of the given moment
wants, but what *he himself* wants to do. From being the master, *A*
must become the servant.

*The first stage of work on oneself consists in separating oneself from A
mentally*, and then later in being separated from him in actual fact,
in keeping apart from him. But the fact must be born in mind that the
whole attention must be concentrated upon *A*, for a man is unable to
explain *what he himself really is*. But he can explain *A* to himself, and
with this he must begin, remembering at the same time that he is not
A."

Let us notice that in the above quotation it is emphasized that a
person cannot change as long as he takes himself as *one*. But when he
divides himself into an *observing side* and an *observed side*, the first step
towards possible change has been taken. That is, a man must become
Observing 'I' and *Personality*. Everything that a man can then observe
in himself he must take as *A* to begin with—that is, as personality.
Now people suppose that only one thing acts in a man, and as long as
people take themselves as one, they cannot think otherwise, so they
find the idea of self-observation very difficult. "What should we
observe?" they ask. The answer is: "Everything"—to begin with.
"But," they will say, "Whatever I can observe is surely myself?"
The answer is: "No and Yes, in the sense of the Work." All you observe
you must take at first as personality in you. This personality in you
governs you and the part which can observe it is helpless in face of it
at first. The order of things is wrong. The command is in the wrong
place. The inner cannot control the outer. What should command is
subject, and what should be subject commands. The inner part which
observes sees the outer part calling itself 'I' and so acting in its name
and can do nothing at first. Notice here that the part which observes
is always deeper than the part observed—i.e. the inner can observe
the outer but not vice versa. Now, although the inner or observing
side is helpless at first, it becomes strengthened by the ideas of the Work
which feed it. The *inner* can only become stronger by the Work. Life
cannot feed it. A man then begins to wish to get free from personality,
from *A*, from the machine he is in the power of. The neutralizing force
of life keeps the personality active: the neutralizing force of the Work
nourishes the inner observing side. A man, in short, begins to understand that his whole aim is to free himself from *A*, from personality.
"And," to quote again, "since he cannot in fact free himself from *A*
because it is himself, he must therefore master *A* and make *A* do, not
what the *A* of the given moment wants, but what *he himself* wants to do.
From being master, *A* must become servant."

281

INTERNAL CONSIDERING
AND EXTERNAL CONSIDERING

IX—On being Passive (3)

In the last paper it was said that a man's work on himself starts from the moment he begins to feel *two men* in himself. One is passive and the most it can do is to register and observe what is happening to it at the hands of the other. The other, which calls itself 'I', is active. It speaks of itself in the first person. It regards itself as being the real man, the man himself. Let us notice that it is said that a man's work starts from the moment he begins to feel *two* men in himself, one passive and the other active. Now how many, do you suppose, reach this stage? Let me ask each of you this question: "Have you reached this stage distinctly, so that you constantly realize that there is an active side in you that will keep on taking charge of you at every moment and a passive side that can only look on and be conscious that this is so, and is quite helpless in the face of this active side?" If you can answer with certainty that you have reached this stage, then it is a matter for congratulation because it means that a real and very important inner division has taken place in you, necessary for all further stages of the Work. For it is exactly this passive side, that has become separated from the active side, that can grow. The evolution of a man in the Work-sense is an evolution from the passive and not the active side of him. But it is just because this inner division into an active and a passive side is so difficult to attain, and takes so long a time and is attended by so many initial failures, that personal work halts or moves in a circle.

As this is such an important matter and so difficult to grasp, let me put the question in another way: "Do you realize your *mechanicalness*, and do you continually realize it?" What does it mean "to realize one's mechanicalness?" It means that you begin to realize that you are a machine that *reacts* to external influences. *It* does not *act*, but *reacts*. All that you have taken as individual and conscious action is mechanical. In other words, to realize what mechanicalness is, is to realize that you cannot behave differently from the way you do behave. Now everyone thinks he is *free* and can act as he likes or chooses. Everyone thinks that he or she can say either this or that by choice or do either this or that by choice. The Work teaches that this is an illusion. It says that it is the first great illusion that must be dispelled in practical work on oneself. Man cannot *do*. In order to *do*, a man must be *free* to do. In order to *do*, a man must first *be*. And to *be* a man must become a unity. Then he is *free*. But man as he is is not *free*, although he so fondly imagines he is. Whatever he *does* is dictated to him by his machine—that is, by the kind of machine that has been built up in him by circumstances, education, imitation, phantasy, negative states, attitudes, opinions, and so on. This is one of the fundamental principles in the *psychological* teaching of this Work. *A man cannot do. It* does, in him—that is, the machine "does." This is what is meant by the saying that a man must reach the stage, through long and often painful inner observation, of realizing that there are *two* men in him, one active and the other passive. The active man "does" everything—by reacting to impressions. The passive man—once he has come into conscious existence—can do nothing at first. He can only notice what the active man "does" and for a long time he must submit to it, however much he, the passive man, would like things to be different. Becoming passive to oneself is the first stage of the Work. It requires great inner activity of *attention*. The question of *control* of personality arises later (*not here*). Before any question of control arises, a man must study what it means to become passive to himself, what it means not to identify *with himself at every moment*—otherwise he will all the time be identified with himself. This includes the whole of himself—*everything* he can observe in process of time—not merely what he personally thinks is bad, but *everything*. That is why it is so often said that self-observation must be *uncritical*. If it is critical then you will only observe one part and never think of observing another part—which may actually be connected. The passive man has not yet the strength to change anything in the active man—that is, to control him. Unfortunately, people start off, right from the beginning, trying to control, trying *to do*. This is impossible, unless the right point of control is established. The right point of control comes from the gradual strengthening of the passive man.

★   ★   ★

It is often said in this Work that a man is in prison. The original talks were often about "prison"—and about "escape from prison". But to escape a man must first realize he *is* in prison and see where his prison lies. I will quote something once said on this point: "If a man in prison is at any time to have a chance of escape, then he must first of all *realize that he is in prison*. If he imagines he is free, then how can he even begin to think about escaping from prison? He will regard the idea as nonsense. So long as he fails to realize he is in prison, so long will he think he is free. Then he has no chance whatsoever. No one can help him. No one can liberate him by force, against his will, in opposition to his wishes. If liberation is possible, it is the first requisite that a man feels he is in prison and begins to study the prison he is in, and the means of escape. And he can only gain freedom as the result of long work and effort—and by this is meant conscious effort, directed towards a definite aim. But in order to escape from prison, a man must have help. He must be told what to do and told again and again, by those who have escaped and who in turn have transmitted their knowledge to others who have realized they are in prison and have themselves begun to escape."

In what is said in the above quotation, you must understand that no physical prison is meant nor does it mean merely that the body is the prison. What is meant is a *psychological prison* that must be escaped from. Everyone is in the prison of himself. If a man could really stand behind himself—that is, stand behind every side and every manifestation of himself, whether he thinks it good or bad—then he would be able to see the prison he lives in. But, in order to do this, he must become *passive* to himself. He must see all his reactions, whether he regards them as good or bad, passively. He must see all the opinions he expresses, whether he regards them as good or bad, passively. He must see his attitudes. And when he has reached this stage, by long self-observation, then he is really divided into two men—one active and the other passive. The passive man stands inside or *behind* the active man. The passive man at this stage is powerless but although he is powerless in face of the active man, he is now *conscious of him*. He sees his prison. This is the starting-point of real change. So I ask you again the question asked before: "Have you reached the stage of realizing that there is an active side in you that takes charge of you at every moment and a passive side that can only look on and is quite helpless in the face of this active side?"

The less you identify with yourself, the more will you become passive to yourself.

Birdlip, May 9, 1943

INTERNAL CONSIDERING
AND EXTERNAL CONSIDERING

X—On being Passive (4)

On Identifying with Oneself

Part I.—If you have to pass from one room into another room, it will be impossible to do so if you are fastened to something in the first room. Suppose you are stuck to your arm-chair. It will be impossible to move, except with the arm-chair attached to you. And if the door is narrow, you will be unable to get through. And you must imagine that we are fastened to many things that prevent us from passing to a new level of being. I remember, on one occasion, that Mr. Ouspensky spoke of us as wearing an enormous number of coats. He said that it was necessary to strip off these coats one by one. Otherwise we were too bulky to pass through the door. A person who believes in himself, in his virtue and merit, and so on, is bulky in a psychological sense. So he cannot pass through the "narrow gate"—or through "*the eye of a needle*". He is a camel. A camel is a big and obstinate creature. Of course, a person who is *psychologically* a camel is meant.

In the Gospels, a person who is very much identified with himself is called a *rich man*. He has a firm idea of his own worth. He thinks that he knows, he is certain he can do and is sure that right and wrong are clear to him. Such a person is very much *identified with himself*. This is the *rich man* of the Gospels of whom Christ said it was easier for a camel to pass through the eye of a needle than for a rich man to enter the Kingdom of Heaven. In the case given in the Gospels, the rich man felt he possessed goodness and had obtained much merit in everything he had done. He was identified with himself. So all that he did went into the wrong part of himself. Because of this, Christ said to him: "Go, *sell* all that thou hast." The rich man was sorry, for he had "great possessions"—that is, he was identified with himself and his value. Yet he was not so much identified with himself as the Pharisee who prayed, saying: "God, I thank thee, that I am not as the rest of men, extortioners, unjust, adulterers, or even as this publican. I fast twice in the week; I give tithes of all that I get," while the publican prayed: "God be merciful to me a sinner." The Pharisee is an extreme example of identification with oneself. Let us clearly understand that a man may be very good in life and do his duty and follow all he is taught faithfully and meet danger with heroism and yet be the *rich man* of the Gospels. This means that he is identified with himself in all that he does and is satisfied with himself. Now you know that there is a phrase in the Work which says that until a man reaches the stage of realizing his own *nothingness* he cannot change. To begin to realize one's own nothingness as a *practical experience* is to begin to cease to be a "rich man". In other words, it is to begin to cease *identifying with oneself*.

*   *   *

Part II.—Let us now speak of identifying with oneself from different sides. Let us begin by saying that *where* you are identified with yourself, *there* you cannot be passive to yourself. To be identified with yourself means that you are fastened to something in yourself which you take as yourself. Suppose you are fastened to the idea that you are a truthful person. This means that you are fastened to this picture of yourself. You picture yourself, to yourself, as being always truthful. So wherever you are, as it were, you take with you this picture. You have no existence apart from this picture. You *are* this picture. It accompanies you everywhere, no matter even if you are not telling the truth. This makes no difference to the picture that you have of yourself and to which you are firmly glued. If for a moment circumstances make you feel you are not being quite truthful on some occasion, then at once you will begin to justify yourself and explain and argue and so on until you feel again quite comfortable inside, and at peace with this picture which dominates you. This is being identified with yourself. It is an example belonging to the class of *identifying with pictures of oneself*. Of course, pictures are legion. But everyone has special pictures of himself or

285

herself with which he or she identifies. One of the sources of our inner disharmony and of our negative states lies in pictures. When a picture is, as it were, touched, we shew our touchiness either by being depressed or by being angry, or, in short, negative. When we carry a great many pictures about, we are very identified with ourselves. And the more we are identified with ourselves, the more liable we are to be upset, discouraged, disappointed, and so on. Of course, it is not only pictures that make a person liable to be upset. But pictures form a very definite source of instability in ourselves. Pictures are formed out of vanity and imagination—that is, they belong to the False Personality, which is *Imaginary 'I'*. And with everything belonging to the False Personality we are especially identified. If we could really see by direct insight that we are not at all as we imagined, then the power of False Personality would be weakened. On one side we would lose, but actually we would gain far more than we would lose. But we always defend ourselves, even when we know better. This is because those two giants called *pride* and *vanity* will not allow us to yield—at least to others. And for this reason only *self*-observation can help. You yourself, by seeing yourself, can yield to yourself. So a division must be made *in oneself* between the observing and the observed sides. And, at first, everything must be observed passively, and placed in the light of consciousness without criticism. If you have a picture of yourself as always being truthful, then you must observe over a long period how often you lie. Only this *inner realization* will destroy the power of the picture with which you have been identified and to which you have been a slave.

★   ★   ★

Part III.—"So long as a man takes himself as *one* person he will never move from where he is." Yes, but why? Because he is then completely *identified with himself*. His work only begins when he feels two men in himself. One is passive and this is the man who observes: the other is active and this is the man who is observed. This active man calls himself 'I'. The passive man is the beginning of the path to *real 'I'*. But it is for a long time weak and can do nothing. But as the feeling of 'I' is drawn out of the active man so does the passive man become strengthened until the time comes when the passive man becomes active and the active man passive. That is, a reversal takes place and the inner controls the outer, not the outer the inner.

Let us understand this more clearly. So long as a person takes himself as one he cannot become different. Do you see why? He cannot change, because he is *identified with himself* and takes everything in himself as himself. His thoughts, opinions, moods, feelings, sensations, and, in fact, everything, he takes as 'I'. He says 'I' to them all. You will remember what the Work says about *identifying*. I will quote a few things: "Identification is so common a quality that for the purposes of observation it is difficult to separate it from everything else. Man is always in a state of identification and for this reason he cannot remember himself . . . 'Identifying' is one of our most terrible foes. It is necessary to see and to study identifying to its very roots in oneself. Identifying is the chief obstacle to self-remembering. A man who identifies with everything is unable to remember himself. In order to *remember oneself* it is necessary not to *identify*. But in order not to identify a man must first of all not be *identified with himself*. He must remember that there are *two* in him, one that can only observe at first and another that takes charge of him at every moment and speaks in his name and calls itself 'I'. He must try not to identify with this other man who controls him, and feel that he is different from him and that there is *another* in him. But unless this separation is made and continually made, he remains *one man* and nothing can change in him."

You will see that the Work teaches that the state of man is such that he identifies with everything. For example, a man *identifies with his knowledge*. One person has one kind of knowledge, such as knowledge of the world, another has knowledge of science, a third knowledge of cooking, a fourth knowledge of business, a fifth knowledge of books, and so on. But in each case a person will identify with his or her knowledge. You know how people having similar knowledge quarrel and how, in the so-called learned world, all sorts of extraordinary jealousies exist based on identifying. Doctors, for instance, always disagree. And they are always identified with their knowledge. Cooks also do not agree, nor do literary people, nor soldiers, nor parsons, nor mothers, and so on, and so on. Perhaps you remember in childhood when you first began to identify with knowledge and how pleased you felt when you were told something that others did not know and felt a kind of power. Identifying gives a sense of power. It was not, of course, the knowledge you were interested in, but the fact that you could "shew off".

Now let us take the subject of identifying with Intellectual Centre. Here exist among other things *attitudes, opinions* and *thoughts*. Do you know, or rather, have you observed, that you identify with your opinions? This is another form of identifying with oneself. Of course, an opinion is not you, but quite distinct. But if you are identified, the feeling of 'I' becomes fastened to it. Perhaps you feel you do not have opinions. In any case, we all have thoughts. Can you say 'I' to your thoughts? or rather, do you say 'I' to them invariably? Certainly, if you believe that everything in your inner world is 'I' then you cannot help doing so. But you might as well say that everything in the external world is yourself. Often very depressing and complex thoughts come. If one identifies with them they exert their full power. Then one is identified with one's thoughts. But it is quite possible not to identify with one's thoughts. In fact, it is very necessary to learn this, and as soon as possible. It helps one a great deal in work on oneself, and in every way. It is impossible to stop thoughts. You can try this, but merely as an exercise in self-observation. But one can learn not to identify with thoughts, and one must begin by observing them. Some thoughts are very interesting to observe, tangled, complex, heavy thoughts that it is very dangerous to identify with. If you do not identify with something in yourself, you begin to be free from its power. Next time we will speak more of identifying with oneself in regard to the Intellectual Centre and later in regard to the other centres.

Birdlip, May 15, 1943

INTERNAL CONSIDERING
AND EXTERNAL CONSIDERING

XI—On being Passive (5)

We continue to-day to speak on the subject of non-identifying with *oneself.* I remind you again that people take this thing called oneself for granted, and also take it not only as *one* thing but allow it to say 'I' to everything it does or thinks or feels.

*   *   *

We spoke last time of identifying with oneself from the standpoint of centres and began with the Intellectual Centre. When you are first taught about self-observation, you are told to try to observe the work of the different centres so as to see the three people in you corresponding to them. The activities of the Intellectual Centre are very many. Last time something was said about *opinions* and *thoughts* which belong to the Intellectual Centre. A man usually identifies himself completely with his opinions, which are borrowed from others, from the papers, etc. Then we spoke of identifying with our thoughts. Our thoughts are not *visible* to other people, nor to ourselves. But they are quite definite things, composed of definite substances. We can be *more*, or *less*, conscious of our thoughts. Now when you *observe* a thought, you are not identified with it. What does that mean? It means that unless you observe the Intellectual Centre and what is going on in it you tend to take its activities for granted. You will *believe your thoughts* or take them for granted. You identify with them. You give them the quality of truth and either say: "*I* think" or, more internally, you take the thoughts as *you.* Then they have power over you and exert their influence upon you. An unpleasant thought, a dreary, heavy thought, a suspicious thought, a pessimistic thought, an evil thought, and so on —all these thoughts *become you*: and so you *are* them, through identifying with them. But *you* are *not* your thoughts. *Any* thought can enter the mind. All sorts of hopeless, bad, useless, stupid, formless and imbecile thoughts can enter the mind. And if you say 'I' to them all, where will *you* be? You will say 'yes' to them all. You will consent to them.

You will, in short, be identified with them, because all the time you will be saying 'I' to them and believing that 'I' is thinking them and that they are *your* thoughts. But, as I said, any thoughts can enter the mind, just as any people can come into your house. Very few of our thoughts are worth following and in order to begin to think rightly, nearly all the thoughts that casually come into the mind have to be rejected as useless or worse. A person may indeed have very dangerous thoughts, especially when he accepts them as if they were his own. He is so naive as to believe that all thoughts coming into his mind are his own and that he himself thought them. And so he says 'I' to them, not knowing any better. But if he begins to understand that he must observe his thoughts, he will soon have quite a different viewpoint.

I remember that many years ago when Mrs. Nicoll and I left the Institute in France and went to Scotland to my grandfather's house, I spent many months looking through the theological books in my grandfather's library, written by various Scotch divines. They were all, of course, purely formatory. They were all about matters of doctrine and about the letter of the law and they indulged in all sorts of hair-splitting arguments. But one of them struck me. The writer said that people must remember that the devil sent many thoughts into our minds and that we must never think that they are our own thoughts. He explained this idea at some length and even often emphasized the phrase: "Our thoughts are not our own." Here was a man beginning to understand *something psychological* and reading him was like a breath of living air, amongst all those dead and terrible volumes, in which there was no trace of understanding, and nothing was said on the psychological level, and everything was taken on the literal level—on the level of *stone*. This writer said that we are not responsible for our thoughts but responsible for our thinking. You can think a thought, or not. A thought enters the mind and seeks to attract you. If it does, you begin to "think it"—that is, think from it. You begin to enlarge this thought, by paying attention to it and thinking from it, until it grows in all directions, and forms, as it were, a little tree of thought in you, that bears fruit, and seeds other similar thoughts. This is clear enough in the case of suspicious thoughts.

You understand that a *thought* and *thinking* are not the same. Let us suppose that the thought enters your mind that Mr. X is lying. This is only a thought. You probably say to yourself: "I must think about that." But if you believe the thought at once you identify with it. Your thought has now transformed Mr. X. into a liar. What thoughts we identify with change things very much. For instance, some people habitually identify with a gloomy, tortuous, mistrustful class of thoughts. They like thoughts of this shape and colour. So they accept such thoughts and reject others. These thoughts alter things for them, like dark glasses. Now they are identified with these thoughts so that they cannot see them. They *are* these thoughts so they cannot observe them and see they are certain kinds of thoughts and that all sorts of other thoughts exist, with quite different shapes and colours. A man can have any kind of thoughts. Any thoughts can come into a man. In the Gospels it is pointed out that it is not what comes into a man that defiles him but what comes *out of a man*. Any sort of thought can enter the mind, but whether you identify with it and act from it—or rather, re-act—is another question. If you identify with a thought you say 'I' to it and you believe it. So you will *think* from it or *act* from it. How you think and how you act is what comes *out of you*. The thought that enters the mind is what goes *into a man*. What he thinks and does from this thought is what comes *out of him*. A thought that is a lie, a wrong· thought, wrongly joined together, a false thought, a depressing thought, a thought that takes hold of one thing and ignores everything else, or that kind of thought that can only deny and contradict, etc.—if a person identifies with such thoughts, he will think and act from them. His mind will be a mess. The ideas of this Work are to build the mind up in the right order so that everything can be related aright. In the centre of the mind stands the Ray of Creation—that is, the *Scale of Being*. From the highest to the lowest all things fall into their places. But unless the mind is changed by the Work, it continues to think that all its thoughts are real and true. The mind is then like a tent lying in a heap on the ground without a central upright pole. All its parts are touching each other wrongly. They are not stretched out. By means of the training of the Work and learning to think from what it teaches, a man begins to be able to distinguish between right and wrong thinking. He begins to learn how to think on the right scale, and how not to mix scales, and so on. All this helps him not to identify with all his thoughts. It gives a centre of gravity to his thinking.

This Work is to make a man think aright. That is why it is so important to try to take in what this Work teaches. You know that in learning, say, Chemistry, or, if you like, a foreign language, it is very important to listen to what is taught you, and to arrange it in your mind, and think about what is being taught you. Many people never think of what they are being taught. But in the Work, it is necessary. Why is it necessary? Because it builds up a new system of thought and of thinking in your minds. Actually, it makes your minds begin to work in the right way—so that they can really begin to think.

Now let me emphasize that a *thought*, and *thinking* a thought, are not the same. A thought may enter your mind, but you may or may not *think* it. And even if you *think* it, you need not necessarily *identify* with it. But there are many different kinds of thoughts, higher and lower, big and little, that enter the mind, and this belongs to later teaching. What it is necessary to realize at present is that thoughts are of every possible kind and that they are not yours, but that you make them yours by identifying with them. And if you do so, then they can pull you in any direction. There is a science of thought. This Work, with all its ideas and teaching, and instructions, has to do with a right *science of thought and thinking*. For that reason all of you who have heard the Work for some years should know what it means to *find fault with your thoughts and with your thinking*, and should be able to see wrong thoughts and inadequate and unrelated thinking, poor thoughts, negative thoughts, useless thoughts, lying thoughts, and so on. The first change demanded in this Work, as in the Gospels, is *change of mind*. But for "*change of mind*" to take place, you must begin *to think from this Work* and what it teaches. Then later, perhaps, you can begin to *act from the Work*. But first of all a new way of thinking is necessary. Now in this paper we are speaking of what the Work teaches. It says that any thoughts can enter your minds, and they are not *your* thoughts. It says you can think them or not. And it says you can identify with them or not. When you hear this, as a part of the teaching of the Work, and apply it by observing yourself in Intellectual Centre, you will see that it is quite true. When you realize this, you will be *thinking in a new way* about yourself.

If you can realize practically—that is, by experience—that you can be passive to your thoughts by non-identifying with them, you have already reached a definite stage of work on the Intellectual Centre. But if you take yourself as *one* you will never get to this point. You will remain stuck in the illusion that all your thoughts as well as all your feelings and moods are *you* or rather "I myself". You will have no insight into the enormous inner world of height and depth containing thousands of inhabitants, good and bad, that you take for granted as one person, which you regard as *yourself*, and in *the customary state of sleep* say 'I' to at every moment. Everything that takes place in yourself you will call 'I'. So you will never move from the position you are in, because you take *yourself* as one, and so you will never understand what it means to become *passive* to *yourself*.

In the above paper we have been speaking of practical work that leads to becoming passive to *thoughts*. This belongs to intimate work on the *Intellectual Centre*. This is the subject of the paper. The paper is about long practical work on non-identifying with thoughts.

INTERNAL CONSIDERING
AND EXTERNAL CONSIDERING

XII—On 'Being Passive' (6)

Last time we spoke of the necessity in the Work that a man should be able to find fault with his thoughts and not identify with them. To-night we speak of the necessity of finding fault with our emotions. The activities of the Emotional Centre are far more difficult to become passive to than the activities of the Intellectual Centre. A man can *think differently* more easily than he can *feel differently*. It is quite possible to become passive to many thoughts that one has been accustomed to follow and identify with, but it is not the same in regard to the sphere of the emotions and feelings. The reason is that we are identified with our feelings far more than with our thoughts. Our feelings, our emotions, our moods, grip us. Notice yourself, when you are vexed. Is it easy to non-identify with this usual daily emotional state? You may smile and say cheerful things and pretend you are all right, but inside you are held as if in a vice. Although one side of you may not want to be vexed, yet some other side insists on being so. Or let us say that something belonging to the self-importance, to the vanity, is touched—is it easy to cease being identified with it? Is it easy not to be offended? One reason is that the emotions are very quick. They work with a very "quick" energy, a far quicker energy than that used in ordinary thoughts. Another reason is that we rarely look at our emotions. We do not observe them because we take them for granted. Our emotional life is a very poor thing. But we do not notice how poor and unpleasant and mean it is. If we did, we would begin to dislike it. We would begin to dislike our usual emotional states—even begin to hate them. But it takes some considerable time before we reach this stage of consciousness. It is scarcely too much to say that we are not really conscious of our usual daily emotions, which are practically always negative, mean, jealous, and paltry—or, in short, unpleasant. Our love of unpleasant emotions is extraordinary and we like very much not only to communicate our unpleasant emotions to others and infect them but to *hear* about unpleasant things, scandal, and so on. *We do not know what we are doing. We do it all in sleep.* We cannot see our emotions because we are so identified with them. If we could see plainly our usual emotions we would be horrified. But fortunately we are not able to see them, simply because we could not endure it. It would drive us mad to see the quality of our emotional life. We all have noble pictures of ourselves. And the Work never allows us to *see* what we cannot bear. Its action is very slow, very gradual, very gentle. But we can see the *results* of our emotions and this is the starting-point. We can see that we hurt people, for example. But even if we realize this, it may take us years of self-observation before we realize that we have unpleasant, treacherous or nasty emotions, which cause others to be hurt, and that it is our fault. You must understand that *awakening* is a very long process and a painful one. Awakening means becoming more and more *conscious of oneself*—of what one is really like. In the emotional sphere this is very difficult. How often do people imagine that they have done their best for others, when, in actual fact, they have done nothing but express their unpleasantest, most stinging and harmful, and often nastiest emotions, of which they should really be ashamed. In fact, expressing unpleasant emotions is what in life is so often called "being sincere" or "trying to help", and so on. People actually think it is a kindness to say all sorts of unpleasant and wretched things to one another and they imagine that if they smile sweetly they are exercising charity and goodwill. That is the trouble in regard to our emotional states. We are not charitable nor have we goodwill, and one of the first things is to realize this to the very bottom and hate it. We love ourselves in everything. We love everything that gratifies our vanity and so we do not love our neighbours unless they flatter us and we feel that we dispense their lives. And even though we may have better 'I's in us that can understand other people more and even care for them, even if they do not flatter us, yet the smaller, meaner 'I's belonging to the self-love, the self-interest and the self-conceit, usually prove to be far stronger—save perhaps after a long interval of time of self-observation, or when they are rendered quiescent by the exhaustion of severe illness, which renders the personality passive. On the point of death people wish only that others should forgive them. That is because they are no longer in small 'I's. But this humiliation can *gradually* take place by the action of the Work—that is, through increasing consciousness of what one really is like—by means of long and patient self-observation and all the inner pain of realizing that life cannot be as it was in our imagination.

Now let us sketch the person who is full of vanity, self-merit, self-admiration, self-love, self-estimation, self-worthiness, self-conceit, self-importance, self-esteem, self-excitement, and so on. This person is very identified with himself or herself. This person is *rich*—"the rich man" (or the rich woman). Such people have no idea that they *cannot do*. This idea would startle them. They also have no notion that they *do not know*. They are sure they know best. They feel depressed only when their vanity meets with a check, or no doubt they feel furious. But they cannot see themselves. They may be very kind so long as they are gratified with thanks and praise. They help the poor, they give money to those in distress, provided they get proper recognition and feel they are properly treated. Such people may be very useful in mechanical life, but in the Work, which is under a *reverse sign* from life, they may find themselves at a loss. I remember many years ago that some people of this kind who were in the Work decided to get together and make the Work "really go". They felt that it was all too slow and that they could rapidly make it a great success and they no doubt pictured themselves sitting on the platform at some great meeting at the Albert Hall or some such place bowing to thousands of people. They felt that out of their "richness"—I am speaking psychologically —they could enlarge the Work. But it is out of a man's "poorness" that the Work grows. It is not from the rich personality that the Work grows in a man but from the starved and real essence. This is why the Work *reverses everything*, and makes the active passive and the passive active. Do any of you really imagine that if this Work were a great success in life and were broadcast night and day it could retain any inner secret force and meaning? I advise you to think out this for yourselves. For my own part, I realized very early that this Work could never be a success in life and that it could never be written about openly, save indirectly. And if you think deeply you will see why this must be so—that is, if you think from the idea of active and passive signs, in regard to personality and essence.

Now let us take the question of becoming passive to *likes* and *dislikes*. This is part of the Work on Emotional Centre, in regard to the general teaching of becoming passive to the active "oneself" that takes charge of things and controls us. Try to observe your likes and dislikes and how you *waste* yourselves in silly likes and dislikes. There is an exercise in the Work to this effect: "Try for a time to like what you dislike and dislike what you like." There is a similar exercise in regard to the Intellectual Centre which I should have mentioned before—namely, "Try to observe what opinions you side with and speak in favour of the other side." Being identified with one's mechanical liking and dis-liking holds a person down to *emotional habits*. It so often happens that you find that what you dislike you can easily like and *vice versa*. Our mechanical likes and dislikes are based on very little. They change every moment. Yet we attach so much importance to them. And often in the Work you find that people you disliked you begin to like. This is a sign that you are changing. But you cannot change if you identify with every one of your momentary likes and dislikes. One thing can help here—namely, not always *talking* endlessly of your likes and dis-likes, and making a fuss about them. Sometimes people's sole form of conversation is about what they like and they do not like. As if they really imagine it is important! No form of talk is more egotistical or exhausting. To practise for a short time, at intervals, being consciously passive to one's mechanical likes and dislikes is very useful, but not always, particularly in those who mechanically are too timid to say what they want. Speaking in general, Work is always against what is *mechanical in you*. If *mechanically* you have not enough likes and dislikes you should have more, and *vice versa*.

Let us now speak of one side of being passive to likes and dislikes. Let us speak of being passive to *associations*. You know that the Work says that we see everything from association. Yet we may have feelings of being in a familiar place and of being in an unfamiliar place at the same time, but these feelings are not in the same part of us. To our small 'I's living in mechanical divisions of centres, things may seem familiar by mere association which when seen from more conscious 'I's become unfamiliar. Thus we sometimes "behold" one another —as for the first time. We see *for a moment without associations.* Impressions then fall beyond the machinery of mechanical personality. Then everything is strange, unfamiliar and vivid. Impressions then fall on essence. We get used to things owing to associations so we no longer *see* each other or indeed anything, but only our associations with which we completely identify. We take another person by our associations. We identify with these associations and so think we see and know the person. Now it is quite possible to observe *associations* at work with which we identify, and so get misled. It is quite possible to observe associations about others especially if one begins to realize *one does not know them.* For instance, people take it for granted that they know each other. This is illusion. We are nearly invisible to one another. But if you think you "know" you will not be able to "see" without mechanical associations. This means that you must start from the realization that you do *not know* other people, however familiar to you they are. And so also with everything. We do not really *know.* But we are sure we know. Start from the idea that you do not know and have never known. Start, that is, from *ignorance.* This is the "poor" side. And this gives new life because you begin to get new impressions, new viewpoints, new understanding. If impressions fall on essence you see in a new way. Now a "rich" person, very identified with himself, cannot expect to see things without associations or to get any new impressions falling on essence, which is the growing point of a person. He will live always in associations—in the past. Also an opinionated man, a man or woman convinced that he or she knows right and wrong, a man or woman openly or secretly in love with themselves, and certain of themselves and their virtue, and standpoint, such a man or woman, wholly identified with themselves, will not be able to divide themselves into two. That is, they will not be able to shift their position but must always remain *where* they are and so *what* they are in the Scale of Being. *Where* and *what* are the same in this scale. That is, the level of being *where* a man is, is also *what* he is. If you begin to see yourself passively you begin to see the level of being you are chained down to by the active, self-acting side of you—the side that calls itself "I" and which, in my case, expects to be called "Maurice Nicoll". This side, in everyone, usurps the throne and sits on it. There are endless legends, parables and myths, referring to this wrong psychological situation of man. One has some difficulty in believing that such a thing actually happens to everyone and that everyone has a wrong Ruler on the throne, and that it happened long ago to oneself. One at least thinks one is *master* in one's house. This is precisely not the case. You have no real *master* on the throne of your inner world—that is, in your own psychology. You must understand that if we see everything from past associations we will not be able to see anything in a different way. We may imagine we see another person but it will be from our associations. In this way, we keep one another in the prison of our associations about one another. We have already formed our own opinions about others. So we do not allow others to exist beyond what we think of them by associations. This is a great tragedy. To let people go, as it were, let them be different, depends on *our* letting them go. That is, it depends upon our not trying to keep them to what we imagine they are by our mechanical associations. All mothers and fathers have this difficulty with children. But it applies to all sorts of other relationships in life. Remember that we see one another by our associations, once we become "familiar", as it is called, with each other. What we do not understand is that seeing a person by one's own associations with him or her has nothing to do with what the person really is. Try to see another person *without associations*. That is the beginning of something new. And it so often happens that people have got quite wrong associations with others and never even catch a real glimpse of them. I personally have found in this Work that I "know" others less and less. Certainly I would never say: "I know this person—I have known this person all my life." That is exactly saying, in so many words, that you know nothing save your few associations with the person.

*　　*　　*

One of the most difficult things in this Work is to go on steadily with it when one's vanity has been hit at. This shews merely how much we do things from vanity, without realizing it. All the explosive, bristling, quarrelling touchiness of life is due to the two emotional giants, Vanity and Pride. Can you stick to a thing when you have been told you are not good at it? Your vanity may be offended, but your pride may help. Anyhow, if you can, then you may be fairly sure that you are not acting from personality entirely but perhaps from something genuine, and deeper, and so more real. Yet it may only be pride, turned *outwards*, which comes to the rescue of offended vanity. At the same time one can stick to this Work through pride turned *inwards*, and eventually find genuine reasons which have nothing to do with superficial feelings, but spring from a real valuation of the Work itself. This is to reach emotion beyond self-emotion. You must remember that in a fully-developed school of this Work, your Vanity would be hit almost every day, and that many would leave in indignation. At the Institute in France we were told on entering that "personality has scarcely any right to exist in this place." But we merely heard the phrase. We did not realize what it meant—save later. Speaking on a far higher scale, let us recall how many people left Christ because "they were offended in him." This means they were identified emotionally with the vanity of their own worth. To be so is really a nuisance. You will find out why I say this, if you do not know it already But there is a deeper side to all this—that is, where the Work really brings you up against yourself. Here lies the point where people forget to work and simply feel lost. Here is the place where it is possible to long not to be so identified emotionally with what one is. It is like being stuck to an illusion that you cannot get away from and that can no longer galvanize you. You must, however, begin to realize that you have been "stuck to" an illusion that you have called 'I' and that beyond the illusion you can begin to have real things—that is, the same things, but differently.

Now let us take another aspect of being identified emotionally, which illustrates one of the many difficulties of becoming passive to oneself—to this person called *A*, to this active Frankenstein-monster that one has been led to make, and which now stalks about in one's little world and takes charge of one, and speaks as if it were 'I' and keeps on singing all sorts of things, grandiloquent and boastful as well as pious and timid. This monster, this *machine*, that you are fastened to —what do you think of it? Do you like it? Everyone is attached to his or her machine. Remember the Work teaches that everyone is a machine but that machines are of different kinds—some are loud like Bren guns, or chattering like typewriters, and some are as silent as the electric meter in the hall outside. Now people compare themselves with others. That is, machines compare themselves with machines and identify through comparison with themselves. If you are a noisy machine you perhaps feel you are superior to a quiet machine. And if you are a quiet machine you thank God you are not a noisy machine, and so on. This is one source of identifying emotionally with oneself—that is, it is one source of liking oneself. In the Gospels it is said that a man must come to *hate himself*. This Work uses different language but has the same deep meaning. The Work says a man must become passive to himself. But it is very painful to go against the usual way one has reacted to life. You feel you are losing so much. Yet you are losing nothing real and after a time you begin to feel new forms of living passing into you. You come back to the same scenes, but you are different. It is the same outer world but you take it quite differently. It is the same kind of thing, the same kind of events, but you are related to them quite differently. It is even the same people, but you see and feel them quite differently. In passing from one level of being, and experience, to a new level, there is a gap that is painful. It is like leaving something familiar. If you hold on to the Work, after a time you find that you can once more experience everything fully, but at a different level—that is, *in a new way*.

INTERNAL CONSIDERING
AND EXTERNAL CONSIDERING

XIII—On being Passive (7)

Associations

The mind should become accustomed to think of the ideas of the Work. A man can only think from his ideas. If you think always with your usual ideas, your thoughts will always follow the same circles. You will go round and round in your minds. As a rule this is our usual state. When did you last have a thought that led anywhere? The ideas of the Work are to change the mind. They are very powerful. To think from an idea of this Work—such as that man is asleep on this earth and that is the real reason why everything is in the mess it is in —to think from such a powerful idea is to think in a new way. This means that *new* connections and associations are made in the mind and the psychic energy begins to traverse new paths. This is always a good experience. This making of new connections opens up the mind and gives new force. To think always in the same way is, as has often been said, like walking up and down a lawn always in exactly the same narrow track. The result is that the grass is worn out just in these places. But owing to the tremendous mechanical pull that we are subject to on this far-down planet, habits of thought form very quickly and persist throughout life. That is why it is so difficult to become passive to typical associative ways of thinking, especially since we take them for granted as being true. Truth is, for us, our habits of mind. Nothing is surely more evident than the fact that people become so identified with their ways of thinking that nothing can alter them. But this does not apply only to other people. It applies to ourselves. We do not realize that we have *habits of mind*, as the Work calls them, just as we have habits of feeling, habits of movement, and habits of appetite. Habits exist in all centres because centres become overlaid with a network of associations, like railways running across country. If we could start with a new machine things would be different. But we start with a dirty and worn machine. Yet, even though this is so, by not identifying with typical habits of mind and feeling (to begin with), very much that is worth while can be achieved.

Let us take another illustration. The physical instrument of thought is the brain. The brain contains something like 14,000,000,000 distinct nerve-cells, each with about 100 branches or connections, with other nerve-cells. Let us picture this on a very reduced scale, as a mere diagram.

Diagram shewing three brain-cells

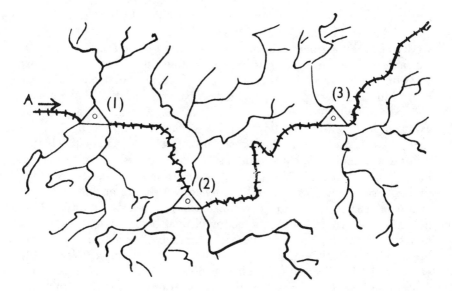

This small diagram shews a nervous or psychic impulse entering the field under observation at A and passing through nerve-cells (1) to nerve-cell (2) and then to (3) *via* one path only, shewn in thick lines ⊢⊢⊢⊢⊢⊢⊢. But you will notice that this impulse entering at A might take many other paths. And if you remember that there are some 14,000,000,000 brain-cells, each with 100 arms or branches or connections, then you will realize in how many ways a thing can be taken —that is, along how many different paths an impulse can travel theoretically. But owing to habit impulses find habitual tracks and so produce the same results.

Try to visualize the infinite number of possible paths an impression might take. But actually the matter is like the lawn upon which we walk always along a few well-worn paths. That is, we live by *associations*. We think by associations and we feel by associations. And certainly we move by associations, and this is just as well, speaking in general, but as we so often move wrongly, some of these associations must ultimately be broken down. But we speak here only of associative thoughts and associative feelings or emotions—that is, mechanical thinking and mechanical liking and disliking, mechanical negative emotions and so on. Speaking from a rather different angle, the Work says that we live in the *basement* of ourselves. The basement means the mechanical divisions of centres. The basement of the Intellectual

Centre is the formatory part—that is, the moving part of Intellectual Centre. The basement of the Emotional Centre is the moving or mechanical part of it. In these parts we live almost entirely by mechanical associations. We get up, yawn, eat breakfast, make our usual remarks, express our usual opinions, use our usual phrases, make our usual jokes, exhibit our usual likes and dislikes and so on. In this sense we live in the basement and also, in much the same sense, we live by *association*. If anything is missing, or if anything is unusual, we are astonished and probably make a fuss. But provided we recognize everything at a mere glance, provided everything is routine, and familiar, we are satisfied. This is our mechanical life. We should all be well aware of it by self-observation. And if we feel no desire to be different then there is no reason why we should. But a man may reach that point of awakening, or that point of self-consciousness, where he realizes his mechanicalness and begins first to be rather surprised, and then perhaps to feel discomfort, and finally to feel dislike of himself. It is, of course, useless merely to feel dislike of oneself in a vague way. Many do. Many alternate between a feeling of their own worth and a feeling of despair. But that leads nowhere. It is merely the swing of the pendulum. What we dislike must be pinned down. For example, in regard to work on the Intellectual Centre from the side of *associative thinking*, one must observe some typical chain of associations or thoughts that one wishes to change and become *passive* to it. That means, one must not say 'I' to it, nor believe it is 'I' thinking it, but that it is the machine of associations thinking it. *It* is thinking it, not 'I'. To non-identify, you must take all feeling of 'I' out of a thing. But as you know, for a very long time we take every psychic happening in us, that is, every thought and feeling, as 'I'—as oneself— as *me*. And this attitude to our inner psychic world is as foolish as a corresponding attitude to the external world by our senses. I do not take the table as *me*, as 'I'. Nor need I take my thoughts in that way.

Now we spoke of "living in the basement"—that is, in associations belonging to the mechanical parts of centres. To-night I wish to speak of *three* categories of associations that are possible for us, according to the Work teaching—namely, associations produced involuntarily, associations produced voluntarily, and associations of a higher order, that are established in us by connection with the ideas of the Work. Let us take these three categories one by one.

The main part of our associations are produced *involuntarily*. These are associations that simply happen by circumstances—such as, that as a child one was eating a pear and a nasty worm crawled out of it. "Pear", its taste, smell, shape, etc. become connected with "nasty worm", simply because the two things happened together. So an association is laid down between these two things, one pleasant and the other unpleasant. If the same experience happens again, it is probable that one will never like pears very much—and that will be due entirely to a path of associations laid down *involuntarily* in the machine. The object "pear" will ring up the object "worm" automatically. Or the secretary on hearing of the word "pear" will at once add the word "worm". Or more strictly, the sight of a pear will start a roll turning that will automatically start another roll turning on which the memory of "worm" is recorded. The point is that it is all mechanical—a bit of mechanism—and that it was formed *involuntarily.* I will only add here that a great many illnesses are due to involuntary associations that become habitual.

Now to come to the next class of associations, called voluntary. To this class belong the associations formed in the machine by training of all kinds. These associations are not involuntarily laid down but are laid down voluntarily, although they may be mixed up with involuntary associations. A man who is taught to read and write has a special and very complex set of associations laid down in him *voluntarily,* partly by the will of another, and partly by his own will. A man who is taught to ride or skate has again *voluntary associations* connected with moving centre. A man who becomes a mathematician has similarly very complex voluntary associations formed in his mind over a long period, that he has deliberately acquired. Briefly speaking, all education is to lay down associations that are *voluntarily* formed, but these are not necessarily so formed. They may be partly laid down unconsciously —that is, involuntarily formed. But if a man *labours* at learning something and uses his directed attention, then voluntarily formed associations are laid down in him.

The third class of associations is formed, briefly speaking, in moments of self-remembering and work on oneself. When a man sees both into himself and into the object, or sees himself and the other person simultaneously, then the results of this higher psychic activity form associations of their own class.

Now in giving this brief outline I have used the terms "involuntary and voluntary associations". Strictly speaking, I should have said "associations formed by involuntarily perceived impressions and associations formed by voluntarily perceived impressions." I shall now quote from a conversation which took place many years ago. Mr. Ouspensky is speaking of what he was taught:

"The modern man never acts of his own accord, but only manifests actions stimulated by external stimuli. The modern man does not think, but something thinks for him; he does not act, but something acts through him; he does not create, but something is created through him; he does not achieve, but something is achieved through him.

In a newly-born child, the three diverse parts or centres of the general human psyche may be compared to a system of blank gramophone rolls upon which begin to be recorded, from the day of its appearance into the world, the external significance of objects and the subjective understanding of their inner significance, or the sense of the results of all actions taking place in the outer world, as well as in the inner world already forming in him; all this is recorded in accordance with the correspondence between the nature of these actions and the nature of those distinct systems which form themselves in man.

All kinds of these recorded results of environing actions remain unchanged on each of these 'depository-rolls' for life, in the same sequence and in the same correlation with the impressions previously recorded, in which they are perceived.

All the impressions recorded in these three relatively independent parts, composing man's general psyche, later produce, in the period óf responsible age, all kinds of associations in diverse combinations.

That which is called 'reason' in man, as well as in all other external forms of life, is nothing more than the concentration of the results of impressions of different quality formerly perceived; and the stimulation and repetition of these provokes different kinds of associations in the being. The recorded impressions have three sources of origin and are subject to three different law-abiding influences.

One category of associations is formed by impressions perceived involuntarily and coming directly from the outer world as well as springing from man's inner world, as a result of certain previous, constant and automatically repeated associations.

The second category is formed by voluntarily perceived impressions either springing from the external world or crystallizing in man's inner world by means of deliberate active thinking and verifications of reality.

The third category originates from the process known as the *transformation of impressions*, where impressions of all kinds whether arising without or within, are consciously perceived and related with similar impressions, already recorded, and connected with their right centres."

Birdlip, July 3, 1943

COMMENTARY ON SELF-OBSERVATION AND 'I's

I

As long as a man takes what he observes *as himself* he cannot separate from it. It is like standing on a plank and trying to lift it. To take what you observe in yourself as yourself is to identify with it. Then you cannot change it. For a long time we are asleep to the significance of self-observation and its real goal, which is *inner separation*. But if everything inside, in the psychic world of yourself, to which only *you* have direct access, is for ever turning and turning and you take it all as *yourself*, you have not begun the journey to find yourself, which you lost.

Let me ask you all a question: "Why is it so difficult to establish *a Work relationship to yourself*?" Because everything in you is taken as one, as 'I'. This is our strongest illusion and day after day it defeats the action of the Work upon ourselves. And like all the many powerful illusions we live under, its object is to prevent us from awaking. Yet what does the Work, which tries to awaken us, say insistently about our state of Being? It says that it is characterized by lack of unity, lack of oneness, by multiplicity, manyness, by many 'I's, instead of one big permanent 'I' whose gaze covers the whole field of our life. By this time we should know practically some of the 'I's in ourselves and whether we can trust what they say or not. It is very easy to fall amongst thieves, who not only steal from us but harm us, leaving us almost dead, like the man who "went down from Jerusalem to Jericho and fell among thieves, which stripped him of his raiment and wounded him, and departed, leaving him half dead." (*Luke* X 30). Notice he went *down*. Everyone has in him'I's that wish to drag him *down*. This is the remarkable discovery that we can make for ourselves—namely, that we have 'I's in us that, if we follow them, drag us down in regard to esoteric ideas, that, indeed, fight against all new understanding and wish to kill us in this respect. Yet we take ourselves quite calmly as if there were nothing wrong with us. This means illusion. This means we have not begun to observe ourselves in the light of esoteric teaching —whether of the Work or the Gospels or of any other source more ancient. It is *within a man* that the struggle of Yes and No must begin, in regard to esoteric ideas. And this means that everyone has 'I's which will resist the Work, resist every form of esoteric ideas, so we have to observe our trains of thought. From which 'I's do they come? If you have no *Work relationship to yourself*, you will take all your thoughts, any idle thoughts, as 'I', and say "Yes" to them. How then can you work on yourself? Are you so foolish as to trust in any and every train of thought? Can you not see where Work on yourself lies in regard to the sphere of thinking? Do you suppose that you yourself think your thoughts? Do you still take every personal, psychic event—that is, every mood you have, every thought you have,—as you yourself, as 'I'—and give it the sanction and signature of yourself? If so, you do not understand what *Work on yourself* means. You take yourself as one person. You are trying to do this Work without even starting to do it, without even seeing where it starts. You are like some kind of dung-beetle continually rolling up masses of negative filth and storing it up in the cupboards of your mind as your personal possession. Why should you go with all your thoughts? Why believe in them when they originate in negative 'I's? Why follow so intently chain after chain of negative thinking as if it were all *you*, all 'I' myself thinking, when you only have to *wake* up a little and realize that you need not take these thoughts as *you*, that you need not go in those directions? We spoke recently of being *passive* to thoughts. I assure you all it would be useful if you would realize particularly what this means, every day. I said that once you realize this part of the Work *practically* it is like pure magic. You suddenly wake up out of a train of evil negative thoughts and realize you need not wallow in them. You can separate from them, as when

303

getting out of a mire into which you sank. Yes, but who really knows this yet? If one still loves negative states before all else, one certainly will *never* know it.

Now you must all understand that you have many 'I's in you that are against the Work. If not, there would be no basis of personal Work. Whatever you gain through the Work is therefore *individual*—the result of your own struggles. If you simply accepted the Work, nothing could happen. If you record all the teaching of the Work in note-books in beautiful typing and so on—well, *Work* for you has not yet begun. No change will take place. It is like a chemical change. A salt is made from two *opposite* elements. These are psychologically: *life* and *Work*. So you must understand that the Work sets up a struggle between opposites, which grows and grows in strength, between 'I's that wish to work and 'I's which do not. Purely life 'I's do not wish the Work—and they are the cleverest 'I's in us. You remember that it is said in ancient esoteric literature that "the children of this world are in their generation wiser than the children of light." This refers to 'I's in us. Life 'I's are cleverer than Work 'I's. So our negative emotions and thoughts appear cleverer than anything else—at first. Perhaps some of you know how very plausible some 'I's can be, how they begin to advance arguments in your mind, and apparently wish to assist you. Such 'I's are self-justifying 'I's of which we have a great number. These 'I's appear often like one's reasoning power, and, like bad lawyers, they always start from something that is not quite true. Now supposing you meet a person who tells lies, at first you do not realize how he speaks, but after a time you become more wary and you realize he is a liar and you cannot trust what he says; but when we are asleep—that is, when we are taking ourselves for granted—'I's of this kind, that are inveterate liars, continually take charge of us and of our thoughts, and twist them into all sorts of false patterns, false associations. This makes, as it were, a kind of mess in us and if it goes on long enough the whole of the mind becomes poisoned and cannot think clearly about anything. It is very necessary to see and to observe lying 'I's. We have so many of them. They are continually distorting everything. But once you begin to see them you can notice how they are weaving their material and you need not go with them, need not believe them, need not take their inner talking as truth, and this reality is magic. You shake yourself, as it were, like a dog coming out of the water, and get rid of the whole thing instantly. You feel at peace. You feel that something has happened inside you that is quite wonderful, that you have escaped from some danger that you never realized before.

Try, therefore, to see different 'I's and what they say in regard to the Work—that is, in regard to esoteric ideas as distinct from life-ideas. And remember that if you cannot see this struggle in yourself, if you identify with every train of thought, with every kind of inner talking, with every mood, you do not yet know what this Work means practically. You will simply say: "*I* feel negative towards the Work." This means that you take yourself as one thing, one mass, which is sometimes negative, sometimes positive. In that case, you will get nowhere. It also means that you do not understand what it means to observe yourself and do not notice different 'I's in yourself. In that case you will always be identified with your state, and you will always say 'I' to any state of yourself. How then will you realize what it means to *transform* your states? You will *be* them. You will be incapable of *separating* from them, so that *your states* and *you* are identified—are the same. So you are *one by identifying*. Everything is *you*.

*   *   *

Many of you think that Self-Observation consists merely in noticing that you feel moody, that you feel unwell, that you feel negative or bored or gloomy or depressed and so on. Let me assure you that this is *not* Self-Observation. Self-Observation begins with the establishing of Observing 'I' in your own inner world. Observing 'I' *is not identified* with what it observes. When you say: "*I* am feeling negative," you are not observing yourself. You *are* your state. You are identified with your state. There is nothing distinct in you that is standing outside your state, something that does not feel your state, something that is independent of it, and is looking at it, something that has a quite different feeling from your state. If you say: "*I* wish *I* were not negative," this is quite useless. It is 'I' speaking the whole time. You are taking yourself as one mass. You are not dividing yourself into two, which is the beginning of Work on yourself. You are not saying: "Why is *it* negative?" but "Why am *I* negative?" You are taking *it* and *you* as the same. Try to understand what it means to divide yourself into two—an observed side and an observing side—and try to feel the sense of 'I' *in the observing side* and not in the observed side. This is the whole point. Remember that *unless a man divides himself into two he cannot move from where he is*. It is like this: we are all fastened inside to wrong things which we take as *ourselves*—wrong thoughts, worries, etc. We take them as *us*. Work is to separate ourselves from them. This is the beginning of *inner freedom*. This is what the Work is about. If you can *observe* your thoughts and worries, then you establish the starting-point of the Work in yourself. It is this observing side that is the new point of growth in you. So try to feel the sense of 'I' *in Observing 'I'* and not in the observed side. Try to be conscious in Observing 'I'.

COMMENTARY ON SELF-OBSERVATION AND 'I's

II

Let us all understand that in order to renew the force and feeling of this Work we must always return to fundamentals as the *Source*. Last time we began to speak again of one of the fundamental teachings in this Work—namely, that this Work, in its practical application, begins with *Self-Observation*. But when the Work says that you must begin with Self-Observation, you must not assume that you already know what is meant by this term Self-Observation, which has such depths of meaning. People sometimes say: "Oh, yes, all this is nothing new to me. I have always observed myself." And yet they remain as they are. Why? Because they *imagine* that they already know everything about themselves and so that they have no need for Self-Knowledge. All this is illusion, sheer imagination. To imagine one knows oneself is to be a slave to one of the powerful illusions that keep humanity asleep. Let us speak for a moment about *imagination*. Everyone imagines he knows himself. Now the peculiar thing about imagination lies in this fact: that if you imagine you are something or have something, you no longer wish for it. For example, if you imagine you know yourself, then you will not seek to find out how you can gain Self-Knowledge. So you will make no real attempt to practise Self-Observation. You will both take yourself for granted and imagine you know yourself already. You will go about behaving as you always behave, imagining that you do everything consciously. In that case you will never be able to set up the inner struggle between *Yes* and *No* that is the basis of practical work on oneself and the source of change of being.

Now it is very difficult to discern even a single thing about *oneself*, and this is due to more reasons than one. For example, the whole natural movement of ourselves must be turned completely round in order to observe ourselves. Naturally speaking, we look out through our external senses at that aspect of the world they register according to their very limited powers. This external scene, registered by sense, full of people and things, brightly coloured, we suppose is the sum-total of what we call the real, or the existing, or, in brief, *reality*. But reality is not confined to the small range of our senses and does not only lie outside us, in the show of life. There is the reality of our inner thoughts and feelings and desires and sufferings—that is, there is a reality even more real than any external reality transmitted by the senses and which can only be penetrated by each one himself. Outer reality is common to us all. But inner reality is individually approached. This other inner reality, to which each person has his own access, lies invisibly within us. It is to this invisible inner reality in which we dwell psychologically or psychically (this inner confusion) that the Work applies. Science, turned outwards, *via* the senses, seeks how to conquer nature. This Work is about conquering oneself, about self-mastery. So it begins with observing, not external nature, but *oneself*. But all kinds of psychological difficulties arise here and in this respect we all have very defective sight—that is, *insight* as distinct from *outsight*. And one of these difficulties is due to imagination. We imagine we see ourselves and know ourselves thoroughly and this prevents us from awaking to the realization of what real Self-Observation means and of what it means really to begin to know oneself. Let us remember that Self-Knowledge from most ancient times was regarded as the highest knowledge. All esoteric teaching speaks of Self-Knowledge.

Let us hear again the Work speaking to us about *imagination* and the part it plays in life in preventing us from changing our being. The Work says:

"There are a thousand things which prevent a man from awakening, which keep him in the power of his imagination and dreams. In order to act consciously with the intention of awakening, it is necessary to know the forces which keep man in a state of sleep. First of all, it must be realized that the sleep in which man exists on this earth is not normal, but hypnotic sleep. Man is hypnotized, and this hypnotic state is continually maintained and strengthened in him. One would think that there are forces for whom it is useful and profitable to keep man in a hypnotic sleep state and prevent him from seeing the truth and understanding his position.

There is an Eastern tale which speaks of a very rich magician who had a great many sheep. But at the same time this magician was very mean. He did not want to hire shepherds, nor did he want to erect a fence about the pasture where his sheep were grazing. The sheep consequently often wandered into the forest, fell into ravines, and so on, and above all they ran away for they knew that the magician wanted their flesh and skins, and this they did not like. At last the magician found a remedy. He *hypnotized* his sheep and suggested to them first of all that they were immortal, and that no harm was being done to them when they were skinned, that, on the contrary, it would be very good for them and even pleasant; secondly, he suggested that the magician was a *good master* who loved his flock so much that he was ready to do anything in the world for them; and in the third place he suggested to them that if anything at all were going to happen to them, it was not going to happen just then, at any rate not that day, and *therefore* they had no need to think about it. Further the magician suggested to his sheep that they were not sheep at all, to some he suggested that they were *lions*, to others that they were eagles, to others that they were *men*, and to others that they were *magicians*. And after this, all cares and worries about the sheep came to an end. They never ran away again, but quietly awaited the time when the magician would require their flesh and skins.

This tale is a very good illustration of Man's position. In so-called

307

'occult' literature you have probably met with the expression 'Kundalini', the 'fire of Kundalini' or 'the serpent of 'Kundalini'. This expression is often used to designate some kind of strange force which is present in Man, and which can be awakened. But none of the known theories gives the right explanation of the force of 'Kundalini'. Sometimes it is connected with sex, with sex energy—that is, with the idea of the possibility of using sex energy for other purposes. This latter idea is entirely wrong because 'Kundalini' is not anything desirable or useful for Man's development. It is very curious how these so-called occultists have got hold of the word from somewhere but have completely altered its meaning, and from a very dangerous and terrible thing they have made something to be hoped for, and to be waited for, as some blessing. In reality, Kundalini is the power of the imagination, the power of fantasy, *which takes the place of a real function*. When a man dreams, instead of acting, when his dreams take the place of reality, when a man imagines himself to be an eagle, a lion, a *man*, or a magician, it is the force of Kundalini acting in him. Kundalini can act *in all centres* and with its help *all the centres can be satisfied with the imaginary* instead of the real. A 'sheep' which considers itself a lion or a magician lives under the power of Kundalini. Kundalini is a force put into men in order to keep them in their present state. If men could really see their true position and could understand the horror of it, they would be unable to remain where they are even for a second. They would begin to seek a way out and they would quickly find it, *because there is a way out*; but men fail to see it, simply because they are hypnotized. Kundalini is the force that keeps them in a hypnotic state. To 'awaken', for Man, means to be 'de-hypnotized'. In this lies the chief difficulty and in this lies also the guarantee of its possibility, for there is no *organic* reason for sleep, and Man *can* awaken. Theoretically he can, but practically it is almost impossible because of the *psychological forces* acting on Man. As soon as he awakens for a moment and opens his eyes, all these forces that caused him to fall asleep begin to act on him with tenfold energy and he immediately falls asleep again, very often *dreaming* that he is awake or is awakening.

There are certain states in ordinary sleep in which a man wants to waken but cannot. He tells himself that he is awake but, in reality, he continues to sleep—and this can happen several times before he finally awakes. But in ordinary sleep, once he is awake, he is in a different state; in hypnotic sleep the case is otherwise; there are no objective characteristics, at any rate not at the beginning of awakening; a man cannot pinch himself in order to make sure that he is not asleep . . . Only a man who fully realizes the difficulty of awakening can understand the necessity of long and hard work in order to awake."

In the above quotation you will see how much importance is attached to *imagination* and in what sense it is used. Imagination is therefore defined in the Work as *that which replaces reality*. Imagination can satisfy all centres, so Man can be satisfied with the imaginary instead of the real. It is for this reason that the Work so often speaks about imagination and about the necessity for struggling with it. As you know, in the practical instructions given by the Work as regards what one must struggle against, *imagination* is mentioned. However, it usually takes a considerable time before a person in the Work begins to observe his imagination. And there are also many difficulties connected with observing imagination, one of which is that as soon as you try to observe it, it stops. That is, as soon as you get into directed *attention*, imagination ceases.

I suppose that few of us yet have really thought about how we would care to face the possibility of the whole of our inner psychical life of secret thought and feeling being laid bare to the observation of other people. Here, in our life on earth, this is mercifully hidden from others. But, at the same time, it is individually accessible to each of us. This is the direction of the Work, on its practical side—to see, by direct, uncritical self-observation, what exists in oneself, what thoughts and feelings, and so on, one identifies with. But in self-observation in the Work-sense it is necessary to observe *facts* about oneself. Now most of us so excuse ourselves and are so much under the pleasant and subtle activity of self-justifying, in co-operation with imagination, that we never really register any distinct facts about ourselves. For example, if we are mean, we really do not observe it as a fact. Others may. But we find all sorts of reasons in excuse. Or let us take ourselves from the angle of how we speak unpleasantly about one another. We do not register the fact by direct and real self-observation. We allow it to go on, chiefly because we like it and it is so very easy and if accused of it we probably smile in that terrible way we do at such a time. Why are we so incapable of registering facts about ourselves? One great reason is that imagination of ourselves prevents us. So we cannot *see* anything real, any real facts about ourselves, save very dimly. Our imagination —or state of hypnosis—prevents any real, direct observation. We imagine we are, so to speak, eagles or lions, or, let us say, respectable and nice people, and cannot see through the mists of self-imagination that we are nothing of the kind. But all these ideas, all these forms of imagination, under which everyone lives, are different examples of 'Kundalini' and the force it exerts on mankind to keep up the state of sleep that characterizes humanity on this earth. People are not what they imagine, nor is anything in life what it pretends to be. Certainly people may begin to see that this is so as they get older—and then, just when this Work is necessary for them—as a rule they become negative and feel frustrated.

You have all heard that the Work teaches us that we are in the power of *Imaginary 'I'* and that this is the source of most of our troubles. This 'I', or this feeling or idea of oneself, is composed of *imagination*. Do not think for a moment that imagination is nothing—"nothing but imagination"—as the saying goes. You have seen what the Work says about imagination. It is the most powerful force acting on mankind. It is a definite and terrible thing, not a "mere nothing". To say that a person is suffering from imagination is to say that that person is suffering from a very powerful, intractable and dangerous force.

★　★　★

Apart from what was said last time about self-observation and its meaning and object, this can be added. One of the objects of self-observation is to break down imagination of oneself—that is, *Imaginary* '*I*'. One is not what one imagines one is. Now imagination has no real memory. But self-observation is to create a special and real memory—a conscious memory—a memory that imagination cannot escape from. Self-observation is to destroy imagination—that is, to create a memory that fights with unreal, sentimental and imaginary memory. If you only possess the unreal memory of imagination, you live in the ideal phantasies of Imaginary 'I' and never see that anything is wrong *with you*. Others are wrong, not you. But what are you really like in yourself? What 'I's control you? What 'I's govern your life? What 'I's do you consent to? Can you bear to break yourself up into different 'I's and see what they say and do and what they think and feel? This is to break up the power of imagination: this is to register unpleasant facts about yourself. Can you move on the "surface of your own waters", as it says in the account of the beginning of personal esoteric work, in the first chapter of Genesis? You remember how our ordinary state of sleep is described: "And the earth was waste, and darkness was upon the face of the deep and the spirit of God moved on the face of the waters. And God said Let there be light." What is light? It is esotericism: it is esoteric ideas. It is the ideas of this Work, which is esotericism. When a man who has right magnetic centre first meets the ideas of this Work, he is himself the "earth that was waste and darkness". Self-observation done sincerely from the knowledge of the ideas of this Work lets *in light* into this inner darkness, this inner chaos of oneself. That is how self-observation is defined in the Work, for it says that self-observation "lets in light" into oneself and adds that many things can take place in darkness, just like certain chemical processes which cannot take place in the presence of light. Light is consciousness. This is the beginning of that possible inner transformation of Man that all esoteric teaching, including the Gospels and this Work, is always speaking about through the centuries.

★　★　★

Having spoken of self-observation from the standpoint of some of the greater ideas of the Work, let us now speak of it on the scale on which the last paper was written. In the last talk, amongst other things, it was said that to observe oneself it is necessary to divide oneself into an observing and an observed side and that the feeling of 'I' or *conscious-*

ness must be given more and more to the *observing side*. That is, Observing 'I' must be given as far as possible the feeling of 'I' at the moment and the observed side given the feeling of "not 'I'". You walk about in life observing houses and people and trees and so on and do not necessarily connect the feeling of 'I' with them. They are "not 'I'" to you. But the same division must be made internally. What you observe internally is "not 'I'", in the same way as the houses, people, etc. you observe externally are clearly "not 'I'". We are not identified with everything we see outside us but ordinarily we are identified with everything that takes place inside us—with every thought, mood, desire, and so on. Self-observation in the Work-sense is to *separate* Observing 'I' from what is observed in oneself. For instance, you can observe the emotion of the beginning of anger. You can observe the thoughts connected with it. If your consciousness of the feeling of 'I' is stronger in observing 'I' than in what it observes, then your anger and the thoughts accompanying it will not have full power over you. The whole inner event *may* die away. But let us suppose that some self-justifying 'I' comes on to the scene, that says your anger is right. What then happens? Answer that for yourselves. If you have never really observed *yourself*, then you will not be able to answer. But if you have, you will know exactly what happens. But the difficulty mentioned already remains—merely, everyone *imagines* he or she is one person, a unity, and cannot realize that he is not one person, and everyone imagines he knows himself. It requires long work and great sincerity and particularly great evaluation of the Work and its meaning to realize that you are not one but many 'I's. Even your very pride will prevent you, unless you feel the existence of something greater than your pride. The doctrine of many 'I's is a stumbling-block to everyone. Yet it is true and is the secret that begins to make change of oneself possible. Now remember that if you identify with an 'I' in you, you give it force and you give it the sanction of yourself. That is, you sign its cheques in your name. Surely some of you must recognize unpleasant or rather, evil-minded 'I's? Then if you identify with them they become you. You *will* them. As soon as you extend your will to possess something, as soon as you take something into your desire, then it is the same as yourself, and so it works in you as yourself and you believe it.

Now I will quote this question: "*How can we make use of the observations we have made on ourselves?*" This is a very interesting question. I would like to hear what you think of this.

COMMENTARY ON SELF-OBSERVATION AND 'I's

III—OBSERVATION OF 'I's

After a certain time in the Work, a person should be able to recognize quite clearly one or two 'I's in himself. He will, of course, be unable to do so if he still remains wholly under the influence of "Imaginary 'I'", for in that case he will have the illusion that he is one 'I', one solid person, one permanent ego. This will prevent him from even beginning to look seriously for 'I's in himself. But, as you know, the Work teaches that the Personality is made of a large number of egos, which all call themselves 'I' and take charge of us at different times. Thus our life is in the hands of a great many people unknown to us who live in and on us, some of whom may be desirable but many undesirable. Ordinarily we do not see these people, mistaking them for ourselves. This is a curious illusion, if you think about it. Actually, you should be constantly thinking of it, and noticing how it works. Then you may begin to see into the trick, and how clever it is and how simple.

Some egos in us are very dangerous and should never be allowed either to speak through us or to call themselves 'I'. However this is easy to say and very difficult to do. Some are dangerous in one way, others in another way. Let us take suspicious 'I's as an extreme example. These 'I's are amongst the most dangerous in us. They have an extraordinary power of binding a man or woman to their influence. Their action lies in transforming things or rather connecting them up in another way. Their representation in the Intellectual Centre is very subtle. They transpose facts to fit in with their central theory—that is, with the nature of the suspicion. They alter the arrangement of things in the memory and in thought so that everything seems to corroborate and confirm everything else. In this way, they build up an organized mental system—not of truth but of falsity. In the emotional centre they arouse their own peculiar feelings which are distinct from jealousy or envy or revenge or hatred, and give a curious excitement like all destructive emotions. The action of suspicious 'I's is such that they in a short time spread like a ferment in all directions within us and set or fix the materials of the mind and emotions as if they were coagulated. They also act on the moving centre, giving rise to stealthiness, odd silences of the bodily movements and so on. Suspicion takes everything on the lowest plane and is therefore closely connected with the "sin against the Holy Ghost" mentioned in the Gospels which refers to seeing the worst side of everything and everyone. Suspicious 'I's are fond of whispered conversations, if you notice them in action.

Now the idea of the Work is to make one big Observing 'I' that stands outside the Personality and takes photographs of all the 'I's in the Personality. The more photographs you take, the stronger will the Observing 'I' become and the more chances you will have of coming into a new life freed from the compulsion and habits of the old life. But, apart from the fact that it is difficult to take any photographs at all, at least to begin with, it becomes clearer later on that some 'I's are exceptionally difficult to photograph. This is because of their hypnotic power over us. Remember that all 'I's are specialized—that is, of different kinds. One is fond of this, another of that. One likes to say or do this, another to say or do that, and so on. Some of these 'I's attract us more strongly than others do. Their inner hypnotizing power is greater. This applies particularly to suspicious 'I's. These 'I's, present in everyone, may play only a small rôle, or may assume far greater proportions. They are amongst the most subjective of the 'I's and can eventually employ the reasoning power of the formatory centre for their own purpose, so that a person begins to live in another inner world of his own invention, quite distinct from the objective or real situation. Every 'I' makes, as it were, a little momentary world into which we pass when we identify with it, but suspicious 'I's, if consented to and nourished by the will, invade all the inner life and organize it into another and *permanent* world of hell.

The power of Observing 'I' not to identify with what it observes varies with the kind of 'I' it observes. You must all have noticed this. The hypnotizing power of suspicious 'I's like that of jealous or revengeful 'I's or envying 'I's is so strong that the independent power of Observing 'I' is often overcome. That is, Observing 'I' identifies with what it observes. This will not be the case so easily if Observing 'I' has behind it many strong thoughts about the Work—that is, some definite Work 'I's—and also strong feelings. But when people take hold of the Work and indeed the whole idea of esotericism very loosely and in a trivial way, and therefore actually place small value on it, then Observing 'I' is very weak and unsupported and is easily swamped, like a little boat without keel, rudder, sail, compass or master. A weak Observing 'I' is due to lack of seeing what the Work is about and if one does not see what the Work is about it means that one does not try to think about it. Esotericism, throughout the ages, is something very big. One cannot take hold of it with little trivial 'I's. Best not even to attempt to do so.

Let me say one more thing about this extreme example that we are taking of suspicious 'I's. The less you realize *your own deceitfulness* the more will you tend to be suspicious of others. The key is to see that they are 'I's, formed by long habit, that you can separate from and not go with—not believe in—not consent to. Of course, if you consent to every 'I' of the moment in yourself, you are not working, and you do not understand what work on yourself means. Work on yourself means to get into a new way of living—of living consciously inside yourself instead of mechanically. It means to work against your mechanical ways of reacting to everything, and so on. Work on yourself means simply *Work on yourself*. This begins when you observe yourself and begin to see different 'I's in you that have preyed on you and enslaved you all your life. But all this is impossible if you imagine you are *one* person.

Another set of 'I's is based on slander. Their activity and, in fact, the delight of these 'I's lies in various forms of slandering or vilifying or twisting. This constitutes in the Work one bad form of wrong talking, in general. Their strength varies in different people. When they are marked, a person must struggle to see them and separate from them with all his available willingness and desire. They are very dangerous 'I's because they act against the person himself or herself eventually— that is, they turn on you and slander *yourself* and drag you down internally and so prevent you from understanding, slandering everything you try to do, even quite sincerely. Remember that there is a reason why the Devil was called the *Slanderer* in the Gospels. Try to observe when you are slandering, both in your mind, and in words, and notice and remember it and try to see that it is certain 'I's in you that are doing it and notice what they wish to say and feel pleasure in, and how they come to wake up in you and become active, and so on. 'I's that belong to the domain of suspicion, slander, hatred, revenge, envy, jealousy, and so on, must be struggled with to the end of one's life. To realize that *you need not go* with these various habitual 'I's is the dawn of a new life. It is the beginning of understanding what personal Work means. Yes, it is actually so. Nothing sentimental or foolish is meant here. But this dawn does not come as long as you take yourself as *one* and live under the hypnotic power of "Imaginary 'I'" which is a cloak for all the different 'I's in you and worn by each in turn. Remember that the secret lies in seeing these 'I's as *not you*—or rather, as *not 'I'*. If you take them as 'I', then nothing can be done. You are standing on the plank that you are trying to lift—and that is impossible. You are standing in your own way.

Now let us speak of different kinds of 'I's, some of which may also be very important. Some time ago we spoke of worry and worrying 'I's. These form a strong group of 'I's in most people. Their action is very interesting to observe. Their sole object is to upset you and make you depressed or, in short, worried. They lead to nothing else. They are quite useless, as are so many 'I's in us. But you have to notice for yourself, by direct and sustained self-observation, what they do and say and what their main object is. Worrying 'I's act in two main ways. You all have your worrying 'I's—about one another, about business, about money, about your state of health, and so on. And you also have to meet other people's worrying 'I's. Try to see even one worrying 'I' distinctly in yourself, study it, see how it only loves to exhaust you and leads nowhere. Then you will see others. Also notice how some of your worrying 'I's connect themselves with the Work. You begin to worry about the Work in one way or another, whether you are working, and so on. They are like flies, and can settle on anything. They are all small 'I's living in small parts of centres. They cease when we get into directed attention. We might imagine that worrying 'I's have a kind of foreman who looks out for jobs to give them. If you cannot see your own worrying 'I's, notice those in other people—how as soon as one worry is over they almost arrange to have something else to worry over. These 'I's disperse force and exhaust people and cause illnesses. They are, so to speak, rampant in Western people.

Now let us take 'I's that like to complicate and muddle things. They form a considerable group of somewhat various 'I's. Their object, of course, is not to help you but to make everything extraordinarily difficult. They delight in misunderstanding everything. They delight in calling your attention to something unimportant, in delaying you—especially last minute 'I's, as Mr. Ouspensky once called them, 'I's that come on to the stage just as you have to go somewhere or catch a train and so on. Again, let us take the sensational 'I's—'I's that love to create a scene, to get excited, and which lead even into hysteria. Their object is to exaggerate everything and when they express themselves in the Moving Centre, they like to scream, or make violent movements. In the Intellectual Centre they shout "gramophone sentences", such as: "I can't stand this any longer," or "This is too much." They produce frantic states, which again only exhaust and deplete the nervous system. They are our own enemies. Only people like them.

You must realize that a great many 'I's—in fact, most of them— are against you and wish to destroy you in various ways, openly or more secretly. That is why we have to be awake *towards ourselves*. Now about negative 'I's, which are often exceptionally subtle and dangerous, I am not going to speak in this paper. I will only say that negative 'I's form a very great part of our inner life and that they always eat our force and weaken us, both for life and for the Work. There is only one thing that can fight for us here and that is the Work itself—and it will fight for us only in relation to our evaluation of it. Negative 'I's are created by life, as are other 'I's. Life as third force keeps them alive. The Work is a contrary third force that weakens all 'I's formed by life save those that can understand esoteric ideas—that is, those who begin to understand that there is another way of living and thinking and valuing and feeling and acting, and wish to re-interpret everything that happens to us in terms of another set of ideas. Then, again, notice 'I's that like to be ill and attract illness. The habit of illness can be formed early and that means that a group of 'I's form themselves that wish to occupy the stage whenever possible. They wish to make you ill. It used to be taught (by G.) that 80% of our illnesses have a psychological cause of this kind—that is, are due to 'I's, just as in the same way, if you form the habit of taking some drug, the 'I's formed and nourished by it will seek to dominate and destroy you. Now look for different kinds of 'I's and try to observe them practically. All 'I's are specialized. More or less similar 'I's form groups and these may form "personalities". For example, a doctor's medical 'I's will be various but will form a "personality" within the Personality in general. Or a person's social 'I's will do the same, etc. Often there are useful 'I's in us that have been formed earlier and which we do not nourish in after life. This is a great mistake. People often drop their best 'I's in this way quite early. They get swamped by life and its exigencies and make no effort, in continuity with what they have already gained. Then it is like a garden becoming overgrown with weeds—that is, with useless, poor or negative 'I's. Everything in nature has to fight, to make effort. Animals and plants cannot, so far as we know, make *psychological effort*. But we know that we can. All this Work is effort—not effort such as lifting a weight but psychological effort on this inner world called *oneself*. We have specialized 'I's formed by previous interests and education. One 'I' is fond of poetry, another of mathematics, another of music, another of writing, another of reading, and so on. When our first education ends, very often these 'I's fade, and become weak because they are not nourished by attention—that is, we make no further effort about them. To direct the conscious attention in anything requires effort. This is psychological effort. Attention, will and consciousness are very closely connected. Once we have started on our second education—that is, the Work—we should all know to some extent when we should make some effort in connection with useful 'I's. Then if you notice you do not, try to observe what 'I's prevent you from doing so. This is seeing "second force" in you—that is, the force of resistance to effort. When we leave good and useful 'I's unvisited too long, they lose heart, as it were. It is much the same inside as outside. What I am saying is that, in regard to different 'I's in oneself, one should also work on good 'I's. It is not merely a question of working on bad 'I's. The Work has two sides. It walks on two legs. When you observe genuinely good and useful 'I's that want to know, to be taught more, do not neglect them. And this applies to Work 'I's. You cannot work on bad 'I's, if you neglect Work 'I's—that is, if you do not keep them alive by thought and feeling and effort. It is necessary to strengthen Work 'I's not only by remembering what you are doing but by re-understanding the esoteric ideas of the Work, again and again, and constantly re-learning and re-seeing the meaning of the Work until it forms your sky. This strengthens the side of Observing 'I' and makes it possible for it to keep outside and to resist the influence of what it observes. All new life and inner vigour forms round Observing 'I' which leads finally up to "Real 'I'". When this is reached, then this world, which is really, of course, a school, has fulfilled its task, and you have fulfilled your task in regard to it. But this goal is very far away from us all at present.

*   *   *

Now as regards the question asked at the end of the paper read last time: "How can we make use of the observations we have made on ourselves?" Let me say first that you must realize that you can do nothing in regard to *changing* yourself unless you *observe* yourself. Self-observation must precede all change of oneself. You cannot change what you do not observe. To observe a thing in yourself is to know it. This begins self-knowledge and the first step in self-knowledge is to see that you are not *one*. If you know nothing of yourself and your many 'I's how can you change yourself? You have to see what is meant here very clearly. I ask you to discuss this point later on.

I will now quote five answers to the above question given when the paper was read here on Tuesday last:

(1) The observations that we have made help us to have *aim*. They give us force to go on working.

(2) Our observations begin to create *Work-memory*. They cause an alarum-bell to ring next time the event happens. We can observe the same thing more deeply next time. They increase *consciousness*.

(3) Your self-observation collects 'I's round Observing 'I'. It will be a step towards inner separation. (This answer is obscure).

(4) Our observations will make us less mechanical next time.

(5) Our observations help us to see our being.

Birdlip, July 26, 1943

SELF-REMEMBERING

To-night we will speak of Self-Remembering. It is necessary to remember oneself every day, at least once. Many different descriptions have been given in the literature of the past. I will quote one given some three centuries ago. A disciple asks his master how he can come "to the supersensual life and hear God speak." The master replies: "When thou canst throw thyself into THAT, where no creature dwelleth, though it be but for a moment, then thou hearest what God speaketh." The disciple asks him if the place where no creature, or nothing created dwells is near or far away. The master says: "It is in thee", and he adds that it is to be reached by ceasing, even for a moment, from all one's thinking and willing—"when thou standest still from self-thinking and self-willing and canst stop the wheel of the imagination and the senses." In another place he says that this act must be done once a day at least and only for a short time. It certainly must not be attempted too often. He is really describing what in this Work is called Self-Remembering. It is very often difficult to hear the Work speaking to us. As a rule we are immersed in life and self-interests of various kinds and cannot hear the Work. In the example just given the disciple asks how he can come "to the *super*sensual state and hear God speak". This means to a state that is above the life of the senses. Have you ever really thought what is the life of the senses? It is all your daily worries, all your cares, your daily contacts, all you see and hear, etc. through the senses. You see there is not enough food, or your

317

pots and pans are wearing out, or you miss the bus, and so on. All this is life of the senses. You see war! You see money! You see the table is broken; you see a letter with bad news; you see disease; you see an earthquake; you see your own face—and so on. All this is *sensual*—that is, life transmitted by the senses. How many of us are upset because of the electric light failing or because of another man, or a woman, or because we cannot buy what we want and so on. All this is *sensual*: it is the sensual life. It is life as you experience it *via* your five senses. You might ask: "Is there any other kind of life apart from my business, my job, my daily cares, my house, family, my sick child, my this, my that, and so on?" In other words, you are asking: "Is there any other life than the sensual life?" Esotericism speaks of *another life*. The Work speaks of it. You know how often the Work says you must transform incoming impressions. Yet, glued to that sensory reality that masters us at every moment and makes us its slaves, we cannot easily see beyond the particular life-event that is exerting its influence on us at the moment, as, for instance, we have lost our ticket or our bag or some-one has been rude to us. When we are in a particular outer *event* everything seems to be that event, does it not? Then it passes and we wonder what happened. You remember what was once said—that life is a series of events, or, if you prefer, that passing time, hour by hour, day by day, is composed of a definite structure of events, that crowd in all the time on different scales—that is, as personal events, family events, local events, national events, world-events, all on different scales. These are due to the 48 orders of laws we are under. Now you can never be *without some event* that is trying to take force from you. Ill news is an event, for instance. Certainly war is an event. But they are not on the same scale, of course. There is a common phrase that "life is one thing after another." It is necessarily so since we are under definite laws. We are not free. This takes us probably all our life to grasp—and then we cannot grasp it. If you notice the kind of being you have, then you will get to know that it weaves a thread continuing the same series of events. Our level of being attracts our life—that is, the events belonging to it. You may feel how bad it is that these things always happen to *you*. Yes, but what has the Work to say? Have you ever made the connection? Have you ever observed your life and its events from the angle of what the Work teaches about being?

There are times when self-observation is no good. Then you can say: "I wish to remember myself." You will find that the Work will help you.

Recently Mr. Ouspensky suggested that people should remember themselves at certain definite times, as an exercise. The Work empha-sizes the importance of Self-Remembering from the start. Very often we forget to remember ourselves. We wonder what to *do*, but forget to remember ourselves. Perhaps we think of it but we do not try to do it. We are always thinking of but not doing the Work. When we make no attempt to self-remember, our inner continuity with the Work is broken. The Work moves away from us and we pass into life. When this happens it is necessary to self-remember. This opens us again to the influences of the Work. This is quite a definite experience, but, as I said, we usually forget to self-remember and try instead to *do* something ourselves. To remember oneself is a surrender of oneself. One realizes one's helplessness. It is impossible to self-remember if one does not realize and understand that better influences can reach us. In one book written some eight centuries ago, by someone belonging to the Sufi schools, the writer compares Self-Remembering with coming to the surface of the sea and drawing in air. "This air," he says, "is miraculous, and will last a whole day, even when one is at the bottom of the ocean."

When one is very much identified with life it is difficult to self-remember. It is also difficult when one has a wrong inner attitude to the Work. Again, it is difficult to understand anything about Self-Remembering when one is identified with oneself. When you make a practice of Self-Remembering every day, you begin to be aware of a continuity running through your life. On the other hand, you become aware when this continuity is lost. When you feel this continuity and the loss of it, you have a point in the Work in the Emotional Centre. This is like "inner taste," the starting of real Work-conscience.

Birdlip, July 27, 1943

THE OPPOSITES

Part I.—To-night we will speak about the Law of the Pendulum. By the Law of the Pendulum is meant the swinging of things between opposites. A pendulum swings from one side and then to the opposite side. We can see the Law of the Pendulum at work in nature as in the change of the seasons from winter to summer and back again, to and fro without ceasing, and in the movement of the tides, and in the motion of the waves, up and down, and so on. We also have many pendulums in ourselves, *for what is in the Universe is in ourselves.* We can observe that we have pendulums swinging between "like and dislike", between "desire and disgust", between "happiness and dejection", between "love and hate", "affirmation and negation", "certainty and doubt", and so on. These pendulums have different periods—that is, length of swing—and, like clocks, some go faster, some go slower, in the same time. That is, they swing faster or slower between opposite signs. Also there is the period of our lives which swings between the opposite signs of birth and death. This is the period of life. We swing physically from birth to death: we do not, however, see the opposite swing.

Many things are said in ancient literature about the opposites between which all things swing to and fro, as between checking or limiting forces. You must not think that when it is said that things swing to

319

and fro it means that there is no law governing it all. It means that there are checking forces at work. It is said in the Book of Ecclesiasticus (not Ecclesiastes): "All things are double, one against another." (XLII 24). Let us take this phrase: "All things are double, one against another." What does it mean that a thing is double? It means that to everything there is an opposite through which it exists and by which it is opposed. As a rough example, darkness implies light as its opposite and light darkness, and together they make one thing, a double thing that we might call "light-dark", one thing that divided becomes light *or* dark. Or, to take a psychological example: sorrow and joy are opposites. They are one against the other and together are a "thing" which is double, which we might call "joy-sorrow". Notice also that sorrow destroys joy, and joy sorrow. They are opposites and so are mutually destructive. Or again, hunger and satiety are opposite states. As hunger is appeased by eating, the opposite—namely, satiety—or even disgust, appears. Then the swing of the pendulum into satiety is followed by its swing back to hunger. What we must see is that hunger and satiety, although so contrary, form *one* thing, which we can call "hunger-satiety", and they are inseparable, although one is against the other—that is, you cannot have one without the other, any more than you can have a stick with only one end. In this connection compare the above remark of Ecclesiasticus, "all things are double, one against another," with an observation made by Philo in the first century A.D. Philo, who was associated with a school in Alexandria, says : "That which is made up of both the opposites is *one*, and when this one is dissected the opposites appear." This is a very interesting view of life if you care to reflect on it.

Let us take another ancient reference to the opposites, in this case from that strange piece of esoteric writing found in the second book of Esdras, from the third chapter onwards, in the Apocryphal Old Testament:

"The woods of the trees of the field went forth, and took counsel together, and said, Come, let us go and make war against the sea, that it may depart away before us, and that we may make us more woods. The waves of the sea also in like manner took counsel together, and said, Come, let us go up and subdue the wood of the plain, that there also we may make us another country. The counsel of the wood was in vain, for the fire came and consumed it: likewise also the counsel of the waves of the sea, for the sand stood up and stopped them." (II *Esdras* IV 13-17)

In this passage the idea is expressed that everything is kept balanced by means of the law of opposites. One thing checks another. That which checks or destroys another thing can be thought of as its opposite. The wood thinks it will dominate the world and the fire consumes it: the sea thinks it will over-run the plains but the sand checks it. The unknown writer of Esdras is using physical images to represent *forces* that act in nature that keep everything between certain limits and so prevent any one thing from getting the upper hand permanently. You can think of endless other illustrations of one thing checking another. Think for a moment of how every living creature is attacked and eaten by some other creature so that a balance is kept going. This balance is the result of the work of the opposites. The Law of the Pendulum indicates that there is a swing to and a swing fro in all things, but after a point in either direction there is a check and the opposite force begins to exert itself. We can see for ourselves that as a pendulum swings further and further, say, to the right, it gets slower and slower until its motion reverses and it swings to the left. That is, the opposites, if we term them "right" and "left", alternately have power. Notice that when the pendulum is fully to the "right", the "right" is *weakest* and the "left" begins to have power, and vice versa. Sometimes you can see this expressed in psychological experience, as when a man is violently against something and takes an extreme attitude, and suddenly swings to the opposite viewpoint. Many of the phenomena of sudden "conversion" belong to this pendulum swing. There is the case of Paul, who persecuted the early Church with the utmost energy and hatred, and suddenly had an experience that turned him in the reverse direction.

Now, at this point, I must say to you all that it is not at all easy to understand the opposite forces and their work, which is always double and so requires double thinking. We think in terms of one thing, comparing it with another thing. We do not think in terms of *two* things simultaneously. We think in terms of *one* force and find it difficult to think in terms of *two* forces and impossible to think in terms of *three* forces. At present, however, we are speaking of two forces, opposite in their nature, which govern or limit all things and prevent too much excess or deficiency. All phenomena, all visible things, all events, all earthly life, take place between opposite forces, or opposite poles, now swinging this way and now that, so that war follows peace and peace war, and famine follows plenty and plenty famine, and so on. When we begin to realize this, we can understand that time is different *at different times*. On a small scale we realize that if we have a good time to-day we may have a bad time to-morrow. It is really the Law of the Pendulum. This idea is expressed in Ecclesiastes:

"To everything there is a season, and a time to every purpose under the heaven: a time to be born, and a time to die; a time to plant, and a time to pluck up that which is planted; a time to kill and a time to heal; a time to break down, and a time to build up; a time to weep, and a time to laugh; a time to mourn, and a time to dance; a time to cast away stones, and a time to gather stones together; a time to embrace, and a time to refrain from embracing; a time to seek, and a time to lose; a time to keep, and a time to cast away; a time to rend, and a time to sew; a time to keep silence, and a time to speak; a time to love, and a time to hate; a time for war, and a time for peace."

(*Ecclesiastes* III 1-8)

Notice that the opposites are mentioned throughout the above passage and that the meaning is that in one part of time things go well and in another they go badly—or in one part of time one plants and in another part it is absurd to plant. Just imagine if one should always plant, and always be born, or always build up, or always weep, and so on. The passage quoted above meant that everything comes to an end and turns into its opposite *in time*. I emphasize the last words: everything comes to an end *in time*, so that one thing is replaced by *its opposite*. What do you mean by the *end* of a thing? Have you ever thought? The *end* of sorrow is joy, the *end* of weeping is laughter, the end, in fact, of everything we know in this life of time is *its opposite*. What shall we call the *end* of this war? We shall call it peace—that is, its opposite. And what is the end of peace? Why, it is surely once more *war*. And what is the end of pain? Is it not that relief from pain for which we have no exact word? It is very interesting to try to think of words that really express opposite states.

When we catch a glimpse of the idea that all life lies between opposites, we begin to realize what controls events and also that life is controlled. We might at this stage say that everything is the result of two opposite forces that tend to counterbalance one another and so to produce a balance in all things. We find an example of this in the physiological working of the body, where it seems as if health is the result of a balancing of opposite or antagonistic systems, chemical and otherwise. The ancient Greek physician Hippocrates, who lived in the fifth century B.C., taught that health was a harmony or balance between different forces or elements and illness the result of one or another becoming too strong. We might also think that the psychological health is of a similar nature—the result of two or more factors in balance.

In the ancient sacred temple of Delphi two inscriptions were written for those to read who entered to consult the oracle. One was composed of the famous words: "Know thyself". The other, less known, was: "Nothing too much". This does not mean that it is too much in the sense that a man cannot do or give too much. The Greek does not bear such a meaning. The phrase means: "Nothing in extremes". Notice the order of these two sayings. First a man must know himself and *then* he must not go to extremes—that is, once he knows himself and so knows what are extremes in himself. To know what is in oneself takes long years of self-experience. Self-knowledge implies, amongst many other things, knowing the opposites in oneself—that is, becoming conscious of them. Then one can begin to understand and apply the second aphorism: "Nothing too much."

THE OPPOSITES

Part II.—We can picture a tightrope expert who keeps his balance by swinging now to the right, now to the left. Of course he already knows how to do this by long training and study of himself. Without knowledge he could not do it. Suppose we ask him Pilate's question: "What is truth?" and say: "Is it to the right or to the left?" If he said it was both, our sense of truth would be offended, because we all imagine that truth must be rigid and inflexible. It is said that, once upon a time, a man dreamed he had discovered the secret of the universe and woke up and wrote down his dream. Next morning he found he had written down: "Walk on both legs". In the sphere of our own psychology, the place we live in with our consciousness, having no real self-knowledge, we walk on one leg, regarding truth as something invariable. We think we know what is right and wrong, or good and bad, and because of this we have no idea what it is to keep a balance in ourselves. We do not see the opposites in ourselves save in the sense of all *that* being bad and *this* being good. I once heard it said in this Work that the devil is **also** necessary. At the same time we are constantly swung about by the events of life which is always changing its aspect. And as we are swung we do not try to assimilate the opposites. We ignore everything that does not correspond to our viewpoints: what does not correspond to our viewpoints is, for us, the devil. So we walk on one leg. Yet we can understand that it would be a mistake for a tightrope walker to regard the left as the devil and the right only as desirable. For we would say that at different times he has to lean to the right or lean to the left, and that only in this way can he advance. This is the idea expressed in the passage from Ecclesiastes quoted above that there is "a time to keep and a time to cast away." At one time a man should speak and at another he should keep silence. What does this mean? It means that if people are looking for a rigid code of truth, if they regard truth as a rigid series of fixed rules, they will never find her. Nothing is the same in time. Time is change. Everything changes in time. And everything in time changes between the opposites. It is now one way and now the opposite way. Everything in time is governed by the opposites and swings between them. This is the significance of the passage quoted from Ecclesiastes. Things that will go well at one moment will not go well at the next moment. There is a time for everything under the sun and everything is excellent *in its time.* However, people expect things always to be the same, and when things do not correspond to what they wish they are incapable of adjusting themselves and taking in impressions from that side of life that does not correspond to their viewpoints. I suppose that there is nothing more difficult for us to learn than that time is not the same. We want the same and expect the same, although we complain about it. Our inability to assimilate the opposite, to see things from an adverse point of view, to be conscious on both sides of the pendulum, renders us liable to monotony. And this is deeply based on our general attitude to life that does not include the idea of the opposites. We insist on taking life in a one-sided way, and regard everything that is contrary to our viewpoints as exceptional or unfortunate. The result is lack of flexibility. We lean to the right and refuse to lean to the left when occasion demands it.

A living thing is in a state of balance: it is balanced between life and death. As long as it makes a distinction between itself and what it lives in, it remains alive. Now you cannot be alive if you take up a fixed view of life. The inter-action between life and yourself then ceases. You become identified with your view of life. Now the Work teaches that you should never become identified with life, whichever way it is swinging, whether into war or peace, comfort or hardship, and so on. But we all want to be fixed. It is as if we wanted to freeze things into a fixed pattern. Then we become identified through our attitudes. The surface of life and the surface of ourselves cease to have their normal interchange. We, then, become life, and there is no longer any living in life. Every living organism is alive because it resists life, and learns how to use it. And from this angle life is the opposite to life. Every living thing is born into life wound up like a spring under high tension. It is more than its surroundings. It has a certain energy that makes it more clever than the life in which it finds itself. It has a surface that meets the surface of life, and between these two surfaces that living thing lives. It lives by opposites, in the sense that life is an antagonist to it. As long as it can deal with life it is alive. But in the case of Man, who is far more complex than any other living creature, we must understand that he has a psychological surface apart from a physical one. His environment is not only a physical one but a psychological one. Have you ever asked yourselves what is your psychological environment? Have you a sense of surface towards it? Do you keep this side of yourselves alive with good interchange? Or are you nothing but your psychological environment, going with everyone's opinion, with everything you hear, with everything you read? In that case you are really dead. Because there is no distinction between yourself and life. Unless you feel that *you* are living in life you are dead. There is no tension between the two surfaces of life and yourself.

Some of you may have heard of the scientific idea of entropy. The idea is like this. Everything tends to become, let us say, at the same temperature. If you put a boiling kettle in the room it will warm up the surroundings until everything is at the same temperature. Now once life and death become, as it were, at the same temperature, you are dead. You can only work if you have a higher temperature than life, and Man has in him ways of keeping himself at a higher temperature than life. The sense of the surface, whether intellectual, emotional or physical, that separates you from the surface of external life is necessary. It is really another aspect of Self-Remembering. All things have an outline, or surface, that distinguishes them from life. We are all different shapes—animals, insects, plants, and so on—but every one of them has a particular shape that distinguishes it from what it lives in. They meet at their surfaces the surface of life. Life seeks to devour them and they seek to devour life. Every living creature having its own life given to it is capable of devouring external life, according to its own design. But, I repeat, *Man* is not merely a physical shape but also a psychological shape—that is, a mental shape and an emotional shape —because out of all creation Man has a psychological destiny, apart from his physical destiny.

However, we must come back to the point that is essential in the teaching of the opposites. We must realize that we live on this planet between the opposites. Our whole lives, ordinarily, are governed by the Law of the Pendulum. We all swing to and fro. When you are in one opposite you are unconscious of the other, and vice versa. You may have idle dreams of rising and rising, of progressing and progressing, of getting better and better, but all these are indeed idle dreams. You cannot escape from the opposites unless you know how to do so. You have to see both sides of yourselves and how one side helps the other side. This requires double thinking. One might even say it requires double consciousness. In other words, it requires self-knowledge. What do you think self-knowledge means? It means knowledge of all sides of yourself. What do you think self-consciousness means? It means being conscious of all sides of yourself. First "Know thyself": then "Nothing in excess." What does excess mean? It means going too far to the right or to the left. But it means not only this. When you are too far to the right you are in excess and must go to the left. Nothing is more painful than excessive goodness. For example, take people who are excessively kind. Does it not at once arouse the opposite in yourself, just as people who are excessively cruel? Naturally all forms of vanity and pride (which form the false personality) enable us to think that we can do only good, and that we should be regarded with admiration. But I am afraid that finding one's balance has nothing to do with pride or vanity. What is said in the strange reports of the Sermon on the Mount? Surely something is said about "Blessed are the poor in spirit"? What does this mean? Have you ever thought how much your vanity and pride put you in the opposites? To be poor in spirit means not to identify with oneself. Now, supposing I only identify with what I think is the best side of myself, will I be poor in spirit? Will I then ever be able to walk on two legs? Will I ever be able to assimilate both sides of myself, both opposites in myself, and in others, and in life? When people say: "Thank God I am not as other men", do you think they are one-sided? Certainly they have buffers which enable them not to see their contradictions. But if you can see both sides of yourself, what you call your good side and your bad, then you begin to be conscious in opposites at the same time. And this is where some strange secret lies that is spoken of so much in past esoteric literature. There is a

Sufi saying: "All true life is the peace and harmony of contraries. Death is due to war between them."

Birdlip, September 2, 1943

THE OPPOSITES

Part III.—In the esoteric Greek thinking, when one opposite encroached on another a state of *injustice* was said to exist. *Justice*, or *righteousness*, was regarded as a state of balance. You know how often the word *righteousness* is used in the Gospels, as, for instance, when it is said: "Except your righteousness exceed the righteousness of the scribes and Pharisees, ye shall in no wise enter the kingdom of heaven." (*Matt.* V 20). The Greek word for righteousness (δίκη) has the original meaning of being *upright* and so, *between* the opposites. The "just" or "righteous" man, both of the New Testament and of the Socratic teaching four centuries earlier, and of the teaching of Pythagoras as early as the 6th century B.C., is the "upright" man, the man who stands balanced between the opposites and is *neither* of them. This is a very difficult idea to understand. But the idea of the just man was directly derived from the ancient teaching about the opposites. A one-sided man could not be a *just* man. A fanatic, a bigoted or scrupulous man, could not be just. Nor could a man who lived in some small part of himself be just. To be righteous, to be just, is *to be balanced*. Do not misuse this word *balanced*, imagining that perhaps because you do not feel things so strongly as others, you are more balanced. To be balanced is not to be stupid but to be alive to every side of existence. In speaking of the idea of the just or balanced man, we can use the conception of the development of all the centres, where it is said that a one-sided man cannot be balanced. But here we are speaking of justice or balance from the angle of the pendulum and the law of opposites and cannot bring in the centres, save to this extent: one centre may sometimes appear to act as the opposite of another and again in each centre there are different pendulums swinging at different rates. As was said before, when one opposite encroached on another, a state of injustice was said to exist. This is constantly happening in ourselves and in life around us now and in history. Take history: is it a steady line of progress, or is it a swinging to and fro and a continual encroachment of one nation on another? Once the Egyptians were powerful, then the Jews, then the Greeks, then the Romans, then the Goths, the Arabs, and so on. All this is a to and fro swinging, not a line. And it is the same in the case of one's own life, of which one gets a not very clear impression. Or take one's thought—has it not continually swung to and fro? Has not doubt encroached on assertion, and so on? Or take your emotional life, if you remember it. Is it a steady line, or can you say, for instance, that some emotions have encroached on others, and are always doing so? What is it we have to keep steady?

Now ancient teaching saw the world as kept between the opposites, not in a single line of progress, but in a swinging movement. One opposite encroached on another and was overcome and in turn encroached upon. It is like a continual raiding of one camp on another. In this continual strife everything was contained. In this tension of opposing forces, life manifested itself. To pray for the end of this tension and strife is to pray for death, as one Greek said. It is best to think of the opposites as forces having opposite signs, not as things. A "thing" may conduct one or another force. We know that behind visible matter, in the régime of the atom, only two forces are met with—positive and negative—to begin with. They are *opposites*. It is very strange to think that this is so. Matter is built up of primary *opposite* forces. Do you see what I mean? The world appears out of a tension that is sometimes harmonized.

The primary opposites were called by an ancient Mediterranean school "love" and "hate"—or "attraction" and "repulsion". What was meant was that there is a force that unites and an opposite force that separates and that these two forces lie behind all things. When love or desire for union is uppermost all things tend to come together, and creation appears. When hate and strife predominate all things break up and vanish. This school taught that the Universe comes together and breaks up in a vast time-cycle, or pendulum-swing. The pendulum-swing is only a cycle seen, as it were, sideways. This idea of things coming together in the cosmic creation and sundering into chaos is also found in ancient Eastern schools. For example, Brahma is said to breathe out and then breathe in the Universe. From this point of view the properties of the physical Universe will never be constant, since the tendency of particles to unite or otherwise will not be the same at every point of time. Everything will change—not merely fashions and viewpoints and theories, but the properties of things—so that what worked once will not necessarily do so to-day. Seen in this light science will be always re-discovering itself and re-casting its ideas. A remedy that once was effective will cease to be, and so on. And the same process will affect human affairs. As "love" cosmically gains the upper hand people will unite: as "hate" grows they will separate and be scattered. This view is really the same as that expressed in Ecclesiastes where it is said that there is a time for gathering and a time for scattering, etc. only it is expressed in terms of a vast pendulum-swing and not in terms of lesser and even little pendulums. In both statements what is meant is that the tendencies of things are not the same at different times. Consider for a moment our position to-day. What is the tendency of things? Do you see any tendency? At least we can say that the tendency of things to-day is not the same as that of a century ago.

If you look at a pendulum swinging against a wall, you will see that it covers the same ground, to and fro. Any point at which it is may be in a forward or reverse direction. That is, things may be at the same point as before but moving in the reverse direction. In studying the swing of the pendulum in ourselves we notice we come to the same points, but that often the tendency is different. Things are the same but moving in another direction. We are, say, irritable and becoming pleasant, or pleasant and growing irritable. The Work teaches that we are most unconscious, most asleep, when any pendulum in us is passing the mid-point. Here it is moving fastest. So we live, as it were, in extremes —at either end of the pendulum-swing—and do not know what lies in the middle. We swing, as I have heard it said, between red and green, between blue and yellow, but cannot see the white light in the centre which is a combination of all colours.

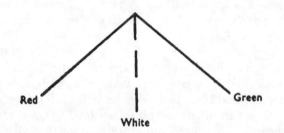

Red   Green

White

If we could retain full consciousness and memory right through the swing, we would not only remember the two opposite states at each end, but would begin to catch sight of a *third* factor which lies in the middle. But our consciousness works with too slow an energy ordinarily. Of this we will speak at another time. At present it can be said that we should try to see pendulums in ourselves and in life and try not to identify with the two ends of the swing. Our moods are all hung on to pendulums. *We should not trust them.* Unfortunately we identify with them. We take them as ourselves. We say: "I feel", "I think", and so on. We forget that "Real I" is in the centre of the pendulum-swing, and we allow ourselves to swing between excitement and dejection, between enthusiasm and depression, between over-valuation and under-valuation, between conceit and humility, and so on, endlessly. In all this there is no centre of gravity. Remember that by identifying with one side of the swing, you will be under the power of the other side when it takes charge—and you will see no connection. "Why", one says, "they cannot be connected because they are *opposite.*" That is exactly why they are and this is what we are talking of in these papers.

THE OPPOSITES

Part IV.—We have previously spoken of the original conception of the *just* man. It was not a sentimental idea. The just man is between the opposites, in a state of equilibrium. By knowing how to withdraw force from the opposites, his centre of gravity is not pulled to one side or the other. This is only possible by reaching a definite feeling of one's own *nothingness*, as was said. To feel one is something prevents one from reaching a position between the opposites. When the Work says that a man must come to realize his own *nothingness* before he can be re-born, it does not mean that he must humble himself and so on, but that he must by long self-observation actually begin to realize that he is nothing and that there is no such person as himself. The object of this is to get into a position, psychologically speaking, between the opposites. I mean that it has a definite object. Why is it so important to get somewhere into the centre of the pendulum and not swing to and fro? Because here, between the opposites, lie all the possibilities of growth. Here influences from higher levels reach us. Here, in this place where one can feel one's own nothingness and where one is therefore free from contradictions, influences and meanings coming from higher centres, *which have no contradictions*, can be felt. Not regarding yourself as good or bad, not priding yourself on being just or otherwise, not thinking you are well-treated or badly-treated, not being caught by either movement through identifying, you come into this mid-position. This is not easy! With personality active, it is impossible. Sometimes, when the opposites are drained of force, as in severe illness, a person is brought into it. Then all his centres are in focus and he understands and sees clearly.

*　　*　　*

The Work teaches that there are three forces in every manifestation. We see only two—if we see as far as that. We do not see the third Force because the formatory centre works between the opposites and everything for it is either "it is so" or "it is not so", either "yes" or "no". The harmonizing of the opposites is in the mediating force between them. Not that the Third Force is merely a union of the opposite forces. It is a distinct force to which we are not sensitive in ordinary states. It is called "Neutralizing Force" in the Work and "Holy Spirit" in the New Testament. At the top of the Universe is the Unity of the Absolute. Creation begins with the three forces or first trinity proceeding from this Unity. These three forces are equal. At the bottom of the Universe is the greatest antithesis to Unity. Here the opposites are most widely separated and there is no Third Force to reconcile them. So the Work speaks of the lowest matter in the Table of Hydrogens as being "without the Holy Ghost". One must imagine what it would be like to be imprisoned in a world of that kind, at that lowest level of creation, where there is no hope of harmonizing anything or of reaching any new state.

★   ★   ★

Third Force lies between the opposites and so we can picture it as the mid-point of the pendulum-swing. If you take the feeling of 'I' out of both sides of the pendulum, then you do not feel yourself through the opposites and the feeling of 'I' moves to the centre, into nothingness, or, if you prefer it, into not-somethingness. Here in the middle is the place or state where Real 'I' is. Real 'I' or *Master* comes from "above" —that is, from a higher level. We cannot reach it from one or the other opposite. This is why so often in ancient symbols you find the two opposites on either side and the Third Force in the middle, in the representations of the mysteries of re-birth. To attain Real 'I' is to be re-born. For example, there is Christ on the Cross between the two thieves. Or in the close rival to early Christianity, the religion of Mithra, you find the bull being slain between the two opposites. Those of you who have looked at the Liber Mutus will remember the two animals on either side and the rays of light descending between them. An ancient and very simple device found on seals was the sun rising between two hills.

The opposites are thieves because what you build on one is undermined by the other. Or, to put it differently, joy leads to sorrow. But whatever is built in the centre cannot be taken from you. Let us take understanding as an example. If you really *understand* something, if you have seen the truth of it yourself, it is in the middle, and stands in the Third Force.

Birdlip, September 15, 1943

<h2 style="text-align:center">THE OPPOSITES</h2>

<h3 style="text-align:center">THIRD FORCE</h3>

Part V.—To-night we speak of Third Force. As was said, the Work teaches that there are three forces in all manifestations, in all events, in all created things, and they are called *Active, Passive* and *Neutralizing* or First, Second and Third Forces. The concept of Third Force is not yet known to science in any distinct way, save that to the positively and negatively charged particles of the atom there has been added the *neutron*. Science was primarily built up on the concept of two forces—that is, on action and reaction. This is in accordance with our usual way of thinking

330

according to the formatory centre which cannot see Third Force. It cannot comprehend it and so a new mind is necessary—a new way of thinking. Action and reaction we can all understand: *cause* and *effect* we can see more or less. You knock a passive table and it resists you. Your toe is active and the table is passive and you get hurt. But the conception of Third Force is far more difficult to understand. Yet it is at work amongst us all and it sometimes takes the form of what seem miracles—as synchronicity, or the same kinds of things happening together, which we call coincidences.

Now I want to call your attention to the word used by the Work to designate this not-seen and not-acknowledged Third Force. Why is it called *Neutralizing Force*? Let us take this point first of all. The term obviously contains the idea of *neuter*. What does neuter means? Neuter means in the dictionary-sense simply *neither* (from Latin *ne uter*).

Of gender, neuter means neither male nor female. Of a verb it means neither active nor passive, and so intransitive—that is, not passing into a definite object. In general it means belonging to *neither* of two specified contraries or defined states. From neuter comes *neutral*. *Neutral* means politically to remain *between* two opposing parties. In chemistry, a *neutral* salt is neither acid nor alkaline. Militarily, to be neutral means to assist neither one side nor the other, and so to remain in a state of relative independence and freedom. In the sphere of electricity it means having neither a positive nor a negative charge. In mechanics it means a point where different forces are in equilibrium. Again, *neutrality* means "the condition of being inclined neither way: the absence of extreme views, abstention from taking a one-sided view-point, etc." Now let us pass from neuter and neutrality to the verb *neutralizing*. To neutralize, in the dictionary-sense, means "to render neither active, nor passive: to counterbalance, to render ineffective by means of an opposite force, to produce equilibrium." The above dictionary definitions only partly give the real meaning in which the term "neutralizing force" is used in the Work. This is not surprising because the terms and conceptions and ideas of this Work are not to be found in any dictionary. At the same time, many Work-terms have reference to terms in ordinary usage. There is a correspondence. When the Work calls Third Force the Neutralizing Force it means that its nature is such that it is neither active nor passive force and is quite distinct from them. So it is neuter in the dictionary meaning of the word —that is, *neither*—but, though *neither*, it is something. Also, when the dictionary says that to neutralize can mean "to counterbalance, to render ineffective by means of an opposite force," this is correct in a Work-sense, because sometimes the first effect of neutralizing force appears in an increase of either active or passive force, so as to preserve an equilibrium. But Neutralizing or Third Force is a separate and distinct force originating from the first *trinity* or *triad* of forces, which create the first order of worlds at the note *Si* in the Ray of Creation and give rise to all subsequent levels of creation by reduplication. In the first order of created worlds three forces and no more act, and they reflect the will of the Absolute, but in three forms: in the second order of worlds six forces—that is, two triads—act: and so on until at the level of our far-down earth 48 forces—that is 16 triads—act, far removed from the will of the Absolute and so *mechanical* by comparison. For it is the inter-action and criss-crossing of all these forces that produce both the complications and the mechanical limitations of our existence in this extremity of the Universe. No freedom down here is possible, whatever social laws are made, because of these forces or laws. To speak of freedom is impossible. But a man in himself by work on himself can pass under fewer laws.

In order that this may take place the first thing he must do is to *remember himself*. In life a man does not remember himself. It is from this point of view that I wish to speak to you about the Third Force to-night. The point where a man can begin to become more free lies between the opposites, in the region of the middle of the pendulum-swing, and by the act of remembering himself he begins to approach this place, psychologically speaking. It would be impossible to describe all the different ways of remembering oneself, even if one knew them. The emotional realization of our position on this minute, far-down, insignificant planet, of the unimportance of our personal existences, can bring about some degree of self-remembering. Sometimes merely look-ing externally at the heavens at night, at the myriads of stars, produces a momentary state akin to self-remembering by withdrawing us from personal feelings. Everything that takes force from personality may bring about a trace of Self-Remembering. But it is the recognition of the *taste* of the state that is important. For it is in this state and only in this state that "help" can reach us. The feeling of the Work and all the background of esoteric teaching can bring about a state of Self-Remem-bering and it is to the development of the mental and emotional evaluation of the Work that the power of Self-Remembering eventually belongs, apart from transient forms induced more or less by accident. The increasing feeling of the Work as stronger than life and all its ups and downs and swinging to and fro between the opposites brings about a state of Self-Remembering that is not due to chance nor is merely a fleeting experience. But for a very long time we mix the Work with our associations, with the machine of personality, which is driven by life and reacts to it mechanically. And this is inevitable because only a gradual separation is possible. A person cannot be torn suddenly away from personality. It would destroy him. So even though we try to work, we identify with the reactions of personality which seem more distinct and real, or more 'natural' as we say. At the same time we may know well enough that we should remember ourselves and even want to do so, and are unable to do so. We are unable to because we are identified with the reactions of personality. We view the incident, whatever it may be, through personality—that is, through all the attitudes, buffers, associations, pretences, pictures, negative emotions, and so on, in short, through all the typical reactions that belong to our personally acquired personality. That is, we see it from the life point of view and not from the Work point of view—and this though we are not forgetting the Work and are even trying to work. Now if we are identified with the reactions of our personality and at the same time try to remember ourselves we find it impossible. To be identified and to be in a state of Self-Remembering is impossible. It is not merely that the taste of each is contradictory. It is rather that the two states are incompatible. The more identified we are, the more are we in life under the mechanical laws of this planet. The more we are in a state of Self-Remembering the more are we under conscious influences. In the Work the idea of Self-Remembering—that is, the Third State of Consciousness, where help can only reach us—is always given in conjunction with non-identifying. The Work as Third Force reaches us only when we are relatively *awake* —that is, in some degree of Self-Remembering. The original idea of prayer was to put us in a state of Self-Remembering, to let go our troubles, or, as it were, to ask for help and acknowledge our powerlessness *to do*. But prayer, in this sense, is very difficult. To pray mechanically, or violently, or tragically, or out of duty, or piously, cannot give results. Prayer can only be answered when all three centres co-operate. And the three centres can only co-operate when they are "in focus" and this is when we are somewhere in the middle of the pendulum-swing and not one-sided. The *act* of Self-Remembering is an attempt to put us somewhere in the middle of this swing. Being in the middle is to be in the *state* of Self-Remembering. Working on being identified is separating oneself so that one is not swung from one side to the other. It can be said that Self-Remembering is striving to be in Third Force and that non-identifying is striving not to be in the two opposite forces. When we try to act from one side or the other side of the pendulum, as when we say in life: "This is too much,"—that is, when we act from identifying —we cannot expect anything more than the usual action-reaction work of the opposites. I hit you: then you hit me: then I hit you. And so on endlessly. For a longer or shorter period I triumph, then by the mechanical swing of things you triumph, and so on. Now you are first: now I am first. Now I am on the top: now you are on the top. This is life, swinging between the opposites. This is "going up the hill", and then "tumbling down". In all this play of opposites there is no *solution*. That is why life is called in the Work insoluble. You have only the satisfaction of the opposites, which are thieves. Take, for instance, jealousy and its unpleasant triumphs. This satisfaction—as, say, of triumphing over your enemy—is transient. If, however, you work on your mechanical reactions, you begin to escape from this two-cylinder engine of life, in which one piston is always moving up and the other down, and vice versa. When you feel the strange force of the Work you begin to understand that you cannot *solve* difficulties by any one-sided and so violent action. But this takes much time and labour to realize. To reach anything like *solutions* we have to learn how to move in one direction a short way but then move in the opposite direction a short way until you get into the middle. This is very difficult. But by this method you can reach Third Force, in which both good and truth lie—that is, the real meaning, and so the solution.

Now I want to add only one thing to-night. It is about inner silence In working on yourself and noticing how the swings of the pendulum go in yourself and how now you think or feel this, and now you think or feel the opposite, and in not identifying with either side, so far as possible at one's present stage, there is something called in the Work "inner silence". Different 'I's, ranged along the orbit of the swing, wish to say now this and now that, as the light of consciousness touches them and wakes them to momentary life. To a limited extent one may permit them to speak, provided one has a distinct idea that neither side is right. Inner silence means being silent *in oneself*. It means not taking sides in yourself and so being silent. This is impossible if you identify with every 'I'. You may let talk take place on one side or the other, but you observe it and are in yourself silent.

This paper is about reaching the middle of the pendulum where Third Force can touch us. The object of Self-Remembering is to reach this place, which is neither one nor the other of the opposites, but a new experience, and so a new consciousness and understanding. All identifying belongs to the opposites.

Birdlip, September 29, 1943

THE THREE LINES OF WORK

We speak briefly to-night of the three lines of Work and of External Considering. All three lines are necessary. The first is work on oneself. This includes work on the side of knowledge and work on the side of being. To work on knowledge means here to work on knowledge of the Work. To work on being means to observe oneself from the standpoint of what the Work teaches so that one actually sees one's own personality, one's negative states, internal considering, identifying, mechanical talking, mechanical disliking, self-justifying and so on, and to struggle with them. Mechanicalness and sleep prevent change of being. It is necessary to understand that knowledge of one's being is required before we can work on ourselves, and this is gained through the effort of attention called self-observation. The first step is the realization that we are not one but many, and that our being is characterized by absence of unity. Self-study is different from the study of the knowledge of the Work. Both require effort, however. You have often heard it said that this Work is to make us think. It is impossible to get to know this system of teaching unless one makes the effort of thinking for oneself. Writing it down in note-books is not the same as thinking, but remembering what was said requires the effort of directed thinking. The first line of Work is to make us know our state of being and state of knowledge. Otherwise we cannot change. To *observe* is the first thing, but it must be without criticism or analysis. It has been said, on one occasion, that you can change nothing until you know *all* yourself.

The second line of Work is work in conjunction with other people in the Work. Unless you practise the first line of Work you cannot practise the second. Again, unless you practise the second, you cannot practise the first rightly. There are several reasons for this, which it would be useful for the Group to discuss.

The third line of Work is—for us at present—to help the Work in general and try to see what is required of us and not talk wrongly or harm the Work. Right valuation and right attitude to the Work belong to the third line, but they enter into everything, because unless one has valuation and right attitude one will work neither on oneself nor with others nor for the Work. As was said already, all three lines of work are necessary. A man working by himself and only for himself cannot get anywhere. To begin with, he has not the force to do so.

Now, to return to the first line of Work and to personal work on oneself. It is necessary to know the Work and apply its ideas to oneself. It is then possible to begin to understand the Work. But you cannot apply the ideas of the Work to yourself unless you observe yourself and what goes on within you in their light. Self-observation lets a ray of light into our inner darkness, but only when the Work accompanies it —that is, when one observes oneself in the light of the teaching. What does the Work teach you to observe in yourself? It is very useful to make a list and then notice if you put it into practice—that is, whether you actually apply the Work or whether you dream you are working.

The second line of Work cannot be done unless you gain knowledge of your being. Unless we observe ourselves and notice how we think of or speak to others who are in the Work we cannot put ourselves in their position. This brings us to *external considering*, which belongs to the second line of Work. External considering is putting yourself in the position of your neighbour. In the New Testament it is called "love of neighbour". In order to put yourself in the position of another person in the Work, you must know your being—the kind of person you are. Otherwise you will leave yourself out. Your neighbour, of course, sees you. But if you do not see yourself, how can you put yourself in another's position? One should think of this because it explains why so much wrong and false "external considering" exists, which only causes irritation or perhaps hatred. Another practical thing about the second line of Work, to prevent useless friction, is not taking in negative impressions of other people in the Work. They accumulate and produce a poison. To see only the worst sides of others is, of course, to be fast asleep. When an impression falls on a negative part of a centre there is a brief moment

335

in which, if you are awake, you can render it null and void by not accepting it. If, however, you identify with it, however little, it lodges in you and collects others like itself. The last point that I will mention is that everyone should try to stop mechanical liking and disliking and the kinds of conversations that arise from them. We cannot expect to get much force from impressions if everything falls either on mechanical like or mechanical dislike. Nor can we expect any development of the second line of Work in us, in which case the first line will be held up.

Birdlip, October 10, 1943

THE DIGESTION OF IMPRESSIONS

Last time, after the answers to the first three questions had been read out, something was said about the talk at Birdlip on the previous Saturday in which I spoke about the digestion of impressions. It might be just as well to give a further talk on this very important subject.

We have often spoken about the transformation of impressions. You all know the Work continually points out how we receive incoming impressions. The Work teaches that impressions are the highest food that we take in and therefore the most important. It has often been said that everything you see, everything you hear, the people you know, the books you read, enter as impressions. Other people are impressions to you. You touch them, you see them, you hear them, and so on.

Now the first place of work on oneself is designated as the place of the First Conscious Shock. The meaning of the First Conscious Shock, which is sometimes called in a general way Self-Remembering, is to transform impressions. You can accept some impressions and reject others, just as ordinary food coming in to the body as *Hydrogen 768* is either accepted or rejected by the stomach. So first of all there is the acceptance or rejection of impressions, and then comes the digestion of impressions which is exactly comparable with the digestion of food in which you extract, as it were, certain parts, and excrete or get rid of other parts. To make a right stomach in the top compartment of the 3-storey house is the object of this Work. The Work can form, when it is sufficiently understood, a stomach that rejects or accepts—that is, a stomach that digests. The transformation of impressions is exactly comparable with the transformation of food in the stomach. Food is taken in and digested—i.e. it is transformed into finer and finer matters. You remember that *768* passes to *384* and then to *192*, and so on. Impressions enter the human machine in the top-floor as *48* and can become transformed into *24* and *12*. But the Work teaches that ordinarily this does not happen except in very small quantities. When you begin to become active to your life, when you begin to take things often

336

from the Work point of view and not from a natural or mechanical point of view, you begin to digest impressions. This idea of the transformation or digestion of impressions is met with in the Gospels, as you all know already. We have to take everything in a new way. Ordinary people will take things in an ordinary way but in the Work we must take ordinary things in quite a new way. This was called in the Gospels μετάνοια. As you know, many people have written about the meaning of this strange word which is so wrongly translated as repentance. De Quincey suggested 'transformation of the mind'. I suppose you have all realized that you take in impressions through the present form of your minds. You see things, as it were, through your mental apparatus. Take a very simple, mentally uneducated person who sees an elephant. She will probably say: "Tut, tut." Perhaps you see what I mean. You all have mental attitudes, mental apparatus for reception, a set of ideas that you take as completely veracious, as completely right, true, and so on. When you become more educated your mind changes to a small extent, so it becomes transformed slightly. What you previously thought was quite impossible, or wrong, you now see is not as you thought. Every one of you is limited by his or her thinking. Of course you do not see this yet. For some reason or other, we all think we already have all points of view, all possible thoughts. This is utterly wrong. Each one of you is limited completely and totally by the small range of thinking that you have acquired by your mental prejudices, attitudes, and so on. Life appears as it does to you because of your mental level. You cannot take things in a new way unless the way you think changes, unless your mental level is changed. As I said, it is extraordinary that we all think we are capable of taking in any kind of experience or of understanding anything just as we are. Do you see that we have not the apparatus, we have not the power of reception, to understand beyond our limited mental outlook and limited mental functions?

Now μετάνοια (so wrongly translated as repentance) means to get beyond one's present mind—not to pass out of one's mind, but to get beyond one's present mind, to transform one's whole way of thinking about oneself, about other people, and so on. *A new mind in a new body* means the development of a completely different understanding which leads to the formation of a *second body* in one. The Work teaches you many quite new ideas about the meaning of life in general and about your own lives. Unless these ideas are taken in and thought about individually your minds will remain exactly the same kind of dung-heaps as they are at present. You have often heard the expression that *this Work is to make us think* and *think in a new way*. Now take this phrase and apply it to every place in the Gospels where the word *repent* is used. Let us suppose that it was already translated as "think in a new way". Then perhaps you will see how the Work is designed to change the entire furniture of the mind and re-arrange the whole mental being.

Now with regard to the digestion of impressions—digestion of impressions depends on a stomach, and the stomach in this case is the Work. The Work is to give you a mental stomach to digest impressions with. You can only digest your day by having something to digest it with, something that has been established in you by the assimilation and consent and valuation of the Work. When you refer things to the Work you will find at once something that will help you to arrange your daily impressions rightly. You will learn to take things in a light and easy way which ordinary people would take very negatively and heavily, and you will also learn to take things in a serious way that ordinary people take very lightly. Let us take an example: Someone speaks to you in a way that you do not like—you feel all the mechanical reactions arising in you, you feel how you dislike this person and so on. Now suppose that you identify with all these typical mechanical reactions, which means consenting to the feeling of 'I' and going into these mechanical reactions automatically aroused in you, so that you say: "I can't stand this," or "I can't bear this," or "I dislike so much this kind of person who looks like this, behaves like this," and so on. Well, of course, if this happens, you are not transforming impressions, you are not working on yourself at all. Let us take another example: a person you do not like mechanically happens to say something to you of which you see the truth. You may perhaps despise this person, mechanically speaking—i.e. from a life point of view—yet this person has said something that rather penetrates. Now you may think it ridiculous that a person of this kind can say anything of the slightest value to you, possibly because you think you are far better, yet at the same time here is something that you must accept and digest. What you must excrete are your feelings of despising and so on. You will usually find that your best advisors, your best sources of knowledge, are people whom you would normally completely disregard. I always think it is very interesting to reflect a great deal on the fact that Christ was born in a manger, the place of least importance from the life point of view. Since I am talking about this subject I would like to mention something that was said long ago—a phrase that has not been used for a long time. *Try to see what you are resting on*, all of you. Try to see the basis of your self-satisfaction. You will understand that unless this basis is completely broken up there can be no change of being.

Now you can see clearly from these examples that I have given that if impressions come in and ring up the usual place there can be no digestion of impressions at all. You are not then attempting to transform impressions. You may talk a great deal about the First Conscious Shock but you are not practising it because the First Conscious Shock is to transform impressions. Now suppose you are sufficiently interested and sufficiently conscious to notice how these impressions fall on you mechanically, and suppose that you have sufficient valuation of the Work to wish to transform these impressions, which means not letting them simply fall on their usual place, exciting your usual dislikes and hatreds. In order to do this you must have some power of digesting impressions, and this is where the Work comes in. You know that the

338

Work says that people are mechanical. Now suppose you apply a Work idea of this kind at the moment when you notice that someone is making a customary negative impression on you. If you understand something of what it means when it is said in the Work that people are mechanical, then you will not accept the impression so easily. You will realize that it is not the person's fault. You will realize that the person always does this, always says this, because he is a machine. But of course you all know already that you will never really see in the right way the mechanicalness of other people unless you see your own mechanicalness and how you are constantly doing the same thing. Perhaps you will see what I mean by these illustrations of transforming impressions. If you have these Work-thoughts in connection with this person the impression will fall in a quite new place in you. It will be digested. But first of all you must have a new kind of thinking, some degree of μετάνοια, before you can transform or digest these impressions. If you can do this you will find yourself entering on a very strange path that you cannot understand for a long time. You may tend to go back to your old ways of thinking because you cannot understand it, but if you do it will be a great mistake. To think in a new way about other people means that you yourself are beginning to change and when you are beginning to change you will feel that you are losing sight of yourself. But if you always remain in sight of yourself—that is, if you always remain as you were, you cannot change. To change, you must lose your ordinary feelings of identity. For instance, if I wish to change I cannot remain Dr. Nicoll or even Nicoll. Change of being, change of oneself, means that you become quite different. Now if you apply the Work as a transforming agent to your life, to yourself, and to people around you and the impressions they make on you, you begin to change. The Work is designed to make you change. Taking things in a new way—namely, from the Work teaching—is bound to make your whole relationship to other people change, but this will not happen unless you digest impressions by means of the alchemy of the Work.

Now I will speak of the digestion of impressions *at the end of the day*. If we could work more consciously we would digest impressions at the moment of taking them in, but since we have not this power, since we are not conscious enough yet, we can digest impressions taken in during the day at night-time or even the next day. That is, we can re-arrange them in our minds in terms of what the Work teaches as good and evil. You remember that it is said in the New Testament that we should not let the sun go down on our wrath. It is important how we go to sleep and it is equally important how we get up. Past moments of sleep, past moments of identifying with wrong 'I's in ourselves, can be to a certain extent cancelled by consciously going over the whole situation in our minds afterwards. You must never think that you cannot work on a thing in your past. Never think that you cannot alter it. You can alter the present, you can alter the past, and you can alter the future.

Now I will tell you one of the most important ideas of this Work teaching. This life on earth cannot be understood save in terms of another life, of another world. All that this Work teaches is about how to educate ourselves in terms of another life, of another level of being, of another level of humanity called conscious humanity. This is one of the greatest transforming ideas contained in the Work. You know we must begin to imitate a higher level of humanity. We are all in the basement but we might get up to the drawing-room. All the Work-teaching about non-identifying, about negative emotions, about self-remembering and all the rest of it, is about going upstairs. Of course if you take this life and all that happens in it as the only thing and have no idea that there is anything else, you will never be able to transform impressions. You will always remain under A influences.

Birdlip, October 24, 1943

NOTE ON "WHAT YOU ARE BASED ON"

You know that many things are said in esoteric literature, and of course the Gospels are included here, about what a man is based on, and in connection with this idea you have to think about what can be taken away from you by life. You all understand that if you are based on someone else—i.e. completely identified—then this basis can be taken away from you and you will be unable to remember yourself. Or again, if you are based on your property, your possessions, your position, your money, your reputation, your past, and so on, all this can be taken away from you and then you will feel a total loss of yourself and perhaps feel that only suicide is the way out—I mean, if your chief basis is on such things that are not *you*. There is one thing that can never be taken from you and that is your understanding. If you have a point in the Work, which is the only thing that gives understanding in a real sense, you will be able to stand the loss of many external personal things. You remember the parable about catching hold of the rope. If you find this rope *in your own way*, which everyone in this Work must do, then you will be held by something quite distinct from life and its vicissitudes. This is really called having a point in the Work. Other people may fail you, disappoint you, and so on. Outer life may assume very unpleasant forms. Yet you are held by something beyond life—that is, by a new force.

You remember some of the parables in the Gospels about what a man is *based on*. For instance, there is the parable in which Christ speaks of the foundation on which a man builds his house:

Christ says: "Everyone therefore which heareth these words of mine and doeth them, shall be likened unto a wise man, which built his house upon the rock: and the rain descended, and the floods came, and the winds blew, and beat upon that house; and it fell not: for it was founded upon the rock. And everyone that heareth these words of mine, and doeth them not, shall be likened unto a foolish man, which built his house upon the sand: and the rain descended, and the floods came, and the winds blew, and smote upon that house; and it fell: and great was the fall thereof."

(*Matthew* VII 24-27)

Then there is the parable about the man who stored up wealth in barns:

Christ says: "The ground of a certain rich man brought forth plentifully: and he reasoned within himself, saying, What shall I do, because I have no where to bestow my fruits? And he said, This will I do: I will pull down my barns, and build greater; and there will I bestow all *my* corn and *my* goods. And I will say to my soul, Soul, thou hast much goods laid up for many years; take thine ease, eat, drink, be merry. But God said unto him, Thou foolish one, this night is thy soul required of thee; and the things which thou hast prepared, whose shall they be? So is he that layeth up treasure for himself, and is not rich towards God."

(*Luke* XII 16-21)

Here "God" is contrasted with "my".

I remember that G. once gave a talk in France about *what could be taken away from us*. You will understand that if we are based on "False Personality" we are standing on a basis that will give us constant trouble as regards keeping our balance. G. said that a man could be compared with a flat containing three rooms. He spoke for some time about this 3-room flat and about everything that was in disorder in it and how the utensils were in the wrong place, etc. Then he went on to say how a man was always in *debt*, always insolvent, always liable to be summonsed, however much money he possessed. Of course you must understand that he was speaking of Man's insolvency in a particular way—in fact, in the way that Man is spoken of so often in some of the parables as, for instance, in the parable of the servant—that is, *you*— who owes his Lord millions of talents. G. said the *bailiffs* may enter your flat at any moment and they have a "legal" right to take away everything except your "bed" which is in the inner or third room. So please think what you rest on most internally. There is something which cannot be taken away from you. Have you got to this place? Everything else can be taken away by these "bailiffs" that may come at any time and remove everything that is not your own.

A SHORT COMMENTARY ON THE IMPORTANCE
OF INDIVIDUAL WORK EFFORT

To-night I would like to remind you of a subject that we often spoke about some time ago. I recall that many people were interested in it, so I will try to formulate the subject again. It has to do with the Work-idea that everyone is "a self-developing-organism" and must make *individual* effort. Each person must develop himself or herself on all sides.

Let us begin like this. Most people make no effort beyond their daily routine, because they think that if someone else is able to do something better than they can it is useless to try to do it. Certainly this is a common viewpoint in life. People say: "What is the good of my trying to do this or that, when others do it far better?" This is an entirely wrong attitude. To make effort beyond this point is the beginning of individual growth. It is exactly this attitude that prevents people from having individual experience, or rather, from growing in their own centres by personal experience. Let us try to understand what is meant. If you—that is *you* sitting there now—think it is no good going beyond your present circle of daily life, then you do not understand what *individual* effort means. You may say: "What is the good of trying to understand this or making effort beyond what I am doing at present?"

You have all heard that everyone has to make mechanical effort. Organic life makes conditions such that every rabbit, every fox, every animal, every plant, and every man and woman, has to make *mechanical effort*, in order to live. But *Conscious Effort* lies beyond this level.

You can either practise this Work or not. But you must all understand that if you practise this Work, now, at this moment (not to-morrow) you are making effort beyond mechanical effort. The point of the Work is to transform daily life. So it is said that if you merely listen to this Work and do not practise it, nothing will change in you. Suppose, for example, that you hear many times that you must observe your different 'I's and try not to identify with some of them? Well, of course, you can hear this day after day, and year after year, and say that you know all about that, and why is nothing else said. However, you have heard that the Work tells you here to practise a certain definite thing *on yourself*—now, at this moment—yes, at this very moment.

Now as regards the example given—the selection of 'I's in yourself and the rejection of other 'I's—there is an interesting parable about this. It means, on one level, what we are speaking about. It is about inner selection and inner rejection of 'I's. You have heard how often the Work says: "Do not go with wrong 'I's". This means that you must realize by self-observation that you have different 'I's. (Here I would like to ask each of you if you realize this yet.)

The parable about the selection of 'I's is as follows:

"Again, the kingdom of heaven is like unto a net, that was cast into the sea, and gathered of every kind: which, when it was filled, they drew up on the beach; and they sat down, and gathered the good into vessels, but the bad they cast away."

(Matthew XIII 47-48)

Think what it means to "put the good into vessels". Have you a vessel? Have you yet attained through self-observation any power of *inner selection*—that is, of throwing away negative 'I's, and negative thoughts and emotions, and keeping good ideas and feelings and experiences and discarding the rest?

Birdlip, November 2, 1943

FURTHER NOTE ON "WHAT YOU ARE BASED ON"

In respect of various things said last week, it is quite right to say that we rest on something that is not ourselves and which therefore can be taken away from us. It seems to me that this is the best way of starting to think at all deeply about this question—namely, what you really are. One person rests on his or her position, another on reputation, appearance, the past, and so on. Think what can be taken *away* from you—say, in revolution. All this question belongs to what you feel yourself through, what 'I' you feel yourself. You thank God in all sorts of different ways that you are not as others. Do you remember the parable about the two men who prayed? It was addressed "unto certain which trusted in themselves that they were righteous and set all others at nought." Christ says: "Two men went up into the temple to pray; the one a Pharisee, and the other a publican. The Pharisee stood and prayed thus with himself, God, I thank thee, that I am not as the rest of men, extortioners, unjust, adulterers, or even as this publican. I fast twice in the week; I give tithes of all that I get. But the publican, standing afar off, would not lift up so much as his eyes unto heaven, but smote his breast, saying, God, be merciful to me a sinner. I say unto you, This man went down to his house justified rather than the other: for every one that exalteth himself shall be humbled; but he that humbleth himself shall be exalted." (*Luke* XVIII 10-14). I heard it once said that one of the most difficult things for a man who reaches that stage of development where he begins to come in contact with the highest teaching is that he has to give up his "religion". He may feel himself a very good "Catholic", a very good "Quaker", a very good "Protestant", a very good "Mahometan", and so on—i.e. he rests on this basis, thanking God he is not like other people, other unbelievers. In the highest stages of inner evolution all such *distinctions* have to go completely. Perhaps you can think for yourselves how this must be so. And this applies to many other sides.

343

To become *nothing*, or rather to *begin* to realize one's own *nothingness*, would be quite impossible as long as one is *certain* one is better than others by reason of reputation, religion, position, cash. Can you yet grasp this idea? No one can pass through this "eye of a needle" as long as he is *rich*. You remember that Christ said to the rich young man: "It is easier for a camel to go through the eye of a needle than for a rich man to enter into the kingdom of God." (*Matt.* XIX 24). What you base yourself on is what makes you feel rich and is therefore what turns us all into "camels" in regard to the Work.

Talking on a different scale, try to see where you are easily offended, where you feel that you have not been properly treated. If you can observe this you will see a part of the basis on which you rest psychologically, a part of the sand on which your house is built. Or again, try to observe where and when you despise other people and think yourself superior to them, or at least think they are inferior to you and quite unimportant. This again will shew you part of the basis on which you rest. Or again, try to observe where you feel flattered, where your vanity is gratified. This again will shew you part of the basis on which you rest. But all this must be done quite practically by observation and not discussed theoretically.

When you begin to cease to have any ideas about yourself, any pictures of yourself, you can then begin to change your inner state. To change one's inner state is to go on a long journey. There are physical journeys and psychological journeys. You cannot change your inner state if you cling to what you are based on, just as you cannot leave your room if you persist in clinging to all the articles of furniture in it and keep on saying: "These are mine—i.e. *me*". You can come to a state where you go on very long journeys that do not exist in physical space. You may meet new kinds of people who live elsewhere. But you cannot do this as long as you cling to yourself, cling to *me* and *mine*, cling to the basis that each of you rests on in so imbecile and self-complacent a way. You know how people who have to leave a burning house often catch hold of something quite imbecile and silly, such as a parrot. That is because they feel themselves by means of such outer things. They are based on them. They have no feeling of themselves at all otherwise. The feeling of Real 'I' can only come to you when all such false 'I's are diminished in you. All of you may think that you never speak like that man who prayed: "Thank God I am not as other men", but have you actually observed how often you do enact this without actually saying it, how often you act from this basis? We often think that we do not do the silly things that we see other people doing, and conclude therefore that we are really better than they are; but we do not see the silly and mean things we do ourselves. People's ways of being silly and foolish and mean vary very much. Everyone is different. The giraffe thinks the wart-hog is ridiculous, the jay thinks the nightingale has a wretchedly weak voice, and so on.

Have you ever stood in a place in yourself in which you can almost say: "There is nothing of me here," either by a sense of comparison or a sense of vanity or by any other estimation? Perhaps when you have been very ill you have touched such a state. Here everything falls away and you are quite alone but without any fear. From such a state one can see what one is usually based on. One can catch a glimpse of all the 'I's that are constantly feeding on one like clouds of vultures and jackals and insects. It is very interesting to take the Work from the standpoint of studying how to be free in oneself. Esoteric knowledge can make us free but only by its practice. You remember the phrase: "The truth shall make you free." But how long does it take before the teaching of the Work becomes truth for us even in the remotest sense?

Birdlip, November 6, 1943

COSMOLOGY

We will now speak for a short time about Cosmology. I will put this question to you all: What different cosmological systems do you know about? Do you know what ideas of the Universe and its construction have existed? Strictly speaking, a cosmology means a system which regards the Universe as an ordered whole formed on some definite plan. The word *cosmos*, which means *order*, was first applied to the Universe by the Pythagorean School from which all European science was derived. All esoteric teaching regards the Universe as ordered and formed on a definite plan. But the word *cosmos* has come to mean simply any view of the Universe apart from any idea of order or origin. Since it is clear to us all that we live in a Universe and that this earth is a small part of it, many thinkers in the past have advanced different cosmological ideas which can roughly be divided into those that explain it as haphazard and accidental and those that regard it as ordered and so intelligent.

You may think that it makes no difference to a person whether he believes in one cosmological system or another, or even if he never thinks about the matter at all. You will be wrong if you think in this way. A man from the Work point of view has different centres, different parts of centres and so on. He cannot possibly be in higher parts of centres or higher centres, if he has wrong cosmological conceptions governing his mind. You know that this Work can only begin with those who have Magnetic Centre—i.e. who are convinced that there is something higher than themselves. How can you expect to reach anything higher in yourself if you do not believe that anything higher exists?

Let us begin with the cosmological system taught in the Work. This system starts from the Absolute and descends in degress or notes down

345

to the most remote and the smallest parts. Here you have very clearly expressed the idea of a *higher*. Again, from this cosmological conception is derived the idea of higher and lower Man—of conscious and mechanical mankind. This conception teaches us that there is meaning beyond meaning, level beyond level, and it also teaches us that everything starts from meaning. The whole Universe in its great and small divisions is derived from *ultimate meaning* and therefore from *mind* and *intelligence*. It also teaches us that everything small and low down is derived from something greater and higher up. From this comes the Work-idea that the whole scale of creation is seeking to grow, to ascend, to reach something better than it is. So the Work says that our moon, our little twig of the terrific cosmic tree, is seeking to grow and reach the state of the earth, and again that the earth is seeking to become eventually a sun and so on.

Now you know that we have the idea of evolution in science, as Darwin formulated it. But of course the idea of evolution existed long before Darwin and is as ancient as esoteric teaching. You know how this idea stares out at us in every page of the New Testament. Man is capable of undergoing an evolution—i.e. an ascent in the *Ray of Creation*. Here you remember the *Side-Octave from the Sun*, this *Jacob's Ladder*. Darwin saw evolution under the aspect of mechanical selection out of chance variation that takes place over vast periods of time. I mean that he saw the idea of evolution, but he got it in a certain way, upside down, as it were. He thought that a monkey somehow or other became a man. He could see no mind, no meaning, controlling the Universe, and therefore it is not surprising that he complained of having lost his "higher aesthetic tastes".

You know that you can always explain a thing by its small parts; you can explain a house by its bricks, but you know quite well that the whole house existed in the architect's mind long before it became manifest in time and space. You can explain a picture in terms of the mineral colours but do you think that the tubes of paint make the picture or the mind of the artist? Now when you see the explanation of an organic whole, such as the human body, solely in terms of its small constituent parts, and cannot understand that a thing must be related in all its parts and that they could not have arisen by chance, your mind is shut to all higher meaning. You then explain the higher by the lower. You explain a motor-car by its nuts and bolts and so on and not by the idea behind the motor-car that has related all its different parts together. Certainly you can argue that a motor-car could not exist without its different parts or that an oil-painting could not exist without its tubes of paint, but do you think you have got the right explanation in thinking in this way? Can you not see that if you think only in this way, from below upwards, your mind remains shut to thinking from above downwards? Surely the idea of a motor-car preceded the construction of it. Now do you think that the idea is prior to its working out in visible terms such as a motor-car that you can touch and handle?

Which comes first? Is mind first or is mechanism as the vehicle of mind first?

You all know that there has been a great loss of meaning in the last century or so, or rather, since the Reformation, which has made it possible for scientists to exist. An entirely new cosmological system was conceived when the so-called Renaissance took place which was more or less synchronous with the Reformation. This was certainly necessary, inevitable. Previously the cosmological conception was that at the head of all things stood God. This conception became as it were worn out and abused to such an extent that no one was allowed to think for himself: only the canon of Scripture was allowed. Then an entirely different cosmological conception came in. In the first place the earth was no longer the centre of the Universe and secondly the whole Universe was seen as under mechanical laws. It has often been said that once it was proved that the earth was not the centre of the Universe a great revolution in thought took place. I would add that a revolution in feeling did not take place. We seem to be as vain as ever. Science is reluctant even now to admit that there is life anywhere in the vast Universe save on our earth and still ascribes to itself its own discoveries, not realizing that it is studying a given Universe that transcends the human mind and its capacity.

The task of the future is to reconcile the older and newer standpoints. That is why the Work says that one of its aims is to unite "the Wisdom of the East with the Science of the West." Unless science discovers what is called religion and unless religion discovers what is called science the mind of Man will be split into two irreconcilable sides and indeed we might think that the whole world to-day suffers from Schizophrenia.

Now if your cosmological system (if you have one) is based on the idea that there were somehow or other a lot of atoms derived somehow or other from somewhere or other, which condensed to form billions and billions of worlds and galaxies, and that somehow or other life started and somehow or other made different animals, trees, fishes, birds, men, women, gradually, little by little, then your mind is not properly furnished with the requisite ideas and understanding for you to reach the higher parts of centres, and finally higher centres themselves, which compose the very complex organism of Man. You will be looking down like cattle and will be incapable of looking up. You will see the explanation of the most wonderful things like consciousness, thought, feeling, sensation and so on in the little small instruments that render them possible. You will be boiling up the artist's picture and analyzing its chemistry. Then what happens is that you will be more and more under the domination of matter, seeing in matter the explanation of everything. The result will be that internally you will be more and more under the influence of machines, of external organisations coming from outside. But if you begin to think that there is not a single thing that you can study in any branch of science that is not a miracle, if you realize that the properties of matter cannot be solely explained in terms of matter, then something inside you will turn the other way round and begin to look at the source of meaning.

You remember the definition that Plato gave of the difference between a man glued to the senses and a man of understanding? He said: "The first believes that matter created mind, whereas the second believes that mind created matter." Which do you yourself think is prior in scale? Do you think that mind and consciousness arose accidentally out of some chance combination of atoms whose origin you cannot explain, or do you think that mind created matter and all its possibilities and that you live in an intelligent and ordered Universe? It is on these two questions that the whole future of humanity at present depends. If you say there is *nothing*, then well and good. If you say there is *something*, then, well, and much better. I have never any quarrel with science itself. Science is obvious. The Mother of Europe (i.e. Greece) laid down all the formulations of science long before Christ. Then came the Christian teaching in this short 2,000-year era of ours, in this experiment upon Man created as a self-developing organism. It seems that the idea was to unite the two aspects of truth, outer and inner, and this idea has no doubt failed, although in the beginning Pythagoras taught both religion and science together and in those times no one thought there was any contradiction between scientific facts and the gods. Every centre has two sides, one turned towards the external senses and the literal meaning of everything, and the other side turned towards higher centres which represent higher levels in the *Ray of Creation*. Balanced Man must learn to use both sides and to understand them and bring them into relationship so that there is no contradiction, and if he excludes one in favour of the other he is undeveloped.

NOTE

I repeat that it is not science that is wrong. The facts of science are perfectly correct, although fluctuating. It is the interpretations of science that are wrong.

Birdlip, November 13, 1943

ON RE-BIRTH

G. said on one occasion that many things appear in the Gospels about the inner teaching on Man's nature and possibilities but that usually the essential points are left out. They are either left out or given in the wrong order and appear without connection. In the extract from G.'s talks that I am now going to quote, three main ideas are spoken about: death, birth and sleep. Everyone knows that the New Testament says that a man can be re-born, or born again, or born anew, or born *from above* (literally interpreted). Christ says to Nicodemus: "Unless a man is born again, he cannot see the kingdom of God." (*John* III 3). This means in the language of the Work that a man cannot enter the Conscious Circle of Humanity unless he is born anew or born from the Work. Strictly speaking, the Work would say: "*Unless he is born*", because physical birth is not being born in the esoteric sense. When a man ceases to be mechanical man, when he becomes conscious, when Real 'I' appears in him, then he is a *Man*. In the 7 categories of men given in the Work, Nos. 1, 2 and 3 men, which comprise the bulk of humanity, belong to the circle of mechanical men, the circle of confusion of tongues, of Babel, where no one can ever agree and no one can understand the other person. We can say that those who are *born* agree with one another and understand one another, for the two things are the same. Amongst Conscious Humanity there is understanding. We seek in this Work to learn a common language in order to understand each other a little better. We seek ultimately to be *born*, but in order to be born we must die, and in order to die we must first awaken. Christ in the words attributed to him, says simply: "A man must be born again before he can enter the kingdom of God." In another place he says: "We must awaken (translated as 'watch') and pray." In another place Christ says: "Except a grain of wheat fall into the ground and *die*, it abideth alone . . ." (*John* XII 24). You will see in what follows how things are wrongly arranged, indeed as if by people who did not really understand what they heard. Suppose the teaching had been clear in the Gospels that a man must *awaken* before he can do anything else and that in this is included becoming conscious of what he is like. One would imagine that in that case the whole course of exoteric Christianity would have gone differently. If you think for a moment you will see how impossible it is to *die* to oneself unless one *awakens to oneself*, however painful the awakening may be.

I will add one thing more here. You remember that it is said that C influences which come directly from Conscious Mankind are always turned into B influences when they pass out into life. From those schools which were connected with Christ nothing emerged into outer life for at least half a century. It is only within the atmosphere of a school that C influences can be really preserved. Without this atmosphere people will adapt them to themselves and to *their* level of understanding and to what *they* think is right or wrong. The consequence is that essential points are missed, things are wrongly arranged, all harsh things are left out, and things that seem incredible from a life point of view are also omitted. Moreover everything is adulterated with the general prejudices, general customs and moral views of the time. Then you must remember that in those days every manuscript had to be copied by hand and the scribes would naturally alter sentences that they did not agree with or understand, or they would insert things that they thought ought to have been said, etc. C influences cannot exist in life, and always turn into B influences. The mind of Man based

on the senses has to be raised so that he no longer—to give one example
—thinks in terms of Yes *or* No about everything.

Now I would like to read you something that G. said many years
ago:

"I am often asked questions in connection with the various
texts, parables, and so on, from the Gospels. In my opinion the
time has not yet come for us to speak about the Gospels. This
requires more knowledge. But from time to time we will take
certain Gospel texts as points of departure for our discussions.
This will teach you to treat them in the right way, and, above all,
to realize that in the texts known to us, the most essential points
are usually missing.

To begin with, let us take the well-known text about the seed
which must die in order to be born: 'Except a corn of wheat fall
into the ground and die, it abideth alone; but if it die, it bringeth
forth much fruit.'

This text has many different meanings, and we shall often
return to it. But first of all it is necessary to know the principle
contained in this text in its full measure as applied to man.

There is a book of aphorisms which has never been published,
and probably never will be published. I have mentioned this
book before in connection with the meaning of knowledge, and I
quoted then one aphorism from the book.

In relation to what we are speaking of now, this book says the
following: 'A man may be born, but in order to be born, he must
first die, and in order to die, he must first awake.'

In another place it says: 'When a man awakes he can die; when
he dies he can be born.'

We must find out what this means. 'To awake', 'To die',
'To be born': these are 3 successive stages. If you study the Gospels
attentively, you will see that references are often made to the
possibility of 'being born'; several references are made to the
necessity of 'dying'; and there are very many references to the
necessity of 'awakening' . . . 'Watch, for ye know not the hour'. . .
and so on. But these three possibilities of man, to awake or not to
sleep, to die and to be born, are not set down in connection with
one another. Nevertheless this is the whole point. If a man dies
without having awakened, he cannot be born. If a man is born
without having died, he may become an 'immortal thing'. Thus
the fact that he has not 'died' prevents a man from being 'born';
the fact of his not having 'awakened' prevents him from 'dying';
and should he be born without having 'died', he is prevented
from 'being'.

We have already spoken enough about the meaning of being
'born'; this relates to the beginning of a new growth of essence—
the beginning of the formation of individuality, the beginning of
the appearance of one indivisible 'I'.

But in order to be able to attain this, or at least to begin to attain it, a man must die, that is, he must free himself from a thousand petty attachments and identifications which hold him in the position in which he is. He is attached to everything in his life, attached to his imagination, attached to his stupidity, attached to his sufferings, and possibly to his sufferings more than to anything else. He must free himself from this attachment. Attachment to things, identification with things, keep alive a thousand useless 'I's in a man. These 'I's must die, in order that the big 'I' may be born. But how can they be made to die? They do not want to die. It is at this point that the possibility of awakening comes to the rescue. To awaken means to realize one's nothingness, that is, to realize one's complete and absolute mechanicalness, and one's complete and absolute helplessness. And it is not sufficient to realize it philosophically in *words*. It is necessary for a man to realize it in clear, simple and concrete *facts, in his own facts*. When a man begins to know himself a little, he will see in himself many things that are bound to horrify him. So long as a man is not horrified at himself, he knows nothing about himself. He decides to throw it off, stop it, put an end to it. But however many efforts he may make, he feels that he cannot do this, that everything remains as it was. Here he will see his impotence, his helplessness and his nothingness. Or again, when he begins to know himself, a man sees that he has nothing *that is his own*, that is, that all that he has regarded as his own, his tastes, views, thoughts, convictions, habits, even faults and vices, all these are not his own, but they have been borrowed somewhere ready-made. In feeling this, a man may feel his nothingness. And in feeling his nothingness, a man should see himself as he really is, not for a second, not for a moment, but *constantly*, never forgetting it.

This continual consciousness of his nothingness and of his helplessness will eventually give a man courage to 'die', and that is, to 'die', not merely mentally, or in his consciousness, but to '*die*' *in fact* and to renounce actually and for ever those aspects of himself which are either unnecessary from the point of view of his inner growth, or which hinder it. These aspects are, first of all his 'False 'I' ', and then all the fantastic ideas about his 'individuality', 'will', 'consciousness', 'capacity to do', his powers, initiative, determination, and so on."

NOTE

I would like to say that we should understand and always try to keep in mind that in this Work we are not trying to remain as we are, but to change, and that change does not mean remaining as we are. All change is inner and starts from the inner—from beginning to see what one is like. No one can remain the same as he is and change. Buffers, attitudes, pictures of oneself, mechanical behaviour, typical forms of internal considering, of making accounts against others, all our ideas of life, and ways of thinking, and forms of self-estimation, above all, the ways in which we identify—all these things in ourselves must change if we are going to change. You cannot, as long as you hold on to your buffers and ingrained ways of taking and judging things, your self-esteem and your typical reactions, become *changed* in yourself— even if you go into a desert and live on a glass of water a day. To change it is necessary that people work on themselves and try to *separate* themselves from what they are, and observe themselves, in accordance with what the Work says.

Birdlip, November 20, 1943

A BRIEF TALK ABOUT DREAMS

[*Dr. Nicoll is here speaking about dreams from the standpoint of the teaching that he had from Dr. Jung.*]

Part I.—This Work does not speak directly about dreams. However, certain things are said about dreams. The main thing said is that it is useless to study your dreams and that all psychological systems based on the study of dreams are fantastic because immediately you begin to study your dreams they alter. Some of you know that in modern Physics the discovery has been made that when you investigate the micro-physical—i.e. the world of atoms—you interfere with what you are investigating. Your instruments for investigation interfere with what you are investigating. Now you all know that one of the difficulties of self-observation, such as observation of your thoughts, is that observation interferes with your thoughts. This is especially the case when you try to observe your forms of imagination. Immediately you try to observe your imagination it stops. That is to say, the instrument for observation interferes with what you observe. To take a gross example —suppose you suddenly strike a match to see whether there is a mouse in the room, you interfere with what you are observing, and probably the mouse disappears. Now in the case of dreams, the Work teaches that once you begin to pay attention to them, you interfere with them and so change them. And it is for this reason that the study of dreams as a psychological method of approach to oneself is definitely discouraged.

But the Work teaches something further about dreams: for example, the Work says that there are many different kinds of dreams not recognized in Western psychology. Dreams, the Work teaches, are of every kind because they can come from every centre and every part of a centre. In a conversation I once had with G. he remarked that most dreams come from Moving Centre, from haphazard connections taking place in Moving Centre. Strictly speaking, most dreams come from

Instinct-Moving Centre—that is, they are echoes of things seen during the day, sensations and movements. Such dreams are echoes of the life of Instinct-Moving Centre during the day-time. They have no meaning and so are of no importance. But dreams can also come from other centres. Instinct-Moving dreams are, generally speaking, chaotic. Then again, some emotional impression such as a fright may enter into these instinct-moving dreams, especially if the fright connects itself with earlier fears which one has consented to and not worked against. But the point that I wish to emphasize now is that the Work teaches that there are different kinds of dreams originating in different centres and different parts of centres. This means that there are intellectual dreams, emotional dreams, sexual dreams, moving and instinctive dreams, and there are also dreams that come from the centres we do not use —i.e. Higher Emotional and Higher Intellectual Centres. I would say one thing at present: that dreams that come from the higher parts of Emotional Centre or even from Higher Emotional Centre are always characterized by what can be roughly called dramatic formulation.

Let us suppose that a person experiences a very dramatic and well-formed dream. He wonders why he had this dream which seems to have nothing to do with his ordinary life. How, he says to himself, can such a dream arise which has nothing to do with my own thoughts or experiences? Why should I have such a dream? From what source did this strange experience come? Has it any meaning or not? Most of us admit that occasionally we are visited by very strange dreams, sometimes very wonderfully worked out and containing some meaning that we cannot catch. Now if you will all think about the Ray of Creation and about how we have in us higher and lower centres and higher and lower parts of centres, and how influences come down the Ray of Creation from higher levels, it is not so surprising if we find that there are influences in us that are trying to cure us, trying to make us understand ourselves and our inner situations and states better. But it is quite clear that the language of dreams is not our ordinary language. Suppose that the Ray of Creation and all that it means is quite true, suppose that the idea of Jacob's Ladder is quite true, suppose that 'angels' are blowing trumpets in our ears to make us hear better, suppose that higher intelligence is working on us and in us at every moment only we cannot hear its words or understand its meaning. Is it extraordinary that we may receive and be in touch with greater mind than our own? Do you remember what the Work teaches about higher centres? It teaches that higher centres are fully developed in us and are always transmitting meaning to us only we cannot hear them. We cannot hear their finer vibrations. We are tuned in to the life of the earth and of the five senses. Very often G. used to say that we must listen to ourselves and that if we would only listen to ourselves before embarking on some enterprise we would realize how useless it was. But what do we listen to in our ordinary daily lives—i.e. in our lives of ordinary sleep? We listen to the crudest 'I's, the most mechanical

353

'I's, the 'I's turned out to external life, and its small adventures. We listen to our jealous 'I's, our offended 'I's, our negative 'I's and so on. And so it is in this sense that we cannot hear these influences that are continually coming down to us from higher centres. We do not even listen to our reason—i.e. to the higher parts of our ordinary centres. And yet all the time there are influences, so clearly expressed in the diagram of the Ray of Creation, that are trying to touch us and make us understand better, and cure us of our life-maladies and so lead us to our own inner development. Sometimes these influences reach us in the form of dreams. When we are cut off from our five senses, the external world registered by them fades away and we pass into another world, the world of our invisible selves which this Work is about.

I suppose that every one of you has had some dream that has made you wonder, some dream that you do not permanently forget, some dream that has some strange quality about it. To those of you who have had moments of Self-Remembering in life, when you have seen some quite ordinary thing or person in an entirely new way, it will not be astonishing if I say that such moments have the same quality or inner taste as have those rare and unusual dreams of which I am speaking. You suddenly see new meaning and in the case of dreams you feel that they have new meaning of the same order (although you cannot grasp it) as when you realize the Ray of Creation in yourselves and particularly the Side-Octave from the Sun. When you begin to see their significance you will not be surprised if I say that there are forces in you working upon you all the time to make you awaken, to heal you, to cure you— if you can only listen to them. The uproar of the personality prevents us from hearing. The continual action of the false personality with all its intrigues literally makes us deaf, blind and dumb, so that everything is pseudo, even what we call our most sincere moments. You understand what a dumb man means in the Gospels? A man who can never speak from his understanding is a dumb man; a man who is always talking from the 'I's of false personality is a dumb man—dumb because he can never *say* anything *real*. Just in the same way a blind man is one who can never see anything, never see the meaning of anything: and a deaf man is a man who can never hear anything even when it is said time and again. He has no mental ears to hear with. We are all deaf, dumb and blind as regards the teaching as given throughout the ages, and only Christ—i.e. the Work—can cure us. Not only this, but we are deaf, dumb and blind to ourselves, to those higher centres in us that are continually telling us what to do, only we cannot understand their language. So please realize that you have the Work in yourselves already, all of you, and that the external form of the Work and the teaching and study of it and the practising of it is to open you to what is already in you, to something that we have all lost contact with owing to falling asleep. So it is not strange that sometimes we have experiences that seem to have nothing to do with what we believe is our sole form of life, and that sometimes when the external senses are stilled we experience dreams that are quite extraordinary about which we understand nothing.

Now as regards dreams that have a trace of Emotional or Higher Emotional Centre in their formation, I will simply say that they are practically always about oneself. They tell you about your inner situation and inner state. Sometimes they represent your inner state in terms of people and situations. The people may or may not represent different 'I's in yourself. The general situation you are in psychologically speaking may be represented as buildings, scenery, and so on. The dream may be entirely subjective—i.e. entirely about yourself and your inner state—or it may have a certain objective reference as well, and refer to how you are behaving to an actual person and so on. Or it may represent your inner state in such a way as to shew you how you are taking something quite wrongly as from some former life-way of taking things. You know that we have to take everything in a new way in the Work. Sometimes a dream which has a trace of Higher Emotional Centre behind it will give you a picture of the Work and your relationship to it. Of course it will be mixed up with personal associations—i.e. with personality—but the general form and meaning may come through, as it were. I will quote an example of a dream of this kind which is about life and the Work and about the danger of mixing the two in one's thinking and in one's evaluation. It relates to the fact that if one wishes to work one must be very careful how one walks in life. The dream is as follows:

"We were living at a kind of farm. Work people were around us. The peculiarity of this farm was that wherever you walked you had to travel on duckboards raised on stilts above a swamp of all kinds of filth and muck, such as you find in a farmyard. If you slipped you plunged into it and anything you dropped was lost in it. When we sat at table and in conversation forgot what was beneath us, we would suddenly awake to the fact that our feet were dangling in the filthy stuff. We had to remember all the time to hold them up above it . . ."

Here is a strange dream. If we take it literally it is about duckboards, mud, stilts, and so on. One might very well say, on waking up, "What have I to do with this farm lying on mud, in which it is necessary to be very careful where one walks?" But why should this well-formulated dream come? What does it represent in its imagery? What ideas lie in this dream? For instance, do you think that it might represent *identifying* with life? Do you think that it might represent how one must always remember oneself in walking about in life? In this dream it is said that if you drop anything it is lost. The Work says that everything you do mechanically is lost to you. And what does the Work say about *talking*? Does it not say that here we forget ourselves most of all? And yet I say that this dream was dreamt just as quoted, without knowledge of what it meant. Think about this dream, for, in a sense, it is for all in the Work. Do you think life should be like what you expect—or have you grown up and seen the necessity of making your own life? Life is *filth* unless you learn the science of duckboards and stilts and so on.

But most people are immersed in this "filth" and like to stay in it.

The language of dreams is not our formatory language. A dream is not put in the form of words. It is put in a language of imagery. It is exactly comparable with the language of parables. It is quite true that parables are expressed by means of words but they indicate images. You all know you do not dream in words but if you want to describe your dream you have to turn it into words and you soon lose its meaning. In fact you cannot express it in words save in a very poor way. Parables are the other way round. They are expressed in words usually very simply but they transmit imagery. The parable gives the imagery by means of words: the meaning however does not lie in the words but in the imagery. A literal-minded person may think that an actual sower went forth to sow and actual seed fell on stony ground, etc. but the whole parable of the Sower and the Seed transcends the words completely and passes into the language of Higher Emotional Centre which uses only images and so is universally understandable—i.e. we see the beginning of a universal language which is the language of Higher Emotional Centre.

*   *   *

One of the most extraordinary things is that people imagine they are related only to the external world. The Work teaches that we are related to an inner, invisible world and that where we are in this invisible world is the most important thing. Many dreams refer to where we are in this inner invisible world from which our nightmares arise and from which much of our unhappiness comes. Each one of you is related to different 'I's, to different parts of, as it were, an enormous building, about which you may sometimes dream. Which room are you in ? Within ourselves we have rooms where we can live in discomfort or comfort and in ourselves we have a radio that we can switch on to one set of influences or another set of influences. The world to-day has gone so far into the external senses and into matter that it seems extraordinary to most people that there is another world to which they have to make relation in order to have any peace of mind and any centre of gravity, an internal world that one can only begin to realize by means of self-observation, by Observing 'I' which is an internal sense-organ. Try to notice where you are in yourself at this moment, to what thoughts you are consenting, with what feelings you are identified. Have you yet attained any power of inner freedom from yourself, from your mechanical reactions, your mechanical thoughts and feelings induced by external circumstances? Or are you taking everything in the way you have always taken everything? Your inner invisible world is much larger and contains far more interesting things than this external world that you are always looking out upon through the five windows of your senses, and in this inner invisible world of yourselves influences are always playing upon you from higher and lower levels, and all higher influences are trying to heal you, trying to make you understand how to live in this world. But, as you know, as long as we are identified with all our sufferings, all our false personality, buffers, accounts, self-pity, memory of the past, with what we think will give us happiness, then we cannot feel these influences that can free us and make us grow.

Birdlip, November 27, 1943

COMMENTARY ON VANITY AND PRIDE

COMMENTS ON ANSWERS TO A PSYCHOLOGICAL QUESTION

QUESTION: "It is said in this Work that two giants called Pride and Vanity walk in front of us and arrange everything beforehand. Can you draw any distinction between them from personal observation or observation of others? Do you think that these two are the only giants that walk in front of us and arrange things?"

The first thing to be said about Vanity and Pride is that they must be studied in *oneself* by personal observation. One may know theoretically about them without having the slightest idea how they manifest themselves in oneself. Everyone has their own forms of Vanity and Pride which differ in different cases and you must remember that they seem quite reasonable, quite natural, so that people do not notice them.

Both Pride and Vanity are connected with self-love but although they have this connection their manifestations can be quite different so that one opposes the other—for instance, you are paid a compliment and your Vanity is delighted but your Pride makes you feel awkward.

On the whole people were agreed in their answers that Vanity is based on the unreal part of us, but that Pride is connected with something real. I will quote an interesting answer:

"From personal observation, I would say that vanity comes from false personality only. Pride can belong to the good 'I's of personality and perhaps essence. With the right neutralizing force, 'I's that are now proud might become part of will. One is always acting and reacting from vanity, but pride can be a passive or restraining force . . ."

Yes, it is quite true to say that Pride can become part of the Will but Vanity cannot. We can see in a sense that the density of Pride is greater than the density of Vanity and so more can be done, more can be endured from Pride, and in this way it resembles the Will. By the way, do you think that Lucifer fell from Heaven owing to Vanity or Pride? These two giants that walk in front of us and decide everything beforehand may sometimes co-operate and sometimes be antagonistic. This is why it is difficult to define any particular action as being due exclusively to either one or the other. *Vanity has a different internal taset*

357

from Pride. One person says "You may be proud of a new motor-car and vain when you are sitting in it." This is quite true and the feelings taste differently. You can also be even more proud of an old car and certainly not vain of sitting in it! Women do not like old cars as a rule.

Several people point out that Vanity is usually connected with making an impression on other people. It is true that Vanity always needs an audience. Even when you are cossetting yourself alone in your bedroom you will imagine the effect of people looking at you later. You would not think of making up if you were the only inhabitant of the earth, but if you were one of two you probably would, and particularly if you were one of three inhabitants. But Vanity is not necessarily concerned only with the outward appearance, as one person mistakenly says. The ugly hunchback Pope was notorious for his Vanity: he had no illusions about his looks but was vain of his wit and his position in the literary world. In one answer the distinction made between Pride and Vanity is that "Vanity may want me to shew off, be important, and it may be that Pride would prevent me from doing this." Another distinction that I have observed is that Pride can make you ashamed of not knowing something, whereas Vanity can make you pretend to know it. I do not agree with the person who says that "Pride self-justifies a great deal". It is usually Vanity that causes self-justifying, which latter is an expression of the false personality defending itself. Pride can make us ashamed of self-justifying. One of you quite rightly attempts to distinguish between Pride and Vanity by the facial expression—i.e. by the way in which these two emotions are represented in the moving Centre in expression and posture. I think you will agree that a proud look is quite different from a vain look. This is a useful angle to reflect on. Which causes you to blush most?

One person says that "Pride lives more in the Intellectual Centre." But the centre of gravity of Pride is not in the Intellectual Centre. It is an emotion arising from the self-love which may manifest itself in any of the emotional parts of centres including the emotional part of the Intellectual Centre. Several people discuss right and wrong Pride. I quote from one answer:

"When Pride is turned outward it can be an accomplice to Vanity . . . If it is turned inward it can be of use to us in helping us to make effort in remembering our aim in the Work."

Yes, when one's Pride is directed inwards towards oneself, it can, for instance, make us ashamed of not keeping our aim. I will quote another answer where a good distinction between Pride and Vanity is made:

"Although in many ways so alike, pride and vanity seem to me to be so different in quality as to be two quite different things, as different in intensity as jealousy is different from envy. Vanity seems to be connected with the more ephemeral things of life, the more external things, whereas pride seems to belong to a much more permanent and inner part of oneself. One may be vain of what one does, but one seems to be proud of what one *is* (or thinks one is). Blows at one's vanity make one angry, offended, more than hurt. A hard blow at one's pride hurts deeply and makes one feel murderous—as if it aroused an instinct of, so to speak, psychological self-preservation. I think one's false personality is kept going by vanity and pride, but particularly by vanity. One can take pride, say, in one's work, be proud of it, or one can be vain of it. In the former case, although one does not like criticism, I think one accepts it for the sake of the work, whereas if one is simply vain one resents and rejects criticism. I think it is vanity which blows its own trumpet. Pride is silent.

Pride seems to go deeper than false personality, or personality. Sometimes it seems to me to be even connected with essence, it seems such an integral part of oneself. I cannot see how vanity can ever be directed otherwise than on to externals (one's achievements, for example), whereas I feel that pride could be re-directed if one could observe it and its roots deeply enough. I believe it may be capable of directing force interiorly instead of exteriorly, though I cannot see clearly yet how. It might become shame. I think it might even lead eventually to sense of one's own nothingness—not just by a swing of the pendulum; pride does not seem to be subject to the same swings of the pendulum that vanity experiences—if it could really be seen and directed. Vanity, I think, must eventually disappear; pride, I feel, might be used if it were not one's master, but this may be only because it is so close that I do not see it for what it really is . . . "

This is a very good answer. Now we have to think of Pride and Vanity from the side of what is useful and what is useless in connection with the Work. Pride can turn into Shame and genuine Pride can turn into real Shame and Humility in the presence of what is higher. A man without proper Shame and so without proper Pride is not really suitable for the Work. There is no depth in him. But Vanity is always wrong except, as it were, in very small doses. As you know, it was always said by G. that personality has *scarcely* any right to exist. When you ascribe some success to yourself, it goes to strengthen the false personality and so increase the Vanity in you. One is allowed to ascribe a very little to oneself, for a short time, but our trouble is that we like to talk about our successes or about what we did and what we said. And even if we are silent, we think it.

Now about giants. Some of you give an enormous list of giants and one of you invents a giant called "Highbrow" but surely this giant is Vanity. I agree with those who say that one great giant is Laziness and that these three giants, Pride, Vanity and Laziness are constantly striving for possession of us. One person describes them thus:

"I think that Laziness is also a giant which walks in front of us and arranges everything beforehand. It pre-arranges our actions mechanically to avoid exertion almost as much as Vanity or Pride.

Fortunately this giant is apt to walk in an opposite direction to the other giants and our days become a battle between them. Pride often refuses to let one give in to Laziness, where Vanity will arrange something which will suit them both."

This is good. Then there is the giant Fear. We should really say that Pride, Vanity, Fear and Laziness control us mostly. I disagree with all those who think that buffers are giants. Buffers are like wooden blocks that prevent us from seeing contradictions. It is our Vanity that creates them. Buffers are not giants. Nor again is false personality. It is what it is made of and is founded on—i.e. Vanity and Imagination. You can say that Imagination is used by the giants and you will be speaking very deeply if you say this, remembering perhaps the story of the sheep, and the magicians who made them imagine they were lions and tigers. You know how closely Vanity and Imagination are connected and how closely Fear and Imagination are connected. I am speaking of Emotional Fear, not Fear arising from Instinctive Centre. The negative emotions, and especially Self-Pity, are also giants.

There are some very interesting giants in literature. There is an interesting giant described in the early part of Peer Gynt. Then there is Giant Despair.

Now I would like to read you some words of G.'s about Vanity:

"The fundamental cause of almost all the misunderstandings arising in the inner world of Man, as well as in the common life of people, is chiefly due to a psychic factor formed in Man's Being at an early age and due to a wrong education, the stimulation of which gives birth in him to impulses of "Vanity" . . . I affirm solemnly that the happiness and self-consciousness—that is, self-remembering—which should be in a real man depend in most cases exclusively on the absence in us of feelings of Vanity . . . And I have made it my aim in working with my people to hit mercilessly at every manifestation of this factor which hinders all development and prevents any genuine and real relation to one's inner life, in the harmonious adjustment of which all true happiness only can be found."

I must once more refer you to what I said at the beginning: that you must study Pride and Vanity in yourselves and all their different gradations. Do you know your own forms of Vanity and how much they occupy you? Do you know where your Pride lies? Where do you feel that you love yourself, that you admire yourself? Where do you most feel that you are utterly different from other people? Where are you most conceited? What do you boast about? What are you silent about? Vanity is frequently very talkative, whereas Pride is silent. Which is the deeper wound, wounded Vanity or wounded Pride? What is it you cannot forgive? You know that if you cannot forgive it is because of some form of self-love which, ideally speaking, has to be smashed out of you.

ON DREAMS

Part II.—In our last short discussion on dreams, it was said that dreams can come from every centre and that one of the most interesting things about dreams is that although your eyes are closed you see things and people, even people you have never met, and you walk in buildings and feel embarrassed or confident. In other words, all that you experience in external life through your senses appears to take place when all your senses are cut off—i.e. when your external senses are not seeing the light of the sun or the light of searchlights or anything of that kind. Yet you can enter now a world that is perfectly real to you. I suppose that this is the first thing to make us begin to wonder whether the external world registered by our senses is the only world we live in. People can have nightmares, people can be plagued by unhappy dreams which appear quite real, if they have not learnt to non-identify. Our troubles do not lie only in the external world.

Now to revert to the dream that was spoken about in the last paper. I will quote it again:

"We were living at a kind of farm. Work people were around us. The peculiarity of this farm was that wherever you walked you had to travel on duckboards raised on stilts above a swamp of all kinds of filth and muck, such as you find in a farmyard. If you slipped you plunged into it and anything you dropped was lost in it. When we sat at table and in conversation forgot what was beneath, we would suddenly awake to the fact that our feet were dangling in the filthy stuff. We had to remember all the time to hold them up above it. . . ."

You remember that there are many dreams that have no meaning, but this dream has meaning. Whether a dream has meaning or not depends on which centre it comes from. Influences reach us of every kind in the scale of things. If you have begun to understand the Ray of Creation you will know that influences are reaching you all this time and that these influences are of different qualities. These influences are registered by our psychic apparatus according to its level, or, put in other words, we receive lower or higher influences according to our level of Being. We are told in this Work to try to listen to ourselves. Of course, if there is nothing to listen to this would be absurd advice, but if you contemplate the Ray of Creation and all those influences coming down it, you may not think it absurd. We have to remember always that there are higher influences playing on us at this moment but that if we are glued to our senses and completely identified with all that we are doing, we cannot become aware of these influences.

Now you may remember what is said in Ecclesiastes: "A dream cometh through the multitude of business." (*V. 3*). Something speaks to you. It is as if a person were trying to say something to someone who will talk very seriously to him about his affairs with which he is completely identified and which he takes as everything that has any meaning for him. He will be deaf to what is said. The multitude of business in which we live makes, as it were, a daily uproar. We cannot hear. Later on, perhaps, we begin to listen, when we decide that we must become simpler and can detach ourselves from our rôles in life.

Now let us think of this dream that we are discussing from the standpoint that "a dream cometh through the multitude of business." You will notice that the structure of the dream concerns mire, swampy ground, and that one has to learn to walk upon this and be very careful about it. I said very briefly that this meant life and how we walk upon it. One can always be completely engulfed by the situations that are continually produced by life, whether in business, in domestic or in personal affairs or in the wretched aspect of general life, such as it' is at present. But the whole of the Work is about *non-identifying* with all this mire and, expressed in the visible sensory language of parables, the meaning is that we have to learn to keep our feet out of this mire. Now the mire is not outside oneself but inside oneself. Take, for instance, the mire of negative emotions. Is it inside oneself or outside oneself? Take all one's forms of making inner accounts, feeling that one is owed, feeling bitter about it, and so on. We know a little about this by now. What does it mean to have duckboards and stilts and to be careful not to stand on all this mud. It means that we have to be very careful how we walk *in ourselves*. It is psychological—that is, about oneself inside.

Now I will quote some interesting passages that I have found in the Old Testament that you can understand in connection with this dream that we are discussing. I must introduce the word *pit*. You will realize that the dream speaks about not going down into the pit, not falling into the mire. You can easily get into the stage in life (and most people remain in this stage) of making for yourselves a pit of negativeness, hopelessness, self-pity, internal considering, and also of attributing everything to external circumstances, to outside people —and finally of being totally identified with outside things that have no value at all. Also one can go down into the pit of making no effort about oneself.

I will now quote from the Sacred Scriptures a few passages that refer to all this:

"God brought me out of the pit, out of the miry clay, and set my feet upon a rock." (God is esoteric teaching).

Again, "I went down to the bottom of the mountains, the bars of the earth were upon me yet thou broughtest my life up from the pit." (The Work can bring one up from the pit).

Again, "O God, thou hast brought up my soul from hell, thou hast kept me alive from those that go down into the pit and into the mire." (If you feel you have something to hold on to, then you can keep alive).

And again, when the Psalmist is in despair about himself, he says: "I am accounted with them that go down into the pit, I am accounted as a man of no strength. Thou hast set me a pit in the lower regions, in the darkness and in the depths." (He feels he is falling asleep.)

One more example: "Exult greatly . . . behold thy king cometh unto thee. He is just, wretched and riding upon an ass . . . he will deliver thee out of the pit wherein is no water."

This last phrase has very deep meaning but you will realize that "the pit wherein is no water" means "a state where there is no truth and no understanding."

Let us turn to the Gospels. Christ said to the Pharisees—i.e. to the people who are quite sure that they are right and who attribute everything to themselves: "Let them alone. They are blind leaders of the blind. If the blind lead the blind both shall fall into the pit."

It would be possible to quote, I suppose, a hundred other examples from the Sacred Scriptures about the significance of this pit, this mire, this filth, which each one of us must see in himself and realize its significance for him or her. You will see from the dream we are discussing that it is this subject that is being dealt with. It is, so to speak, an esoteric dream—that is, a dream coming from higher centres. If one has a dream of this kind, one must not attribute it to oneself, to one's own cleverness. It is a formulation about the Work, and, as you have heard many times, this Work is what higher centres would teach us if we could hear them. The Work is not invented. It is not a psychological system invented by some ordinary man. It comes from higher Man, from conscious influences, from those who are in touch with higher centres, only, because we cannot hear higher centres themselves owing to our state of deep sleep, their continual inner teaching, to which we are deaf, has been turned into an external system of Work formulated by those who are already in touch with higher centres. In other words, we have to learn externally, from outside, from our senses, what we could already know if we could only listen to ourselves and render quiet the uproar of the daily wheels of personality.

Now let us speak about what the duckboards might mean psychologically. Can you think what this image, exactly comparable with an image in a parable, might mean? Or can you think what stilts might mean, psychologically? I would like you to discuss this and also what it means that when you are talking, as the dream says, you are liable to get your feet in the mire. You must all have noticed that when you have been talking at random or saying all sorts of unhappy things about others, you lose force, but if you have not been doing this you feel stronger in yourselves. "Silence gives strength". One must learn to be silent even when speaking. It is this inner feeling of integrity that means strength. Of course, you can always say a thousand things, you can always poison others with your negative emotions, you can always hand on unpleasant things, you can always hint at something that has been said—all this takes you down into the mire, which is exactly what a person must try to escape from sinking into. Everyone must see his own mire. Often it is what a person does not think is mire at all. He thinks, for instance, that he has a right to worry, to be continually talking about life-things, or talking about his business, about his own affairs, his private difficulties. To talk consciously about one's affairs is quite different from talking mechanically. To talk consciously, I repeat, is quite different from talking mechanic-ally. What does it mean to talk consciously about your troubles, for example? It means to formulate, and formulation means to be conscious of both sides, of what you are like, of what the other person is like, and so on. Just try to do this. You will notice that it means that all sorts of mechanical 'I's in you are checked and deprived of their desire to speak. If you do this you will understand what strength means. You remember how the Psalmist complains that because he had no inner strength he was sunken into the inner pit. Remember that your lives are your own and that in a sense no one else can help you. But the Work can help you if you apply it. We reach a certain stage, perhaps, of personal work, and then fall again into this mire. At first we may not notice it but after a time we really become aware of our inner state, and then, if the Work means anything to us, we begin to feel that we cannot bear to be in this mire. This means that the inner taste of the Work has begun to act on us. Then we are no longer made unhappy simply by adverse external conditions but we begin to be unhappy in quite a new way—namely, with regard to our inner state, to where we are in ourselves. When this stage is reached we may be sure that the Work has begun to act on us directly and then we will know that the only thing that can save us from this "Mud Farm" is to practise what this Work is teaching us. Give way to a negative 'I', give way to negative imagination, feeling that things are not fair, identifying and thus con-senting to every doubt, and so on, then you are using neither duckboard nor stilts nor any of the apparatus of this Work. All this Work is about lifting us off what we might call in these papers, which are merely commentaries, "Mud Farm", but remember that this Mud Farm is in yourselves. The Work is to get us to a new level of understanding. It is to get us to the next storey in our personal evolution where there is no mud.

I am taking this dream because it shews the first stage or level. It does not reach the next level. It represents what we have to do in regard to the level we are on, the level of Being we are on, which is represented as mud. At the same time it shews that, on the side of knowledge, there are certain things that we must practise—i.e. the use of duckboards and stilts and walking delicately on this mud in ourselves. In other words, it represents the first stage of this Work, practically applied to ourselves. You will notice how beautifully Higher Emotional Centre formulates about the Work. Its formulations of the Work are as beautiful as those in the Parables in the Gospels.

COMMENTARY ON THE RELATIONSHIP
OF A MAN TO HIMSELF

Each of us is related to three things. First we are related to our bodies, about which we know practically nothing. The body is sometimes ill, sometimes well, and so on. We may get certain knowledge of our bodies but we never really know about them as their complicated organisation is far beyond our comprehension. There is however a quite definite side in our lives that concerns our relationship to our physical bodies. In general, the Instinctive Centre looks after us in this respect provided we do not abuse our bodies too much. This is our first definite relationship. If a person has had no trouble with his body he is quite surprised when trouble of this kind begins.

Our next relationship is to the external world, to things, to people, to affairs that take place around us, and such things as friendships, business, politics, war, and all our relationships with matter in general, with dealing with things, with cooking, with carpentry, with building, and also with managing people, finding jobs, making both ends meet, and not only with making both ends meet but with tying a bow.

Generally speaking, most people's lives are concerned with these two relationships, and failure and success are possible in both cases. I mean that a person in the first relationship may have great trouble with the body, may be often ill, and so on, or he may find out how to keep in better health. And as regards the second relationship, the relationship to external life, he may fail to adjust himself to anything or anyone or he may be more successful. He may find, for example, something in external life that he is good at.

Now we must speak about the third relationship which is really the subject of this teaching—namely, the relationship of a man to himself. For most people this relationship is unnecessary. A man is concerned usually with the first two relationships only and to a certain extent these two are connected; if a man is starving, for instance, he has a bad relationship to his body and therefore must find a better relationship to external life in order to nourish the body. But this third relationship is different. For the purposes of mechanical life it is unnecessary. In a young country you will generally find that it is only the first two relationships that count. Food, health, business, are the main preoccupations. Now both the body and the affairs of the world are external to us. In what sense are they external? They are external in regard to the third possible relationship.

In thinking of myself from the angle of this Work, I have sometimes found it useful to think of these relationships and, keeping them clearly in mind, to try to observe in which relationship I am, especially, at fault. I may be in a wrong relationship to my body or again I may be in a wrong relationship to external life, or I may be in a wrong relationship to myself. That is, as regards the third relationship, I may be thinking where I should feel, or feeling where I should think, and so on. Or again, I may be asleep to myself. This applies to everyone. If we feel something is wrong, we tend to look outwards. We may decide we are ill—i.e. we look outwardly at our bodies—or we may decide that other people are wrong, in which case we look outwardly once more. However, one may decide that one is wrong in oneself, that one is not in right 'I's, that one has not sufficiently nourished this third relationship to oneself. Perhaps one has not really worked on oneself for some time. Perhaps one has not connected one's thoughts that have come in from higher parts of centres—that is to say, one has not been listening to oneself and has missed what is being said to one. There are many sayings in ancient esoteric literature bearing on Man's relationship to himself and to all the different parts in him, both higher and lower, that refer to the necessity of keeping a certain heat within him. You know that an egg that is being hatched must not be allowed to get cold too long. You have heard also in this teaching that a fire must be lit to heat the alchemical retort in which the metallic powders are contained which must eventually be fused together. As long as this is not so, every tap on the walls of the retort shifts the powders. This means that every change incidental to life shifts us inside and we have no power of inner resistance to the external world and its changing events. Or you can compare Man as he is to a kaleidoscope of which every tap changes the pattern. The object of the third relationship to oneself is ultimately to form something permanent. First of all, in the hierarchy of development, comes the establishing of Observing 'I'. Then above this comes the formation of Deputy-Steward which is a collection of 'I's that wish to work. Some of these 'I's may really wish to work and some may only pretend that they do. But when Deputy-Steward is strong enough, then there is a possibility that Steward himself may come and above him lies the possibility of the coming of Real 'I'—i.e. something permanent and unshakeable. When this happens there is a *real man*—a man such as we do not know in ordinary life.

Now in this commentary I wish to talk to you about this third relationship. We miss many opportunities for work because we forget about this third relationship. We may be depressed by illness or by the external situation in life to which we happen to be related at the time and, finding no particular comfort in either of them, we may feel at a loss. But over and above both these relationships lies the possibility of the third relationship. We forget to summon the Work just at the very time when we should summon it. Our ordinary thoughts connected with our ordinary daily affairs do not lead into the ideas of the Work. We have to jump: we have deliberately to make a connection with the Work and we must all find different ways of doing this. You all realize how life puts us to sleep, how our pre-occupation with our life-problems cuts us off from the influences of this Work. I would define two different conditions in which anyone in this Work can find himself. One is simply that a man finds himself in the condition in which he feels immersed in things; he feels rather depressed, worried, anxious, and so on, and being as it were, unable to lift his head up, he views life along the vistas of his own negative feelings. The second condition occurs when a man *knows* he is in a bad state from the Work point of view and cannot find out how to get rid of it. I think that it is this second state that is most interesting to study in oneself. One knows one is asleep, one recognizes that there is something all wrong, but one does nothing to help oneself. It is just here that some of the worst negative thoughts about the Work can arise. One is, so to speak, out of the Work in one-self, out of the 'I's that can conduct or transmit it and yet, although one knows this, one does nothing about it. Now this state can again be divided into two. You may be in some kind of heavy, indifferent state and not wish to do anything at all, although you realize your situation. Or you may be in that interesting condition which is called "tempting God". You may feel you should be helped. But in both cases you have no technique developed in you that can re-establish some kind of harmony within yourself. Here one of the many aspects of Sly Man comes in. You may go about in a miserable mood complaining that you cannot feel the Work and expecting to be helped from on high. But if you feel that you have lost contact with yourself, if you feel that this third relationship which the Work is about has gone wrong and wish to re-connect yourself, you may find some way to do it and deliberately apply it without spending time in being miserable.

What is one's task under such circumstances? One's task is to get into different parts of centres and into different 'I's that can feel the influences of the Work. Recently observing myself under such a condition I began quite deliberately to think of the Ten Command-ments. I tried to repeat the first five Commandments from memory and found I did not know them distinctly enough. As you know, the first five Commandments are psychological, and although the second five Com-mandments are also psychological in their ultimate meaning they refer in the first place to our relationship to external life. But the first five Commandments refer only to our relationship to ourselves. Take the opening Commandment: "Thou shalt have none other gods before me." If this teaching coming from Conscious Influences were so power-ful that one worshipped nothing else—namely, that every thing else was in the second place—one would be in a position to resist all the evils of the body and of life. Perhaps you see what I mean. You would be held up the whole time by a strength that nothing could break. Then I thought of what Christ said: "Thou shalt love the Lord thy God with all thy heart, and with all thy soul, and with all thy mind, and with all thy strength: This is the first commandment." (*Mark* XII 30). And just by thinking of these references to following the Will of Higher Beings from which the teaching of this Work comes, I felt a complete transformation taking place in me which was like a shock, and suddenly everything looked different—people looked different and I felt throughout the whole of my body a certain lightness. You know how the Work teaches that if you give yourself the shock of Self-Remembering it changes even the whole working of the body so that all the cells in the body receive a different food. I assure you that this can be experienced often by every one of you. Remember that always what you value highest is God for you. What you value most you worship and what you worship is God. What you value most controls all your being. In this sense God is a reflection of you and God is according to your level of understanding. We worship strange things and have strange gods.

But there are many other ways of getting oneself out of a bad inner state. You must understand that *no work is possible unless you get into these bad states* because they are tests or, if you like, temptations, which are absolutely necessary in order to make us skilful in dealing with them. You will not learn to swim well unless you are often dropped into the water. And it is always surprising that some of you think that if you pass into a bad state it is because you cannot do the Work. It is just in these bad states that one can work and learn what it is about. It is quite an interesting view, that was once given a long time ago, to regard bad states as something about which you must be clever and use, as it were, every possible intelligence and technique to get out of them. There are many different forms of Self-Remembering, and Sly Man was once defined as "he who knows how to remember himself in different ways at different moments." Sometimes when one is in a bad state and attempts to get out of it and fails to do so, one can be consciously passive to it, without being negative and without identifying with it fully, having the inner certainty that it will pass provided one does not let negative imagination work and does not consent to its presence. This is a form of Self-Remembering and is just as if one has to wait, and knows that one has to, because it is raining too heavily and one cannot go out just at present and yet remains certain it will clear. The Work exists for one as an additional way of living. It is extra. All right relationship to oneself depends on the feeling of integrity in regard to the Work as something extra and valuable. Once this has been established in you—namely, that you see clearly in your inner vision that the Work is something extra and valuable—the Work will begin to touch you and find a way for you.

Now, in conclusion, as regards the Work finding a way for you when you begin to give it a place in yourself, let me say this. Everyone has problems and troubles. No one is without them. We try to find solutions—final solutions—as if afterwards there would be no further trouble.

Remember that there are no final solutions to anything. To try to find final solutions to things is like trying to do away with the waves of the storms of the sea. You have to have a good ship, a good rudder and a good compass. The solution to things lies in seamanship. Or, to change the metaphor—it is said in this Work that it sells leather from which you can make good shoes. You cannot clear away all the mud and stones and pebbles, but you can construct good shoes to walk over them.

Birdlip, December 14, 1943

INTRODUCTORY NOTE ON PRACTICAL WORK

In talking about inner states it is useless to begin with some vague generalization. For instance, to talk about "chaotic states", as one of the London Groups did last time, is useless. To talk in this way is to talk chaotically. One of the objects of self-observation is *actually to observe something.* Now I must say here that to take the Work-phrase "Man cannot do" in such a way that one makes no effort is a very good example of chaotic thinking in the Work. There is one thing that you are told you can do in regard to yourself and that is that you can observe yourself, that you can observe the working of different centres and that you can observe different 'I's in yourself, that you can observe when you are internally considering, that you can observe when you are negative, that you can observe when you are identifying, that you can observe when you are justifying yourself, and so on. This Work is to pull a person together, to brace him, and to make him have a more distinct relationship to all that goes on inside him. For this reason, you are taught first of all to observe yourself, and then to observe yourself from certain well-defined angles. A man must get hold of himself, he must steady himself, he must try to let light into himself in order to see what is going on in him and so where he is going in himself. Also he must observe where he is talking wrongly, where he is complaining and not working, where he is saying things mechanically that should belong to self-observation.

The Work must be practised. In every wrong state it is absolutely necessary to review oneself from what the Work teaches and try to see where one is. If you never call upon the Work to help you it will not be able to help you. Your relationship to the Work is an internal matter that lies between you and the Work right down, deep inside you. A person can talk as much as he likes about his difficulties with the Work. He can let the whole of the Work discharge itself into small 'I's. He can connect the Work with some feature in himself and turn it into a source of perplexity and worry. A man can treat the Work in a thousand different ways. But it is important how one treats the Work. It can produce very great tensions within one. Its object is to do so. But it is necessary to keep the Work, as it were, inviolate, as something utterly pure that cannot be contradicted and which at the same time is telling one something if one will only listen to what it is saying, if

369

one will only relate oneself to what it is teaching. It is quite easy to say that one does not understand the Work, but there is a right way of saying this and a wrong way. It is quite useless to shrug one's shoulders mentally speaking and again it is quite useless to think that one should understand the Work after a few years' casual practising of it. A great deal of patience is necessary, and patience is the Mother of Will. We find ourselves in a crowd of people within us and some of them say one thing and some say another. If there is valuation and if in spite of all difficulties we can feel that here is something that can eventually lead us away from our present states, and if in spite of all the failures this valuation persists, then a centre of gravity will be formed, a point in the Work will be established, and when this is so it is a very blessed condition.

So do not complain too easily, because, as you all know, it takes a very long time to learn anything in a real way even in life. You remember how often it was said that if you wish to learn Chinese thoroughly it will take you all your life. So do not have too short a view. Do not think that when you begin to observe yourself and find a chaos within you you need be pessimistic. It is actually the first step in the Work, the first step to realization. What then, a person may ask, must I do? The answer is that you must begin to follow as sincerely as you can all the practical things that the Work tells you to observe and separate from. The intelligent scrutiny of oneself, the practice of a directed noticing of oneself, the application of non-identifying with certain states of oneself, remembering that certain 'I's weaken oneself and undermine everything one does—all this is being led by the Work. All this is following the Work. People do not surrender to the Work for a long time. They keep on trying to do things by themselves according to their own lights instead of doing things according to the Work. They continue to make the same life-efforts as before but they do not make Work-effort. But all this it is necessary to pass through, and one must pass through this jungle, through this tangled forest, this kind of darkness, until one discerns the Work and what it is saying. For a long time the last thing that we ever think of doing is to work on ourselves in accordance with what the Work teaches. We wriggle about, as it were, like a fish on the end of a line and will not submit to the gentle pull of the line which will lift us into another atmosphere. We get into a bad state and we identify with it right away. Then we see everything through the medium of this bad state but we do not think of practising non-identifying with this bad state, of seeing that it is not 'I'. On the contrary, we say 'I' to it, and we argue about everything from this bad state which is quite incapable of leading us anywhere save into a worse state. We are like people standing in the drenching rain complaining that they are catching cold and saying how miserable they feel, when their own house is standing close beside them into which they can go. Very often when we stand in this drenching rain and this bad inner state, we think vaguely of trying to work on ourselves and separating

370

ourselves from it internally by an act of consciousness and Will, but some small 'I' pipes up and says: "Oh, the Work is too difficult for me."

In connection with the idea of rendering things more distinct within ourselves I have written a short commentary on three different sorts of relationship that can occupy our attention. It is very necessary to try to establish a distinct awareness of where one is. I do not mean by this where one is in physical space but where one is in the world of relationship which is the real world in which we live. Everything lies in relationship, in how you relate yourself to things. You cannot change the thing itself but you can change your relationship to it. All this Work is about changing our relationship, both to ourselves and to life. To say that you can do nothing is to take the idea of the Work quite wrongly. You cannot change life. You cannot *do* in this sense but you can change yourself and your relationship to everything. This is what the Work emphasizes time and again. We can change ourselves through the medium of C influences provided we recognize them— that is, provided we recognize the existence of Greater Mind. But we cannot change life in general nor can we change other people. You cannot make a new world and if we think we can we are what is called "lunatics" in the Work. Remember that the whole question lies in changing our relationship to things, in taking things in a new way and so in thinking in a new way about everything.

NOTE

In this connection remember that duckboards and stilts are things that change your relationship to this mud that is both life itself outside, and our ordinary state of sleep inside. To change the metaphor the Work teaches that we are in prison and not at all a pleasant prison. Some inhabit better cells and some worse. Some even enjoy the prison. But there is a way out of this prison and the secret has been handed on from generation to generation. It is a curious secret just as the prison is a curious one, for the prison is not composed of literal stone walls and ramparts and guards or literal chains and dungeons. And the fact of its existence is due to our looking the wrong way round, in the wrong direction. I advise you all to read the Myth of the Cave in Plato's Republic and think about what it means. It will help you to realize how ancient and how authoritative this teaching is.